Doing Business in Europe

Doing Business in Europe

Gabriele Suder

SAGE Publications
Los Angeles ▪ London ▪ New Delhi ▪ Singapore

First published 2008

Apart from any fair dealing for the purposes of research or private study, or criticism or review, as permitted under the Copyright, Designs and Patents Act, 1988, this publication may be reproduced, stored or transmitted in any form, or by any means, only with the prior permission in writing of the publishers, or in the case of reprographic reproduction, in accordance with the terms of licences issued by the Copyright Licensing Agency. Enquiries concerning reproduction outside those terms should be sent to the publishers.

SAGE Publications Ltd
1 Oliver's Yard
55 City Road
London EC1Y 1SP

SAGE Publications Inc.
2455 Teller Road
Thousand Oaks, California 91320

SAGE Publications India Pvt Ltd
B 1/I 1 Mohan Cooperative Industrial Area
Mathura Road, New Delhi 110 044

SAGE Publications Asia-Pacific Pte Ltd
33 Pekin Street #02-01
Far East Square
Singapore 048763

Library of Congress Control Number: 2006939053

British Library Cataloguing in Publication data

A catalogue record for this book is available from the British Library

ISBN 978-1-4129-1846-6
ISBN 978-1-4129-1847-3 (pbk)

Typeset by C&M Digitals (P) Ltd, Chennai, India
Printed and bound in Great Britain by TJ International Ltd, Padstow Cornwall
Printed on paper from sustainable resources

To David, Caroline and Chantal, my parents Ingrid and Rudolf Schmid and my grandfather Anton

Contents

Acknowledgements

The author would in particular like to thank the following persons, firms and organizations for their valuable help, suggestions and submission of materials.

First of all my family, in particular David, Chantal and Caroline, and my parents for their everlasting love, patience and support, and the role they play in the intellectual and emotional foundations that made yet another book project possible.

Secondly, my colleagues, friends and contributors, who made important suggestions, provided information and, for some, submitted essential case study material, amongst them, Jean-Philippe Courtois, Ray Pinto, Vojtech Jirku, Mario Rebello, Jan Muehlfeit, Nicole Fontaine and Claire Holveck, Vincent Lacolare and Nicolas Rougy, Christophe Aulnette, Dirk Feldhausen, Delphine Foucaud, Nathalie Pigault and Ricardo Monteiro, Christiane Issa, and others.

Thirdly, Airbus at Toulouse, BASME Macedonia, Microsoft, Altran, Dari Couspate, Domaine des Tourelles, Daniel Lefevre, EuroRSCG, Gijs van IJsel Smits, Michael Lucas, Trygve Sten Gustavsen, P.A. Havnes, Jerome Reboul and Christine Lalonde, Philippe Bucaro, Beti Delovska and Vlatko Danilov, Joel Lequette and Celine Dusser, Francine Gittins, Martin Seppala, the European Union, WTO, World Economic Forum, DBO International B.V., EastWest Institute, Altran, Synops6 International, BASME CT, Philips International and Groupe Consultatif Actuariel Europeen, Schneider Electric, Carrefour, EuroInfoCenter Nice, Agderforskning AS, Volvo Group, and from academia, among others, David Gillingham, Robert Isaak, Lyvie Gueret-Talon, Michael Payte, Claude Chailan, David Weir, Gerard Valim, William Lightfoot and my anonymous reviewers.

Thank you to Ingrid and Rudolf Schmid, Alain Lavaud, Olivier Domerc, Wladimir Sachs and many others.

Also, my research assistants, in particular Laetitia Darnis, Camille Bomal, Amine Bouhassane and Verena Bracke, Michele Ryan, and my proofreaders at CERAM, among them my assistant Christine Lagardere but also Ruth Samson, Laura Cooney, Rini Monnot and Gill Rosner, all the contributors, all my students, and last but not least, Delia Alfonso, Jim Collins and especially Anne Summers at Sage Publications for their professionalism, and their never-ending willingness to provide advice and friendship.

I am grateful to the following for permission to reproduce copyright material:

Professor Michael Czinkota, Wilf Greenwood, Wladimir Sachs, Jacqueline Fendt, William Lightfoot, Gerard Valin, Microsoft International, EuroRSC, Christiane Issa, Mohamed Khalil, Daniel Lefevre, Ricardo Monteiro, Gijs van IJsel Smits, Dirk Feldhausen, Laetitia Darnis, Nicolas Rougy, Per A. Havnes, Jerome Reboul, Joel Lequette, Michael Payte, Delphine Foucaud, Martin Seppala, Carla Irene Coen, Sak Onkvisit and John Shaw.

Eurobarometer Interactive Search System Satisfaction with national and EU democracy (http://ec.europa.eu/public_opinion/cf/subquestionoutput_en.cfm), the flag of the EU (http://europa.eu/abc/symbols/emblem/index_en.htm), Geopolitical and river map of the EU after enlargement to 25 Member States in 2004 and of the candidate countries except Croatia (http://ec.europa.eu/avservices/photo/photo_thematic_en.cfm?id=&mark=PRO, CART), table 1 European Divergence of Asylum Policy taken from CEC Asylum statistics (http://europa.euant/comm/justice_home/doc_centre/asylum/statistical/docs/2001/total_number_decisions_en.pdf; http://ec.europa.eu/justice_home/doc_centre/asylum/statistics/doc_asylum_statistics_en.htm), extract from European Coal and Steel Treaty (http://europa.eu/scadplus/treaties/ecsc_en.htm and http://eur-lex.europa.eu/en/treaties/treaties_founding.htm), the Directorates-General and Services (http://ec.europa.eu/dgs_en.htm), Six European Legislative Tools – The three objectives of the structural funds (http://europa.eu.int/scadplus/leg/en/lvb/I60014.htm), A Council, Parliament and Economic and Social Committee conclusion about Single European Market needs (http://ec.europa.eu./internal_market/strategy/docs/comstrat_en.pdf), The first Report on Competition Policy 1972, Evolution of the exchange rate between US Dollar and the Euro from January 1999 to July 2005 (http://www.ecb.eu/pub/pub/stats/html/index.en.html) and the table 'Share of EU exports % …' (http://ec.europa.eu/comm/external_relations/asia/rel/ eco.htm).

Permissions are granted and all acknowledgement is given to the European Communities and to the source © European Communities. Figure 5, Source: Map of Europe with 25 members, © European Communities [2007] [http://europa.eu/abc/maps/index_en.htm.]

The European Communities consider legislative and quasi-legislative documents published in the *Official Journal of the European Union* and related COM and SEC series as well as charters and treaties and ECJ case-law to be in the public domain. Prior written permission is thus not required for their reproduction, and they may be reproduced freely without restriction, including for the purpose of further non-commercial dissemination to final users, subject to the condition that appropriate acknowledgement is given to the European Communities and to the source, and provided that the additional guidelines set out below are respected.

For whenever a document is reproduced verbatim from a source other than the printed version of the *Official Journal of the European Union*, we attract your attention to the following disclaimer that

'Only European Community legislation printed in the paper edition of the *Official Journal of the European Union* is deemed authentic.'

Noting that the EU moreover, does not consider a 'further commercial dissemination' the inclusion, as reference material for consultation purposes, of small amounts of relevant legislative texts in articles/thesis/studies/reports/books issued by third-party authors or publishers, whatever the means, and disseminated subject to payment.

WTO Publications for all WTO quoted statistics and tables, as well as 'The EU at WTO negotiations: The United States call for countervailing measures concerning certain products from Europe (Recourse to Article 21.5 of the DSU by the European Communities)' and 'GPA – A case of diversity in multinational negotiations re: government procurement' material. AB Volvo for the mini case study.

Thank you for the advice and agreement of all companies and organizations mentioned in this book.

Whilst every effort was made to trace the owners of copyright material, in a few cases this has proved impossible and I would like to offer my apologies for such cases that I may unwittingly have infringed. I would appreciate any information that would enable me to trace the owner of such copyright and include them for the right tribute to their work.

The testimonials, case studies, case study teaching notes and other support material are intended to be used as a basis for classwork and discussion rather than to illustrate effective or ineffective handling of business operations or management issues.

1 Introduction: The New European Business Environment

1.1 Centrepiece: The idea of creating a 'unified Europe'

The idea of creating a 'unified Europe' to maintain peace and to create a common European culture has resurfaced repeatedly over European history, although the ideal of a united Europe has its origins in classical philosophical thinking. In the fourteenth century, for example, Pierre Dubois[1] proposed a European confederation that was to be governed by a European council, while in the nineteenth century, Victor Hugo[2] envisaged a political, federal Europe, uniting nations and unifying people. In a speech to the French National Assembly on 1 March 1871 he said:

> Plus de frontières! Le Rhin à tous! Soyons la même République, soyons les États-Unis d'Europe, soyons la fédération continentale, soyons la liberté européenne, soyons la paix universelle!*

Through industrialization and the evolution of trade across frontiers over centuries, nations came to expand their knowledge of different economic systems and trade mechanisms. The end of the feudal system, the mercantilist era from *c.*1600 to *c.*1800, and colonialism shaped societies and their economic and social functioning. The term 'mercantilism' originates from the Latin word *mercari*, meaning 'to run a trade', and from *merx*, meaning 'commodity'. It sets the scene for economic and political interest in internationalization. Mercantilism ideologically underpinned cross-border trade long enough to leave its mark driving exports rather than imports, in so far as a country needed a positive balance of trade to gain more precious metals (gold and silver), and determining that governments introduced tariffs that would inhibit other countries from gaining an economic advantage. The political economist Adam Smith, who is generally considered the father of economics, popularized the term in *The Wealth of Nations* (1776) where he analyzed the exchange mechanisms that drive economies – and indeed, every economic system embraces some exchange activity.

The appeal of harmonious trade for economic growth and welfare developed increasingly from the mid-eighteenth century onwards: more than the dream of peace and stability

---

* 'No more borders! The Rhine to all! Let's be the same Republic, the United States of Europe, let's be the continental federation, let's be the European freedom, let's be the Universal peace!'

across peoples and nations, the idea of welfare through profitable economic relations was easier to share among all peoples. Adam Smith's book set the foundations for a classical trade theory that evolved strongly on European grounds, and that was complemented in later years by the mainly Anglo-Saxon school of international business research, which analyzed transactions and investments of corporations across borders. It is important at this stage to recognize that the convergence of Europe stems from a basis of economic and philosophical history, and that during the twentieth century this convergence led to pressure on states that had seen their power and sovereignty erode to the benefit of regionalism and globalization. International trade relations thus became key to the fulfilment of the European idea and ideal.

In Europe, economic and political integration have been driven by one predominant fundamental objective: 'Keeping peace among nations'. Interaction between people and their economies has indeed maintained peace for longer than in any other region of the world. Certain European countries have joined together to create a unique organization for this purpose: the European Union (EU). An organization of states, not a confederation, nor an organization of the types generally known in international relations, but rather the most advanced form of economic integration worldwide that is flirting closely with the temptations of political union. As such, the Member States have created a single market that marries competitiveness with certain social ideals (welfare, human rights, equality and many others). The European market place is both the driver and the stimulus of Europe, as it has shaped and is being shaped by the European ideal. It represents the largest economy in the world, the largest trading partner and the largest donor of development assistance.

This market offers opportunities to those corporations that recognize the pros and cons of convergence, and that make the most out of the diversity of cultures, languages, business practices and management styles. At the same time, the challenge for the European institutions is to maintain European developments close to its citizens and to balance a productive economy with social welfare.

The objective of this book is to prepare future managers to face up to the resulting challenges and opportunities for doing business in Europe – a Europe enlarged and deepened through continuous integration. Whether you will be working in a local, a European or an international company, you will be confronted with the issues dealt with in this book. Globalization and Europeanization expose any company operating in or dealing with Europe to those challenges of diversity.

In this introductory chapter, we take a brief look at attitudes among citizens and at some European foundations and symbols, and then introduce some terms and concepts that have a bearing on discussions later in the book.

1.2 Europe: For European citizens and abroad

The European idea and ideal are centred on the citizen and her/his welfare. It is driven by economics and politics, in symbiosis with European competitiveness and its role in the world.

Box 1   The European Union

The EU, originally known as the European Economic Community (EEC) prior to 1993, is a highly advanced form of economic integration. It is a market grouping of more than 27 countries that promotes the economic wealth of its members not only through barrier-free trade, but also through many other coordinated activities such as a common competition policy, internal and external trade policy, research and development policy, industrial and social policy, and so on. The creation of a central European bank and the adoption of a common currency, the euro, significantly contribute to its singular nature in the world. The EU operates as one economic unit in international trade negotiations.

The EU therefore regularly studies the attitudes of its citizens.[3] Among the statistics that are found in these surveys, it is noteworthy that more than 9 in 10 EU citizens feel that it is extremely or very important to help others and to value people for who they are, while more than 8 in 10 believe that it is important to be involved in creating a better society. These societal values are strong in each Member State.

At the same time, EU citizens seem to appreciate specific identity and traditionalism. Nearly 7 in 10 want to live in a world in which people live by traditional values. We are a long way from a standardization or homogeneity of the peoples of Europe; for business, this is where challenges of values and diversity unfold.

Box 2   EU Member States: Who are they?

In 2007, the EU comprised the following 27 Member States: Austria, Belgium, Bulgaria, Cyprus, Czech Republic, Denmark, Estonia, Germany, Greece, Finland, France, Hungary, Ireland, Italy, Latvia, Lithuania, Luxembourg, Malta, Poland, Portugal, Romania, Slovakia, Slovenia, Spain, Sweden, The Netherlands, United Kingdom (UK).

Is there a European identity among citizens? Again, EU statistics, as well as student surveys conducted by the author at several business schools, illustrate that the majority of EU citizens feel to some extent 'European', in particular those who travel or work across frontiers, while they preserve a strong feeling of adherence to particular roots and culture. Eurostat (the Statistical Office of the European Communities) notes that this feeling of adherence differs greatly among countries: people in Luxembourg are most likely to feel themselves to be European only. This is much higher than in any of the other countries and

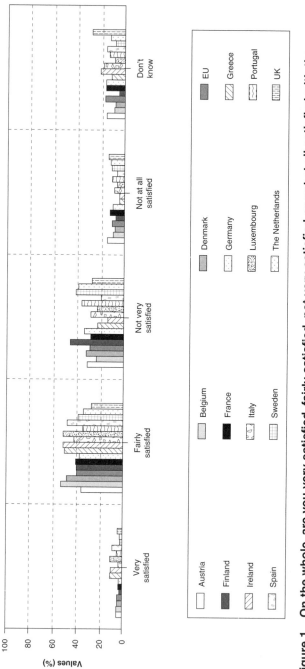

Figure 1 On the whole, are you very satisfied, fairly satisfied, not very satisfied or not at all satisfied with the way democracy works in your country?

Source: (© European Commission: 2004) Eurobarometer Interactive Search System Satisfaction with national and EU democracy, CEC April 2004 (EB61)

1   On the whole are European citizens satisfied with the life they lead?
2   On the whole, are European citizens satisfied with the way democracy works (in your country and in Europe)?
3   In general, are European citizens in favor of or against efforts being made to unify Western Europe?
4   Generally speaking, do you think that (your country's) membership of the European Union is a good thing?
5   Taking everything into consideration, would you say that you/your country has on balance benefited or not from being a member of the European Union?
6   At the beginning of the next decade, will the European Union play a more or less important or the same role in European citizen's daily life?
7   How much do you feel that you know about the European institutions? Which Institutions? What's your level of knowledge about their functioning? (Self-assessment)
8   As a European citizen, do you think that the European Parliament protects your interests?

Figure 2   A selection of the questions to European citizens and business people (CEC, 2005, http://europa.eu.int/comm/public_opinion/cf/index_en.cfm)

can be explained by the high proportion of citizens from other EU countries that reside in Luxembourg. Nonetheless, there are seven other countries where people who feel to some extent European are in the majority: Italy, Spain, France, Belgium, The Netherlands, Austria and Germany. In the other EU countries, people who identify exclusively with their own nationality are in the majority, although in Portugal, Ireland and new Member States, this majority is very small. In the UK, Sweden, Finland, Greece and, to a slightly smaller extent, Denmark national identity is very strong. The strong adherence of Europeans to the values related to democracy is an essential part of the identity that drives integration. Figure 1 summarizes public opinion on the matter, and reflects a need for the EU to make further progress in that field.

A spring 1997 Euro barometer study surveyed young Europeans aged 15 to 29. This sample is interesting because it represents future employers and employees and decision makers in all spheres of European society. The survey found that 25 per cent felt that the presence of foreigners added to their country's strength. These figures were reconfirmed through a 2001–5 survey of Europeans in several business schools. When asked which areas the EU should prioritize in the next five years, the key issue for these future business and political leaders was employment, closely followed by research and development in new technologies (see Figure 2). In regard to the general image of the EU for young people, the results indicate that it represents:

• the freedom to move within the Member States;
• a better future;
• a better economic situation.

Very few young people felt that the EU represented negative elements, such as too much bureaucracy or the loss of cultural diversity, or that the goals of the EU were unrealistic. We can legitimately conclude that Europe has made unprecedented progress towards its ideal of peace, political and economic stability and welfare, and that this progress has shaped a reality for citizens, politics and economics that more often than not is fully assumed in its diversity.

1.3 Foundations and symbols

1.3.1 Why 'Europe'?

In Greek mythology, Europa was the daughter of a king of Tyre in Phoenicia. Zeus, attracted by her, transformed himself into a white bull, seduced her, and ran away with her on his back to the sea. He took her to the island of Crete and, after revealing his true identity, made her the island's first queen. The semantic root of the name 'Europa' is to be found in the word 'ereb' (dark) – the European continent as seen from Phoenicia was located towards the west where the sun sets. The kidnapping of Europa is a frequently represented motif in Antique arts. The continent of Europe is now called Europa in all Germanic and Slavic languages that use the Latin and Greek alphabet. Also, Isis was often represented standing on the crescent moon, with 12 stars surrounding her head.

1.3.2 The European flag

The European flag (see Figure 3) is the symbol of the EU and of Europe's unity and identity in a wider sense. In ancient Greece, the number 12 stood for harmony. Traditionally it symbolizes perfection, completeness and unity; thus the circle of 12 golden stars represents the ideal harmony between the peoples of Europe. The number of stars is not dependent on the number of Member States. The flag therefore has remained unchanged since the beginning of 1986, regardless of EU enlargements. The European flag is the only emblem of the European Commission. Other EU institutions and bodies complement it with an emblem of their own.

Figure 3   The EU flag

1.3.3 The European anthem

The Hymn of Joy from the Ninth Symphony composed in 1823 by Ludwig Van Beethoven was adopted by the heads of Member States and governments in 1985 as the official European anthem.

Without words, in the universal language of music, it expresses the European ideals of freedom, peace and solidarity. The anthem does not replace the national anthems of the Member States but is symbolically celebrating the values shared by them: United in diversity – along the EU's motto. The anthem can be heard on http://europa.eu.int/abc/symbols/anthem/index_en.htm

1.3.4 9 May – Europe Day

On 9 May 1950, Robert Schuman presented his proposal for the creation of an organized Europe, essential for a prosperous post-war European future and peace between nations. The Schuman declaration is considered to be one of the great landmarks of European integration. Today, 9 May is 'Europe Day', a symbol, along with the single currency (the euro), the flag and the anthem, that supports the shared identity of the EU. It is a day of activities and festivities across Europe, celebrating political and economic stability and integration. More information on Europe Day can be found online at http://www.europa.eu.int/abc/.

1.3.5 The euro

The EU and its unity are also symbolized by the introduction in 2002 of a single currency, the euro, that replaced the currency of participating Member States. This was the result of a long process that began in 1969 and was spread over several stages. The preliminary stage, between 1969 and 1993, saw the development of the European Monetary System (EMS), the transitional stage, between 1999 and 2001, the official launch of the euro on 1 January 1999, and the final stage, in 2002, the introduction of coins and bills for circulation.

1.4 Some terms and concepts

Before you begin to concentrate on the forthcoming chapters, it is necessary to define several terms and concepts that will be used throughout the text.

1.4.1 Globalization

In the context of this book, the term of globalization means the compression of time and space that increases the frequency and duration of linkages between any given actors in the international environment. This implies a complex structure of integrated activities, mainly economic, but also those driven by political, environmental and geopolitical considerations. The compression of time translates into a high sequence of interaction between any of the given actors; for example, impacting on the rapidity of orders over the Internet or of how long it takes to have a product delivered. The compression of space results in a geographical proximity with countries (and thus markets) that appeared very far away some decades ago. The major advances made in transport and in information and communication technology are at the origin of much of this. Therefore, these sectors play an important role in the competitiveness of sectors and markets.

1.4.2 Europeanization

Europeanization is a term that is used in two senses. The first implies the European integration of economies and the development of common policies of EU Member States. Hence, Europeanization is considered here as an advanced case of globalization. Thus the impact of Europeanization in this context can be measured via the importance of EU internal and external trade compared to non-EU – countries and market groupings such as NAFTA (North American Free Trade Agreement). For example, the Organization for Economic Cooperation and Development (OECD) regularly publishes relevant data.

Secondly, when used in connection with business corporations, Europeanization deals with advanced forms of organization that reflect (a) the diversity of markets and cultures; and (b) the diversity within companies as well as in the scope of their operations. One example of a Europeanized firm is Eurocopter, the leader in military helicopters and part of the EADS (European Aeronautic, Defence and Space) group. The company was established in 1986 by a French and a German aerospace leader, and is now a truly European company in terms of shareholder nationality, partners, employees and management. It has taken what it has learned from trading in the European market and developed it into an international competitiveness.

1.4.3 Multinational and transnational firms

International business operations are transactions across borders that may be pursued via different forms of corporate structure and types of transaction, depending on the relation of risks and returns that are expected from investments in those transactions. They may encompass exports and imports, licensing, franchising or subcontracting, outsourcing and offshoring strategies, direct foreign investment into joint ventures, or greenfield investment. The basic definition implies that cross-border activity is different from domestic trade. Therefore, an organization with substantial foreign investment may take the shape of a multinational enterprise (MNE), that is, a corporation that has its headquarters in one country but also operates in others. An MNE is typically engaged in the active management of its offshore assets. Another commonly used form of organization is the transnational company (TNC), defining a firm that coordinates and controls operations across borders through an organizational design that allows for local responsiveness. These firms are typically well adapted through a structure and strategy that responds relatively easily to the changing external business environment, and evaluates the particular advantages of locations at any given time.

1.4.4 The company typology

Large organizations interest us in terms of their ability to profit from Europeanization and to adapt organizational structures and business functions to cross-border networks of decision making, coordination, control, knowledge management and quasi-institutionalization. However, small- and medium-sized enterprises (SMEs) play a particular role in the European business environment: 99 per cent of companies in Europe (i.e. 23 million firms) are SMEs. The European Commission defines SMEs as 'enterprises which employ fewer than 250 persons and which have an annual turnover not exceeding 50 million euro, and/or an annual balance sheet total not exceeding 43 million euro' (Article 2 of the Annex of Recommendation 2003/361/EC, see also definitions in Table 1). We will frequently refer to the role of SMEs and to the importance of flexibility, innovativeness and trade diversion to SME management.

Table 1   Staff headcount and financial ceilings determining enterprise categories

Enterprise category	Headcount	Turnover and/or	Balance sheet total
Medium-sized	<250	≤ €50 million	≤ €43 million
Small	<50	≤ €10 million	≤ €10 million
Micro	<10	≤ €2million	≤ €2 million

Source: *Commission Recommendation 2003/361/EC, Annex 1, Article 2*, Official Journal L124, *20 May 2003, p. 0039*

It is also important here to distinguish between a private and a public sector company. A private company cannot offer its shares to the public and restricts the right to transfer them. On the other hand a public company is owned by the public. There are two uses of this term. It may indicate a company that is owned by stockholders who are members of the general public and is traded publicly. Ownership is open to anyone who has the money and inclination to buy shares in the company; government often owns a minority of shares. A public company may also be fully or mainly owned by a local, regional or national government. Employees may take stock options. For instance, in Belgium between 70,000 and 75,000 employees have received stock options since 1999 and almost all of the 20 largest Belgian corporations (BEL20) operate stock option plans. In Germany they were introduced in 1997 and by 2006 over two-thirds of companies included in the German stock index (DAX) were running employee stock option programmes. In France, approximately 50 per cent of all quoted companies and 95 per cent of companies use stock option plans.

The main European directives on employee participation introduced pan-European structures for a range of business and employment issues in multinational companies over a certain size operating in the EU. Directive (2002/14/EC) sets a framework for informing and consulting employees and/or their representatives for all undertakings with at least 50 employees (or establishments with at least 20 employees) that are required to provide employee representatives with information and/or consultation on a range of business, employment and work organization issues. Directives 2001/86/EC and 2003/72/EC expand employee involvement in the European Company and in the European Cooperative Society – the new optional form of Europe-wide company set up under the European Company Statute. The directives add information and consultation structures, procedures and board-level participation (cf. R. Davletguildeev, Trade Unions Advisory Committee to the OECD Third Eurasian Roundtable on Corporate Governance, 29–30 October 2003, Bishkek).

The competitiveness of business depends on innovation, efficient knowledge management and entrepreneurship. In Europe, the impact of multilateral decision making and policies on competitiveness is recognized by European and third-country business working across frontiers. The results can be measured by the attractiveness of the European market for foreign industrial location and investment, and is a subject of vivid debate in political and business circles. The main advantages are based on the European cost base, on taxation levels, on the availability of skilled, trained labour, on effective linkages between research/academia and the corporate sector business, and on the internationalization opportunities of European products and services. But the European business environment is also subject to the struggle between national interests and the efficiency of economic sectors vis-à-vis each other and the world. The EU is thus a microcosm of opportunities and challenges preparing you for global business.

1.5 Structure of the book

The book is divided into four parts. Part I sets the foundations necessary for doing business in Europe. This section, which follows this Introduction, begins with Chapter 2, which presents an overview of the main European landmarks. It discusses the evolution of the numerous treaties and how the European business environment has developed in relation to them. The chapter is complemented by a review of the impact of certain treaties on business, and presents briefly the tools necessary for the successful implementation of European integration. While Chapter 2 illustrates the depth of integration of the European marketplace, Chapter 3 examines past, present and future waves of enlargement, and looks into the future of an EU with new Member States. The analyses are placed into the framework of integration theories that help us understand the diversity of approaches which Member States may have while striving for further integration. Where does Europe aim to go, why and by which manner? Waves of larger European integration appear to foster trade creation but may also cause trade diversion. What opportunities and challenges does enlargement bring with it? Chapter 4 studies the framework in which European policies are negotiated, streamlined, debated and decided: the institutions and its main actors. The main actors are identified and the key roles highlighted.

Part II is divided into two chapters. Chapter 5 provides a clear understanding of the causes and effects of globalization and the related issues for European and international firms in achieving competitive advantage in increasingly integrated markets. This chapter proposes two complementary perspectives for this analysis. Internally, the single market represents the opportunities that come with the most highly integrated economic grouping worldwide, that is, a business environment that has evolved into a complex but ever-increasing opportunity network for business activity. Externally, the EU is a major actor in the international geopolitical environment, and plays a particular role in globalization. What is this role? What is the implication of this role for international business? What impact does this internationalization have on European firms of different sizes and sectors? Chapter 6 demonstrates how management and knowledge are becoming central to the strategic focus of European firms. In all Member States, distinct management styles, cultures and structures, and resulting management and HR issues can be identified.

Part III focuses on essential 'business activity functions in the European environment'. European economies are characterized in particular by the common policies and the harmonization of rules that attempt to maximize the benefit gained from trade and financial integration through risk-sharing, spill-over of macroeconomic fluctuations as well as product and consumption co-movements. Chapter 7 shows how economic harmonization raises fundamental issues for business and business creation in Europe. Chapter 8 develops the marketing perspective that helps businesses operate with the knowledge of the methodology necessary for approaching and managing marketing in the large European environment. European diversity makes marketing a product or a service at the European level both challenging and worthwhile. But hidden or subtle differences in pricing, consumer attitudes, specific buying processes, cash flow management, the structure of distribution and communication, settling legal differences, and the practice of arbitration also make marketing on a European scale more difficult. The European arena offers opportunities for economies of scale, but requires a sound knowledge of European lifestyles and consumption patterns, the buying process, and the typology and segmentation of the European markets with appropriate marketing strategies and techniques.

Another essential business function in today's Europe is that of public affairs management and lobbying. An increasing number of public and private organizations are represented at the European institutional level: for this reason, Chapter 9 explores lobbying networks, and analyzes the arena, players and competition in the decision-making game. It illustrates the most recognized methods to make your business be heard in Brussels, Strasbourg and Luxembourg. This is where your business environment is shaped, and competitiveness either strives or fails. International competitiveness is the key issue covered in Chapter 10. The chapter examines relations of the EU with its trading partners, and places issues of international competitiveness into a concluding discussion of globalization and Europeanization. It places *Doing Business in Europe* into the international context.

The last part of the book contains case studies related to the concepts developed in the previous chapters. The case studies illustrate the realities of companies that compete in the European marketplace as it has developed, as it exists today and as it will evolve tomorrow. Their cases demonstrate clearly the need to participate in European and international activities.

Throughout the chapters, the objective is (a) to provide you with the fundamentals of theory and concepts; and (b) to link these clearly to the business environment. Every sequence is followed by an evaluation of the impact on business. Short case studies illustrate the way in which corporations experience the realities of the European business environment. The questions after each case study ask you to apply your freshly acquired knowledge and to define the solutions that may be adapted to that very case. Testimonials reflect the intimate thinking of business people as regards the issues raised within each chapter. Finally, the web guide leads you to websites on which you can find valuable information about the chapter topics, and are there to help you with your assignments. Do try to answer the review questions after each chapter to make sure that you have indeed acquired the knowledge, and that you can now go ahead with the next chapter, as the chapters build on each other. Also, the book concludes with case studies that illustrate a variety of business challenges and asks the relevant questions that are crucial for 'doing business in Europe'.

Review questions

1 **What** knowledge is key to success for a company doing business in Europe?
2 **Explain** the ideal of Europe.
3 **What** role does European integration play for business?
4 Vice versa, **what** role does business play for European integration?
5 **Why** does Europe need symbols?

Web guide

General information

http://europa.eu.int Gateway to the EU: activities, institutions, documents, services, etc.
http://www.europa.eu.int/information_society/index_en.htm Europe's
    information society.
http://europa.eu.int/abc/index_en.htm The EU: panorama, treaties, etc.
http://www.answers.com/topic/history-of-the-european-union Some EU history.
http://www.europa.admin.ch/eu/expl/uebersicht/e/#1 The EU in brief.
http://www.europeanvoice.com/ EU news from *European Voice*.
http://www.sme-union.org/ SMEs in the EU.

Public surveys – European citizens

http://europa.eu.int/comm/public_opinion/index_en.htm Public opinion towards the EU.
http://europa.eu.int/europedirect/Answering services European citizens
    concerns by phone.
http://europa.eu.int/comm/public_opinion/cf/index_en.cfm Select a trend question
    and find the related study made by the EU.
http://europa.eu.int/comm/enlargement/opinion/#eurobarometer Public opinion
    about European enlargement – European citizens.

Notes

1 Royal advocate of the *bailliage* in Coutances. He was not only an important figure in France's war against Pope Boniface VIII but also the creative force behind a project to restore Jerusalem to the French king, Philip IV.
2 Renowned poet, novelist and dramatist, but also a senator under the Third Republic.
3 Office for Official Publication of the European Communities (2001) *How the Europeans See Themselves – Looking Through the Mirror with Public Opinion Surveys*. Brussels: European Commission Press and Communication Service (available online through continuous tracking survey 97.8 at http://europa.eu/publications/booklets/eu_documentation/05/txt_en.pdf); and How Europeans See Themselves (available online at http://www.europa.eu.int/comm/public_ opinion/index_en.htm).

Part I

THE IMPACT OF 50 YEARS ON THE EUROPEAN BUSINESS GAME

2

Landmarks of European Integration, or How History and Politics Shape the Business Environment

---

What you will learn about in this chapter

- The historic evolution of the European market.
- The main European treaties and their direct business impact.
- The business opportunities that unfold.
- The new challenges stemming from constitutional plans.

2.1 Origins: Not only a Franco-German reconciliation

Doing business in Europe requires an understanding of a set of historical realities. Understanding the European market, its diversities and characteristics requires us to look back at the historical development of European integration.

The formulation of a plan to work together among European states originates mainly from the period between 1870 and 1945, when Germany and France fought each other three times. The last military conflict in the EU area, World War II, left more than 50 million people dead and economies devastated. Thus the only hope for lasting peace and prosperity in Europe was to strive for unity on an economic and, if possible, political, social and cultural level, and not for further punishment of and revenge on those countries that were in chaos and confusion. A number of leaders, in particular Konrad Adenauer (the first Chancellor of the new Federal Republic of Germany, or West Germany) and Charles de Gaulle (the first post-war President of France), were deeply involved in a process that has been ongoing ever since.

This long-term process of integration spans the initial treaty that created the European Coal and Steel Community (ECSC) up to and beyond the formulation of a European Constitution. The legislation and cooperation within Europe includes many actors and provides the basis not only of its business environment but also for the role of the EU internationally.

Box 3   The PanEuropa movement

In 1923, Count Coudenhove-Kalergi founded a PanEuropa movement with the aim of uniting the European states. Political and economic tensions (in Germany in particular) – caused not only by upheavals between political parties and politically motivated groups, but also by internal and global economic crises – hindered these unification aspirations. Indeed the resentment after World War I harboured among European nations proved to be insurmountable.

Relations between the European states have been transformed: efforts to foster reconciliation and partnerships have evolved into deep economic and political cooperation and competition, while violence and demolition have been replaced by peaceful conflict resolution mechanisms and growth. Political and geopolitical stability has been obtained through reinforced economic interaction – a concept that Kofi Annan, Secretary-General of the United Nations (UN) from 2002–2006, also subscribed to at the international level.

Specifically, the post-1945 period was marked by two phenomena. One was the desire to combat nationalism, leading in parallel to further decolonization, the other was the new power situation in Europe – dominated by United States (US)–Soviet relations during the Cold War. This bipolarity shaped the business environment in Europe into diverging economic, political and socio-cultural systems, divided within Germany and symbolized by the Berlin Wall, that from 1961 to 1989 divided East and West.

In the international business environment, pre-war and wartime experiences led to the creation of several multilateral organizations that were to have a strong impact on international business and a significant influence on the laws and regulations in the development of European integration. The UN is one example, but these also stimulated the creation of new international economic and financial arrangements.

The first fruits of this were realized at the Bretton Woods Conference in 1944, where the representatives of 44 countries, led by the UK and the US, agreed to the establishment of fixed exchange rates and of two new bodies. The first of these was the International Monetary Fund (IMF) as a means to deal with balance of payments problems; it is the first international monetary authority endowed to a certain extent with the power of national authorities. The second body, the International Bank for Reconstruction and Development (the World Bank), was set up as a means to facilitate international trade. In 1947 the General Agreement on Tariffs and Trade (GATT), the predecessor of the World Trade Organization (WTO) established in 1994, was signed by a first group of 23 countries. Its goals were defined to encompass the reduction of customs, tariffs and trade barriers with the underlying perception that a rise in living standards, the provision of supplies and the exploiting of resources on the world market necessitated unhindered competition. One year later, in 1948, the General Assembly of the UN ratified the Universal Declaration of Human Rights in order to complement the rules governing increasing cross-border relations.

Within this multilateral collaboration, led by the UK and the US, an unprecedented degree of cooperation between France and West Germany took shape, and gave birth to a form of

'European integration'. The European Recovery Programme, or the Marshall Plan as it is better known, gave rise to the stimuli necessary for this development, that is the launch of economic cooperation and a customs union on a small scale.

After years of cyclic euro-optimism and euro-pessimism, and after decades of adapting to the interests of the different Member States, a unique organization has taken shape that today comprises (on different levels of integration) the quasi-entity of Europe as one market, and deals as one force in international negotiations, for example at the WTO. The 'Franco-West German engine', that is the power and influence exercised by these two countries, and the experience of the founding members in dealing with each other during the post-war period have driven what was initially a successful peacekeeping measure on towards becoming the largest alliance of countries ever to work together in an economic and (partly) monetary union that is complemented by social, cultural, environmental, security and other harmonizing initiatives.

Figure 4 illustrates the various degrees of international integration. It correlates degrees of market integration with the harmonization of policies, the intensity of the resulting correlation defining the level of integration achieved. The EU has experienced all of the degrees of integration shown by the arrow in Figure 4 and is now at a level whereby efforts are being made for yet, deeper integration. This is clearly a historical and unique development for a business environment. The original Franco-West German reconciliation has clearly overcome historical divergences. A united Europe, launched with the other founding members of the ECSC, Belgium, The Netherlands, Luxembourg (the Benelux countries) and Italy has vastly enlarged its ideas and ideals. Its geographical layout can be studied in Figure 5, which shows the map of Europe after the EU enlargement to 25 members in 2004.

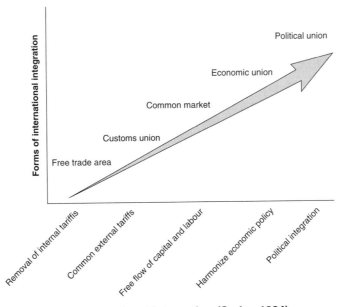

Figure 4   The degrees of international integration (Suder, 1994)

Figure 5 Map of Europe with 25 members

Driving Europe jointly since the early 1950s, France and Germany (West Germany before unification in 1990) often appear to reflect what could be called a hostile brotherhood. Both countries and their peoples deeply believe in the benefits of both European integration and political and economic stability among its members, all the more so due to the difficult history they share. For at least half a century, they proclaimed the mantra that Europe can only develop if the two partners agree. Yet their unique partnership is marked by divisions. France is characterized by a traditionally centralized, Catholic, individualist and hierarchical structure, focusing on the state as a nation principle. Its people are thought to be passionate, sensitive, elitist, used to improvising and to the power of the street, with a belief in the pursued role of the grand nation. Germany is a rather new, decentralized structure, partly Catholic but mainly Protestant, for historical reasons profoundly democratic and egalitarian, its people abhorring any authoritarian system. They are thought to be down-to-earth, well-organized, peace-oriented, and taught to deal with uncomfortable issues and truths. In European integration, these characteristics translate into diverse behaviour. The French elite favour mainly an intergovernmental decision-making process in Europe, avoiding a high degree of supranational power, with different groups of regions working together on a 'variable geometric', preserving sovereignty over issues such as that of foreign policy. In Germany, the tendency is towards a federal Europe, though based on nation-states, with its own constitution and institutions, possibly led by a hard core of countries leading European integration. The country favours a common foreign and security policy both for historical reasons, and because it cannot act unilaterally.

Franco-German tensions have marked much of contemporary history: German unification, recognition of Croatia, nuclear tests and waste, French resistance to the German-inspired stability pact, the choice of Head of the European Central Bank, the reforms of agricultural policy, and the ratification of the European Constitution to mention just a few, and at times shifts of power in Europe have put the Franco-German partnership into question, in particular regarding its role in contemporary Europe. While it may lose some of its power at EU level, the partnership may well continue for a very long time to come, otherwise, both sides would have too much to lose (compiled from *The Economist, Le Figaro* and *Frankfurter Allgemeine Zeitung*, 2005). Across Europe, reconciliation is no longer a motivating force for most generations, but has been replaced by a desire for ongoing social and economic welfare.

2.2 The Schuman declaration

In 1943, Jean Monnet, a member of the National Liberation Committee of the Free French government (Comité Français de Libération National – CFLN), declared to the committee: 'There will be no peace in Europe, if the states are reconstituted on the basis of national sovereignty … The countries of Europe are too small to guarantee their peoples the necessary prosperity and social development. The European states must constitute themselves into a federation.' Monnet, who was in charge of French industrial modernization, is today regarded as one of the main architects of European unity. Together with Robert Schuman, French Foreign Minister, he developed the Schuman Plan for a united European market of coal and steel production. Schuman proposed the plan on 9 May 1950: the creation of an organized Europe, stating that it was indispensable to the maintenance of peaceful relations. This proposal, known as the 'Schuman declaration', can legitimately be considered as the starting point of European integration. Schuman (1950) underlines both the motives for and the planned organization of European cooperation when he states in the declaration that:

> World peace cannot be safeguarded without the making of creative efforts proportionate to the dangers which threaten it. The contribution which an organized and living Europe can bring to civilization is indispensable to the maintenance of peaceful relations. … A united Europe was not achieved and we had war. … Europe will not be made all at once, or according to a single plan. It will be built through concrete achievements which first create a *de facto* solidarity. The coming together of the nations of Europe requires the elimination of the age-old opposition of France and Germany. Any action taken must in the first place concern these two countries. … By pooling basic production and by instituting a new High Authority, whose decisions will bind France, Germany and other member countries, this proposal will lead to the realization of the first concrete foundation of a European federation indispensable to the preservation of peace.

The UK was invited at this stage to participate, but the government thought that such an undertaking would undermine national sovereignty, and so refused.

2.3 Understanding integration: the main treaties

The founding treaties are the result of negotiations between the Member States pursuing two main objectives: to benefit from an efficient and effective European integration, and to promote and defend national interests. You will now learn about the treaties that were the result of these negotiations and look at those that are considered fundamental and provide European business with its contemporary macroeconomic conditions.

The 1950s and 1960s were rather prosperous in terms of setting the foundations for a united Europe. In the mid-1950s the founder members of the ECSC (see p. 27) agreed to explore further economic and atomic cooperation and in 1957 they joined with the European Atomic Energy Community (Euratom) to establish the EEC, also referred to as the Common Market, and later as the European Community (EC). In 1963 the Elysée Treaty become a key component in the eventual creation of the EU because it set the scene for enhanced Franco-German cooperation and, although only bilateral, it is considered as a milestone agreement between two former enemies. It had an important positive impact on how the security of Europe was perceived. 'It is good for our children,' Chancellor Adenauer and President de Gaulle agreed, and set the basis for cooperation in areas as diverse as education and training, culture, research and technology, foreign affairs, defence and security, and the Europeanization of business.

Nevertheless, from the 1970s to the mid-1980s world events, such as the hardening of East–West attitudes during the Cold War, the increasing north–south divide, the oil crises, and, in particular, the geopolitical turmoil in the Middle East, caused a slow down the progress that was being made towards European unity. The Member States were like a small firm alliance that grows bigger and faces organizational, strategic and geographical complexities and has to look into its internal structure and external strategy … but that will not necessarily stop its growth.

This period became known as the years of 'Euro-pessimism' or 'Euro-scepticism'. Nonetheless, the EC grew in size due to considerable enlargement into the north and south. From the mid-1980s, negotiations about treaty reforms crucial to the evolution of European integration intensified and led to the 1986 Single European Act (SEA), the 1992 Maastricht Treaty, the 1997 Amsterdam Treaty, the 2001 Nice Treaty and the Constitution of the European Union. They have tremendous consequences for the European market and for the opportunities for and challenges of doing business in Europe. Table 2 shows the main treaties established since 1951.

2.3.1 The Treaty of Paris

2.3.1.1 The first founding treaty

The Treaty of Paris established the ECSC and was signed by the founder members in Paris on 18 April 1951. The Treaty was conceived from the Schuman Plan and laid the basis for the four main European institutions: the Council of Ministers, a Common Assembly (later the European Parliament), the Court of Justice, and a High Authority. The objectives of the ECSC were to:

Table 2 The main European treaties established since 1951

Date signed	Treaty	Place of signature	Date entering force	Impact on business
18 April 1951	**European Coal and Steel Community**	Paris	23 July 1952	A strong impact on business in the coal and steel industries
25 March 1957	**European Economic Community**	Rome	1 January 1958	Creation of a free trade area evolving into a customs union that removed internal tariffs on goods and harmonized external tariffs
				Establishment of the prohibition of monopolies
				Launch of the Common Agricultural Policy (CAP)
25 March 1957	**European Atomic Energy Community**	Rome	1 January 1958	Organization of Member States European atomic activities
17/18 February 1986	**Single European Act**	Luxembourg and The Hague	1 July 1987	Elimination of physical and technical frontiers
				Liberalization of financial and services markets
				Harmonization of national laws on safety and pollution
				Increased industrial environmental cooperation
7 February 1992	**Treaty on European Union**	Maastricht	1 November 1993	The EU becomes one streamlined market thanks to the single currency, the euro
				Significant change for the competitiveness of European manufacturing, primary and tertiary sectors
				Disappearance of transaction costs between the members of the euro-zone

(Continued)

Table 2 (Continued)

Date signed	Treaty	Place of signature	Date entering force	Impact on business
2 October 1997	**Treaty of Amsterdam**	Amsterdam	1 July 1999	Enhancement of the multilateral promotion of employment, placing national controls into a wider European employment strategy Consumer protection becomes a priority The protection of the environment introduced important challenges to the production sector Support for the farm sectors and rural and regional economies, helps to narrow economic and wealth gaps, especially in candidate countries
26 February 2001	**Treaty of Nice**	Nice	1 February 2003	Preparation of the path for an enlarged and smooth-functioning European business environment Increase in the efficiency and credibility of the EU's foreign policy for foreign and local investors
29 October 2004	**Constitution**	Rome	–	Attempts to streamline legislation, to set strong priorities and to increase transparency, democracy and solidarity

- abolish and prohibit internal tariff barriers;
- put an end to state subsidies and special charges;
- outlaw restrictive practices;
- fix prices under certain circumstances;
- harmonize external commercial policy, for example by setting customs duties;
- impose levies on coal and steel production for budgetary purposes.

Jean Monnet was the first president of the ECSC. The economic success that the ECSC achieved provided enough stimuli to launch further initiatives for economic integration, and led to the establishment of the fundamental treaties governing the EEC and its marketplace. The ECSC ceased to exist in 2002 – the Treaty provided for a limited duration of only 50 years – and its responsibilities and assets were assumed by the EU.

2.3.1.2 The impact of the Treaty on business

The Treaty had a strong impact on business in the coal and steel sectors, and opened the way for further cooperation in the way that the founder members conducted business. Coal and steel were the most important elements to the economic and military power of nations during the post-war reconstruction: steel was the major element in states' post-war economic reconstruction, and was needed for railways, buildings, ships, vehicles and machinery; and coal was the primary energy resource. This treaty was therefore a commercial treaty establishing a regulated market-sharing arrangement under supranational control. It was designed to balance the six states' particular vested interests in coal and steel and to facilitate the achievement of national objectives in these two sectors. In practice, co-operating drove trade up significantly in coal and steel (an increase of 129 per cent in the first five years). Further, unifying the market concentrated supply; this enabled the industry to streamline, leaving only the most efficient producers. However, the treaty rapidly became insufficient from an economic point of view: the coal and steel markets were replaced by economically more durable products over time. Indeed, the decline of coal resulted in one of the first challenges for European state aid policies: the enduring tradition of granting large amounts of state aid for the purpose of delaying structural adjustments subsequent to market developments as long as possible.

In theory, ECSC market integration was perceived as being about the physical movement of goods alone; however, in practice, it proved to be far beyond this. The impact on business conduct was significant, and in this instance a consideration of Italian steel price fluctuations during this period is particularly instructive. Over the first five years of the ECSC's existence, Italy, alone of all the Member States managed to negotiate a gradual reduction of steel tariffs. Tariffs were finally abolished in February 1958. From January 1957, steel prices in Italy began to fall as the country's producers anticipated the lower prices that firms based elsewhere in the ECSE would be able to offer on the Italian market. Italian firms anticipated and indeed expected an attempt by foreign firms outside Italy to supply the Italian market, and acted pre-emptively on the basis of that expectation. At the same time, steel firms in the other ECSC Member States were able to offer low prices in Italy, without lowering their entire price schedule, by aligning with French prices, which were low following currency devaluations in 1957 and 1958. Thus, steel-market integration not only changed business conduct but also confronted Member State governments with the challenges of microeconomic consequences of macroeconomic policy decisions.

2.3.2 The Treaties of Rome

2.3.2.1 The failure of the European Defence Community

The desire for further economic integration coincided with the confirmation of the Cold War and the US–Soviet arms race (the 'Sputnik Effect'). Both superpowers exercised pressure upon Germany; and there were also demands from the American government for Western Europe to assume a greater share of its own defence burden. German rearmament was something that many in Europe would have preferred to avoid: if it could not be avoided, they would try to control it. It became clear that the question of Germany was a key factor for both super powers, and hence for the future of European cooperation and its economic model.

In October 1950, less than six months after Schuman's press conference, French Premier René Pleven proposed the establishment of a European Defence Community (EDC). The Pleven Plan would have set German rearmament under European political control, with German troops serving under the authority of a European defence minister, who in turn would be responsible to the ECSC Assembly. Ultimately, the French Assembly rejected Pleven's proposal. This led to a rapprochement between West Germany and the US with the Dulles–Adenauer friendship that underlined the subscription of West Germany to the Western economic system. In 1955, Germany joined the North Atlantic Treaty Organization (NATO) established in 1949, which assured any member a common defence in the case of outside aggression.

2.3.2.2 The main objectives of the EEC Treaty

The success of the ECSC stimulated efforts for further integration, the outcome of which was the Treaty of Rome, which symbolized the victory of Jean Monnet's gradualist approach to building a European Union. In June 1955, the foreign ministers of the six Member States launched talks in Messina (Italy) where it was decided that the time was ripe for the ECSC to move towards a common European market for all products. On 25 March 1957, the same six countries that had founded the ECSC signed two treaties in Rome, one creating the EEC, the other Euratom, (a sector-specific treaty of limited application, promoting and regulating the nuclear industry). Under what was effectively one treaty, the Treaty of Rome, the two new entities, along with the ECSC, merged to form one organization, the EEC. Both treaties entered into force on 1 January 1958 after ratification by the national parliaments. The Member States committed themselves to removing trade barriers and forming a 'common market'. The Treaty of Rome (the EEC Treaty) set the framework for the institutions governing the communities and its policy framework.

The introduction of a Common Customs Tariff was one of its main objectives. All tariffs and other barriers to trade among the Member States were to be eliminated, while common external tariffs between the six were to be formulated, complemented by establishing the following: a common commercial policy; an agricultural policy; the free movement of people, goods, services and capital; equal treatment for all workers with respect to wages, conditions and entitlements to welfare benefits; and, finally, a European Social Fund and a European Investment Bank. To achieve this the focus had to be on market liberalization (unification of), normalization of competition (control of monopolies, state aids, subsidies), and economic development.

2.3.2.3 The impact of the EEC Treaty on business

The monumental EEC document of more than 200 articles created a free trade area evolving into a customs union that removed internal tariffs on goods and that harmonized external tariffs, thus having a significant impact on import logistics. For a company importing a given product, customs tariffs would no longer differ: choosing a port at which to import a product now became dependent on logistical evaluations rather than pecuniary ones related to customs. In other words, as the customs tariff became equal across the EEC, only geographical or other logistical considerations defined at which location a good entered the market. Internally, competition and competitiveness were enhanced even further. The free movement of citizens, capital and services, however, remained limited.

The Treaty of Rome also launched the Common Agricultural Policy (CAP). It was the very first common policy, that is, a policy under sole EEC decision making. Essentially, the CAP enacted a free market of agricultural products inside the EEC and formulated policies guaranteeing sufficient revenues to European farmers. The aim of the CAP was to prevent starvation as it was experienced by the people of continental Europe during and after World War II. Since its inception the agricultural policy has become subject to a wide range of diverse, complex issues, from how to treat former colonial possessions to the conflict between the desire of the Benelux countries for low tariffs on food imports and that of France, Germany and Italy to use high tariffs to protect their agricultural sectors. Box 4 gives an insight into the development of the CAP up to the beginning of the twenty-first century, and the challenges that it faces under rather different macroeconomic conditions from those of the mid- to late 1950s.

Box 4   The Common Agricultural Policy – victim of its own success

The CAP was established with two prime objectives: to ensure that the people of Europe would never again experience starvation; and the self-sufficiency and independence of the agricultural sector. The system was so successful that it soon resulted in the over production of certain agricultural goods, leading to so-called butter mountains and cereal heaps, due to the system of market price support payments. The question of what to do with this overproduction quickly arose: immediate but unsuccessful solutions included dumping crops on the markets of Third World countries. In Europe, prices became inflated through distorted export subsidies,

(Continued)

> *(Continued)*
>
> with high-volume low-priced produce replacing quality goods. Attempts to reform the CAP has on a number of occasions resulted in quarrels between the Member States and has led to countries such as the UK negotiating a budget rebate, due to the fact that it is not a large agricultural country, much to the annoyance of countries like France or Poland which are high net contributors and receivers of that budget. A heated debate about the distribution and significance of the agricultural budget reflects the many challenges for European leaders in the quest to protect the economic, social and political interests of their respective countries.

The Treaty of Rome also prohibited monopolies, launched some transport policies, granted certain commercial privileges to the colonial territories of the Member States, and set up an investment fund to transfer capital from the more developed to the less developed regions of the EEC.

Despite its post-war role as an ally, the UK – still strongly attached to its Commonwealth – did not join the Community until 1973, having maintained a more independent cooperating role throughout the 1950s and 1960s. Instead, the country joined the European Free Trade Area (EFTA) that was established in Stockholm in July 1959. Members of EFTA entertained bilateral free trade agreements with the EEC, and later, with the creation of the European Economic Area (EEA) in 1994, adopted approximately two-thirds of the EEC's body of law and enjoyed a privileged relationship with its Member States.

Table 3 lists Member States by year of accession to the EEC/EU, while Table 4 dates the accession of Member States to EFTA. While you study both, note the shifts from one grouping to the other. You will find, for example, that Denmark and the UK were among the founder members of EFTA in 1960 but that they left in 1973 in order to join the Community. In 1986, Portugal did the same, as did Austria, Sweden and Finland in 1995. EFTA by this time had become a springboard for those countries that had EU membership aspirations. The European marketplace now started to be vast and well regulated, with different degrees of integration in the region. Note also that 1960 was symbolic for further international multilateral efforts with the creation of the Organization for Economic Cooperation and Development (OECD).

Eurostat shows that trade in industrial products among the EEC's Member States doubled within four years after ratification of the two treaties signed in Rome. The average growth among the economies of the six founder members in the 1960s reached between 5 and 6 per cent. Even with weaker economies, France and Italy increased their trade by far more than the other Member States, reinforcing the belief in the virtues of economic and political integration. Also, barriers to trade were removed more rapidly than had been provided for in the Treaty of Rome.

European integration in the 1960s was an exercise in realpolitik: sovereignty remained largely with Member States and was passed to the supranational level only when and to the

Table 3   EEC/EU membership by year of accession

Year	Countries
1952 *('founding members')*	Belgium, France, Germany (West Germany only, East Germany in 1990), Italy, Luxembourg, The Netherlands
1973	Denmark, Ireland, UK
1981	Greece
1986	Spain, Portugal
1995	Austria, Finland, Sweden
2004	Cyprus, Czech Republic, Estonia, Hungary, Latvia, Lithuania, Malta, Poland, Slovakia, Slovenia
2007	Bulgaria, Romania Candidates: Albania, Bosnia-Herzegovina, Croatia, Macedonia, Serbia, Turkey and Montenegro.

Table 4   The internal market EFTA and EEA membership by year of accession

Year	Countries
1960	Austria, Denmark, Norway, Portugal, Sweden, Switzerland and the UK (the founding members of EFTA)
1961	Finland becomes an associate member (full member in 1986)
1970	Iceland becomes a member
1979	Spain signs the free trade agreement
1991	Liechtenstein becomes a member of EFTA
	Free trade agreement signed with Turkey
1992	Free trade agreements signed with the former Czechoslovakia, Israel, Poland and Romania
1993	Free trade agreement signed with Bulgaria and Hungary
	Protocol on the succession of the Czech Republic and Slovakia to EFTA Czechoslovakia agreement signed
1995	Free trade agreements signed with Estonia, Latvia, Lithuania and Slovenia
1997	Free trade agreement signed with Morocco
1999	Free trade agreements with the Palestine Liberation Organization and with Morocco enter into force
2000	Free trade agreements signed with Macedonia and Mexico
2001	Free trade agreements signed with Croatia and Jordan
2002	Free trade agreement signed with Singapore
2004	Free trade agreement signed with Lebanon and Tunisia

extent that they were willing. The treaties of the 1950s and 1960s were the basis for later progress in European integration, and ensured that progress took place no more rapidly than the Member States were willing to permit, respecting the time it took to negotiate their diverse interests and objectives. This was reflected in the 1967 decision of the six founder members of the EEC to change its name to the European Community (EC), a title which corresponded more with the Community's aims and objectives.

2.3.3 Main developments from the 1970s onwards

The 1970s saw major developments occur inside and outside the EC. On 1 January 1973 it increased its membership from six to nine when Denmark, Ireland and the UK became Member States. This period also saw the Community reinforce earlier agreements with neighbouring countries to enhance free trade, as well as the European Parliament use its newly acquired budgetary powers to finance the EC's external market initiatives. In 1975 the EC negotiated the Lomé Treaty that established economic cooperation with, initially, 46 African, Caribbean and Pacific countries (former colonies), and in the same year a referendum in Norway decided against joining the Community. A major step towards further integration was taken in 1979 when the European Parliament held its first direct elections, for the first time opening the way for a political party system to exist within the Community. Approximately 61 per cent of those eligible voted in these first cross-national elections – not numerically a huge turnout, but symbolically a successful one. The following year saw the introduction of a common unit of currency, the ECU (European Currency Unit), brought in in order to harmonize exchange rates between the Member States.

By the end of the decade a sense of Euro-pessimism haunted the Member States with two areas dominating the debate. First, there was dissatisfaction about the many hurdles still to overcome on the path to economic integration and secondly, there was a resurgence of doubt about whether national sovereignty should be traded off for the benefits of a harmonious Europe.

By the mid-1980s there was a more optimistic outlook within the EC. Greece had joined in 1981, followed by Spain and Portugal in 1986, and the process of integration had received important political impetus, in particular from Jacques Delors, a French socialist who had been elected President of the European Commission. In 1985 Delors published a startling White Paper which pointed out that the expanding Community potentially could become a single market serving 300 million consumers. However, it also showed very clearly that this tremendous potential was being thwarted by particular obstacles: queues at border crossings; technical barriers to trade; and closed markets for public contracts. Delors argued that the cost of doing nothing about these inefficiencies – the 'cost of non-Europe' – would be around €200 billion, but that they could be overcome by the introduction of 282 specific measures. Thus, the pressing challenge of European competitiveness vis-à-vis the US and Japan became a significant driving force for a revitalized Euro-optimism.

On the global stage, the optimism of the 1960s had, by 1970, been replaced by a realization that peace and harmony in the world was still a long way from reality. In Europe, the decade had seen a bipolarity of political perspectives develop: on one side, the concept of larger integration through a strengthening of supranational institutions, and on the other, the Europe of fatherlands, advocated by Charles de Gaulle, resisting the handing over of any sovereignty to supranational institutions – an ideology that led to the NATO crisis of 1965. De Gaulle's attempts to take a leading position in Western Europe between the two blocs resulted in tensions with the US. Internally in Western Europe, the end of the 1960s saw student demonstrations, for example against the war in Vietnam, while those countries of Eastern Europe that came under the Soviet sphere of influence imposed ever-tighter restrictions on their populations. Terrorism also became a terrible threat worldwide.

Individual countries within their own borders also experienced major upheavals. For the UK, Northern Ireland became an area of tension and violence, and relations with the US focused increasingly on economic ties, while the Commonwealth gradually dissolved. Cyprus, which had won independence from the UK in 1960, was invaded by Turkey in 1974. Turkish troops took control of the northern part of the island where Turkish Cypriots had set up a separate community in 1964 after ceasing to participate in power-sharing with the Greek Cypriot community and then refusing to acknowledge a Greek Cypriot government that considered itself to be the government of all Cyprus. After the invasion, the Turkish Cypriots established their own government and state, both of which have only ever been recognized by Turkey. In Spain the following year an era came to an end with the death of Franco, an era that was marked by internal tension, the omnipotence of its head of state, and the growth of the separatist terrorist group ETA (Euzkadi ta Azkatasuna, 'Basque homeland and liberty'). In the same year Sweden further expanded its prominent social system and reduced the powers of its monarch.

There was some cause for optimism in the 1970s. With the Soviet economic system continuing to concentrate on developing its heavy industry at the expense of adequately feeding its people, dissenting voices and calls for reform began to be heard in many of the Eastern and Central European states (such as from Lech Walesa in Poland) that the USSR had systematically undermined and 'sovietized' from 1945 onwards. There were also signs of a definite thaw in East–West relations, when friction with China led the USSR to sign a non-proliferation treaty with the US and the UK.

The 1980s saw the USSR itself undergo change when, between 1982 and 1985, it had four leaders. The last of these, Mikhail Gorbachev, set in motion a series of liberal reforms that paved the way for the eventual collapse of the Soviet system in Eastern Europe. The fall of the Berlin Wall in 1989 symbolized this collapse and was quickly followed by the toppling of the Ceauşescu regime in Romania, while in Bulgaria an attempt by President Schiwkow to make a 'great leap forward' failed and a new constitution proclaimed the country a socialist democracy. Yugoslavia, a country that had been liberated by a partisan army led by Josip Tito at the end of World War II, enjoyed relative liberty from Soviet influence having broken from the USSR (under Stalin) in 1948 and become a federal people's republic. At the time of Tito's death in 1980, the country was collectively led. However, in 1988 Slobodan Milošević became head of state, introducing the systematic discrimination (and, later, elimination) of ethnic and religious minorities that led in the early 1990s to the Balkan wars.

The 1970s and 1980s were also characterized by three important oil crises that put serious strain on the economies of developed countries.

2.3.4 The Single European Act

2.3.4.1 The key points of the Act

With the collapse of the Soviet system, the preoccupations of the cold war vanished, and a multi-polar world map could be envisaged. Geopolitics were shifting, and regional groupings such as the EU or AFTA (Association of South-East Asian Nations) became increasingly important structural variables on the world scene.

In the EU, the 1992 White Paper on Completing the Internal Market finalized under the British Commissioner Lord Cockfield, was presented by the Delors Commission. It gave birth to the 1986 SEA that progressively enforced an internal market by 31 December 1992.

Box 5   Jacques Delors's definition of the Single European Act's main objectives

'The Single Act means, in a few words, the commitment of implementing simultaneously the great market without frontiers, more economic and social cohesion, a European research and technology policy, the strengthening of the European Monetary System, the beginning of a European social area and significant actions in the environment.'

Box 5 provides you with Jacques Delors's definition of the SEA's objectives. The Act covers a broad spectrum of Community law, and contains the first major revision of the EEC Treaty of Rome. It set out a timetable for completing the single market by 1993 for goods, capital and services, and citizens inside the Community. Whether corporations, professions or trade unions, all actors in economic life incorporated the necessary amendments in their operations without delay. As a result, citizens felt the effects of the measures rapidly: a wider range of goods and services became available; and there were less restrictions on travelling in Europe. Most significantly for internal EC administration, the Act extended the scope of qualified majority voting (QMV) at the Council of Ministers (also known as the Council of the European Union) and increased the Commission's powers: a decision is adopted if it receives a given number of votes, expressing the favourable vote of the majority of the members of the institution. More explanation about this will be given in Chapter 4, which analyses the institutional framework of the European business environment.

2.3.4.2 The impact of the Act on business

Once corporations recognized that European integration was the only way forward in an increasingly competitive world market, a Europeanization without precedence followed. For example, the SEA provided the basis for the Directive adopted in November 1997 facilitating lawyers' practising their profession throughout the EU. The elimination of technical frontiers resulted in the removal of nationally regulated barriers on products and services through general agreement or mutual recognition. Steps were taken to make national laws on safety and pollution consistent and, more generally, EU countries agreed to recognize the equivalence of each other's laws and certification systems. A European company law was established for certain legal entities, and the Member States began to bring their national laws on intellectual and industrial property rights (trade marks and patents) into line with one another.

This created an improved environment for industrial cooperation, which was further enhanced with the elimination of tax frontiers. The obstacles created by differences in indirect taxes were overcome by agreeing or approximating VAT rates and excise duty. The SEA also opened the way for even stronger social and cultural cooperation.

2.3.5 The Treaty on European Union – Maastricht

2.3.5.1 The key points of the Treaty

The Treaty on European Union (TEU) signed in Maastricht (the Netherlands) on 7 February 1992 was a turning point in the integration process and changed the official denomination of the EEC to the EU. The Treaty, introduced once the objectives of the SEA had been achieved, is more generally known as the Maastricht Treaty. It was enforced on 1 January 1994. The Treaty assigned the EU with a broad range of objectives, well beyond the politico-economic scope and based on a set of guiding principles, including subsidiarity (the principle that decisions should always be taken as closely as possible to the people and that constant checks should be made to see if Community action is justified if action is feasible at the national, regional or local level) and the respect for democracy and human rights, governed by an institutional structure presided over by the European Council, that is, the Council of the Heads of State or Government of the Member States of European Union.

Three pillars of European affairs embodied distinct sets of policy issues in terms of objective and function, legislative basis, and modus operandi of the appropriate decision-making process. The first pillar is the EC, that is, the achievement, management and improvement of the single market. This pillar comprises quite ambitious objectives for economic and monetary union, manages the Community's legal system, and deals with the Community's institutions and bodies. It is based on the EU Treaty as amended by the SEA and the TEU. The pillar includes customs union and the single market, the Common Agricultural and Fisheries Policy, EU competition law, economic and monetary union, EU citizenship, and education and culture, as well as trans-European networks, consumer protection, healthcare, research (for example the 7th Framework Programme 2007–2013), environmental law and social policy.

The development coincided with important international advancements – with regional free trade zones playing an increasing part in economies worldwide. Among others, NAFTA became the world's largest free trade zone in terms of surface area in 1991, while Mercosur (Mercado Común del Sur – Spanish: Southern (American) Common Market) increased its scale of operations in South America. In 1994, negotiations began throughout the American continent, excluding Cuba and French Guyana, for the establishment of a Free Trade Area of the Americas (FTAA). In Asia, ASEAN (Association of South East Asian Nations) evolved further and the Asia Pacific Economic Cooperation Conference (APEC) proposed progressive trade liberalization measures to its members – the most populated market-group worldwide.

Hence the Maastricht Treaty was coherent in terms of European as well as international movements. It also recognized the internal and external challenges that a deeper and larger union would be exposed to, with its second pillar. To propose and develop a common currency for EU members was a singular development. Giving up one's currency is, sociologically and geopolitically speaking, certainly one of the hardest things to do for a population, as it represents identity, autonomy, sovereignty and culture. Also, the convergence criteria necessary interfered in traditionally domestic affairs, requiring a reduction of inflation and interest rates, the control of government deficit and debt, and a respect for the normal fluctuation margins provided for by the Exchange Rate Mechanism (ERM), of the EMS. By 1999, 11 countries were committed to the Euro-zone: Spain, Portugal, Italy, Belgium, the Netherlands, Luxembourg, France, Germany, Austria, Ireland and Finland. Greece joined later. Pillar two added a Common Foreign and Security Policy (CFSP) to the spheres of European integration. The role of the EU as a whole in international affairs evolved and needed to be strengthened and correlated to the Member States' objectives and international challenges. This pillar comprises the CFSP, foreign policy, EU battle groups, a European rapid reaction force, peacekeeping, human rights, democracy, foreign aid, security policy, European security and defence policy and European security strategy.

The CFSP allows for the establishment of common foreign policy actions – 'One Voice' of Europe. Its long-term objectives encompass the safeguard of EU independence, the strengthening of regional security and the promotion of international cooperation – it is formulated to preserve peace in line with the UN Charter and to contribute significantly to cooperation in disarmament and arms control. The European Council adheres to the principles and general orientations of the CFSP. A precursor of the CFSP was the creation of the Euro-Corps by Germany and France in 1992, a military unit of both German and French soldiers.

The 1990s was a decade characterized by arms reduction. The US and Russia signed START II (STrategic Arms Reduction Talks) in 1993, and in 1995 the Geneva conference reviewing the 1968 non-proliferation agreement decided to maintain regular contact, in particular because new countries were developing nuclear weapons (such as India, Israel and Pakistan). In the same year, New Zealand protested vehemently against French nuclear trials on the Mururoa Atolls. In 1997, an important UN agreement prohibiting chemical weapons was enforced and signed by 165 members.

The decade was also marked by geopolitical crises and war: the US under George H.W. Bush engaged in the Gulf War; and what was then considered the periphery of the EU suffered the Balkan wars – to mention just two areas of conflict. This conflict in the former Yugoslavia demonstrated the difficulties the EU faced in taking decisions and reacting quickly to situations. Sweden (not yet a member of the EU), known for peace and neutrality, had its president, Olof Palme, assassinated in 1986, an event that profoundly shocked the population. Finland became increasingly exposed to political pressure from Russia.

Elsewhere, more challenges arose for the international community: Russia attempted to reinforce its identity and territory in one of its southern republics, Chechnya; and the Chinese leadership, in the aftermath of Tiananmen Square, and despite more economic freedoms, brutally put down the internal criticism made about the Communist Party. The Intifada in Palestine and a rising pan-Arabic nationalism challenged the multilateral peace mechanisms that were of primary importance to European leaders as well as to Bill Clinton, elected President of the USA in 1992 and again in 1996. In the Vatican City State, the first non-Italian Pope since 1523, Polish Pope Jean Paul II, increased his international peace missions and attempted in vain to create relationships with Russia and China. While South Africa became a democratic republic abolishing apartheid and freeing Nelson Mandela, the continent experienced mainly ethnic violence and genocide (for example in Uganda): most of the conflicts originated from former colonial policies and conferred a certain responsibility on the developed world. At the UN, discussions arose as to whether its peacekeeping force should also be peace-installing.

The third pillar includes Police and Judicial Cooperation in Criminal Matters (PJCC), asylum policy, the Schengen Treaty, immigration policy, drug trafficking and weapons smuggling, terrorism, trafficking in human beings, organized crime, bribery and fraud.

It is particularly significant in the context of Italy because it allowed the Italian authorities to take greater measures to reduce the role of the Mafia in internal politics and the economy, and in the a context of police and immigration forces across Europe that were being increasingly confronted with Europe-wide illegal immigration and organized crime.

2.3.5.2 The impact of the Treaty on business

With the TEU, the EU has reached the highest level of international integration as illustrated in Table 2 (see p. 21). The EU has become one market, with added new competencies that refine economic cooperation but also cover policy areas that enforce political and social convergence among the Member States, and include the conduct of monetary coordination and joint monetary actions. The business impact of the Maastricht Treaty is hence tremendous. It has the virtue of having streamlined the European markets in accordance with international and European challenges, and of causing significant improvements in the competitiveness of European manufacturing, in both the primary and the tertiary sectors. It also creates further investment and operational opportunities in Europe and ensures cheaper supplies, goods and services. Some reasons for this are the potential cost-efficiencies in European business stemming from:

- transaction costs disappearing between the members of the Euro-zone not only in terms of currency losses, but also as regards border patrols, customs procedures and red tape;
- reduced uncertainties among those states about the relative price of currencies. Before the new currency, actors deciding to defer payment in a contract ran the risk of the rise or fall of money value. Facilitates selling of securities, raising funds and capital, and recruiting diverse labour;
- credibility and power of a single currency as the demand for the euro will be more important for reserves. European companies potentially save money by having access to lower interest rates;
- increased price and cost transparency on the European markets: easy comparisons of prices facilitate a real competitiveness among companies of EU Member States and encourages efficiencies and economies of scale effects. The competitiveness has also, of course, an impact on companies that are privatized and/or on those that are not competitive on a European scale, and hence is accompanied by a concentration, consolidation and outsourcing and offshoring effect. (This will be examined in Chapter 5.)

The Treaty also facilitates the expansion of operations cross-border, giving access to a great many consumers with 'glocalized' tastes and values, and hence open to a vast multitude of goods and services, studied later in Chapter 8. For both European and international companies, a pan-European strategy may streamline operations in Europe, raise efficiency, improve productivity and the international value chain. Strategic partnerships allow for detailed market knowledge.

2.3.6 The Treaty of Amsterdam (1997)

2.3.6.1 The key points of the Treaty

On 2 October 1997, the Treaty of Amsterdam was signed by the then 15 EU Member States to complement the Maastricht Treaty. The enlargements of 1973, 1981, 1986 and 1995 had both widened the European single market, and challenged the depth of European integration to such an extent that the EU had already started to look even further, in the direction of Eastern and Central Europe. The initial institutional framework, despite some modifications within earlier treaties, was better adapted to the new Europe.

Thus, this treaty complemented earlier ones and focused on the notion of flexibility, of renewal and adaptation of the preceding texts, and on increasing transparency towards the citizen: citizens were granted the right to access documents of the Council of Ministers. The Schengen agreement and convention among the Benelux countries, and Germany, France, Portugal and Spain was also incorporated into the treaty and transferred cross-border formalities from internal to external borders. Among other minor amendments for institutions, it is important to remember that the powers of the directly elected European Parliament were reinforced in Amsterdam, so as to better control the EU internally. As a result, The European Parliament had the power to accept or refuse the Commission President and his college of Commissioners. The Amsterdam Treaty created an enhanced cooperation procedure (flexible cooperation). For political relations among Member States, arenas of cooperation on levels below that of the 15 were installed, allowing for cooperation meetings involving, for instance, only the UK, Germany and France on certain issues, and within well-defined limits. Most importantly, objectives were formalized that focused on sustainable development, human health protection and consumer protection and made firm commitments for cooperation on visas, asylum and immigration. With this treaty the establishment of a new post of head of the CFSP attempted to strengthen a policy that was yet to converge at EU level.

2.3.6.2 The impact of the Treaty on business

The Amsterdam Treaty was widely considered as weak, lacking in a strong foundation for the institutional and legislative preparations for further enlargement. Nevertheless, the Treaty had some impact on business in various areas. It enhanced the multilateral promotion of employment, placing national controls into a wider European employment strategy, with a surveillance mechanism monitoring the coherence of policies whose objective was a flexible, efficient and effective labour market. With consumer protection a priority, the provisions of the Treaty changed the regulatory framework for agribusiness and related sectors and organisms. The quest for sustainable development, responsible business and the protection of the environment introduced important challenges to the production sector's target of profit maximization and installed leadership aspirations into corporations technologically advanced in:

- waste management;
- industrial compliance;
- personnel resources education;
- activities centred on acquiring a migration methodology to environmentally acceptable technologies, quality management and adapted corporate growth strategy.

At the same time, consumer and labour movement has become even easier in the Schengen countries. The Treaty has played its role in promoting a safe and efficient economy of scale facilitating trade and investment. It has also contributed to making the consumer ever more European, resulting in (a) a person aware of the drives and challenges of economic welfare, and (b) a consumer with an increasingly homogenized product need and expectations (price, quality, reliability and fair trade principles), as knowledge and industrialization are diffused.

In July 1997, Agenda 2000, following closely on from the Amsterdam Treaty, complemented it by strengthening Community policies, and providing for a more detailed framework of the tools needed for further enlargement. The negotiations were already under way. At the same time, some of the richest countries, like Germany, complained about the imbalance between their contribution to the Community (around 28.2 per cent of the total) and what they received via the European Structural Fund and the CAP. Poorer countries refused to sanction a rebalance of contributions. The European Structural Fund was aimed at three territories: regions with a GDP per person inferior to 75 per cent of the EU average – these took two-thirds of the whole fund; regions with urgent necessities in terms of social and economic restructuring; and regions not included in either of the former but whose educational, training and employment systems required modernization. A further fund, the Cohesion Fund, focused on helping countries with a GDP per capita inferior to 90 per cent of the EU average. Funds provided through the European Structural Fund are one of the main instruments of solidarity among Europeans, helping to create jobs and economic development by investing in infrastructure and training in less well-off regions.

Agenda 2000 also included a much needed revision of the European model for leaner and greener agriculture that would balance expectations for consumer health and a clean and pretty countryside with competitive farmers, ecological tourism, a high quality of life and stable spending. What had changed over the past two decades was the awareness that future generations would need a heritage of peace, wealth and health.

With specific instruments, the EU not only shaped the means to support the farming sectors and rural economies of candidate countries preparing for membership and to narrow the gaps in wealth and economic prospects between regions, but also strengthened the pre-accession strategy by creating the partnership for accession and offering the opportunity for applicant countries to participate in Community programmes, for instance, in education. The Treaty also made provisions to analyse the effects of enlargement on EU policies towards the former communist countries of Central and Eastern Europe, thus preparing for a historical widening of the European market and business environment.

2.3.7 The Treaty of Nice

2.3.7.1 The key points of the Treaty

Another significant step towards the historic enlargement into Eastern and Central Europe was the Treaty of Nice, concluded on 10 December 2000 after a lengthy meeting of the Intergovernmental Conference (IGC) in Nice, France, and signed on 26 February 2001. Its objective was to increase the role of the Community in several significant ways, classified into seven key issues, and to redefine the size and composition of the Commission by re-weighting the voting system of the Council of Ministers and extending QMV. Two changes were made to the Amsterdam arrangements. The first concerned flexible mechanisms to enhance cooperation and to make it potentially more workable: the minimum number of Member States required for flexible cooperation was to incorporate eight members. The second concerned the first and third pillar, where the Treaty added the possibility of an appeal to the European Council that acts by QMV (a definition of which you can find above and in Chapter 4).

The key issues of the Treaty of Nice concern measures preparing for enlargement of the Union from 15 to 25 and then to 27 Members States, thus adding 75 million citizens to the 380 million already residing there. An extended area of peace and stability and a bigger market for all countries was to be created with the extension of environmental legislation to new Member States, and institution changes were to be defined in consequence. Enhanced cooperation was another key objective, with formal authorization given by the Council after receiving the opinion of the Commission. Within flexible cooperation, no Member State can be excluded, but issues are excluded that deal with military applications or defence matters.

In order for the European Commission to adapt to further enlargement, changes had to be made to its institutional provisions. Before the Nice Treaty, the Commission comprised 20 Commissioners: 2 representatives for each large Member State and 1 for each small Member State. The Treaty, however, stipulated that once the next round of enlargement had taken place, each Member State equally was to provide one Commissioner, thus relieving the large Member States of one Commissioner each but increasing the total number on the Commission to 25. It further stipulated that once the number of Member States had reached 27, the number of Commissioners should not be increased but should be set at a level below 27, to be decided by a unanimous decision of the council. Commissioners would then be chosen according to a system of rotation, all Member States being treated equally.

With regard to the Council of Ministers, the changes in Nice meant that more areas fell under the QMV system (for policies including anti-discrimination, visas, asylum and immigration, and the free movement of people), that is, a systematic 62 per cent of the areas affecting the population of the EU now had to be approved through legislation. Also, the allocation of votes for each Member State were changed so that they were linked to population size.

The European Parliament, whose decisions were made by unanimous voting of the 626 directly elected Members of European Parliament (MEPs) of the 15 Member States, was set to increase its number of MEPs to 700. QMV expanded the powers of the Parliament to enable more efficient decisions, and Nice approved a maximum number of MEPs set at 732 to make room for the enlargement countries. The Treaty set provisions for the European Court of Justice to operate more efficiently, reduce the backlog of cases and reduce the length of time required to process new ones. Indeed, a new distribution of responsibilities was prepared, giving increasing powers to the Court of First Instance.

Nice also widened the scope of the EU provisions on fundamental rights by allowing the Council to recognize any serious violation of those rights by a Member State (a clear sign of citizens' preoccupations with mounting nationalism and extremism in some countries). Any kind of measure against an individual Member State was to be made on recommendation, necessitating the support of four-fifths of the remaining Member States. Moreover, a report on the European security and defence policy was adopted that provided for the creation of permanent political and military structures, through the incorporation into the EU of the procedures for managing crises adopted by the WEU (Western European Union, a body that provided for collective self-defence and economic, social and cultural collaboration among its signatories, the agreement for which was signed on 17 March 1948 by Belgium, France, Luxembourg, The Netherlands and the UK). The aims stated in the preamble encompass assistance to each other in resisting any policy of aggression, and the promotion of unity and the encouragement of the progressive integration of Europe.

In addition, the Nice Treaty increased the EU's capacity to fight international crime. The European Judicial Cooperation Unit ('Eurojust'), formalized in the TEU, was assigned to coordinate action in criminal matters in the Member States, while the European Defence Agency was made an official intergovernmental body in order to coordinate 24 countries' (Ireland decided to remain an observer) military capabilities, harmonize military requirements, coordinate research and development (R&D), and converge natural procurement procedures (for the first time, part of the internal market programme). The Treaty also designated a new committee, the PSC (Political and Security Committee).

2.3.7.2 The impact of the Treaty on business

The foremost benefit of the Treaty is that is has prepared the path for an enlarged and better functioning European business environment with accompanying benefits, advantages and challenges in terms of competitiveness both inside the EU and towards non-member countries. The European common security strategy has increased the EU's foreign policy efficiency and credibility for foreign and local investors, and strengthened the relationships and dialogue among the main trading partners. This deepening and widening market also has helped to reinforce peaceful relationships with its neighbours. Europe counts 27+ members and a vast, integrated and complex market forged through the fundamental treaties.

2.3.8 A constitution for Europe

> The Union is founded on the values of respect for human dignity, freedom, democracy, equality, the rule of law and the respect for human rights, including the rights of persons belonging to minorities. These values are common to the Member States in a society in which pluralism, non-discrimination, tolerance, justice, solidarity and equality between women and men prevail. (European Communities, 2005: art.1–2)

2.3.8.1 The aim of the Constitution

EU leaders reached agreement on a new Constitutional Treaty for Europe at the European Council in Brussels on 17 and 18 June 2004, and signed it in Rome on 29 October 2004. The Constitution enters into force only once ratified by all Member States. Its primary objectives are summarized in Article 1-2 above; they encompass simplification, democracy, transparency, effectiveness and legitimacy for the EU. The Constitution strives to streamline the former bodies of legislation, and to formalize the relevant principles and objectives of European integration. The text was produced by the European Convention, under the presidency of Valéry Giscard d'Estaing (the former French president, born in Koblenz, Germany, in 1926), and included 105 members representing all the Member States, candidate countries, national parliaments, the European Parliament and the Commission, plus 13 observers representing the Committee of the Regions, the Economic and Social Committee, the European social partners and the European mediator. All meetings were public, and a great deal of transparency and much discussion was furnished over the Internet. In addition, there was extensive consultation with civil society.

Political science informs us that a constitution is written when a break with tradition forces a government to define how a country is ruled, as was the case, for instance, after both the American and the French Revolutions, the end of World War II for Germany (with the introduction of the 'Basic Law' in West Germany), and independence was given to formerly oppressed countries. Countries like the UK that have not undergone such schisms, are less likely to have a written constitution, and tend to follow a model of governance where tradition and custom prevail. Nevertheless, it was felt by the leading European thinkers, politicians, business leaders and citizens that with Europe having experienced major upheavals such as those above in the past, there was a need for deeper, wider and more challenging integration.

The Constitution defines the single legal personality for the EU, characterized strongly by the integration of the Charter for Fundamental Rights into the text (see below). This single foundation was created to install a revised institutional framework, with progress relating to the achievement of freedom and justice, as well as common foreign and security policy:

> The Union's aim is to promote peace, its values and the well-being of its peoples. The Union shall offer its citizens an area of freedom, security and justice without internal frontiers, and an internal market where competition is free and undistorted. The Union shall work for sustainable development of Europe based on balanced economic growth and price stability, a highly competitive social market economy, aiming at full employment and social progress, and a high level of protection and improvement of the quality of the environment. It shall promote scientific and technological advance. It shall combat social exclusion and discrimination, and shall promote social justice and protection, equality between women and men, solidarity between generations and protection of the rights of the child. (European Communities, 2005: art. 1–3)

The revised institutional framework clarifies competences by categorizing them into exclusive, shared and supporting, introduces a higher profile for the EU with the appointment of a foreign affairs minister, and limits the right of members' veto to foreign policy, defence and taxation. Also, QMV is extended in the text.

The European Constitution, as it is generally called, is a text that is subject to the rules of international law, and is thus on the one hand a treaty.

On the other hand it answers questions about the distribution of power and its objectives, the functioning of institutions, the means that need to be used to reach the objectives, and the fundamental rights governing the organization of the Member States, and so is also a constitution. It does not, however, replace the national constitutions, and it allows for any Member State to leave the Union if it so desires.

In July 2007, two years after French and Dutch voters rejected a draft EU constitution (after 18 members' ratification and indefinitive deadline postponing), member states agreed to go forward with a simplified version. This is an agreement that from 2009 gives a long-term president of the European Council to the EU, and confirms the confirms the foreign policy high representative in charge of its diplomacy, aid budget and external relations staff. It stresses the legally binding character of the EU's charter on fundamental rights and the single legal identity that the EU became for signing international treaties. This does not diminish the need for further structuring and, in particular, a management of diversity at EU level.

2.3.8.2   The impact of the Constitution on business

The Constitution potentially enhances and streamlines the business environment even further than the preceding legislation, as more transparency and greater and stronger subsidiary powers for civil society are incorporated into its text. The possibilities for interest articulation and interaction between the different actors of the European market and its legislators will increase the applicability of policies: greater outcomes (results) of outputs (policies). Gaining access to EU documents and procedures generally helps stakeholders to obtain information more easily: this is key for companies to define their positions in real time on legislation that will have an impact on operations, markets, opportunities or threats. The enforced co-decision procedure of the legislative body will give a greater chance to focus on specific members of a more powerful European Parliament. In addition, the extension of QMV may facilitate adoption of pieces of legislation.

The aim to create a high level of competitiveness through innovation and information systems potentially implies fast and effective decision making, with the European legislation reinforcing business opportunities and vice versa. The Constitution's explicit aim was from the beginning to create a business-friendly environment, leading to both wealth creation (and therefore employment) and a more secure business environment and better functioning single market. In addition, its provisions accelerate the sanctions procedure.

With the EU, already the biggest donor of financial aid to the world's troublespots, reinforcing its peacekeeping and peacemaking operations, a European legislation adapted to the needs and concerns of globalization allows it to play a role in international organizations, in negotiations, and in running its many projects that help in practical terms to make human rights and democracy succeed. European integration is hence fostering a secure and liberal business environment across borders, inside and outside the EU.

2.4 Objectives of the European Union

The chronological review of the main treaties governing European integration illustrates the consequential evolution of business opportunities and challenges. Doing business in Europe implies first and foremost the respect and enhancement of the objectives of the EU as an area of freedom, law and justice that strives to guide a peaceful, prosperous and independent society through economic, political, financial, social and cultural harmonization. This opens many opportunities. The outputs, or policies, of a governmental body are made to promote defined explicit or implicit outcomes. The definition of what outcomes have to be sought differs, of course, among the different actors of any society, and even more so in a highly diverse, heterogeneous environment. This means that outputs are, in a democratic system, the result of negotiations, bargaining and compromises; their formulation requires collective action and interest articulation from all actors in the society, directly or by representation.

The public policies referred to are classified by Almond et al. (2000) into four types of output. They are:

- the extraction of resources (capital, goods, services and people);
- the distribution of these resources;
- the regulation of their behaviour;
- 'symbolic' actions that stimulate community building.

The outcomes obtainable are then categorized into four activities, that support these goals;

- welfare;
- security;
- liberty;
- international activities.

The evolution of these outputs and their outcomes can clearly be observed in the landmarks of European integration reviewed above. The Europeanization of politics and economics goes hand in hand with that of the citizen. The rights of citizens are ensured at the national and EU level. European countries are making a joint effort to tackle insecurity and to ensure safety. This includes measures to combat international terrorism, drug trafficking and abuse, trafficking in human beings and the illegal exploitation of EU and non-EU citizens for prostitution. Common rules among the police, customs and law courts are to ensure the proper functioning of the policies.

The EU also plays a role in asylum and migration policy, guaranteeing the right to seek asylum. The immigration policies of Member States are still relatively disparate and, with freedom of movement of, and limited intra- EU checks on, people, difficult to control. Countries such as the UK and Spain have a rather lax stance on immigration, and regularly legalize illegal immigrants. Other countries, often with high unemployment rates, are increasingly opposed to this practice. At the same time, the Member States are coordinating their policies for refugees and trying to tackle the problem at source by combating poverty and preventing conflicts in the countries from which people might want to flee. Germany, for example, is known for a particularly humane asylum policy. Table 5 illustrates the divergence among selected Member States' decisions on asylum applications in 2001.

Fewer frontiers benefit the EU as a whole, by safeguarding employment in Europe and creating new jobs. Economic independence is here again a keyword. Some important conditions challenge these objectives: a divergence of labour costs, service and innovation potential, and administrative procedures necessary for the launch of start-ups. In addition, the policy areas that are not yet harmonized produce a serious break in what should be a simple and speedy road to these outcomes.

European industry will not be able to provide more jobs unless the economic conditions are right for what the Union is working to achieve, at the speed defined by its Member States. By

Table 5 European divergence of asylum policy – decisions on applications

	Absolute numbers			Percentages			
	Total	Positive	Negative	Other non-status	Total	Positive	Negative	Other non-status
Germany	103.810	22.719	55.402	25.689	100	21.9	53.4	24.7
France	43.053	7.323	35.730	0	100	17	83	0
Slovenia	10.042	25	97	9.920	100	0.2	1	98.8
Czech Republic	16.974	113	7.042	9.819	100	0.7	41.5	57.8
Estonia	6	0	6	0	100	0	100	0

Source: Taken from CEC asylum statistics © European Communities (2001): European Divergence of Asylum Policy, URL: http://europa.ew.int/comm/justice_home/doc_/centre/asylum/statistical/doc_asylum_statistics_en.htm.

creating a frontier-free single market and a single currency, the euro, the EU has already given a significant boost to trade and employment in Europe. It has an agreed strategy for stimulating growth and generating more and better jobs. Tomorrow's jobs will be created through research, training and education, a spirit of entrepreneurship and innovation, adaptability to new working methods and equal opportunities. The Lisbon agenda objectives strive for competitiveness, sustainable growth, social inclusion, and good jobs – more than just competitiveness, the Lisbon and Gothenburg agendas aim for an EU that is clean, clever and competitive. Moreover, a third of the entire EU budget is taken up by regional funds that promote growth and jobs in less well-off regions, under sustainable development principles. Key to a successful and efficient market are the advances made by the information society, and the EU is increasingly active in helping European research to achieve scientific excellence. In a variety of sectors covering the whole spectrum of modern technology, the Union finances projects such as job creation and improved quality of life undertaken by research centres, universities and industry. Research priorities include, among others, nanotechnology, security, food quality, sustainable development and the knowledge-based society, adopted through the 7th Framework Programme. The decision of the EU to opt for the technical standards of the global system for mobile communications (GSM) has resulted, for instance, in Europe leading the world in the development and manufacture of mobile telephones.

Among the top EU priorities that have evolved over time, anti-pollution has a special priority because its challenges neither respect national frontiers, nor vanish with time. The EU holds over 200 environmental protection directives, applied in all Member States, mostly for prevention and waste management in accordance with the best available technologies. It regulates policies in transport, industry, agriculture, fisheries, energy and tourism. The European Environment Agency in Copenhagen, created in 1993, monitors the environment and aims at the formulation of appropriate public policy.

The timeless challenge for European integration is keeping the EU democratic, fair and efficient by streamlining its mechanisms, its outputs and its outcomes. Judging from the findings of this chapter, business has shaped, driven and streamlined much. As a result, doing business in Europe has, over time, become easier and yet more complicated.

Résumé and conclusion

This chapter has dealt with the long-term process of integration that spans the initial ECSC Treaty up to the European Constitution and further. The legislation and cooperation within Europe includes many actors and lays the basis of its business environment and the role of the EU internationally. The fundamental Treaties of Paris and Rome defined the institutional structure and policy objectives of the European Communities in the areas of coal and steel (ECSC), atomic energy (EAEC) and economic integration (EEC). The SEA of 1986 created the conditions for the customs union to evolve into a single market, extended the scope of QMV and refined earlier legislation. The Maastricht Treaty of 1992 changed the denomination of this unique organization to the 'European Union', expanded former treaties and introduced the codecision procedure and flexible cooperation mechanisms for the Member States. In 1999, the Amsterdam Treaty then set out to prepare the Union for enlargement, and deepened the free movement of people, goods, services and capital. This increasingly integrated organization (in both depth and width) was streamlined by the Constitution, setting top priorities that have the potential of adapting an economic, political, social and cultural union to the challenges and opportunities of globalization. As a conclusion, each treaty has made the European business environment more efficient and more accessible as an entity.

Mini case study: Springer goes East

Springer, the German media group, publishes bestselling tabloid *Bild* and the daily *Die Welt,* among more than 20 other papers. The group originates in the former West Germany.

After decades of both sales and advertising growth, Springer started to look for less saturated markets, and found that the fall of the Berlin Wall opened up unexploited opportunities in Eastern Europe. So, Springer expanded eastwards, buying up certain magazines and launching new ones. For example, *Fakt* was launched in Poland and, one year later, *Reggel* ('Morning') in Hungary. *Reggel,* making full use of the availability of the fast growing Hungarian market, achieved a circulation target of 55,000 by the end of 2005.

Since May 2004, most of the targeted East European countries have joined the EU, integrating laws and regulations and making them even more attractive to investors. Springer Chief Executive Mathias Döpfner stated at the end of 2004: 'Our priority for 2005 will remain Eastern Europe, and that means Hungary, Poland, and the Czech Republic.' He went on to say that the market liked this expansion and that stocks rose 28 per cent in 2004 (*Business Week*, 10 January, 2005).

(Continued)

For the post-communist economies, cash flows of Western media became increasingly attractive, while simultaneously, journalistic freedom and Western style travelled east. Not every expansion was a success, however. For example, when Springer entered the Spanish market in the 1990s and launched a daily there modelled on *Bild*, it failed because it featured topless women and made fun of the Spanish monarchy. Not surprisingly, the mainly Catholic population reacted with indignation. Döfner commented that 'the potential is much greater if you give local management clear business targets but grant it a maximum of freedom' (*Business Week*, 10 January, 2005). The success of Springer lies in the fact that it can sell in other country's markets while continuing to be cost-effective. It does so by putting out local language editions of its bestselling editions like *Auto Bild* and *Computer Bild* the content of which (from text or photographs) does not need to be customized for local audiences.

Sources: Compiled from *Business Week* and *Deutsche Welle*, 2003–5

Mini case questions:

1   Is Springer a perfect example of a firm maximizing its opportunities abroad during European integration?
2   East and Central European media are now largely dominated by Western European newsgroups. Are open and integrated markets threatening (media) pluralism?

Review questions

1   **Explain** the difference between a free trade area and a common market. Which form of integration will better serve trade creation purposes?
2   **Why** does the EU strive towards an increasingly high level of international integration? Which societal preoccupations have driven its evolution over the past decades?
3   **To what extent** have economic issues contributed to the construction of the EU?
4   **Does** Europeanization show a long-term underlying movement towards integration or does it consist of not very well-coordinated responses to specific problems?
5   **To what extent** has the international context contributed to the construction and the development of the EU in its current form?

Assignments

- **Imagine** that you are the CEO of a large British–Spanish company in the year 2003. The text for the Constitution is currently being formulated, and you are asked by the European Convention to express your opinion.
- **Using Figure 4 compare** the threats and opportunities that an Australian exporter faces when dealing with NAFTA, ASEAN and the EU.
- **Case study assignment**: Read and prepare the Airbus case study in Part IV, and discuss the impact of Europe on the company's operations.
- **Internet exercise:** Compare the administrative cost and time requirements for setting up a start-up in three Member States of the EU that joined at different times. How do you explain the divergence of the results?

W W W

Web guide

http://europa.eu.int/abc/treaties_en.htm European Community treaties.

http://www.answers.com/topic/history-of-the-european-union History of European integration.

http://www.germany-info.org/relaunch/politics/speeches/011603.htm Franco-German partnership.

http://www.jean-monnet.ch/anglais/index.php Foundation for European remembrance, research and reflection.

http://www.robert-schuman.org/ Foundation supporting European cooperation.

References

Almond Gabriel A., Bingham Powell Jr. G., Strom, Kaare and Dalton, R. Russel J. (2000) *Comparative Politics Today: A World View*, Seventh Edition. New York: Addison Wesley Longman, Inc. pp. 148–51.

Behringer, W. (1999) *Europa – Ein historisches Lesebuch.* Munich: Beck'sche Reihe, BsR, CEC (2005) URL: http://europa.eu.int/comm/public_opinion/cf/index_en.cfm

Dinan, D. (2006) *Origins and Evolution of the European Union*, New European Union Series. Oxford: Oxford University Press.

European Communities (1951) *Treaty Establishing the European Coal and Steel Community* (ECSC Treaty, or Treaty of Paris), URL: http://europa.eu.int/abc/obj/treaties/en/entoc29.htm.

European Communities (1957a) *Treaty Establishing the European Economic Community* (EEC Treaty, or the Treaty of Rome),URL: http://europa.eu.int/abc/obj/treaties/en/ entoc05.htm

European Communities (1957b) *Treaty Establishing the European Atomic Energy Community* (Euratom Treaty), URL: http://europa.eu.int/abc/obj/treaties/en/entoc38.htm

European Communities (1967) *Treaty Establishing a Single Council and a Single Commission of the European Communities* (Merger Treaty of 1965), URL: http://europa.eu.int/abc/obj/treaties/

European Communities (1987) *Single European Act,* URL: http://europa.eu.int/eur-lex/en/treaties/selected/livre509.html

European Communities (1992) *Treaty on European Union* (Maastricht Treaty) [1992] OJ. C191/1), URL: http://europa.eu.int/eur-lex/en/treaties/dat/EU_treaty.html

European Communities (1997a) *Treaty of Amsterdam,* [1997] OJ. C340/1, URL:http://europa.eu.int/eur-lex/lex/en/treaties/treaties_other.htm, with [1997] OJ C340/145.

European Communities (1997b) Treaty Establishing the European Community (1997 O.J. (C340/173–308).

European Communities (2000) *The Lisbon European Council – an agenda of economic and social renewal for Europe. Contribution of the European Commission to the special European Council in Lisbon,* 23 – 24 March 2000, DOC/00/7, 28 February.

European Communities (2004) Treaty Establishing a Constitution for Europe, URL:http://europe.eu.int/constitution/index_en.htm.

European Communties (2005) Constitutional Treaty for Europe (European Constitution).

Mercado, S., Welford, R. and Prescott, K. (2001) *European Business,* 4th ed. Harlow: FT Prentice Hall .

Northedge, F.S. (1976) *The International Political System.* London Faber and Faber.

Schuman, Robert (1950) Declaration of 9 May 1950, URL:http://www.robert-schuman.org/anniversaire_9_mai2006/anglais.htm

Senior Nello, Susan (2005) *The European Union: Economics, Politics and History.* Maidenhead: McGraw-Hill Education.

Suder, G. (1994) *Anti-Dumping Measures and the Politics of EU–Japan Trade Relations in the European Consumer Electronics Sector: The VCR Case.* Bath: University of Bath School of Management.

Other sources:

Various issues of *Business Week, Deutsche Welle, The Economist, Le Figaro, Frankfurter Allgemeine Zeitung.*

3 Enlargement and the Theories of Integration

What you will learn about in this chapter

- The enlargements of the European market.
- The business opportunities that unfold, using Bulgaria and Romania as examples.
- Challenges for future enlargements.
- The relations between current and future Member States.
- Ways to gain advantages for companies thanks to special agreements with non-EU countries.

Introduction

The open and democratic structure of the European market predestines its future structure for growth. While the treaties establishing the EU and its common policies have deepened the integration of members, the market is also undergoing geographical enlargement.

Economic, political and sociopolitical challenges – from the mid-twentieth century onwards – have given birth to historic ambitions among European nations for freedom, democracy and prosperity; ambitions that have translated into the formal accessions of most European states. The most extensive enlargement of the EU took place in 2004 when, for the first time, former Soviet bloc countries were integrated into the community. Never before had so many countries applied at the same time for membership, nor had so many economies joined that had such a substantial gap in terms of performance. This required an unprecedented scale of adjustment from not only the candidate countries but also the EU internally. Never had an enlargement opened business opportunities of such a scale to both accession countries and established Member States. The fifth EU enlargement had thus taken a strategic dimension that is prolonged through the accession of Romania, Bulgaria and other East European states. It is an illustration of the deep roots that the European ideal has in the values and beliefs that the EU has refined over decades: these key values and beliefs are human dignity, freedom, democracy, equality, the rule of law, the respect of human rights, peace and the well-being of peoples.

The six countries that supported the initial concept of European integration, Germany, France, Italy, Belgium, Luxembourg and the Netherlands, represent the original and persisting common vision of an economic construction that aims for political stability: a pacifist union based on solidarity and economic development. Ideally, the aim of European integration is to progressively and continuously *deepen* and *widen* business opportunities, and it is driven by the challenges of competitiveness vis-à-vis the USA and Asia, which along with Europe constitute the 'triad', that is, the three major investment and trade blocs in the world economy (Box 6). Regionalism is indeed one of the predominant features of contemporary economics on a global scale, and enhances the pressures on states and business to remain competitive.

Box 6   Deeper and wider integration

In the EU, there are some lively debates about enlargement. The fundamental question is whether the EU should integrate more deeply, that is, share more common policies and enhance the authority of the organization, or whether it should increase wider integration, that is, further enlarge not only geographically but also in the number of Member States.

By continuing to deepen and widen European integration the EU has successfully created a European market in which people, goods, services and capital move freely as if in a single country. Supporters of enlargement argue that the business environment has evolved simultaneously on the basis of peace, prosperity and stability; however, critics argue that meeting the challenges is a complex and costly task at every stage. Expansion implies not only trade creation (that is, business opportunities) but also trade diversion, resulting, for instance, from industry that is streamlined and competitive and the replacement of a given outside preference for trade partnership by an internal one.

Every wave of enlargement has not only reinforced competitiveness, trade and investment flows, shared know-how, innovation and technological advancement, job creation and standards and norms on a European level, but also harmonized regulations, economies of scale, and tax revenue gains for governments. On the other hand, it has also resulted in rising unemployment in less competitive sectors, a rethinking of social policy, and a reshuffle of important factor conditions (labour and capital). Less disputed is the fact that European integration improves the weight of the European voice in multilateral trade negotiations, under the condition that all members agree upon one stance.

Why then does Europe experience different levels and times of Member State integration? What is it that drives Member States to have different ideologies about what they want Europe to represent, both in the future and under what conditions, while sharing its fundamental objectives? In order to understand the bigger picture, one needs to be familiar with some predominant integration theories.

3.1 Integration theories

Chapter 2 introduced you to the different stages of integration through which the EU has evolved. This evolution is based on the different integration theories and schools of thought that have been developed since the late 1940s. These beliefs guide the speed and extent to which business has been able to Europeanize. The following introduce these theories, and analyse their meaning.

3.1.1 Functionalism (peak period: 1950s–1960s)

Functionalism originates from a theory which suggests that states cooperate in specific areas only. This cooperation takes place at a minimalized institutional level, and does not strive for deepened political integration. Each state attempts to retain a high level of sovereignty. Functionalism is mainly associated with liberal economies whereby there is little regulatory intervention by the policymaking authority into an economy that is considered to be ruled by the 'invisible hand' of its own dynamics. Issues harmonized at European level are therefore defined by mainly technical necessity. The main subscribers to this theory in recent European history are the UK and Scandinavia. The theory evolves in accordance with ideologies that do not subscribe to fundamental legislative texts or constitutions but are based on common law.

3.1.2 Neo-functionalism (peak period: 1950s–1960s)

As with functionalism, neo-functionalist theory is based on the belief that harmonization and cooperation appear when needs spill over frontiers and economics. Nevertheless, neo-functionalism recognizes the essential role of sociopolitical cooperation in the integration of countries and their economies. Thus an important role is played by supranational institutions that become legitimate and gain sovereignty from Member States in the areas where challenges cross frontiers and lead to sequential cooperation throughout related policy areas.

3.1.3 Federalism (peak period: 1980s–1990s)

The theory of federalism provides the basis for the main treaties governing European integration, and is guided by the belief that a constitutional framework shall govern the relations between Member States. In federalism, much subscribed to by Germany, for example, a formalized framework dictates the roles of government and institutions that coexist with national and local authorities along a set of shared and independent power lines. Consequently, the theory finds its expression in initiatives including a common currency, common foreign and security policy, or a unique constitution. The Treaty of the European Union, for instance, reflects a peak point for federalism.

3.1.4 Further integration theories

Two other integration theories add to our understanding. The collective bargaining orientation of interstate relations is complemented by the need for pronounced independence of Member States, a limited supranational authority, and the preservation of sovereignty via sub-structures of the system, except in areas that are dependent on cross-border solutions. The CAP is a product of this school of thought. Intergovernmentalism reinforces the belief that bargaining is key to European integration and hence gives a predominant role to the Council of Ministers and the European Council.

3.1.5 The meaning of integration theories

This section provides you with an understanding of the reasons why different approaches to integration theory exist. Different governmental actors believe in them and thus use different theories with regard to European integration: hence this is the very basis for the interests and beliefs of Member States, their people and democratically elected governments about the way in which European integration should both advance and be shaped.

Each Member State is subject to its own nuanced system, political culture and heritage, and particular beliefs and priorities. Political culture and heritage shape the orientations of citizens, government and corporations in a manner that finds its expression in mainly three ways: systems and their legitimacy; processes in accordance to public expectations; and outputs and outcomes that may or may not satisfy those they affect (see Chapter 2 for a definition of outputs and outcomes). These levels are dynamic and in constant evolution over time and in response to what are mainly economic, political and sociopolitical challenges. By way of illustration, a comparison of national pride in Germany, Estonia and the UK indicates lower levels in Germany, medium levels in Estonia and relatively high levels in the UK. National identities and the consequent attachment to national sentiments or towards a sharing of sovereignty with supranational groupings can be very different. These sentiments define whether the population desires a solid fundamental text that anchors the rules of law and the processes attributed to the system. Do actors believe in a culture, in a system or in processes for historical, ideological, reasons, or because of participative, corporatist, monarchical, authoritative or religious obligations? The political culture inherent in these issues defines the manner in which the established system governs and the processes are perceived.

The geographic distribution of power varies accordingly, and may allow for a power strain between central and local authorities (horizontal and vertical), and a separation of powers at government (horizontal) level into different bodies or into a governmental body only. For example, because federalism allows member governments to pursue various different policies, if it ruled in Europe actors would experience different outcomes in the different Member States.

In reality, the EU has become a mixed system in terms of the structural separation of authority (marrying parliamentary and presidential structural features). The integration theories are hence based on a diversity of political cultures that characterize the Member States. They smooth the different paths to a single same destiny: the proliferation of any regional economic grouping is dependent on the common interpretation of this destiny. In accordance with the argument above, outcomes need to be in line with the classic expectations of trade creation and diversion.

3.2 Waves of European integration: The past, present and future

3.2.1 Past adhesions

In 1957, six countries signed the Treaty of Rome to create European integration in the shape of the EEC. The main objective of these founding members was to create a customs union. However, trade cooperation led to the launch of an increasing number of common policies, in particular the CAP. The EC, formed in 1967, was enlarged for the first time in 1973 with the accession of Denmark, Ireland and the UK. This led to the creation of the European Regional Development Fund (ERDF) and a regional policy that was adapted to the UK's agricultural budget.

The second and third enlargement saw Greece join in 1981 and Spain and Portugal in 1986. This expansion added poorer and more agriculturally oriented states to the membership of the EC and led to the creation of the Structural and Cohesion Fund, which became increasingly important. In 1987, Turkey, after 23 years as an associate member, decided to become a candidate for accession but its application was refused by the 12 Member States.

The fall of the Berlin Wall and collapse of the Soviet system gave birth to new enlargements. German reunification added 16 million citizens without holding an official ceremony in 1990. Five years later, Austria, Finland and Sweden joined the EU, while a referendum in Norway resulted in a rejection of accession. This enlargement was fuelled by increasing efforts of European policymaking in terms of social policies, and the creation of the CFSP. With 15 Member States, the time had come to think of streamlining the institutions and their decision-making procedures.

In 2004, the EU underwent its biggest ever expansion, of 10 new Member States from Eastern and Central Europe, mainly to solidify the political and economic stability of the region. The accession of Bulgaria, Romania and other East European states has since followed. The enlargements are based on the requirement that the candidate states fully accept and apply the *acquis communautaire*, that is, the full body of laws and regulations governing the EU, and different transition periods. The obligation includes the general principles of the EU. The 2004 accession countries have adopted the *acquis*, which was negotiated in 31 chapters and accompanied by pre-accession assistance from the original members of the EU. The chapters include the free movement of goods, services, capital and people; competition; and the application of rights and rules. In the accession of the 10 Countries of Central and Eastern Europe (CCEE), which were formerly part of COMECON (Council for Mutual Economic Assistance, which united communist and socialist countries in the cold war period), the transition periods were defined as less than five years for certain domains such as pharmaceutical products, the period up to 2011 for the free movent of goods etc., the period up to 2012 for agriculture and the full integration of the CAP, and, finally, the period up to 2015 for the application of the environmental rules. These transition periods are now judged costly and are not applied to any other accession.

Common rules harmonize access to countries and market opportunities. Nevertheless, opportunities differ and are diverse. For example, the Czech Republic offers opportunities in automobile equipment, the agri-business and fishery; Poland in the environmental sector; Estonia in hotel and restaurant equipment; Cyprus in food and perfume. For business, the main impact of enlargement lies in the opening of the markets. The questions to answer internally focus not only on the choice of internationalization strategies, but also on which forms and insensitivity of competition the firm will encounter in these markets, from local, European and international competitors. In particular, the Euro Info Centres are there to help define threats and opportunities, find partners and provide information about prevalent legislation, in particular helping SMEs to answer to the challenges (Box 7).

Box 7   SMEs and enlargement – a significant challenge for European competitiveness

1 External challenges for SMEs:

- resist market internationalization and globalization impacts (economies of scale, strong competition and pressure on margins, access to distribution networks, etc.);
- adapt to the tendency of large companies towards offshore production and services;
- access financial markets, ensure long-term/reliable financing and cash management.

2 Internal challenges for SMEs:

- reach critical size;
- transform development and diversification opportunities;
- develop and implement innovation strategies;
- recruit or access specific competencies;
- benchmark ambitions, performance, results.

3.2.2 Future adhesions

With the 2004 enlargement of the EU, the Copenhagen summit also anticipated further accessions, and in 2007 Bulgaria and Romania became the newest members of the Union. At the borders of geographical Europe, during the twentieth century these two countries suffered extensive oppression from totalitarian local communist dictatorships. It is therefore important to solidify political and economic stability in the areas surrounding the EU even further. The western Balkans and Ukraine are close partners, following the example of Macedonia and Croatia.

Turkey remains a candidate for accession In addition, several Mediterranean partners have expressed their interest for closer ties. The following text deals with two recent accessions and one candidate in particular, as an illustration of the prospects for further EU enlargement.

3.2.3 Romania

3.2.3.1 Historical overview

Romania became a state in 1859. Prior to World War I it was the principal power in the Balkans; after the war the Treaty of Saint Germain in 1919 doubled its population and

Table 6   Basic data – Romania

	General information
Population	21.7 million (2003)
Capital	Bucharest
Neighbours	Bulgaria, Federal Republic of Yugoslavia, Hungary, Ukraine, Moldova
Area	237,500 sq km
Ethnic groups	Romanian (89.4%), Hungarian (6.6%), Roma (2.4%), Ukrainian (0.3%), German (0.3%), other (1%)
Official language	Romanian
Religion	Orthodox (86.8%), Roman Catholic including Greek rite (6%), Protestant (6%), others (1.2%)
Life expectancy (at birth)	71.2 years (males: 67.6 years; females: 74.9 years)
Total GDP (2004 est.)	€48.4 billion
GDP per capita	$7,700
Currency	1 leu = 100 bani (pl.: lei)

Table 7   Political situation – Romania

	Political situation
Constitution	Adopted in 1991 and revised in October 2003
Head of state	The President
Current government	Government formed by the Social Democrat Party (PSD) and supported by the Democratic Union of Hungarians in Romania (UDMR)
Parliament	The parliament comprises the Chamber of Deputies (lower house) and the Senate (upper house). The two bodies wield equal powers. Parliamentarians are elected through a proportional system at the national level. Elections are held every four years simultaneously for both houses. The Chamber of Deputies and the Senate have 345 and 140 seats respectively

territory. During World War II, under Ion Antonescu, Romania sided with Germany. It was sovietized after the war. The dictatorship of Nicolae Ceauşescu from 1965 to 1989 left Romania with a complex and difficult political and economic heritage.

After Ceauşescu, the country faced serious difficulties with its economy, the administration and its legal system. In addition, minority issues and moving borders in Central and Eastern Europe required redefining through bilateral treaties. Tables 6, 7 and 8 provide essential data about Romania.

Table 8   Economic situation – Romania

Structure of production	
Agriculture	13.1%
Industry	33.7%
Services	53.2%
Economic situation in 2004 (est.)	
GDP growth rate	8.1%
Inflation rate	9.6%
Labour force	9.66 million
Unemployment rate	6.3%
Budget balance (% of GDP)	−1.49%
Current account balance	−$3.6 billion
Account deficit (rate of GDP)	Revenue: $22.1 billion; expenditure: $23.2 billion
Public debt (% of GDP)	23.6%

Source: Compiled data

3.2.3.2 EU–Romanian relations

Romania was the first of the CCEE to engage in official relations with the EC. In 1974, an agreement included Romania in the Community's Generalized System of Preferences and an Agreement on Industrial Products was signed in 1980.

Romania's diplomatic relations with the EU date from 1990, and a Trade and Cooperation Agreement was signed in 1991. The Europe Agreement entered into force in February 1995. Trade provisions entered into force in 1993 through an 'Interim Agreement'. Romania submitted its application for EU membership on 22 June 1995. In July 1997, the Commission published an 'Opinion on Romania's Application for Membership of the European Union'. The following year, a 'Regular Report on Romania's Progress towards Accession' was produced. In its second 'Regular Report' on Romania, published in October 1999, the Commission recommended starting accession negotiations with Romania, conditional on the improvement of the situation of children in institutional care and the drafting of a medium-term economic strategy.

Romania's accession negotiations began on 15 February 2000, and EU membership was obtained in January 2007. From 2000 onwards, accession was supported by EU pre-accession aid supplied through the PHARE Programme, which provided funding for institution-building and investment in support of EU accession preparations at €1.5 billion per annum, and the 'ISPA' (the pre-accession instrument that provided investments in transport and environmental infrastructure) and 'SAPARD' (the financial instrument supporting agriculture and rural development), which together provided funding to a level of approximately €700 million per year. These instruments were phased out after the 2007 enlargement, and replaced by DG Enlargement with IPA 2007–2013 (instrument for pre-accession assistance) and National Implementation initiatives. In addition, CARDS (Community Assistance for Reconstruction, Development and Stabilization), which also funded Turkey, Croatia, Macedonia and others, was redefined.

Table 9   Basic data – Bulgaria

General information	
Population	7.824 million (2003)
Population distribution	67.8% urban population; 32.2 % rural population
Capital	Sofia
Neighbours	Greece, The Former Yugoslav Republic of Macedonia, Serbia, Montenegro, Turkey
Area	110,910 sq km
Ethnic groups	Bulgarian (86%), Turkish (9.4%), Roma (4.6%)
Official language	Bulgarian
Religion	Orthodox Christian (83%), Muslim (13%), Catholic, Protestant and other (4%)
Life expectancy	71.4 years (male: 68.5 years; female: 75.3 years)
Total GDP (2004 est.)	$61.63 billion
GDP per capita (2004 est.)	$8,200
Currency (currency exchange rate)	1 euro = 1.995 leva

3.2.4 Bulgaria

3.2.4.1 Historical overview

After a period first under Byzantine and then under Turkish rule, Boris I and his son Simeon I founded the first Bulgarian state in 865. Its people represented a mixture of Slavs, Byzantines, Greek, Russians and Occidentals. In 925, Simeon was declared emperor of both Greece and Bulgaria. Invaded by the Mongols in 1396, Bulgaria then underwent a period of Ottoman domination that lasted five centuries.

In 1878, the Ottomans lost control of Bulgaria, a consequence of Turkey's defeat against Russia and the subsequent Treaty of San Stefano. After the Young Turks' revolution in Turkey in 1908, Bulgaria declared independence through Ferdinand, Prince of Bulgaria, who then assumed the title of Tsar. Bulgaria then joined Greece and Serbia in the first Balkan War, and after defeating the Ottomans, fought against the allies in World War I. The Treaty of Neuilly in 1919 resulted in the loss of some territory and access to the Aegean Sea. Like Romania, Bulgaria allied itself to Germany during World War II, and was sovietized after the war.

With the fall of the Soviet system, the opposition leader Jelyu Jelev became president in 1990, but still with a majority of communists in the National Assembly. Transition was hence rather slow and complex. Tables 9, 10 and 11 provide essential data about Bulgaria.

The Bulgarian economy benefits from high growth and stability, which is denoted by a steadily decreasing unemployment rate and decreasing public debt figures. In its 2004 Regular Report, the European Commission reiterated its recognition of Bulgaria as being

Table 10   Political situation – Bulgaria

Political situation	
Form of state	Parliamentary republic
Constitution	Adopted in July 1991
Head of state	The President
Head of government	The Prime Minister
Council of Ministers	The Government, chaired by the Prime Minister, is the principal body of the Executive Branch and presently comprise 20 ministers. The Prime Minister is nom inated by the largest parliamentary group and mandated by the President to form a cabinet
Parliament	The 240-seat National Assembly, or Parliament, is vested with legislative power. The members of the parliament are directly elected for a 4-year term on the basis of proportional representation. Parties and political coalitions need 4% of the popular vote to qualify. The last elections took place in summer 2005

Table 11   Economic situation – Bulgaria

Structure of production in 2003 (% of gross value added)	
Agriculture	11.4%
Industry	30.1%
Services	58.5%
Economic situation in 2004 (est.)	
GDP growth rate	5.3%
Inflation rate	6.1%
Labour force	3.398 million
Unemployment rate	12.7%
Budget balance	Revenue: $9.67 billion; expenditure: $9.619 billion
Current account balance	$682.9 million
Public debt (% of GDP)	41.9%

a functioning market economy (first recognized as a market economy in 2002). Furthermore, the Report concludes that Bulgaria should be able to cope with the competitive pressure and market forces within the EU. The private sector plays an increasingly important role in the economy through privatizations and the reduction of state aid, the development of the banking sector, and improvements in the regulatory environment.

3.2.4.2 EU–Bulgarian relations

Bulgaria has successfully established stable and democratic institutions, and has overcome the severe economic crisis of 1996/7 by accelerating its reforms and changes in order to join the EU. Efforts in regard to its labour market and the restructuring of the energy sector, such as the renovation or closing down of the Kozloduy nuclear power plants, were the main challenges to achieving accession.

Financial aid from the EU significantly supported Bulgaria's accession process well into 2007. Bulgaria received approximately € 400 million per year reaching 2 per cent of its GDP in 2004/6. As with Romania, the pre-accession aid to Bulgaria was provided mainly through the PHARE Programme, the 'ISPA' and 'SAPARD' (see above). Trade relations between the EU and Bulgaria have continued to develop strongly. The amount of foreign trade that Bulgaria does with other EU countries has continued to increase. Its main industrial exports to the EU are textiles, clothing, iron and steel. Bulgaria's main agricultural exports to the EU are cereals, oil seeds, oleaginous fruits, and meat. In 2003, imports from the EU were slightly down by 0.6 per cent on 2002, accounting for 49.6 per cent (€ 4.40 billion) of Bulgaria's total imports. Bulgaria's main industrial imports from the EU include textiles and clothing, while agricultural imports are fats, oils, fruits and nuts.

Technical Aid to the Commonwealth of Independent States (TACIS) countries, as well as those of MENA (EMP: Euro-Mediterranean Partnership and part of CARDS are eligible for the 2007 European Neighbourhood Partnership Programme (ENPI), including the NIS and southern Caucasus, for cross-border cooperation and for joint programmes managed by the European Commission and its Directorate – General Relex and EuropeAid. Support from the Macro Financial Assistance budget and the Instrument for Stability (fight against crime and insecurity) are also available.

3.2.5 The Occidental Balkans

3.2.5.1 The position and history of Turkey

The Occidental Balkans, the region that separated the Ottoman Empire from the Occidental, were under Turkish control from the end of the fourteenth century. During the eighteenth century, Christianity became established as the major religion in the area, but it nevertheless remained an area stricken by conflict and war well into the twentieth century: Russia against Turkey from 1877–8, Greece against Turkey in 1897, the Balkans from 1912 to 1913, and both world wars. Moreover, ethnic conflicts and the war of 1999 had shaken both the region and Europe, although the region has since been stabilized through the involvement of NATO, the USA and the EU. Hence, it has great geopolitical importance and retains important international military contingents. The challenge of political economic stability is complex.

The five Balkan countries (Albania, Bosnia and Herzegovina, Croatia, Macedonia: The Former Yugoslav Republic of, Serbia and Montenegro) are part of the EU stabilization and association agreements that established CARDS in 1999, which was developed for the period 2000–6 with an allocation of € 4.65 billion, and prolonged through new initiatives and the ENPI. The primary objective of these was to develop relationships with and within the region, and to promote democracy, civil society, education, institutions and cooperation regarding justice and internal affairs, as well as political dialogue.

The Stability Agreement for South-Eastern Europe complements this work. It was adopted in Cologne in 1999 to ensure peace, stability, democracy, human rights and economic prosperity. This agreement encompasses the Member States, the Commission, the countries of south-eastern Europe (Albania, Macedonia, Bosnia-Herzegovina, Bulgaria, Croatia, Hungary, Moldavia Serbia-Montenegro, Romania, Slovenia and Turkey), other countries (USA, Canada, Norway, Japan, Russia, Switzerland) and international organizations.

The early 2000s saw significant advances towards democracy in the region, mainly because of the will of its people. For example, in 2000 the opposition leader in Croatia,

Table 12   Turkey's basic data and economic situation

General information	
Population	67,803,927
Population distribution	64.9% urban population; 35.1% rural population
Capital	Ankara
Neighbours	Armenia, Azerbaijan, Bulgaria, Georgia, Greece, Iran, Iraq, Syria
Area	779,452 sq km
Ethnic groups	Turkish (80%), Kurdish (20%)
Official language	Turkish
Religion	Muslim (99.8% – mostly Sunni), other (0.2% – Christian and Jewish)
Life expectancy (1995)	Male: 66; female: 71
Total GDP (2004 est.)	$508.7 billion
GDP per capita	$7,400
Currency (currency exchange rate – Oct. 2002 info-euro)	1 euro = 1.619 Turkish lira

Structure of production	
Agriculture	11.7%
Industry	29.8%
Services	58.5%

Economic situation in 2004 (est.)	
GDP growth rate	8.2%
Inflation rate	9.3%
Labour force	25.3 million
Unemployment rate	9.3% (plus underemployment of 4%)
Budget balance	Revenue: $78.53 billion; expenditure: $110.9 billion
Current account balance	–$3.631 billion
Account deficit (rate of GDP)	5.1%
Public debt (% of GDP)	74.3%

Table 13   Political situation – Turkey

	Political situation
Official name	Republic of Turkey – Türkiye Cumhuriyeti
Constitution	7 November 1982, amended in 1995, 1999 and 2001
Electoral system	18 years of age, universal suffrage, separate parliamentary and local elections (both every 5 years), 10% threshold
Head of state	President
Internal administrative organization	The central administration, headed by the Prime Minister and ministers, is represented in the territory by 81 governors in the 81 provinces. There are sub-governors at district level. Though similar to the French 'prefet', the governor is assisted by a directly elected provincial council, and district councils. Several ministries have offices at both provincial and district level. (There are 7 geographical regions in Turkey, essentially for statistical purposes.) An autonomous local administration exists at the municipal level (16 large metropolitan municipalities (MM) – subdivided into sectors – and 3200 other smaller towns) which elect a mayor and a municipal council. Istanbul MM has a population of 8.5 million, Ankara over 3 million, and Izmir over 2 million. In 50,000 villages a Council of Elders and a village headman are directly elected by the village assembly

Stipe Mesic, was elected president, taking the place of Franjo Tudjman; democratic forces in Serbia ousted Slobodan Milosevic through the ballot box, and he was eventually arrested and transferred to the International Court of Justice; and in Kosovo, Ibrahim Rugova won the elections in October. The 2000 Zagreb Summit reinforced political dialogue between the Balkans and the EU, while Turkey has continuously confirmed its desire to join the EU.

3.2.5.2 EU – Turkish relations

At the World Economic Forum's annual meeting held in Davos in 2005, Turkish Prime Minister Recep Tayyip Erdogan stated:

> The EU is no longer a union of steel and coal ... It is not a Christian club. It is a totality of political values.

That said, EU–Turkish relations are mainly governed on the basis of a customs union that was established in 1995; indeed, from 1995 to 1999 trade between the two partners increased significantly on the basis of this agreement. Over a fifteen-year period, Turkey became the seventh biggest export destination for the EU (up from ninth in 1990) and the thirteenth largest exporter to the EU (up from seventeenth in 1990).

Despite this positive development in terms of trade, the relations are governed by several conflicting long-term issues that need to be resolved. With more than 65.9 million inhabitants in 1999, Turkey's population has more than doubled since 1960. With a birth rate of 3.1 per

1000, the population will reach 100 million by 2015. The country will be the largest in terms of territory and people: one European out of five will be Turkish. Consequently, Turkey could account for most of the deputies in the European Parliament and therefore alter the decision-making structure and balance of power in the EU significantly. Member States need also to agree on the question of whether the EU is a Christian grouping. Other questions have been raised about Turkey's candidacy: How far can the EU make concessions in terms of human rights and in terms of equality issues? Can Turkey adapt to the European *acquis*? The question of the Armenian genocide is another issue that has to be resolved. Recognition of its Armenian community is key to Turkey's change of direction, from its military past and towards democracy. Turkey also needs to re-evaluate its position on the status of Cyprus as this was the specific condition under which the EU agreed to open negotiations for Turkey's accession on 3 October 2005. Turkey receives half of the budget allocated to the Instrument for Pre-accession Assistance (INP), that is, a total budget of €11 billion from 2007 to 2013.

Besides these questions, the integration of Turkey potentially provides for a large and powerful European Union both regionally and globally with ever-increasing geopolitical significance, and establishes a unique relationship with Asia. Only 10 per cent of Turkish territory is situated inside Europe (oriental Thrace and European Turkey); the other 90 per cent comprises Anatoly and Asian Turkey, both located on the Asian continent. The US is highly favourable towards Turkish accession to the EU. This accession would illustrate powerfully that Islam does not lead automatically to fundamentalism but can be well-matched to and even integrated peacefully into western principles. This adhesion could have a significant effect on the way in which Occidental powers view the Israeli–Palestinian and Iraqi conflicts, and stabilize the region.

3.3 Enlarging business opportunities

Common regulations for free movement of goods, services, capital and people enlarge business opportunities (Box 8), and help facilitate exchanges, create new opportunities and prolong life cycles. Any new operation also encompasses new risks and uncertainties, new obligations and costs.

EU enlargement results in short-term costs that encompass mainly costs of support. For the 2004 enlargement, support payments began in the 1990s with about $18 billion from the EU, US, World Bank, IMF, United Nations Development Programme (UNDP) financing the adaptation efforts made by Central European and Baltic countries. In 2002, $32 million were provided through the Open Society Institute: this was then reduced to $10 million in 2004. By then, most entrants had already become net donors to the UNDP; only Latvia and Lithuania owed payments to the IMF. All the states included in the EU and its waves of enlargement subscribe to respect all the general principles of the EU.

While the enlargement countries are governed by common legislation, opportunities are diverse. In the example of the 2004 enlargement of 10 new Member States from Eastern and Central Europe, each country is a product of its own potential.

> ## Box 8   Selected opportunities in 2004 – enlargement markets
>
> **Czech Republic:** car equipment, agro food, fisheries
> **Poland:** environment
> **Estonia:** equipment for hotels, cafés, restaurants and IT
> **Latvia:** perfumes, cosmetics
> **Lithuania:** clothing and furniture
> **Cyprus:** food and perfumes
> **Slovenia:** luxury goods

The successive waves of enlargement promise to boost the economies of new members. The costs are compensated by the increase in business opportunities. The growing and rich internal market offers huge potential benefits that balance the saturation of certain sectors in the EU. While current EU markets may not provide any further extension of the life cycle under the favourable conditions that a highly integrated market gives, new markets accessing under equal conditions of legislation and market access enable the expansion of operations, life cycles and marketing strategies. The conquest of the consumer, in the non-EU periphery, responds directly to the need for fulfilment and the aspirations of status long satisfied in the traditional Member States.

The benefits are also relatively large where business of the acceding countries typically starts from a lower economic base. It is estimated in a study that the EU15 countries gained €15 billion in real income while the gain for the 2004 accession countries amounted to €23 billion (Baldwin et al., 1997 and 2004). Though acceding to the EU means abiding by all rules, even those that are costly, some are easier to implement than others. Industry–standards, state-aid and environmental protection rules, for example, reshape economies extensively. The workforce needs to be educated to be competitive, the infrastructure polished, and access to big markets granted. Low taxation rates, such as in Estonia (where some firms pay 0 per cent corporate tax), as well as low labour costs put older Member States under strain because in the first years of membership the new Member States' relatively sluggish regulation attracts high levels of inward investment.

Testimony 1 The future of Macedonian business: The BASME C&T story

When Beti Delovska and Vlatko Danilov decided to leave their steady jobs at the National Entrepreneurship Promotion Agency and at one of the largest Macedonian commercial banks to set up a private business, BASME C & T (Balkan Small and Medium Enterprise Consulting & Training), one of the most successful consulting companies in Macedonia, many of their friends and colleagues found the move very risky. Although Macedonia had spent almost 12 years in transition, private business was still perceived as a career reserved for vocational college graduates and the unemployed. The prevailing mindset of most intellectuals considered steady jobs a much more secure and promising alternative.

However, there was no way back and in 2003 BASME C&T was born. It also took almost the entire savings of the two partners. Suddenly, Beti and Vlatko found themselves in a situation of rapid change. The original enthusiasm and virtues of 'being one's own boss' dissipated very quickly.

'As partners in the team of the first Macedonian entrepreneurship agency, we had hundreds of seminars behind us. We helped many start-ups in their most difficult years. We were teaching them that starting a private business is a very serious, but rewarding adventure; that it takes a lot of dedication, knowledge, personal stamina and managerial virtues, and that very often, family life suffers. While we were good with the theory, in real life we found ourselves making the same mistakes as everyone else. Things were changing all the time. You try to plan your moves, but soon find yourself in the role of a medical surgeon in a military hospital who doesn't know: will the next patient be suffering from a head injury, a bullet in his chest, or will he or she need serum against a deadly snakebite. You get on with the job, with the agenda, but something much more important and critical calls your immediate attention. You need to be alert and vigilant all the time, and able to switch topics "in the blink of an eye"' says Vlatko. This is, they say, a 'go-go' phase, when business is more chaotic than smooth and organized.

Today things are different. BASME is a well-established consulting company known by many European counterparts that implement various EU-funded projects in the region. There are members of the team in charge of planning the activities and personal workload months in advance and there is a network of capable associate consultants. However, it was not easy to reach this stage; challenges were tremendous. Indeed, the founders' private lives were jeopardized, since they were always busy with the company, and had insufficient time for private obligations.

It seems that BASME's small team mastered the virtues of implementing various development projects. Macedonia is now closer to the EU and the profile of the projects has changed from start-up issues to more advanced ones. Businesses now demand assistance in their pursuit of EU funds and in expanding their market in the EU.

'We have no time to rest,' says Vlatko. 'Recently, we have started a project with Invent from Germany, on setting up an export promotion agency for small and medium enterprises, and we are looking for partners to make joint applications on projects which will use various accession funds that we expect to be opened up for Macedonian companies when the country starts its formal accession process. We have to be prepared for that stage, and we have already started acquiring the

(Continued)

(Continued)

necessary knowledge.' Their philosophy is 'we have to be always one step ahead of the others'.

BASME plans to go international. The company recently started to respond to the requests for proposals and expressions of interest for projects in the region. Beti obtained a project in Montenegro and was very successful. BASME has also signed a contract with the UNDP Offices in Tirana, Albania. BASME thinks that it has found a winning business strategy in always taking on assignments in partnership with some established consulting company from an EU country. This strategy allows the BASME team to jump years of learning. It gives fast access to the practices and know-how of the leading consulting houses: 'We learned that the percentage of the share you have in a venture is irrelevant. What really matters is how big the pie is. Plus, the possibility to learn from our partners is priceless. We offer this winning strategy to our clients, too. It worked for us in the consulting business; it will work for any other service and industry, even for the government units,' say Beti and Vlatko. (BASME C&T, 2005)

3.4 Competitive strategies in the enlarged market

How should competitive strategies best target the enlarged market? What are the opportunities for a given company? Should my export strategies be generalised or differentiated? What type of presence in the market is best for my company? Should I go for subcontracting or prefer other options? With regard to the threats of doing business in the enlarged Europe, what type of competition will I encounter? What prices can I target? What product or service is best adapted to the customer in this market? What qualifications and human resources legislation will I encounter?

These numerous questions require an answer before internationalization can take place. In Europe, a certain set of rules and conditions defined by the EU can be taken for granted. Economic theory has shown that internationalization appears to be crucial if companies want to obtain or maintain competitiveness. This is even more so when operational and environmental risks are low. Both internationalization and Europeanization have been detrimental to firms that have not been capable of responding to integration.

While gains and losses are intrinsic to any business operation, choosing the right cross-border location represents an efficient solution to obtain competitive advantage that will make a difference by:

- optimizing or reducing costs;
- providing opportunities for growth;
- developing new strategic strengths.

Typically, the prerequisites of internationalization are based on the certainty that foreign countries offer advantages. These encompass:

- ownership – specific advantages;
- internalization to a certain degree;
- location-specific advantages.

A firm must also assess the operational risks and threats of this move. In its international value chain this includes the assessment of conditions related to:

- procurement;
- orders and invoicing;
- manufacturing and inventory management;
- service provision;
- shipping, integrated logistics, order fulfilment;
- planning and time management.

These elements involve all aspects of management, from human resources management to marketing and sales strategies. Before the internationalization process is undertaken or expanded, a crucial decision for a company is the choice of location. In the case of delocalization, the new location is also crucial to both home and receptor markets. A firm's decision is based on the balance that can be established between risks and returns, costs and benefits – ranging from local externalities – research and development spill-overs, cost of knowledge transfer, and/or transport costs. As an example for the geographical dimensions in Europe, consider that the distance between Paris and Prague is the same as that between Paris and Barcelona (1031 km) and similiar when travelling by motorway (932 and 961 km respectively). The transaction costs may make relocating attractive, as will the gains to be made from cost benefits and from entering foreign markets, and from these markets' resources potential. Entry modes may vary between export – indirect or direct – (for example, through agents), controlled (for example, sales branch), contractual – licence or franchise, management or service contracts – cooperation agreements or investments such as greenfield investments. Other options for market entry are acquisition or joint venture strategies.

Any corporation that engages in business across the enlarged Europe must have appropriate organizational capabilities. It must be able to give leverage to its strengths internally and in sufficient supply to counterbalance external market mechanisms. Corporations possess geographic organizations that are shaped into international divisions (for example, Haribo), geographically linked via a matrix structure combining functions and business units to regions (for example, Microsoft EMEA), and have different degrees of what is known as transnationality (Bartlett and Goshal, 1992). It appears that the particular advantage of the transnational corporation lies in the efficient and effective transfer of knowledge regarding global and local conditions: This definition takes account of the tacit knowledge (that is, experience, accumulated tacit knowledge, networking motivations) and the explicit knowledge (for example, geographical proximity, logistic ease and risk diversification motivations) for location decisions. Management also decides which knowledge and competence is transferred to external parties at a location, and which knowledge is to remain internal (Suder, 2006). Hence, the success of going cross-border depends on the strategic competencies or ownership-specific advantages that a firm may have in order for it to counterbalance a knowledge gap in a particular location and its markets. In Europe, the level of unfamiliarity with enlargement markets is relatively low and access to information easy compared to internationalization towards non-EU countries, but nevertheless Europeanization is challenging for any company.

Box 9   Foreign investment after enlargement – not everything is rosy

Greece joined the EU in 1981. Despite expectations of strong inflows in foreign direct investments (FDI), in 2003 the country had still only received 0.2 per cent of the total investment flow to Member States, as the OECD found. UNCTAD (United Nations Conference on Trade and Development) found that the total investment stock for 2003 only amounted to 9.8 per cent of GDP, compared with 32.8 per cent of GDP in the other Member States. The reasons found for this phenomenon, which is rather exceptional for enlargement countries – they tend to catch up within a decade of accession – may be the isolated location, that is, no direct border with the other EU members, waiting for Bulgaria to bridge the geographic gap, the domestic market of 11 million consumers is relatively small, FDI is often effectively hindered by tax rates (in particular compared to those of newer Member States such as Estonia), and bureaucracies that process applications, licences and permits slowly. The *Financial Times* reported in June 2005 that it still took about two years to complete paperwork required before foreign investment. As a result, most investment is made indirectly through acquisitions.

In 2005, the *World Competitiveness Report* (Schwab, 2005) ranked Greece fiftieth out of 60 countries surveyed. The reduction of structural funds that flow into the CCEE required the Greek government to rethink its domestic business environment from 2004 onwards. For example, corporate tax is reduced to 25 per cent from 2007, Public–Private Partnership (PPP) ventures are encouraged and start-up legislation has been facilitated, and will only require 20 permits and 30 days for the paperwork. Indeed, Greece has enormous potential: it excels in high-quality infrastructure with distinct know-how of local and regional markets. The neighbouring Balkan economies are growing fast, and Greece is an ideal springboard for firms in the older Member States to enlarge operations.

Sources: Compiled from Euro Info Center, the *Financial Times*, UNCTAD, IMD and OECD, 2005

In terms of competition, the highest FDI figures found in 2003 for the accession countries of 2004 were achieved by Poland and Slovakia, and by the 2007 accessor, Romania.

From the foreign investor perspective, the progress of FDI into Romania is significant and reflects an economy coming to terms with its struggles with high inflation and low productivity: the country had been ranked bottom for FDI every year between 1989 and 1997. First movers into these markets were firms from Germany and Austria, followed by the US. Proximity, educational levels and the expected growth of GNP due to consumption of equipment (TV, cars, etc.) led the corporate sector to move rapidly into these markets. A study of the specialized industrial sectors of those new Member States illustrates the investment patterns that have attracted the corporations: plastics and transport mechanics in Poland, Hungary and Slovakia, with production levels that were, in the pre-accession era, limited or for regional consumption only; chemicals in Bulgaria; fertilizers in Lithuania; electronics in Hungary, in particular car security; and pharmaceuticals in Hungary, Poland and Slovenia. There are also opportunities in the agrifood, telecom., electric goods and automobile sectors (the latter dominated by the Czech Republic, Hungary and Slovakia with 60 per cent of regional production due to FDI), and metal. All these opportunities establish a cartography of investments which depend on the geographic approach, industrial integration and level of infrastructure that the firm targets within its Europeanization strategy in an enlarg*ed* and enlarg*ing* Europe.

Opportunities for Europeanization through enlargement are mainly connected to the need to satisfy governmental, business and consumer requirements that arise when newly integrated economies catch up with existing members of the Union. Infrastructural sites, the service sector, and SME outsourcing follow the internationalization of the goods sector, with the evolution of a highly qualified workforce, and ever-increasing regional integration. Investors receive support from the EU in the shape of structural funds that amounted to €40 billion for 2004 to 2006 with respect to the 2004/7 wave of integration. These funds are attributed to regional development projects in particular, encouraging firms to create structures now that will open markets for the future.

Typically, it can be observed that within a decade of joining the EU, increasing regional integration results in the close proximity of European demand structures while the gap between labour costs, public aid structures, harmonization of all norms and standards reduces the main differences between older and younger accession countries.

Parallel pricing in the enlarged Europe can have a significant impact on business. Pricing policies generate the specific pricing objectives of a corporation. Common policies include price skimming, penetration pricing, life-cycle pricing, above/at/below competitors, and customer value in order to develop list or base prices for publication. These prices are calculated via cost-based, competitive-based or demand-based methods of calculations. They need to adhere to certain rules of fair competition set by the governmental body, for example, in accordance with anti-dumping regulations. Discounts are used in order to provide not only reductions from list prices for different consumers, depending on the situation, location and consumer behaviour, in the shape of variations in quantity, season, credit and special sales, but also allowances to the distribution channel to perform services. These services may be advertising, stocking or trade-in. Again, although several types of adjustment are feasible, and always dependent on the industry and on the nature of the products, generally speaking, rebates and discounts must not be discriminatory. Indeed, European competition laws prohibit dissimilar conditions for equivalent transactions. Adjustments are also made for geographic and cultural considerations. The lower income levels in some foreign markets may require a firm to set a lower price to achieve sales and fierce competition may call for a low price level.

Furthermore, even with a lower price, the product may be more expensive in the foreign market because of the transport and tariff costs and other add-ons. A firm may, however, reconsider that costs of exports are actually less important if it decides that research, development and other costs are already covered by domestic sales. It is widely recognized that one main advantage from international operations is the leverage of charging country-specific prices that reflect differences in willingness to pay.

A company's pricing in one country can help create separate channels in another country and affect their pricing. This means that pricing decisions in different countries cannot be made in isolation. A corporation needs to consider the consequences of resulting prices in separable channels and to link these prices to form a coherent pricing policy in accordance with the corporate strategy. Pricing policy that attempts to differentiate prices based on buyers' willingness and ability to pay, in order to extract consumer surplus and maximize profit potentials in different countries, often leads to a price difference for the same product. In many cases the price difference is large enough for a business enterprise to purchase the products in country A (the lower-priced country), ship and distribute them into country B (the higher-priced country), and still make a profit. This is, when the price difference between two countries exceeds a threshold, parallel imports emerge and create a channel of unauthorized product flows. This can be observed between the markets of older EU Member States and those of accession countries in the very early stages. Parallel imports are often costly to the manufacturer since they cannibalize the sales of the manufacturer's authorized channel in country B and deteriorate the relationship with its distributors. When companies are forced to compete against their own trademarked items, profits decrease, prohibiting domestic distributors from continued promotion of the product. The net change may be positive or negative. Overall, the effects of parallel imports on the manufacturer's global supply chain are:

- a shift in the middle market segment's sales volume from the higher-priced country to the lower-priced country;
- the creation of a new market segment at the lower end in the higher-priced country;
- an increase in the total sales volume in the global marketplace and a potential increase or decrease in the total profit depending on the profitability of various market segments;
- a modification of the company image based on product usage information, service, warranty and safety protection.

Economic growth usually leads to increased demand, which will raise price-levels. It can be predicted that price differences will merge in the long term (Terpstra, 1991; Vinoo, 1992; Yang et al., 1998).

Résumé and conclusion

In this chapter, you have studied the widening of the European market driven by the principal values and objectives of the EU. The successive waves of enlargement have offered increased business opportunities to European and international firms operating in the single market; the successful integration of countries boosts growth in formerly weak economies and provides the essentials necessary for corporations and Member States to combine competitiveness with welfare. The European market has grown into a microcosm of the global business environment, marrying unique integration with singular diversity. Trade creation is, as expected, accompanied by trade diversion. The candidacy of further potential members as well as the special relations that the enlarged EU possesses with non-EU countries benefit both intra- and extra-EU trade and both the European and the non-EU countries', economies.

Regarding wider consecutive integration, the key question now is: Where do the borders of the EU begin and end? For many partisans of a strong EU, the Union cannot be built politically if there is no delimitation of its borders. What is a border? If we take the origin of the word, a border is a limit that demarks sovereignty, defines community identity and determines its harmony and hostility relationships within its neighbours. Historically, the question of borders is a sensitive one in Europe. Borders have been at the origin of threat and conflict, expansion and exclusion. Enlargements have ended schisms of the past, but have not really opened this debate. With the Turkish candidature, the opportunity for geographical enlargement outside Europe arises. Where will the borders be drawn? Does the EU need to consolidate and homogenize its policies and obtain deeper integration before it can create a truly powerful and competitive Europe?

Mini case study: Carrefour and the challenges of enlargement

The French retailer Carrefour is the number one retailer in Europe and the second largest worldwide, after the American Wal-Mart, with more than 9632 stores in 30 countries. Carrefour operates via three main formats: hypermarkets, supermarkets, and discount stores. The stimulus for French retail's shift towards hypermarkets was provided by the French administration's long-time resistance to permit the establishment of big supermarkets in its cities. The launch of the concept was a powerful stimulus for the creation and expansion of commercial areas in close proximity to

(Continued)

(Continued)

urban conglomerations, with well-developed infrastructures and flexible opening hours, and marketing adapted to one-stop-shopping. As a result of a very sound home base in hypermarkets, Carrefour internationalized intensively and successfully into the most diverse markets all over the world. Shopping in a Carrefour in South America, Europe or Asia you will notice how familiar is the market space, parking areas and allies (floor space between shelves), but see shelves that are filled up with local goods. For example, in Taiwan, where the name Carrefour is translated phonetically into terms that signify 'happy family', you will find the same photo-, insurance- and after sales service desks at the entrance to the hypermarket, advertisements in the same colours as those in Europe, cash tills arranged in the same way, but counters offering products ranging from Taiwanese noodles and dumplings to green teas and Asian candies.

With almost 400,000 employees (in 2004), Carrefour had a market value of $31 billion. Its development strategy consists of the parallel development of hypermarkets, supermarkets, and hard discount stores in order to cover all types of distribution channel. The retailer's objective centres around having the market lead in the hypermarket segment first of all and wherever the company is operating. Typically, Carrefour targets to open stores in three new countries annually; countries are selected through a screening of markets that have rapidly growing purchase power. To implement this strategy, Carrefour has formulated various criteria based on two approaches. First, a rather traditional approach takes into consideration the market size, low political and economical risk and low competitive intensity. Second, a complementary and more recent approach examines socio-economic criteria such as food culture and people's way of life, as well as the level of education, know-how and expertise. At first glance, the CCEE appeared to fulfil these criteria and their accession to the EU constituted a real opportunity for the retailing business, especially since the retail sector had started experiencing a saturation of the European market of established members. By 2004, Carrefour had engaged in development and takeover activities in the eastern market with 8 hypermarkets in the Czech Republic, 4 in Slovakia, and 13 hypermarkets and 55 supermarkets in Poland.

However, the internationalization plans of the retailer encountered limits that were mainly due to non-tariff barriers. In the Czech Republic, for example, national law stipulates that hypermarkets must obtain a compulsory licence to trade. Elsewhere in many of the other East European countries people were more accustomed to shopping at grocery stores and had to be actively convinced of the merits of super- and hypermarket shopping.

The limits of internationalization were above all linked to the high degree of international competition, for example in Poland and the Czech Republic. The British retailer Tesco and the German Spar are established almost everywhere, and the

(Continued)

American giant Wal-Mart has actively gained market share. A quick quasi-saturation has taken shape and Carrefour needs a market presence.

Mini case questions:

1   Why did Carrefour actively expand into the Eastern and Central European markets at an early stage?
2   Why does Carrefour need a market presence in enlargement countries despite the rapid saturation of the retail market there?

Review questions

1   **Which** integration theories drive integration the most? Which integration theory would be supported by a large US corporation operating in the European market? Why?
2   **Should** long-time Member States contribute to EU structural funds that help enlargement countries financially, and that may then help to lure jobs and industries away to countries with cheap labour and low tax rates? Why?
3   **Discuss** the future of Europe. Would business benefit more from a deeper or from a wider integration?
4   It was reported by major analysts that the 2004 enlargement countries are losing out to India on wage costs and skilled labour, and to China for R&D investment location. **Why** then are the Baltic countries booming?

Assignments

*   **Imagine** that you are the CEO of a Turkish corporation producing Turkish delight. To what extent does the customs union with the EU enhance your international business opportunities? What would full membership to the EU mean for your company?
*   **Compare** the threats and opportunities of further enlargement across the European geographic delimitations.
*   **Case study assignment**: Read and prepare the Synops 6 International case study in Part IV, and discuss the impact of Europe on the company's operations.
*   **Internet exercise**: How do corporations make their international location decisions? Prepare an analysis on the basis of statistics and find a short case example.

www

Web guide

http://www.europa.eu.int/comm/enlargement/index_en.html The enlargement website of the European Commission.

http://www.dree.org/elargissement/def2.htm Enlargement towards Central European countries.

http://www.robert-schuman.org Foundation supporting European cooperation.

http://www.gov.ro/engleza/guvernul/cabinet.php Government of Romania (constitution, programmes, objectives, etc.).

http://eu.eu.int/en/info/eurocouncil The Council of the European Union.

References

Baldwin, R.E., Francois, J.F and Porter, R. (1997) 'The cost and benefits of eastern enlargement: the impact on the EU and central Europe', *Economic Policy*, 24: 125–70.

Baldwin, R. and Wyplosz, C. (2004) *The Economics of European Integration*. Maidenhead: McGraw-Hill.

Bartlett, C. and Ghoshal, S. (1992) '*What is a global manager?*', *Harvard Business Review*, September–October: 124–32.

Czinkota, M. Ronkainen, I. and Moffet, M. (2005) *International Business*, 7th edn. Mason, OH: South-Western Thomson.

Dinan, D. (2006) *Origins and Evolution of the European Union*, New European Union Series. Oxford: Oxford University Press.

European Communities (2002–2005) *Eurostat Metadata in SDDS format*, URL http://europa.eu.int/estatref/info/sdds/en/gov/gengovt02_sm.htm

Herder (ed.) (1989) *Der farbige Ploetz*, 12th edn. Freiburg: Herder Verlag.

Iyer, Vinoo (1992) *Managing and Motivating Your Agents and Distributors*. London: Financial Times/Pitman.

Komet (ed.) (2003) *Der grosse Ploetz*, 32nd edn. Cologne: Komet Verlag.

Mercado, S., Welford, R. and Prescott, K. (2001) *European Business*, 4th edn. Harlow: FT Prentice Hall.

Sarathy, R. (1991) *International Marketing*, 5th edn. Dryden: The Dryden Press.

Schwab, K. (ed.) (2005) *World Competitiveness Report*. Davos: World Economic Forum.

Senior Nello, Susan (2005) *The European Union: Economics, Politics and History*. Maidenhead: McGraw-Hill Education.

Suder, G. (ed.) (2006) *Corporate Strategies under International Terrorism and Adversity*. Cheltenham: Edward Elgar.

Terpstra, V. and Sarathy, R. (1991) 'Pricing in International Marketing', in *International Marketing*, 5th edn. Fort Worth: The Dryden Press.

Yang, B., Reza, H. and Kent, B. (1998) 'Pricing in separable channels: the case of parallel imports', *Journal of Product and Brand Management*, 7 (5): 279–94.

Other sources:

Primary sources from EuroInfoCentre, Nice, and various articles and data from the *Financial Times*, UNCTAD, IMD Lausanne European business school and OECD as acknowledged.

4 Institutional Players: Rule- and Agenda-Setting

What you will learn about in this chapter
• Which main EU institutions does business need to be familiar with?   • How is EU decision making handled?   • What are the EU's main tools for implementation of its projects and initiatives?

Introduction

The institutions of the EU were set up on the basis of the Treaty of Rome, which established the EC in March 1957 and came into force on 1 January 1958. As discussed in the previous chapter, at this stage the EC comprised six Member States. These Member States met in Messina in June 1955 to consider the setting up of a European Union, a term that was eventually to come into being some 38 years later when on 1 November 1993, with the ratification of the Treaty of Maastricht, the EC became the EU.

Such an ambitious project necessitated the setting up of a certain type of organizational structure large enough to run the different projects, initiatives and programmes, and, of course, to carry out all negotiations.

When the Treaty of Rome came into force, a general economic framework was set up in order to provide a legal structure for activities and policies shared by the Member States. The Treaty simultaneously gave the EC institutions wide discretion for further integration and a closer union among Member States; it dealt with present needs and it also prepared for the future.

Because economics and business was to drive European integration from the earliest stages, the original design of the institutions entrusted them with the task of establishing a common market and a convergence of Member States' policies. By this means, the aim was to harmonize economic activities and to encourage business across borders. The objective was to benefit the community of countries via the progressive improvement of living standards through the continuous evolution of common activities. Business would increasingly share resources, streamline and become more competitive through a larger home market. However, the Treaty of Rome did not confer on the institutions exclusive tasks or specific instruments for implementing them.

Since their inception, the European institutions have, of course, undergone changes. These concern less their structure than their weight in the power balance of EU decision making. The Constitution of the European Union project made efforts to streamline these changes and to create greater transparency. These aims were pursued in response to, among others, major demands from the private and public sector.

During all stages of EU decision making, the institutions of the EU play an essential role in policy formation, in the legislative and in the executive sphere. Consequently, firms operating in Europe are subject to EU and Member State legislation. Understanding the institutions' role and nature is therefore essential for a good understanding of the European business environment.

4.1 The institutions

4.1.1 The European Commission

The European Commission, or Commission of the European Communities (CEC), was, at the outset, established on the basis of the EC Treaty's Articles 155 to 163, that regulate the CEC's relations with the Council of Ministers(Council) as well as with the European Parliament (EP). Article 4 of the EC Treaty prescribes the function and operation of the EC four principal bodies: the CEC, the EP, the Council, and the European Court of Justice (ECJ), empowered to carry out the tasks assigned to the EC. The CEC's powers (Box 10) are mainly of an executive nature, but are also political, legislative and administrative in cooperation with the powers entrusted to the Council and the EP. The CEC possesses exclusive powers to initiate legislation and the setting up of proposals, with a resulting diversity of the workload. The functioning of the CEC is often complemented by and embedded in expertise from the outside, whether through national civil servants via committees or other knowledgeable parties like, for instance, Eurogroups (pressure, interest or lobbying groups). Participation from outside the institutional setting is considered pluralist in its dependency on input of data from public and private sources in exchange for this participation. We will come back to these issues in Chapter 9.

***

Box 10   Main objective of the Commissions

The main objective of the Commission is to ensure the proper functioning and development of the Common Market.

***

4.1.1.1 Composition

The composition of the CEC is of a pluralist nature: it is headed by a president and his or her vice-presidents. The Treaty of Amsterdam strengthened the role and position of the President of the European Commission in terms of organizational and cohesion powers. He or she sets the broad policy lines and directs the allocation and possible reorganization of portfolios. The governments of the Member States designate the person they intend to appoint as president by common agreement. Through the amendments made by the Treaty of Nice, since 1 February 2003, the Council meeting at the level of the Heads of State and Government (the European Council) designate the President by a qualified majority. The EP is then asked to approve the appointment.

The CEC is organized around Commissioners, nominated by national governments, who are in charge of directorates-general. However, until Nice, each Member State was entitled to have at least one but not more than two Commissioners. In practice, France, Germany, Italy and the UK were the countries that normally nominated two Commissioners due to the size of their populations. Since Nice, each Member State can only propose one Commissioner. The confirmation procedure comprises two stages, the first relating to the President, the second to the Commission as a whole, with an important role played by the European Council that has been enhanced since the Treaty of Nice: it validates the list of the Commissioners prepared by the national governments and approved by the President. Finally, once the President and the members of the Commission have been approved by Parliament, they are appointed to the Council by qualified majority vote. With European enlargement, the Commission enlarged too. As noted above, the Treaty of Nice limited, provisionally, the number of members to one Commissioner per Member State per the 2004–9 Commission. The draft of the Constitution had envisaged a reduction of the Commission to two-thirds of the number of Member States as from 2014. The Commissioners were stipulated to be chosen by a rotation system based on equal rights of all Member States.

The Commissioners are appointed for a renewable term of four years. This term of office may be terminated early by either death or resignation. The Commissioners are required to be independent of any national government or other agency in the performance of their duties, and the CEC is politically independent. The body of Commissioners is often referred to as the College. Within the College, a specific policy area is assigned to each Commissioner's responsibility. Subject to the approval of the College, the President of the CEC may ask a member of the Commission to resign. The EP may, however, force the whole CEC to resign by passing a censure motion by qualified majority vote.

The Commissioners are assisted by a cabinet or departmental staff headed by a director-general. Each director-general is responsible to a particular Commissioner and in each case, the nationality of the director-general is different from that of the Commissioner. The staff of each Commissioner is appointed at his or her discretion and personal choice. When the Commissioner's term of office ends, the staff also leave. They are based in Brussels, Belgium. The directorates-general vary in size and are differentiated by the policy area transferred to them (Box 11).

Box 11   The Commission's policy areas

- Agriculture and rural development
- Competition
- Economic and financial affairs

(Continued)

(Continued)

- Education and culture
- Employment, social affairs and equal opportunities
- Enterprise and industry
- Fisheries and maritime affairs
- Environment
- Health and consumer protection
- Information society and media
- Internal market and services
- Joint research centre
- Justice, freedom and security
- Regional policy
- Research
- Taxation and customs union
- Transport and energy.

The CEC also hosts external relations including:

- Development
- Enlargement
- Europe-aid
- External relations
- ECHO – the humanitarian aid office
- Trade.

Its general services comprise:

- European anti-fraud office
- Eurostat
- Press and communication
- Publications office
- Secretariat general.

and nine directorates for internal services.

Source: © European Communities, 2006, The Directorates-Generals and Services, URL: http://ec.europa.eu.dgs_en.htm

4.1.1.2 Role

The CEC constitutes a collective body which commits its members and Member States to a shared responsibility for actions and policies that often cut across sectors, concerning, for example, anti-competitive practices as well as consumer, environmental and R&D issues. The CEC's major responsibilities are the initiation, formulation and coordination of

Community policy. The cabinets in particular can be considered important players in the decision-making process. Within these cabinets, private senior officials reporting to each 'Chef de Cabinet' specialize in a given subject and play a central role in developing regulations and decisions. The CEC implements, manages and controls, checks the proper application of EU law, plans and implements common policies, executes the budget and manages Community programmes.

Altogether, the CEC functions through the articulation of European interests. These interests are based on a maximum consensus of diverging approaches, attitudes and impacts which are brought upon the CEC. It acts as an observer of what is enacted by the treaties and takes violators to the ECJ. It also suggests policies and is in charge of drafting proposals of EU policy. Agricultural and trade policies may also, in certain cases on a day-to-day basis, be implemented by the CEC. As its negotiator, the Commission officially conducts the relations with international organizations as well as with non-EU countries. Box 12 provides you with an illustration of these activities, and the weight of one strong European voice for business.

Box 12   The European Union at World Trade Organization negotiations: the United States call for countervailing measures concerning certain products from Europe (Recourse to Article 21.5 of the DSU by the European Community)

Representing the EC at the WTO, the EU requested consultations with the US in regard to rules set out in the *Understanding on Rules and Procedures Governing the Settlement of Disputes (DSU)* and the *Agreement on Subsidies and Countervailing Measures (SCM Agreement)*. These rules referred to the new privatization methodology established by the US. Their application to the determinations was set out in the request, and the findings in the sunset reviews (review initiated before termination of duties) regarded certain corrosion-resistant carbon steel flat products from France, cut-to-length carbon steel plate from the UK and cut-to-length carbon steel plate from Spain, and was in the media referred to as the 'steel war'.

The EC represented the three Member States and its industry at the WTO with one voice, driving negotiations against the limitation of access to the US carbon steel market. After examining the arguments of both parties, the WTO asked the US to bring its measures into conformity with its obligations under the SCM Agreement and the GATT 1994.

Source: Articles 4 and 21.5 of the Understanding on Rules and Procedures Governing the Settlement of Disputes (DSU) and Article 30 of the Agreement on Subsidies and Countervailing Measures (SCM Agreement), URL (consulted November 2005): http://www.wto.org

4.1.2 The European Parliament
Within the Treaty of Rome, the proceedings of the EP (Box 13) (sometimes referred to as the 'Assembly') are laid down in its rules of procedure.

Box 13   The European Parliament's main powers

The powers of the EP can be split into two main types:

- advisory;
- supervisory.

4.1.2.1 Composition
The EP is the only directly elected institution of the EU. It consists of Member States' representatives, who hold annual sessions as well as extracurricular sessions held in case of requests either by a majority of its members or by the Council of Ministers or the CEC. The EP's President is elected from among the MEPs; the number of MEPs must not exceed 750. MEPs do not sit in national blocks, but in political groups. Those groups represent the political ideology (as closely as it can) of the national party to which the MEP belongs. The groups encompass, among others: a European People's Party (Christian Democrats) and European Democrats group; a Socialist group; an Alliance of Liberals and Democrats for Europe group; a Greens/European Free Alliance group; a Confederal group of the European United Left–Nordic Green Left; an Independence/Democracy group; and a Union for Europe of the Nations group. MEPs can be contacted directly. The EU websites provide a listing by name or political group.

The EP comprises delegates of Member States who may act as 'representatives of the peoples of the States brought together in the Community' (European Communities, 1957a: Art. 137). Since June 1979, its members are not designated from the Member States' parliaments but elected to the EP by direct universal suffrage. The MEPs are elected for a five-year period, and hence vulnerable to the forces and risks of re-election. EU citizens residing in another EU Member State normally have the right to vote or to stand as a candidate in elections to the EP. The EP meets for its main plenary sessions in Strasbourg but its main business is conducted in Brussels.

MEPs are seconded by administrative staff that the European Communities Personnel Selection Office (EPSO), established in 2002, recruits. It organizes open competitions to select highly qualified administrative staff for positions in the institutions of the EU, that is not only in the EP but also in the Council, the EC, the ECJ, the Court of Auditors, the European Economic and Social Committee (EESC), the Committee of the Regions (CoR) and the European Ombudsman.

4.1.2.2 Role

Because the entire Assembly and the committees consist of political and national representatives, neither the EP's organization nor its operations are determined by any political party majority. Due to this composition, the EP did not always work as a parliament in the sense national parliaments do. Historically, it has been more a consultative body of the EC with powers to suggest amendments of CEC or Council proposals, the power to delay legislation, and the right to dismiss the entire CEC. The consultative duties of the EP consist in consultations by the Council on proposals received from the CEC. This gives some importance to the EP's opinion because the CEC may consider the necessity of an alteration of a proposal as advised by the EP, provided that the Council has not enforced it at that stage.

In general, parliamentary formal opinion is required on most proposals before they can be adopted by the Council; on the basis of the SEA, most single market proposals as well as those concerning social policy, economic and social cohesion and research are subject to the cooperation procedure, that is, the EP giving a first opinion when the CEC makes a proposal and a second after the Council has reached a decision in principle.

The treaties stipulate that a citizen, resident or registered office in the EU, has the right to address, individually or in association with other citizens or persons, a petition to the EP if the issue of the petition concerns EU activity affecting the petitioner directly. An independent ombudsman is empowered by the institutions to manage complaints from any citizen, resident or registered office in the EU that may concern maladministration in the activities of the European institutions or bodies, with the exception of the ECJ and the Court of First Instance, which have a judicial role.

As noted above, the role of the EP includes the power to approve the designation of the Commissioners and to dismiss the CEC as a whole via a motion of censure. Moreover, a supervision of the CEC's administrative function includes questions, both oral and written, put to the other EU institutions, and the right to be heard by the Council. The EP sets up committees for inquiry into Community policy and its application. In addition, since the Treaty of Nice, co-decision powers are expanded, the Assembly sharing legislative powers with the Council, and any new areas to be covered will be as encompassed in the Constitution. The Assembly has the right to bring issues forward to the ECJ. The budgetary powers of the EP include control not only over its own budget but also, increasingly, over that of the Community as a whole, thus once again sharing powers with the Council, and its president's signature gives approval to the annual budget. The EP also controls its implementation.

4.1.3   The Council of Ministers or Council of the European Union

The Council of Ministers or Council of the European Union (herein called the Council) (Box 14) is of foremost importance in European decisionmaking. This institution was set up by Article 145 of the Treaty of Rome.

> ## Box 14   Main objectives of the Council
>
> The main objectives of the Council are to:
>
> - ensure the coordination of the general economic policy of the Member States;
> - use its power to make decisions.

Generally, the Council acts upon a proposal from the CEC, and decides jointly with the EP under the 'co-decision procedure' that we will study a little later in this chapter.

4.1.3.1 Composition

The Council, in its different configurations, is typically composed of one representative from each Member State. The representatives join together at different levels, in either ministerial meetings or working groups of officials. Their composition depends on the matters to be discussed. There are General Council meetings, as well as those of the Council of Ministers that deal with major issues of policy in areas such as foreign affairs, finance, labour, industry, research, internal market, budget, environment and social affairs , with the Foreign Affairs Council coordinating the activities of the specialized Councils. So-called specialized Council meetings hence refer to meetings to decide on one particular area of policy.

The members of the Council are appointed by their national governments. They are the relevant ministers from Member States that normally meet in Brussels and, less frequently, in Luxembourg, plus permanent representatives and experts. One representative of the CEC also attends the meetings without having a right to vote. Decisions are prepared by the Committee of Permanent Representatives of the Member States (Coreper), assisted by working parties of national government officials.

4.1.3.2 Role

The Council is a truly intergovernmental tool in which Member States negotiate outcomes along their national and transnational agenda of priorities. The meetings are chaired by the Member State holding the Presidency.

The Presidency of the Council, and thus also of the EU, rotates every six months in alphabetical order of the Member States's names as they appear in their mother tongues. The state holding the Presidency, together with the preceding one and the state that will follow constitute the so-called Troïka. The Troïka has particular functions, because it represents the EU in external relations within the CFSP, assisted by the CEC and by the Secretary-General of the Council who acts as High Representative. The European Constitution stipulates that the Presidency of the different Council configurations will be held for 18 months by a team of three Member States. Each of them will then hold the Presidency for a period of six months, assisted by the other two states and driven by a common programme. The

Minister for Foreign Affairs, a newly created position, then chairs the General Affairs Council. A difficulty with the rotation system is that when a particular country's Presidency coinciding with that country's national elections or important national issues may result in either an inefficient Presidency or a postponement of issues on the agenda that may not lie in that country's direct interest. Integration can thus be promoted or delayed by a country's Presidency of the Council.

The Council is assisted by Coreper as well as by the General Secretariat, which has its own legal service to cover EU activities. Coreper serves the Council as the 'ambassador' of the EU Member States and mainly prepares for Council meetings. Both the Council and Coreper are assisted by civil servants, council officials, technical advisers, the CEC, the Council working groups, the EP and the ESC, which provide opinion on any drafts before they are officially passed on to the Council.

As the main decision-making body, the Council takes decisions by simple majority voting, QMV or unanimously. QMV now applies in most cases, in areas such as agriculture, the single market, environment, transport, employment and health. Verbal translation into the official languages of the EU is assured at all meetings, and all official documents are translated into these languages. This also applies to the other institutions. The Constitution set out to radically change the QMV system in the Council in accordance with the requirements of the enlarged EU. The weighting system of votes by qualified majority stipulates that the number of votes given to a Member State depends on the size of its population, though a certain adjustment is made to preserve the power of small countries. Since the Treaty of Nice, it was stipulated that from 2009, heavily populated states have 27 or 29 votes, medium-sized states between 7 and 14 and less populated states 3 or 4. This means that a decision will need only 232 votes out of 321 in order to be adopted.

4.1.4 The European Council

The European Council is the institution that defines the general political guidelines of the EU.

4.1.4.1 Composition

The European Council is composed of the Heads of State or Government of the EU and the President of the Commission. It meets twice a year at a European Summit, and is then chaired by the Member State currently holding the EU Presidency. The Constitution previews a permanent, elected President.

4.1.4.2 Role

Set up in 1974, the European Council was legally recognized by the SEA in 1986. The TEU provided it with official status in 1992. Its role consists of providing the EU with decisions that are the major impetus in defining the general political guidelines. This includes setting priorities, political direction and resolving certain issues.

At each Summit opening, the President of the EP makes a presentation. Also, the European Council reports to the EP after each meeting and through an annual report.

4.1.5 The European Court of Justice

The supremacy of EC law over Member States' national law provides the ECJ with a powerful role (Box 15), set out by Articles 164 to 189, with its practices based on rules of procedure that are adopted by the Court by unanimous approval (Treaty of Rome, Article 188). The ECJ is, in the draft Constitution, called 'the General Court'.

Box 15   Main objective of the European Court of Justice

The main objective of the ECJ is to ensure that in the interpretation and application of the Treaty of Rome, the law is observed.

4.1.5.1 Composition

Judges appointed to the ECJ are drawn from the Member States of the EU, and are chosen by common agreement of the Member States' governments within the Council. Their number corresponds to that of the Member States at a given time. They are assisted by advocates-general, and are appointed for six years. The President of the ECJ is elected from among these judges for a renewable term of three years.

Typically, the judges sit in a full court, in a grand chamber of 13 judges or in chambers of 3 or 5 judges. Cases are generally brought to the ECJ by the CEC or transferred to it by national courts. The cases are examined in three procedural stages the first stage, in writing, initiates procedures by the submission of a complaint with the Registrar. The President of the Court then appoints a juge-rapporteur who is one of the Court's judges. The juge-rapporteur has the task of reporting on this particular matter, for the consideration of the court. Subsequently, the First Advocate-General assigns one of the judges to the case.

4.1.5.2 Role

The general ECJ procedure consists of an exchange of submissions, that is, the claiming and defending statements of the parties concerned (Schmid, 1989: 69). These cases may concern the breaking of European rules or the conduct of policymaking procedures or implementation. For example, cases in the area of EU anti-dumping policy concern the interpretation of rules, such as on the determination of the like product or the calculation of constructed values (SEC(92)716final: 18), and can be initiated by any interested party, such as consumer associations or enterprises. A preparatory inquiry, if necessary, has to be approved by the ECJ, presenting the juge-rapporteur's report orally, followed by the questioning of agents and counsel by the judges. After the parties' arguments are heard, the judgment of the ECJ is drafted by the juge-rapporteur and delivered in open court when approved by unanimous vote. It is binding from that date onwards. The main procedures of the Court are distinguished into written (in the shape of direct actions and appeals, or references for a preliminary ruling) and oral proceedings (Hearing, Opinion of the Advocate General, Deliberation of the Court, Judgment).

The ECJ is assisted by the Court of First Instance which was set up in 1989. The role of the Court of First Instance is to determine the direct actions brought by individuals and the Member States at a first level, so as to lighten the workload of the ECJ to only those actions directly oriented to it. Its composition is similar to that of the ECJ, though it does not consist of permanent advocates-general. All cases heard first by the Court of First Instance may be subject to a right of appeal to the ECJ on points of law only. The Treaty of Nice provides since 2003 for the creation of 'judicial panels' in certain specific areas and in 2004 the Council adopted a decision establishing the European Union Civil Service Tribunal due to the increasing number of cases. The Constitution speaks of an enlargement of legal action that citizens and corporations may bring to the courts even if not personally affected. Subjects of direct actions include matters in regard to agriculture, state aid, competition, commercial policy, regional policy, social policy, institutional law, trademark law, transport and staff regulations.

Another court of the EU is the Court of Auditors. This court is independent and since 1977 has been responsible for auditing the collection and spending of EC/EU funds, analysing and recording as well as making sure those funds are subject to legal and regular execution and ensuring their economic management. Again, composition is similar to the terms of the ECJ.

4.2 The decision-making process in the European Union

On the basis of the role played by the main European institutions, and within policymaking, the decision-making process in the EU is both multi-institutional and multilateral. The enlargement of the Union underlines the increasing nation-state bargaining character of decision-making, parallel to the alteration of relative powers by the SEA and the Maastricht Treaty and between electorate and executive organs of the Community. This is why one objective of the Constitutional text of 2005 contained the streamlining and adjustment of institutions given a setting that is quite different to the initial number of actors.

Decision-making is prescribed by the relevant issue concerned and can relate to policy sectors, thus involving a large number of actors competing for influence and power in the process. Every proposal for a new law is based on a treaty article, referred to as the 'legal basis' of the proposal. This basis determines the legislative procedure that applies to the decision-making process in this case. There are three main areas that need to be explained, 'consultation', 'assent' and 'co-decision', and are discussed below. The decision-making process is normally initiated by a request of the Council on behalf of a Member State, or by the CEC itself or on behalf of third parties, or of the EP within a general debate. Following this request for action, a first proposal will be drafted by the directorate-general concerned in the CEC. The proposal is then sent to one or more study groups consisting of CEC officials as well as national civil servants and experts. After the discussion of the draft proposal, the final draft is produced and must be formally approved by the CEC Commissioners.

The proposal is then send out for 'consultation', for 'assent' or for 'co-decision'. Under the consultation procedure, the Council consults the EP as well as the EESC and the CoR. The

EP may approve the proposal, or reject it, or ask for amendments. If the EP makes amendments, the CEC considers the suggested changes, but is not obliged to accept them. If the EP does accept any suggestions, then it sends an amended proposal to the Council. The Council Secretariat typically transfers the proposal to the Permanent Representatives of the Member States. The governments then put forward their official opinion. Meanwhile, advisory opinions are sought at the EESC, which links civil society organizations to the EU. This is a committee whose functions are very similar to those of the EP. The Council examines the amended proposal and either adopts it or amends it unanimously; it then enacts the proposal after approval as a directive, a regulation or a decision. On less important issues, decisions are adopted without debate if Coreper agree unanimously to it. Otherwise, more important issues are discussed in detail during Council meetings.

In the assent procedure, the Council has to obtain the EP's assent before decisions are taken. This applies to decisions of foremost importance to the EU. The EP cannot amend a proposal, but will either accept or reject it. Acceptance requires an absolute majority of the vote cast. In all other stages, the procedure is equivalent to that of 'consultation'.

The co-decision procedure applies to most EU lawmaking. Here, the EP not only gives its opinion but shares legislative power with the Council on equal terms. If they cannot agree, then a conciliation committee, composed of equal numbers of Council and Parliament representatives, is asked to reach an agreement. Following that agreement, the text is sent back to the EP and the Council for final adoption of it as law.

In any case, given the number of members of the EU, most decisions are taken by 'qualified majority voting' rather than requiring every single country to agree. The Constitution evolves further by asking EU ministers to hold law-making discussions in public, and the other institutions to hold other meetings publicly too. In addition, Member States are given powers to monitor better CEC proposals, and create the post of EU Foreign Affairs Minister.

4.3 Tools for getting there

How does the EU implement its objectives and outputs, and reach what its Members consider the right outcomes? There are several instruments that help the institutions and Member States in getting there. We will study the two main tools at this stage: legislative instruments and the EU budget.

4.3.1 Legislative implementation tools

In the decision-making process, its implementation and control, the EU institutions are supported by many agencies. Among them, you will find the EESC (mentioned above in different contexts), which expresses the opinions of organized civil society on economic and social issues. It benefits from a membership consisting of a cross-section of European society and its economy.

The CoR expresses the opinions of regional and local authorities and is charged with subsidiarity (see p. 39a, 97 and 103). It is the EU's youngest institution; its first session was held in March 1993. Its officials count regional presidents, mayors, chairpersons of city or county councils and are elected for a four-year term. Consultation of the Committee is compulsory in the EU decision – making process when it comes to issues related to trans-European networks, public health, education, youth, culture, and economic and social cohesion.

The European Central Bank (ECB) is responsible for monetary policy and managing the euro, while the European Investment Bank (EIB) helps achieve EU objectives by financing investment projects. In this context, the European Ombudsman deals with citizens' complaints about maladministration by any EU institution or body. The ECB stands behind the diverse powers of the EU, based on and in charge of Community law, which can be distinguished as constitutional legislation (primary law), the conventions between the Member States, and the Community agreements (secondary law). The origins of Community law are divided into primary sources and secondary sources. Secondary sources may create their legislation on the basis of primary sources in the shape of obligatory and non-obligatory acts. The binding legal instruments include regulations, directives and decisions. Non-binding instruments are resolutions, and opinions, and a series of legislative tools, such as the institutions' internal regulations and Community action programmes.

Community law has priority over Member States' national law, with judicial legislation enacted by the ECJ through case law. This does not mean that national governments have no say; they are the key actors in the formulation of primary law (that is, the main treaties), and within all EU decision-making processes due to their representation in the EU institutions discussed above. EU policymaking results in rules that are enacted as directives, regulations or decisions, with different degrees of obligation to implement them into the national framework.

Table 14   Six legislative tools of the European Union

Legislative tools	Nature	Institution
Law	Legislative Acts	Proposal from the Commission, adoption by the Parliament and the Council of Ministers
Framework law Regulation	Non-legislative Acts	Commission or Council of Ministers (delegated regulations or execution acts)
Decision Recommendation	Point of view	Commission, Council of Ministers, European Central Bank
Opinion		

Source: © European Communities, 2004: Six European Legislative tools, URL: http://europa.eu.int/ scadplus/leg/en/lvb/l60014.htm

Thus, other than the primary law that was reviewed in Chapter 2, the EU uses international agreements and secondary legislation that comprise recommendations, opinions, joint actions, decision, framework decision and common position, as well as binding regulations, directives and decisions. Table 14 gives a brief summary of the main legislative tools, their nature, and the institutions engaged in issuing them.

Note also that the different institutions issue communications, case law, judgments and orders. Some apply in a more direct and immediate manner to a region, Member State or business than others, and it is most useful for business to know the difference between legislation and its applications. This helps to evaluate which legislation is relevant for a given business sector, a corporation or a business operation.

The relationship between Community law and national law is rather complex, and the Constitution attempts to streamline some of it. The aim is ideally a uniform application and common acceptance of treaty obligations, taking into account three major principles: the autonomy of Community law with regard to each nation's legal system; the supremacy of Community law; and the effectiveness of Community law in national legal systems. EU-wide common policy implementation always takes places under the auspices of the EU, which acts as policy formulator and decisionmaker on behalf of Member State authorities.

4.3.1.1 Binding legislation

The following come under binding legislation:

Regulation: Regulations are 'binding in their entirety' and addressed to everyone. They are used as an instrument guaranteeing uniformity within the EU, and are directly applicable in all Member States as law. They are adopted by the Council in co-decision with the EP, or by the Commission alone. A regulation creates law that takes immediate effect in all the Member States just like a national legislation, without any further action by national authorities. Regulations such as an anti-dumping duty on the applicants' exports of retail electronic weighing scales also applied retrospectively to imports of these products registered in accordance with Commission Regulation (EC) 1408/2004 (Council Regulation (EC) 692/2005 of 28 April 2005). They come into force on the date of publication in the *Official Journal* (OJ) and the Member States are authorised to implement them by their own civil service. Another example is the Council Regulation (EC) No 1590/2004 that established, on 26 April 2004, a community programme on the conservation, characterization, collection and utilization of genetic resources in agriculture and repealing Regulation (EC) No 1467/74 (European Communities, 2004c).

Directive: Addressed to the Member States, a directive is adopted by the Council and the EP, or through the Commission alone, to align national legislation. While the Member States are bound to the directive in terms of outcomes, they have entire discretion about form and method of adoption. In the case that a directive is not transposed into national legislation, or only incompletely, or with an important delay, citizens can directly invoke the directive in question before the national courts. The case of *Sintesi SpA* v. *Autorità per la Vigilanza sui Lavori Pubblici* is one example of the application of directives. In reference to a preliminary ruling of the Tribunale amministrativo regionale per la Lombardia in Italy, the Directive 93/37/EEC on public works contracts and awards of contracts stipulated the right of the contracting authority to choose between the criterion of the lower price and that of the more economically advantageous tender (European Communities, 2004e).

Decision: A decision is a legislative tool that is adopted either by the Council, or by co-decision, by the Commission. It provides the Community institutions with a binding ruling, in its entirety, on a particular issue. It can ask a Member State or a specified citizen to take or refrain from taking a particular action, or confer rights or impose obligations on a Member State or a clearly specified citizen. For instance, the Commission Decision of 18 February 2004 established a model health certificate for non-commercial movements from third countries of dogs, cats and ferrets (European Communities, 2004b), which is a text with EEA relevance.

4.3.1.2 Non-binding legislation

The following come under non-binding legislation:

Recommendation: A recommendation allows the institutions to make their views known and to suggest a line of action without imposing any legal obligation on those to whom it is addressed (the Member States, other institutions, or in certain cases the citizens of the Union). The Commission Recommendation, 2004H0345, from 21 October 2003, for instance, deals with the enforcement of road safety measures. The Commission reminds Member States that they should be more effective regarding speed control, road infrastructure, drink-driving control and seat belts in the context of fatalities on roads. (European Communities, 2004a).

Opinion: An opinion is an instrument that allows the institutions to make a statement in a non-binding fashion, in other words without imposing any legal obligation on those to whom it is addressed. The aim is to set out an institution's point of view on a specific question.

Joint action: A joint action is a legal instrument under Title V of the Treaty on European Union and is thus of an intergovernmental nature. Adopted by the Council of the European Union unanimously or, in certain cases, by a qualified majority, a joint action is binding on the Member States. The Member States have to achieve the set objectives unless major difficulties arise. Joint action in police and judicial cooperation in criminal matters is based on decision, framework decision and joint action (police and judicial cooperation in criminal matters); since the entry into force of the Treaty of Amsterdam, decisions and framework decisions have replaced joint actions in the field of police and judicial cooperation in criminal matters. These are legal instruments under Title VI of the Treaty on European Union and are intergovernmental in nature. Decisions and framework decisions are adopted by the Council of the European Union unanimously following the initiative of the Commission or a Member State.

Framework decision: This is binding on the Member States as to the result to be achieved and leave to the national authorities the choice of form and methods (like the directive in the Community context). Decisions are used in the field of police and judicial cooperation in criminal matters for any purpose other than the approximation of the laws and regulations of the Member State, which is the preservation of framework decisions.

Common positions like those in the CFSP, and in police and judicial cooperation in criminal matters: the common position in the context of the CFSP and police and judicial cooperation in criminal matters is a legal instrument under Titles V and VI of the Treaty on European Union and is intergovernmental in nature. Adopted unanimously by the Council of the European Union, it determines the Union's approach to particular questions of the CFSP or police and judicial cooperation in criminal matters and gives guidance for the pursuit of national policies in these fields. International agreements (CFSP and police and judicial cooperation in criminal matters) are legal instruments under Titles V and VI of the Treaty on European Union that were not provided for in the Treaty of Maastricht. In the context of the second and third pillars there was thus no legal basis for concluding international agreements. In order to prevent each agreement signed by the Council from having to be formally concluded by the Member States, the Treaty of Amsterdam made provision for the Council to be able to authorise the Presidency to enter into negotiations when necessary. The agreements are binding for the institutions of the Union, but not on the Member States whose constitutional provisions lay down particular rules for concluding such agreements. In such cases the other Member States meeting within the Council can decide that the agreement will nonetheless be applicable on a provisional basis.

4.3.2   Other important documents

Other important documents include:

Commission communication: The vast majority of communications from the Commission (COM documents) are legislative proposals. The other most important COM documents are listed below. For example, in its communication COM(2004)636 on 6 October 2004 the Commission explains how to move to the deployment and operational phases of the European satellite radio-navigation programme in many detailed issue (European Communities, 2004d). Therefore, it is sometimes more of a recommendation than real communication.

Green Papers: Intended to stimulate discussion and launch consultation at European level on a particular subject. The consultations that result from a Green Paper can then lead to the publication of a White Paper that will propose a set of concrete measures for Community action. This leads, for example, to communications such as that from the Commission to the Council and to the EP concerning national allocation plans for the allocation of greenhouse gas emission allowances of Belgium, Estonia, Finland, France, Latvia, Luxembourg, Portugal, and the Slovak Republic (European Communities, 2004a). These emission allowances potentially inflict cost increases for corporate manufacturing or combusting activities.

White Papers: Contain a set of proposals for action by the Community in a particular field. They sometimes follow from Green Papers, the purpose of which is to launch a consultation process at European level. If a White Paper is favourably received by the Council it can lead, if appropriate, to an EU action programme in the field concerned. For example, a White Paper on the review of Regulation 4056/86, applying the EC competition rules to maritime transport, was presented in Brussels on 13 October 2004 (European

Communities, 2004). The purpose of the discussion and the proposal presented was to give a framework to adapt the European legislation (via its legislative tools) to specific points. Within this White Paper, we find considerations to repealing the currently applicable substantive provisions of block exemptions or liner conferences and the exception for technical agreements, and a proposal in regard to competitive position of the EU liner shipping industry in a global context, among other issues.

Report from the Court of Auditors: The annual report of the Court of Auditors presents its comments on the handling of the Community's finances. The report is forwarded to the Community institutions and published in the *Official Journal.* The report highlights the points where improvement would be possible, or indeed desirable. The institutions then reply to the Court of Auditors' observations. These reports are thus interesting sources of information for business.

Case law: All the decisions handed down by bodies exercising judicial powers constitute case law. The ECJ and the Court of First Instance are the judicial institutions of the EU. It is the task of the Court to ensure that Community law is respected in the interpretation and implementation of the founding treaties. The Court is assisted in its work by advocates-general, who draw up opinions, as developed above. This case law provides business with interesting guidelines when it comes to contradiction between corporations or the public and private sector in Europe.

Judgments: The ECJ and the Court of First Instance hand down judgments, which are decisions that conclude a litigation procedure. There is no appeal against judgments of the ECJ. An appeal against a judgment of the Court of First Instance can be brought before the ECJ. These instances are important in case of recourse against European legislation.

Opinions: The EP, the Council, the Commission or a Member State can seek the opinion of the ECJ on whether an agreement between the Community and non-member countries or international organizations is compatible with the provisions of the EC Treaty. An agreement on which the Court has given a negative opinion can enter into force only under the conditions laid down in Article 48 of the TEU (procedure for amending the treaties). This is an opportunity for European business in case of international frictions.

Orders: The ECJ and the Court of First Instance issue orders in a variety of instances, as laid down in the Rules of Procedure, which fall broadly into three groups: instances during the investigation of a case (for example, acts ordering the preservation of evidence, or separating, joining or suspending cases); instances where the Court takes a decision without considering the substance of the case (for example, in the event of manifest inadmissibility of the case or lack of jurisdiction); and instances where the Court takes a decision on the substance of the case. The orders are in fact simplified judgments that are used when the case is identical to others on which a judgment has already been handed down. Orders can, in principle, be amended or revoked.

The above selection of EU legislation is important for business activities in the single market because they set the legal business environment that may add threats and opportunities to corporate activity. Given its diversity in the manner in which it is applied, to whom it applies and to what scale, the EU has a powerful tool at hand to drive the integration and regulation of the business environment for matters that concern the Union. The implementation is legal in nature but also has financial implications. This is where the EU budget becomes important. Where do funds come from, and on what are they spent?

4.3.3 Budgetary tools

European income comes mainly from value added tax (VAT), averaging typically about 40 per cent of the budget. About the same percentage can be attributed to national contributions. The GNP-based resource is obtained by applying a rate fixed each year under the budget procedure to a base representing the sum of the GNPs at market price. It is calculated by reference to the difference between expenditure and the yield of the other own resources. Own resources ideally furnish the great part of the EU budget. They encompass customs duties that are levied at external frontiers on imports. Agricultural levies are charged on trade in agricultural products with non-member countries, and vary according to price levels on world and European markets. Besides agricultural levies, there are also levies on the production and storage of sugar and isoglucose. The latter levies are internal to the EU only.

Historically, VAT own resources were introduced by a 1970 Decision because the traditional own resources were not sufficient to finance the Community budget. Currently, each member has to pass on the equivalent of a 1.4 per cent VAT rate to the EU budget that ideally will target only the 1 per cent. Other 'specific resources' are yielded through taxes and contributions paid by staff, income from interest, guarantees and diverse other charges.

For reference, the EU had a budget of €109 billion for 2004. Its financial system is based on medium-term expenditure plans within the so-called financial framework that is based on an agreement between the CEC, the EP and the Council. The agreement typically lays down ceilings for budget periods for categories of expenditure in agriculture, cohesion policy, internal policies, external policy and preparation for enlargement, administrative expenditure.

Once the budget has been allocated for a given year to policy areas, the Commission implements it according to EU rules. Mainly, these rules are laid down by the DG budget that internally monitors the budgetary procedure and is responsible for the annual accounts. The Court of Auditors externally controls the legal and continuous implementation. Also, on recommendation by the Council, the EP may grant a discharge in respect of the management of Community funds. Each directorate-general and service is in charge of the efficient use of its corresponding budget. This use of the budget includes spending of a sector and a regional nature. Its four structural funds are there to help specific regions, sectors or activities in the member states.

They are the:

- European Regional Development Fund (ERDF);
- European Social Fund (ESF);
- Guidance section of the European Agricultural Guidance and Guarantee Fund (EAGGF);
- Financial Instrument for Fisheries Guidance (FIFG).

We distinguish between the ERDF, the ESF, the Guidance section of the EAGGF and the FIFG. All of them operate under a common set of rules which ensure EU grants, classified into three objectives: support for regions lagging behind in development; support for regions in structural crisis; and regions needing support for education, training and jobs. Table 15 illustrates the importance given to each objective.

Table 15   The three objectives of the structural funds

Structural funds	Objective 1	Objective 2	Objective 3
Why?	Regions lagging behind in development	Regions in structural crisis	Regions needing support for education, training and jobs
EU funds available 2000–6 (in billion €).	135.9	22.50	24.05
Percentage of structural funds budget[1]	69.7%	1.5%	12.3%
Which funds?[2]	ERDF, ESF, EAGGF, FIFG	ERDF, ESF,	ESF
Percentage of population covered	22.2%	18%	(not relevant)

1   The remaining share is dedicated to Community initiatives
2   The EAGGF and FIFG funds also finance certain other types of action outside Objective 1 regions

Source: European Communities, 2004: The three objectives of the structural funds, URL: http://europa.eu.int/scadplus/leg/en/lvb/l60014.htm

In all, more than 40 per cent of the EU budget is dedicated to *agricultural markets*, causing regular discussion between Member States whose markets are agriculturally, industrially or service oriented. Another approximately 35 per cent is typically spent on the *structural funds* mentioned above. Less then 10 per cent is used for, in declining order, overseas aid, administration, R&D and miscellaneous.

Both the budget and the legislative tools of the Union ensure the smooth functioning of the EU objectives as a whole. They are the result of a complex formula of Member State negotiation, of the willingness of members to give up or retain sovereignty and power, and of structural complexity that needs to suit many varying wishes and needs. Business in Europe is well advised to keep afloat in the who's who of European institutions. They are the past, present and future of doing business in Europe because, together with the Member States, they are essential actors in the regulation of the European marketplace.

Résumé and conclusion

This chapter has shed light on the different institutions that govern the European decision-making process. CEC is the driving force and executive body of the structure; the EP is the only directly elected body, elected by the peoples of the Member States, and is gradually experiencing an increase in power. The Council of the European Union represents the governments of the Member States. The ECJ guarantees compliance with the law, while the Economic and Social Committee has a main role to play in the representation of opinions of organized civil society on economic and social issues. Other institutions, agencies and bodies complete the structure that operates in three alternative decision-making modes, depending on the policy area and issue that is to be decided. The consultation, assent or co-decision procedures shape the legislative tools that the EU is in charge of and that regulate the business environment for both European and non-European firms in the single market, as well as international affairs of the EU. The EU budget is an essential utensil in the management of the given EU objectives. It is made up of VAT, agricultural levies, customs duties and own resources, and benefits the business environment through, for instance, sectoral and regional spending and funds.

Mini case study: SMEs benefit from institutional initiatives

European structural and cohesion funds are the main instruments for supporting social and economic development, in solidarity across the Member States. They are grants administrated by the EU Commission to help fund measures and projects within the EU along specific common objectives. The 2007–2013 round accounts for a budget of €308 billion.

Applications for finance from these funds must be submitted by recognized organizations, which are supported by a public body. Eligible bodies include the public sector, local authorities, the voluntary sector, registered charities, community groups, training organizations, educational establishments and the private sector. Some bodies will use the funds to operate support schemes for business, especially SMEs, or to support training or (re-)employment schemes for individuals. The funds are designed to help reduce disparities in the development of regions, and to promote economic and social cohesion within the Union. The EU co-finances regional and horizontal operations in the Member States through programmes in the fields of agriculture, regional policy, employment and social affairs. As for the kind of projects that obtain funding from the structural funds, it varies from region to region.

(Continued)

Each region writes a single programming document: the structural funds are implemented within the framework of European programmes known as DOCument Unique Programmation (DOCUP). In order to achieve economic and social cohesion in the EU, objectives include specific measures for SMEs: In Objective 1, for the development of the least favoured regions, help is provided to SMEs by developing and strengthening their support structures. This is the most important objective because its aim is to promote development and adjustment of regions whose per capital GDP is less than 75 per cent of the EU average. Objective 1 funds focus on convergence, Objective 2 funds on competitiveness and employment, and Objective 3 funds on European territorial cooperation. ERDFs for innovation, RTD, environment, risk prevention and accessibility) are complemented by theESF (for social inclusion, equality) and the Cohesion Fund (adds on Trans-European networks and energy), for which only Member States with a GDP under 90 per cent of EU25GNI are eligible.

For each region concerned, a DOCUP describes the development strategy. Any project must in any case find co-financing. The DOCUPs are elaborated by management authorities of each Member State in a partnership with local groups and social partners. The coordination between these parties, for instance in France, is the responsibility of the Délégation a l'aménagement du territoire et l'action régionale (DATAR) for Objectives 1 and 2; and for Objective 3 the Mission of the European Social Funds (Ministère des Affaires sociales, du travail et de la solidarité). Once these parties reach an agreement, the DOCUPs are negotiated with the European Commission. After the adoption of the DOCUP by the Commission, the Member State and the regional *préfecture* adopt the programming complement that determines the measures, the allocations and the potential benefits. The local projects are then typically selected by a programming committee, under the authority of the region prefect, in accordance with the programming period. Committees of monitoring and programming are co-presided by the region prefect and regional counsel, group together representatives of the EU, state, territorial groups and social partners. Here again, local groups, consular chambers, training institutions, SMEs, unions and associations can participate in this process. The participation conditions vary according to every objective and region.

The EuroInfoCentres provide the general public with business support networks that promote entrepreneurship and SMEs in particular. Their archives of case studies tell the tales of many other initiatives that have been taken for SMEs, through the EU institutions and on basis of European decisionmaking. For instance in 2000, the Centre in Genoa helped an Italian company that operates in the machine construction sector present a proposal to the Competitive and Sustainable Growth RTD programme of the European Commission. The SME was helped by the Centre during its negotiations with the institution and signed a contract for €1200.000. The

(Continued)

DG Enterprise of the Commission also directly assists SMEs to find their way through the decisions of the EU: the '2003 call for tender Impact of Basel II regulation: guide for SMEs' on how to prepare for the new rating culture attributed a budget of €95.000, on the demand of the EP in regard to the new Capital Adequacy Directive submitted to the Commission in 2004, and entered into force by the end of 2006. DG Enlargement supports schemes such as the European Business Cooperation Scheme for SMEs with a framework which finances actions that exploit business opportunities originating in the enlargement of the EU, through the development of cooperation between SMEs within the EU and SMEs in accession or candidate countries – preparing both sides to work together. Further support is provided through networks such as the European Centre for Innovation and Spin-Offs(ECIS), SME-net, an e-content project analysing the viability of EU-wide business portals for SMEs, and numerous other public and private initiatives.

Mini case questions:

1   Under what conditions can private business benefit from regional funds?
2   What assistance does DG Enterprise provide to SMEs?

Review questions

1   **Draw** a graph or diagram that visualizes the EU decision-making process clearly. Consider what impediments to the smooth and expedient operation of EU decision-making might exist.
2   **What** is the sense of the regional funds? Does business benefit from these budget lines?
3   **Why** has it been important that the EP increases its power in the decision-making process?

Assignments

• Find the most recent examples of the different types of legislation analysed in this chapter. **Imagine** the consequences for a given business sector.
• **Compare** information regarding the balance between the smaller and bigger countries in EU decision making. Draft a 'constitutional text' that equally balances the sides. What are your suggestions?

(Continued)

- **Case study assignment:** Read and prepare the Microsoft and Lisbon Dialogue case study in Part IV, and discuss the impact of Europe on the company's operations.
- **Internet exercise:** Some legislation is not at all, not entirely or lately implemented in the Member States. Analyse the latest statistics and try to find explanations for the phenomenon.

Web guide

www

http://europa.eu.int/youreurope/nav/en/citizens/home.html Practical information on rights and opportunities in the EU and its internal market.
http://europa.eu.int/eur-lex/en/ Portal to EU law.
http://curia.eu.int/en/instit/presentationfr/index_savoirplus.htm ECJ and legal institutions.

References

Deards, E. and S. Hargreaves (2004) *European Union Law Textbook.* Oxford: Oxford University Press.

Dinan, D. (2006) *Origins and Evolution of the European Union*, New European Union Series. Oxford: Oxford University Press.

European Communities (1951) *Treaty Establishing the European Coal and Steel Community* (ECSC Treaty, or the Treaty of Paris),URL: http://europa.eu.int/abc/obj/treaties/en/entoc29.htm

European Communities (1957a) *Treaty Establishing the European Economic Community* (EEC Treaty, or Treaty of Rome),URL: http://europa.eu.int/abc/obj/treaties/en/entoc05.htm

European Communities (1957b) *Treaty Establishing the European Atomic Energy Community* (Euratom Treaty), URL: http://europa.eu.int/abc/obj/treaties/en/entoc38.htm

European Communities (1967) *Treaty Establishing a Single Council and a Single Commission of the European Communities* (Merger Treaty of 1965), URL: http://europa.eu.int/abc/obj/treaties/

European Communities (1987) *Single European Act*, URL: http://europa.eu.int/eur-lex/en/treaties/selected/livre509.html

European Communities (1992) *Treaty on European Union* (Maastricht Treaty), [1992] OJ (C191/1), URL: http://europa.eu.int/eur-lex/en/treaties/dat/EU_treaty.html

European Communities (1997a) *The Treaty of Amsterdam*,[1997] OJ C340/1, URL: http://europa.eu.int/eur-lex/lex/en/treaties/treaties_other.htm, with [1997] OJ C340/145).

European Communities (1997) Treaty Establishing the European Community, [1997] OJ C340/173–308.

European Communities (2004a) *Commission Recommendation, 2004H0345, Communication from the Commission concerning the Commission recommendation* of 21 October 2003 on enforcement in the field of road safety (OJ C93, 17.4.2004)

European Communities (2004b) *Commission Decision of 18 February 2004 establishing a model health certificate for non-commercial movements from third countries of dogs, cats and ferrets* (notified under document number C (2004) 432)-(2004/203/EC).

European Communities (2004c) Council Regulation (EC) No 1590/2004, *Community programme on the conservation, characterisation, collection and utilisation of genetic resources in agriculture and repealing Regulation (EC) No 1467/74, Official Journal of the European Union*, 30 September 2004.

European Communities (2004d) COM (2004)636 on 6 October 2004, *Deployment and operational phases of the European satellite radio-navigation programme in many detailed issue*, URL: http://europa. eu.int/eur-lex/pri/en/dpi/cnc/doc/2004/com2004_0636en01.doc

European Communities (2004e) Judgment of the Court (Second Chamber) of 7 October 2004, *Sintesi SpA versus Autorità per la Vigilanza sui Lavori Pubblici, in reference to a preliminary ruling of the Tribunale amministrativo regionale per la Lombardia in Italy, the Directive 93/37/EEC on Public works contracts and awards of contracts* (Case C-247/02); URL: http://europa.eu.int/eur-lex/

European Communities (2004f), White Paper on the review of Regulation 4056/86, *applying the EC competition rules to maritime transport, 13 October 2004.*

European Communities (2004g) *Commission to the council and to the European Parliament on the Commission Decisions of 20 October 2004 concerning national allocation plans for the allocation of greenhouse gas emission allowances of Belgium, Estonia, Finland, France, Latvia, Luxembourg, Portugal, and the Slovak Republic* in accordance with Directive 2003/87/EC.

European Communities (2001) *Treaty of Nice Amending the Treaty on European Union*, (Treaties Establishing the European Communities and Certain Related Acts), *Official Journal* C 80, 10 March 2001.

European Communities (2004h) *Treaty Establishing a Constitution for Europe*, URL http://europe.eu. int/constitution/index_en.htm.

European Communities (2005) *Commission Regulation (EC) 1408/2004* (Council Regulation (EC) 692/2005 of 28 April 2005).

Schmid, G. (1994) 'Anti-Dumping Measures and the Politics of EU-Japan Trade Relations in the European Consumer Electronics Sector: The VRC Case'.PhD Dissertation. University of Bath, Bath, UK, 1993; Working Paper. Thomson Consumer Electronics External Relations Department.

Van Schendelen, R. (2002) *Machiavelli in Brussels. The Art of Lobbying the EU*. Amsterdam: Amsterdam University Press.

Part II   BUSINESS EUROPEANIZATION

5 | The Europeanization of a Business Environment

What you will learn about in this chapter

- The evolution of the European market observed through the theory lens.
- European sector dynamics and EU issues related to these.
- Competition, competitiveness and competitivity.
- The main business-related common policies.

Introduction

This chapter considers the Europeanization of the business environment. It would appear that internally, the EU has made efforts with the creation of a single market to evolve into an ever-widening and deepening network of opportunity for business activity. But this network of opportunity also contains many challenges because the EU has changed into a vast business environment. Can firms consider this a home market? This question will be studied through analysis of the phenomenon and the capacity of business to evolve therein. This chapter reviews some of the most important international trade theory related to the field and examines the common policies with which managers in Europe need to be familiar.

The European business environment has been subject to a rapid transformation ever since the mid-1990s: the single market has become a reality. The introduction of a common currency in 1999, the extension of the SEA rules to new areas such as e-commerce, and the ongoing trend towards supranational business taxation regulations are developments that have largely contributed to the construction of an increasingly harmonized business environment. On the business side, these developments have led to a diversification of firm structures. More and more multinationals evolve into European transnational companies that compete worldwide, from a sound and vast home market. SMEs frequently operate on a European scale (as micro-multinationals) and are locally, nationally and internationally exposed to large-scale competition and market harmonization rules formulated for all actors within the single market.

European integration has increased the pace of developments throughout Europe and its neighbouring countries; in a similar fashion to that of globalization it has created a rising compression of the time and space factors that rule the business environment. For a better understanding of this compression, consider the following example: during the cold war era it was difficult if not virtually impossible to export goods, services or capital from Western Europe, already integrating, to some Eastern and Central European countries, politically, logistically and culturally oppressed under the Soviet system. Given the developments during the 1990s and the enlargements of the EU, politically and culturally the Member States have become closer than ever, while logistically both virtual and real means of transport and infrastructures seem to have reduced distances dramatically, and take less time. Among leading contemporary thinkers, Buckley (2004) calls upon international business researchers and practitioners not only to examine the world map using conventional representations (such as the role and limits of nation-states), but rather to see the map as a network of firms. If we take into consideration that all maps contain distortions, as they tend to prioritize certain factors or areas, and are therefore limited in their meaning, the cartography of the European business environment and its networks would ideally also represent relative economic power, distribution of income, capital, labour, entrepreneurship, knowledge and corporate risk. Most of these were found by Buckley to be difficult to represent, given that the cartographer is situated in a particular time and location – which, as stated above, both evolve ever more quickly.

Mapping the (business) environment as 'European' gives the EU a clear advantage to communicate worldwide along the lines of power that result from a 'unity in diversity'. This is the true meaning of doing business in Europe. A filtering or screening of its diversity (virtually or by means of maps) through specific search parameters allows any given corporation to target specific market opportunities. These mechanisms will be considered in depth in Chapter 8, 'Marketing in Europe'.

5.1 The main impacts

The main impact of increased levels of Europeanization is twofold: the opening of significant business opportunities is accompanied by the rising competition within markets that either were entirely inaccessible or were difficult to access in the past, for example, as with the deep-seated animosity that historically came between Germany and France or that appeared because of oppression by another country such as in Eastern Europe. With Europeanization, corporations are experiencing inherent lower costs of doing business in an integrated market. These are mainly based on the effects of economic and political integration automatisms. The initiatives that characterize the European business environment under the theory of cost saving are:

- the integration of major, foremost economic, decision-making at EU level;
- the widening and strengthening of the single market;

- an evolving form of federalism through monetary unification;
- common policies;
- intensification of competition;
- liberalization and deregulation;
- the free movement of labour, service and capital;
- the removal of barriers to entry and to trade, and for production and for investment;
- harmonized norms, standards and legal frameworks;
- simplified tax regimes.

Consequently and ideally, it is possible to obtain significant cost economies in the single market if the mix of factor costs and skills is optimal. The resulting trade creation is the main positivism in freer and more integrated trade, and delivers lower prices for consumers within the EU. Nevertheless, the impact of integration with regard to trade diversion and to reinforced competition is negative. The basis of these Europeanization principles lies in business internationalization and is theorized within international trade theory.

5.2 The ideological background

The ideology behind the Europeanization of the business environment in the Member States and partners is based on globalization and free market concepts that were prevalent in the 1990s. The internationalization of capital markets, technological advances, products and people's way of life accelerated globalization across the world, and marked the evolution of trade groupings.

The acceptance of this globalization has turned out to be largely culture-dependent and based on economic development levels. This is noticeable when the diversity of its adoption in the world is analysed. For instance, there is still a large variation in the number of Internet users, and only 17 per cent of the world's population have access to it. In the OECD region, the average penetration rate is estimated at around 37 per cent (Bouchet, 2005). Moreover, the uniformity and standardization of the consumer has not reached the expected levels. Yet, on the one hand, main brands use 'megabrands' with a global reach (see, for example, Inderbrands rankings and compare *Business Week* annual brand rankings) and, on the other hand, other strong brands such as Legrand have not yet designed a unique product for all Europeans.

5.2.1 The main international trade and business theories

Among the leading classical economic and international trade theories, in particular those of Adam Smith and David Ricardo, as well as those of Heckscher-Ohlin, explain the importance of business operations that reach across frontiers. Mercantilism, at the very beginning of international business and colonial commerce, is the theory that a country shall best run a balance-of-trade surplus, in a zero-sum game towards other countries, and calls rather for government intervention in the interests of each trading nation.

In *The Wealth of Nations* (1776), Adam Smith looked deeper into the reasons why trade exists between countries. To summarize, he put forward the theory that any given country

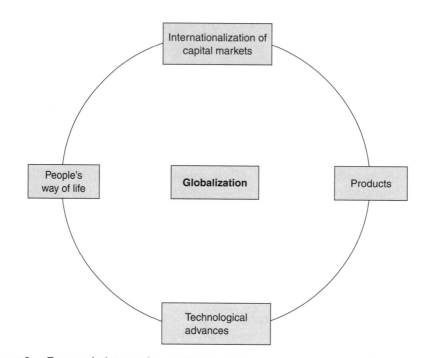

Figure 6   Economic integration and globalization: essential acceleration motives

has an *absolute advantage* in the efficient production of goods; other goods should there-fore be imported. David Ricardo then expanded this theory to that of *comparative advantage*, explaining that within this framework imports may also include goods that could be produced, though less efficiently, in the domestic market. In this manner, free trade without restrictions on the basis of comparative advantage is to turn trade into a positive-sum game that obtains higher world production levels.

The theories of Smith and Ricardo were reinforced by the Heckscher-Ohlin model that analyses international trade patterns based on *factor endowment*. This model indicates that those goods that are imported or exported are defined on the basis of local resource levels. The factors studied in this theory are labour and capital. In short, a country that is rela-tively labour abundant should specialize in the production and export of that product which is relatively labour intensive; the same would apply for capital. Hence, the sense is to demonstrate why certain countries specialize in certain goods and not others, as a rein-forcement of the theory of comparative advantage. However, the theory in itself does not explain the phenomenon completely. For example, some countries have minimum wage laws that result in high prices for relatively abundant labour. The *Leontief paradox* demonstrated in this framework that countries like the United States in the post-war period actually exported relatively more labour-intensive goods and imported capital-intensive goods. A more and more nuanced approach to cross-border trade is therefore necessary. Linder, amongst others, has engaged in research into these nuances; his resulting *Overlapping Product Ranges Theory* holds that trade in manufactured goods is dictated not only by cost concerns, but by a similarity in product demands across countries. This work therefore centred around preferences of consumer demand. Today, we speak of market segments.

In addition, an essential question about the timing of import and export needs to be answered: When is it the right time to engage into trade across borders? Raymond Vernon's *Product Life Cycle* theory was a first valent attempt to respond to this question. The theory suggests that products with technical innovations that lead to new, profitable markets and that are based on large quantities of capital and skilled labour, go through different phases from introduction through maturity to standardization, allowing company and country to switch from product to product at different moments in time in different locations, hence shaping international trade patterns. The complexity of today's operations and productions, and the importance of the service economy, limits the importance of this approach in today's understanding of international trade and business. You may note that the theory mainly still holds for technologically based mass production merchandise.

In the 1970s, the *New Trade Theory* was developed along the lines that with specialized products from a country, economies of scale and low cost of production can be achieved when going across borders. With this, products are relatively cheaper and consumer choice is obtained alongside specializations. Paul Krugman, among other leading thinkers, contributed to the modern understanding of cross-border trade through an examination of internal and external economies of scale that are developed from microeconomics and market structure analysis and that result from *imperfections* of the larger market. He notes, for example, the beneficial role that government can play, thus expanding the study of the political economy. The theory is based on the understanding that the output of firms is differentiated and that market conditions and outputs are heterogeneous (in real or imaginary ways). This stands in opposition to *perfect competition* in which these are interpreted as homogeneous, that is, very similar or equal. The works of Hymer and others explore these imperfections in detail.

The resulting *strategic trade* extracts four essential circumstances in which strategic trade may apply: price, cost, repetition and externalities. Nevertheless, this thinking is challenged by the trends that may seduce governments to turn to protectionism and for companies to seek this protection for themselves, while retaliation from trade partners may result.

In the EU, the free movement of goods, services, labour and capital and market integration is established to allow for cost economies by centralizing production in locations with particular factor wealth and specialization of particular resources, be this raw materials, supplies, human or capital resources, knowledge or cultural factors. The New Trade Theory also explores the predominance of first movers and oligopolies (industries comprising a limited number of large firms, for example, European Aerospace or the petroleum industry), and for government intervention by means of subsidies.

Box 16   Useful definitions

First movers: First movers attempt to gain advantage by preceding their competitors when making a strategic move into a market.

Internal economies of scale: Greater production translates into lower production costs; characteristic for the objective of a common market.

External economies of scale: Free mobility of factors of production translate into lower production costs.

Oligopolies: Few firms dominate a market, in contrast to the monopolistic market in which one firm dominates; both markets show a high degree of concentration of supply structures, in opposition to the low-concentration structure of a competitive market.

Subsidies: Monetary assistance granted typically by a government to a person, organization or business in support of activities.

F.T. Knickerbocker (1973) has suggested that the imitative behaviour found in oligopolies can also be observed in the investments of equity funds abroad and in general in FDI. This is often referred to as herd behaviour. In an extension of the theory it becomes clear that international firms compete in a complex environment at different locations and times and in different industries and markets, like a network of intertwined linkages. In Europe, the increasing competition in Europeanization efforts leads to MNE strategies that favour market share increase through the use of mergers, acquisitions and alliances, or operations through FDI, rather than simple import and export activities. Knickerbocker's theory can hence also help understand the streamlining of, for example, the European mobile telecom. industry and other sectors that compete across the single market.

Michael Porter's theory of *national competitive advantage* is very suitable to get to the point of what are the main attributes to trade of a nation that encompass the so-called 'diamond' of factor endowments, domestic demand conditions, relating and supporting industries, and firm strategy, structure and rivalry. Porter's work underlines (a) that innovation is key to competitiveness and (b) the complexity of a business environment that encompasses many conditions and factors. Porter adds that competitive clusters form in fields that constitute cutting-edge, highly successful markets that locate in a concentrated manner to gain the advantages of stimulating network effects in both the corporate and the public environment, and in particular in knowledge transfer. You may find examples for clusters in Europe in, among others, the R&D technopole of Sophia-Antipolis or the Canceropole in Toulouse in France, the technology park in Brno in the Czech Republic, the Cambridge Avlar Cluster focusing on biotech and venture capital in the UK, the Austrian bioenergy cluster or InternetBay in Sweden.

The writings that constitute international trade theory have substantially helped not only to understand the phenomena but also to structure corporate and governmental thinking about the opportunities and threats of trade across borders. In Europe, the mainstream of thought has gradually driven deep and broad market integration. The *Theory of International Investment* reinforces the concepts above, in that companies are considered to be making a significant investment and hence contribution to the host economy when a company produces in another country. This move is dependent on the mobility of capital at the international level. If the firm invests directly across borders, production, organization, resources management and knowledge management become increasingly complex, while the firm will seek advantages from this diversification of opportunities in resources, factors, knowledge, security and altogether markets. It will strive to profit from access opportunities that may otherwise be difficult (for example, because of import restrictions), from factor mobility and from management imperfections such as managerial or marketing techniques or financial resources. In addition to this, the theory holds that companies will be able to internalize, that is, keep in their possession non-transferable sources of advantage such as trade secrets or other specific expertise, which were the focus of in-depth work by Buckley and Casson as well as Dunning.

Successful European trade and investment is dependent on adaptable approaches of how to exploit opportunities. The European business environment demands careful market segmentation and sound internationalization strategy. It benefits to an important degree from the advantages that trade theories stipulate, and also defines the resulting challenges, depending on sector, production stage and location. Various studies shed light on the market integration effects along trade theory argumentation. These studies confirm that business in Europe remains complex despite the elimination of duties and the progressive harmonization of technical and safety standards, administrative barriers and local fragmentations. For example, the EU has standardized the European government procurement process to create greater efficiency via the Government Procurement Agreement (GPA). Through the GPA, large tenders are published at the European level by its members. Box 17 illustrates this point and provides you with an idea of the challenges that negotiators at the EU may face.

Box 17   The Government Procurement Agreement – a case of diversity in multinational negotiations re government procurement

At a discussion in the heart of the EU institutions in Brussels, on the basis of the latest communication from the European Communities (S/WPGR/W/52), the focus turned to procedural rules in government procurement: a key question was whether there were such rules around for which there could be a greater degree of support.

The representative of the European Communities recalled that his delegation's communication referred to procedural rules that could be developed for government procurement in services; a significant advantage. He underscored that delegations should participate actively and in good faith in all the topics under the responsibility of the

(Continued)

(Continued)

Working Party. Delegations with particular interests in one of the topics could take the lead, as the EU was doing on procurement. However, other delegations needed to participate to ensure progress in the negotiations as a whole. All areas in discussion had to advance at the same pace.

The representative of Hong Kong, China, suggested that he could conduct the negotiations, but, in the light of the discussion on the information exchange mandate, he feared that not everybody shared this view. He was particularly concerned because he had not yet received a satisfactory answer to the question on how the proposed framework for government procurement would square with reciprocity provisions in the GPA. It appeared to him that the EU was relying upon exemptions from the MFN obligation similar to existing exemptions pursuant to Article II of the General Agreement on Trade in Services (GATS) (WTO). He still was puzzled about how this approach would allow for a reconciliation of the reciprocity provisions in the GPA with the multilateral commitments that the proposed EU framework envisioned. He hoped to obtain clear answers in order to progress in the discussions.

The representative of Brazil reiterated that he disagreed with the delegation of the European Communities regarding the scope of the mandate in Article XIII. His delegation was therefore not prepared to engage in any discussion relating to market access or national treatment. He might be willing to address, however, other parts of the communication from the European Communities.

In response to the question from the delegation from Hong Kong, the representative of the European Communities said that under the EC proposal members' commitments would apply multilaterally. If the GPA contained additional elements that applied only amongst GPA members on the basis of reciprocity, these would be preserved by a specific provision to that effect. He did not see a major problem with the relationship between the framework and the GPA, but was open to suggestions. He took note of Brazil's views and welcomed the Brazilian delegation's readiness to engage on some parts of S/WPGR/W/52. 'Should the Chairperson undertake informal consultations on subsidies and ESM, he should also do so on government procurement.'

Source: GATS, 2005

Major studies of the market integration effects in Europe were conducted by the EU (for example, extensively by the European Commission 1996), private sector, research and academia (see, for example, Baldwin and Wyplosz, 2004; and for the US, Campbell and Hopenhayn, 2002) over the past decade. They demonstrate that firm size and market size are interrelated in that industries tend to consolidate and get bigger when markets enlarge and competition grows. It was found that corporations are exposed to an adjustment phase, as integration leads to profit losses through shifting factor advantages, conditions and price decreases. These losses may be short-term because, increasingly, numbers of less competitive firms fall while prices rise, mergers and alliances flourish and consolidation takes place. The faster industry adapts, the less it has to bear.

What do we learn from these theories? For both European and non-European firms, doing business in Europe engages management in strategic decisions, for example that of location, as soon as operations imply investments rather than mere import and export activities. International trade theory underlies these decisions. Location decisions clearly reflect the discussed concepts of international trade theory when it comes to the specific evaluation of corporate and market specialization, resources, factor endowments, and economies of scale objectives. Corporate strategies in terms of first movers may be influenced by those considerations too. Also, government policy is greatly influenced by economic theory. In the defragmentation of the European market and the consolidation of competition for scale economies and profit-sustainability, governmental policy may be seduced by state aid and subsidy solutions to counterbalance the social costs of lay-offs and inefficiency. Trade barriers that are based on some of the theories mentioned above act as impediments to corporations' ability to internationalize; other examples of resulting protectionist policies can be intervention through infant industry protection, local content requirements, voluntary export restraints or anti-dumping duties (Box 18). This is where common European policies play a role to restrict anti-competitive practices.

Box 18   More definitions

Infant industry: An industry, mainly a new and developing sector, that is considered as not sufficiently mature to compete on equal terms with international rivals.

Local content requirements: Some defined fraction of a good needs to be produced locally.

Voluntary export restraints: An exporting country may self-impose export limitations in response to threats of trade barriers from the target market.

Anti-dumping duties: Tariffs in the form of import duties that are established so as to counteract the injurious effects of selling a product (normally a commodity) at a price below cost of production or below domestic price in an export market.

Fair trade principles are the aim and objective of common policies such as the common commercial policy towards non-EU states. These principles are therefore a basis for economic cohesion, but apply mainly punctual, ad hoc specific governmental intervention. While politically, some European states are yet to structure sound governance adapted to Europeanization, corporations have taken the lead in the challenge. Corporate Germany leads the world in export figures and Italy owes a rise in employment figures from its Biagi law, which loosens labour regulations; in France the CAC-40 indexed companies set records in the generation of profits and Bulgaria shows record growth rates.

5.2.2 Business realities

Corporate Europe, that is, business entities and industries in Europe, is business that has the opportunity to move to international markets from a home base provided by the single market and, ideally, is solid and competitive. This objective creates an inherent and incremental advantage of Europeanization. In this context, international trade theory takes its full sense.

However, we need to study this theory just another step further for yet more insight into European complexities: The so-called *market imperfection theories (internalization theories)* stipulate that corporations favour FDI (Box 19) to export or licensing strategies because of market impediments. The Europeanization of business is driven by such internalization: Within the market, these impediments may be trade or tariff barriers, cultural or administrative hurdles. They result in costs or benefits, advantages and disadvantages that vary from one market to the other.

Box 19   Foreign direct investment directions

Horizontal: Equity funds invested across borders in the same branch of activity. Typically this is motivated by cost and market-access considerations.

Vertical: Equity funds invested across borders with product stages in different locations, providing inputs (backward) or outputs (forward) for the domestic production process. Typically this is motivated by the fragmentation of production and relative factor costs.

Because of this, horizontal FDI, that is, that in the same industry of a given company, is of particular interest when market imperfections, transaction costs, location advantages and/or a life cycle serves to decrease the efficiency of less risky modes of international business such as exporting or licensing. Attracted by market similarities and relatively low risk factors among Member States, companies in Europe use the entire range of internationalization strategies (Box 20), including horizontal and vertical FDI (that is, providing input or output for a firm's operations), that may take different forms according to the degree of investments to be made and risk to undertake.

Box 20   Strategic choices for Europeanization

Production remaining in the domestic market:

- direct exporting;
- indirect exporting – via a partner in the manufacturer's home country.

(Continued)

Production partly or fully abroad:

- licensing – the licensor makes an asset available to licensee(s) in exchange for compensation;
- franchising – special form of licensing, with transfer of know-how;
- joint ventures – joining a local partner;
- strategic alliances – collaborative ventures between international firms;
- merger and acquisition – control and ownership of operations outside the home country for corporate growth;
- greenfield – own facilities.

One substantial advantage for firms in terms of subsequent internationalization outside Europe is that their experience curve is at its peak. This is because cross-border trade has become a continuous business reality in Europe. The Europeanized firm is hence an instrument that allows countries and organizations to locate production, service, capital, knowledge and distribution most effectively. It engages into a resource transfer that benefits emitter and receptor of goods, services and capital (Figure 7).

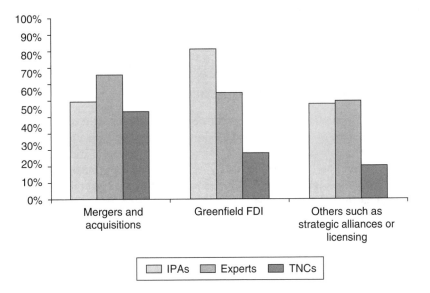

Figure 7   Expected modes of global investment 2005–6 (per cent of responses) (UNCTAD, 2005)

The theoretical and ideological underpinning that we discussed above has succeeded accelerating Europeanization. For example, the UK is one of the Member States that are most open to FDI, but also intervenes when it comes to national interests. Most European countries are rather pragmatic when it comes to the costs and benefits of free trade. The import of skills, capital, technology and know-how, as well as employment, is appreciated and can drive the wealth of an economy, for example that of Ireland. Some Member States actively attract FDI through policies such as tax breaks and grants. Investment incentives may also encompass reduced land prices, infrastructure advantages or personnel training support.

However, it is important to note that there are dangers in Europeanization. Profits from investments may leave the host country; supplies may come from abroad; operations may turn into assembly only. Factor mobility does not benefit each country in the integrated market, therefore, a bargaining for greater benefits than costs leads the general European policies towards FDI.

Adequate competition from inside and outside allows, according to the above theories, for the efficient functioning of markets, in that more competitors will drive prices down and increase consumer welfare and consumer choice. Therefore, again following the theory, competitors will invest more in R&D, personnel training and knowledge and equipment transfer, so as to win the race in competitiveness, productivity and innovation. In this scenario, complementary product and service industries simultaneously flourish. Nevertheless, this does not tackle all the challenges: much thought is increasingly given to the issues of offshoring and outsourcing in Europe (Box 21).

The general public tends to look at these issues fearing unemployment and loss of identity when specific products that are at a population's heart, are produced elsewhere. Typically, however, the European consumer will appreciate the increase of product choice and the decrease in price that comes with these phenomena.

Box 21   Offshoring and outsourcing

Offshoring: Undertaking FDI to serve the domestic market, that is, a relocation of a service, like hotline or any service that can be done remotely from a foreign location. The owner company keeps control of the company involved in the activity but in another country. The local laws, like salary or advantages, apply. European offshoring focuses mainly on eastern or Far East countries as well as the Maghreb countries. For example, France Telecom's 'hotlines' are located in Morocco.

Outsourcing: External acquisition and purchase of services or products that were previously produced in-house, that is, subcontracting to an external company of a part of the service or the business. In some industries, outsourcing is either a company strategy or a necessity because the company does not have the required internal resource. In the pharmaceutical industry, those companies are referred to as contract research organizations (CROs), and they undertake all or part of the R&D process.

When offshore production serves the domestic market, following liberal economic theory, it frees resources so that a country can focus on the sectors of activity that generate comparative advantage. At the same time, prices from offshore production are relatively lower than from domestic production, and companies remain competitive vis-à-vis their international competition which also uses offshoring. Based on this theory, the negative employment effects are outweighted by the long-term benefits to both companies and consumers.

For an employee who loses his job because of offshoring or outsourcing activities, this argument is very weak. For the corporation and the economy as a whole, theory underpins the phenomenon. Ever closer to the consumer and the labour market, therefore, are issues of location. They map out the pattern of Europeanization.

5.3 Choosing your company location

Choosing a location implies that a firm opts to seek direct or indirect gains, in order to avoid loss with regard to its comparative advantages. The theories established by Vernon, Dunning and many others help to understand why and what drives a firm to become international or transnational, with different degrees of host economy integration and linkages across borders (the definition of the terms 'international' and 'transnational' in international business was provided in Chapter 1).

Locations and modes of internationalization are defined by corporate management. This takes place on the basis of the particular advantages that the firm gains from operations that reach beyond the national market. Following Dunning's leading work about internationalization on a global scale, which he called the eclectic paradigm consisting of the so-called OLI advantages (Box 22), **it can be argued that the main benefits of going European in terms of market scale and operations consist in the degree to which a firm remains owner of its resources and the internalization that it may benefit from.**

Box 22   Dunning's OLI theory

- **O**wnership-specific advantages.
- **L**ocation-specific advantages.
- **I**nternalization advantages of certain degrees.

These advantages can differ on a local, regional, national or global scale, depending on the company criteria (nature, organization, sector of activity). Choosing a European, cross-frontier location is therefore a crucial decision and – in some cases – an important first experience for a company in its internationalization process.

Location decisions need to be motivated by either offensive or defensive strategies (Howell, 2001; see Bouchet, 2005: 445). *Offensive internationalization* means that a firm will move faster than its competitors and anticipate market developments on the basis of strong marketing and finances. This is the case, for example, for firms that invest in candidate countries before their definitive accession to the EU. On the contrary, *defensive internation-alization* is conducted to preserve market share and competitive advantage in response to other players in the same or supplementary market. This strategy is different in terms of its timing because it is conducted at a later stage than offensive internationalization. It may require supplementary efforts to succeed in a complex environment that is already domi-nated by competitors: differentiation and knowledge of the terrain are essential require-ments; an option can be the reinforcement of local product or service adaptation, for example McDonald's decision to sell salads in its French fast-food restaurants. The chain is market leader in France despite fierce competition from national and international players in that market (Quick, Kentucky Fried Chicken, etc.).

The decision to go cross-border may be because it is a first move abroad, or because of adding or changing a location to earlier internationalization stages. These decisions are made on the basis of existing alternatives, and may be based on previous experience. While gains and loses are intrinsic to any business operation, choosing the right international location represents an efficient solution to obtain competitive advantage. The main advan-tages to be gained from successful internationalization are:

- optimization or reduction of costs; and/or
- creation of new opportunities for growth; and/or
- development of new strategic strengths.

The firm therefore screens its environment. In the EU this environment can offer impor-tant advantages along the international value chain, that is, the path that links primary and support activities for providing goods and services. This value chain covers all stages that lead from procurement up to order fulfilment, as follows:

- procurement;
- orders, invoicing;
- manufacturing and inventory management;
- service provision;
- shipping, integrated logistics, order fulfilment;
- planning and time management.

The value chain is hence key to the appreciation of a business environment and influ-ences all aspects of management, reaching from human resources management to market-ing and sales orientations.

In operational terms, corporate executives generally use four main criteria for location decisions: operational, financial, location and risk. The operational criterion deals with all aspects relating to operational activities, that is, the quality of transport, logistic and telecommunications infrastructure; the level of local labour skills and education, and their availability; and the proximity of a target market (competition). The quality of operational resources is seen as being more important than the potential of targets markets. The finan-cial criterion directly concerns the finances of the company and its management of revenue. In particular, it concerns not only potential gains in productivity, tax burdens, and the cost of labour, but also public aid, the proximity of financial markets, the flexibility of labour law, special treatment of foreign investments, the availability of grants and subsidies, access to financial investors, and the integration of a particular monetary zone. This criterion ranks mainly second in international location decisions but remains essential, knowing that labour costs and social charges and the level of tax burden are omnipresent. The location, or local, criterion concerns the operating environment of the company of a given country or region and the extent to which they offer the necessary means to develop the firm: this includes the availability of sites, cost of land and regulations, specific skills developed in the region, availability of specific expertise, local language, values and culture, the proximity of centres of innovation and research, as well as the quality of life. In addition to these criteria, the bandwagon or herd-effect that Knickerbocker (1973) explored is illustrated by Europeanization. Competitors follow firms into emerging markets; this move is accompanied by an investment en bloc into a specific region. Chapter 3 on enlargement considered investments made by media corporations in the Eastern European Member States; this is only one example for massive en bloc investments in Europe.

The consideration of relocation or location change is often necessary when a firm needs to adapt to local externalities, research and development spill-overs, the costs of knowledge transfer, and/or transport (Krugman and Venables, 1995). This scenario applies if the costs of operating in a market are greater than the returns. But a firm may also adapt its cost/ return ratio by shifting to a different mode of operation with differently adapted levels of internalization. Box 23 illustrates this phenomenon with the example of the European textile sector.

Box 23   The relocation of European textiles

Italy is at the forefront of European textiles, followed closely by Portugal and Spain. In recent years the European markets have been inundated with textile products from India, which boasts 40 per cent of the world market, and China, with some categories of textile increasing by 1500 per cent a year. This huge shift of activity to Far East countries is due to several factors:

- increasing costs in Europe;
- international competition;
- counterfeit products;
- illegal imports;
- very low labour costs.

This escalating rise in costs in Europe has necessitated a dependence on highly sophisticated machinery and equipment, and has led to a situation where there is an adjustment within the labour market with employers looking for workers who are adaptable and have the competencies to work well in various cultures and teams. The current generation of workers is neither very flexible nor polyvalent. The

(Continued)

(Continued)

labour associations, which represent workers, are finding it increasingly difficult to keep work in Europe.

One of the most prestigious labels in the textile and clothing industry is the 'Made in Italy' label. It is the leading sector in the Italian economy and primarily consists of small and medium-sized companies. In fact, 95 per cent of the companies have an annual turnover of less than two million euros. The Italian fashion industry employs nearly a million people, including about 200,000 self-employed workers.

However, in Europe more than 250,000 workers have been laid off due to international competition, rising costs, counterfeit products, and unfair competition due to illegal importations. Another reason for this phenomenon is the difference between competencies; semi-skilled and unskilled workers have a lower demand profile in many European countries. In Italy, the various employers' associations welcome the introduction of extensive and more efficient training schemes for workers. Employers, as well as the trade unions, agree that to remain competitive in the international market, labour costs must be rationalized and quality further upgraded.

Although it may seem that workers in high-wage countries cannot compete with those in fast developing emerging market countries, steps can be taken not only to balance the actual trends for Europe and Italy, but also to remain focused on luxury brands. In this case, Europe should ideally provide high-quality products. The 'savoir-faire' is a key success factor that Europe can claim in its favour. In addition to this positioning, Europe should also present innovative technologies and processes for the apparel sector such as:

- 3-D body scanning and automated body measurement;
- on-screen visualization of clothes and virtual try-ons;
- 'wearable technology' and multi-functional clothing;
- industrial made-to-measure and mass customization;
- multimedia applications for fashion retailers;
- online retailing and other e-commerce solutions for the sector.

The textiles battle is not lost if we compete in the right direction with the right tools, using European core competencies. In this way, low cost clothing serves a different market.

Source: Compiled data, 2005–7

5.4 A market-serving, resource-seeking Europeanization?

Vernon (1992) and Dunning (1993) argued that firms can leverage resources through FDI, namely in a resources-based perspective. Birkinshaw and Hood (1998) added that the strategy of TNCs is as much market-serving as it is resource-seeking. TNCs may reach scale economies of knowledge (knowledge management (KM)) through its transfer across borders (Buckley and Casson 1976; Kogut and Zander 1993), and link these approaches on a global or regional level. Hence, the mode of entry that a firm chooses reflects the answer to a multitude of variables that are priorities for the European firm, and relatively easily screenable in the European marketplace. Modes of entry that a firm may consider include:

- local advantages: currency, resources, market-related needs, cultures and knowledge management;
- government policies;
- company taxation;
- company law and legal issues;
- regional policies;
- infrastructure;
- sociocultural forces;
- transaction costs;
- organizational structure;
- product life cycles;
- knowledge transfer options;
- risk-diversification possibilities;
- decomposition abilities of activities;
- 'Ecology of firms and places' (Suder, 2006);
- cross-border factor mobility;
- herd behaviour.[1]

The complete and careful screening of these variables encompasses the gathering of information on a European, national and local level. At the European level, CEC databases are particularly useful. In addition, Eurostat is a very complete research tool; it provides, among other data, information about all the main trade areas in Europe and their trends. At the national level, most useful are DTIs (Departments of Trade and Industry) and similar institutions, as well as trade organizations, and business information services such as national and CEC representatives. Company registration offices and local legal offices may also be helpful. The environmental screening process allows the firm to evaluate the potential costs and benefits of locations. Also, operational risk can be limited if managed within a framework of diversification of sourcing and suppliers and flexibility in entry and exit strategies, on the basis of a firm-specific set of location modes. The European market allows firms to apply these diversification modes. Dicken (2003) found that international trade is predominated by a high degree of cross-investment between the highly developed economies, although FDI in developing countries is rising because firms are aware of the importance of this knowledge for their international mapping. **European TNCs favour investment in historically close markets or in markets that are governed in special partnership with the EU: market groupings reduce political risk incrementally as integration improves, and the periphery of special relationships expands this stability.** The reduction of risk encompasses that of economic risk, financial and transfer risk, exchange risk, cultural environment risk, legal and contractual risk, regional contamination risk (spill-over effect), and the systemic risk associated to any global crisis.

5.4.1 Income discrepancies and labour movements

As noted earlier in this chapter, factor mobility does not benefit each country or region in a market grouping in the same way. The benefit can be measured through an examination of the distribution of wealth and profit, and is generally evaluated on the basis of values and the worth of assets. These assets may be stocks and shares, that is, marketable wealth, or assets like property and land resources that are difficult to assess unless sold. Non-marketable wealth may include rights and wealth support by origin and heritage that include the values of networking, creativity and innovation. For instance, in Germany small firms producing innovative machinery and equipment are interlinked.

Gudemann found that the distribution of marketable wealth is more uneven than the distribution of income. Market groupings are often characterized by inequalities in the distribution of income between regions of the same country, and the EU is no exception to this. Within its Member States, parts of Poland, Portugal, Greece, southern Italy and Spain, eastern Germany, eastern Finland, and the west of Ireland traditionally show the lowest income figures. In the UK, there is a north–south divide in the distribution of incomes, in Germany this is reflected in a East-West divide, and in France, the highest incomes can be found in the Île-de-France area including Paris and surroundings, and the lowest incomes in Guadeloupe, Guyana, La Réunion and Martinique.

Generally, five levels of household income (see Figure 8) are taken into account in order to best compare income level and their stages of redistribution. The *original income* is an amount of income or money that is complemented by a system of cash benefits (that is, employment, investments, benefits, etc.). The *gross income* is then subject to the system of direct taxes (deducted income tax).

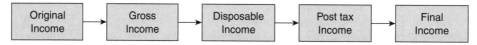

Figure 8   Five levels of household income

The *resulting disposable income* takes into account the impact of the system of indirect taxes (which makes distribution less even), for example VAT, duties. *Post-tax income* is hence the income resulting from the above stages, complemented by benefits-in-kind, that is, free education, free health care, *inter alia*, and is then called the *final income*. In the regions noted above, the bottom quintile of the five levels of household income has little original income. Most of its income indeed comes from cash benefits, that is, there is significant redistribution of income in this stage. Hence, the main effect of equivalization through national and EU mechanisms is to raise the income of the bottom quintile significantly. In this respect, can market mechanisms help solve regional income inequalities?

If one relies on market mechanisms, then the rationale indicates that labour flows to high-income regions (workers migrate), while capital flows to low-income regions due to profit rates. In this case, is policy intervention the key to combating regional income inequalities? Any reflection about international economic history and geo-economy indicates that inequalities occur also in planned economies under strong governmental intervention. While the reply to this question has hitherto been negative, regions differ in regard to high and low resources; the household composition differs in urban and rural regions and educational attainment and skills are not the same. Immigration and minority issues like language, culture and religion can play a significant role in regional income disparity.

5.4.1.1 Labour

In practice, labour is in fact relatively immobile; if labour migrates, it takes its purchasing power with it, and hence further reduces the income of a region. Local commerce then obtains less income, shopkeepers, estate agents, solicitors, etc. reduce their spending: a further reduction of regional income is the result. Moreover, labour is in reality *not* a homogeneous factor, for example a skilled carpenter is not a perfect substitute for a pharmacist or an accountant. In addition, there is no substitute for labour if the population is not sufficiently skilled. Following this, an area with relatively unskilled labour has less attraction for business and FDI. The reverse is true for highly skilled labour. Interestingly, highly educated Finland shows the narrowest gap between income levels in Europe and has lead the World Economic Forum's Competitive Ranking for years.

Highly skilled labour increases the human resource capital of a country, and normally benefits the balance of payments through investment into the host economy. Low-skilled labour exercises a less important impact on the balance of payments because revenues are often sent to the families in the home country. Nevertheless, this labour contributes significantly to the economic health of the host country. This means filling in demographic gaps, counterbalancing labour shortages in specific areas, and offering education and training to a diversity of potentials. Labour may be moving in and out of Europe, or freely within Europe. The Schengen agreement, that was discussed in Chapter 3, encourages labour movement through low-administration common rules and procedures for internal and external border controls for citizens of the participating countries. The Schengen agreement was also signed by some EFTA countries (Iceland and Norway in 1996, and Switzerland in 2005). The agreement facilitates also the transit of goods through increased cooperation of customs.

In terms of labour and employment policies, the overall European focus on a services-oriented economy since the mid-1990s has resulted in employment in services that account for more than double that of industry, and even more of agriculture. In a breakdown by gender, more men work in agriculture and industry, while more women are employed in services. Europe encompasses several socio-economic models: The mainstream models are Nordic, Latin, French, Italian, new Eastern European, and German. In each capitalism model, the labour market models are contrasted. The UK with its limited government, decentralized pay bargaining and flexible working arrangements appears to be the most flexible of the EU economies. Ireland and the Netherlands also provide examples of flexible labour markets.

Under the Amsterdam Treaty and at the Luxembourg Special European Council of 20 and 21 November 1997, Member States agreed to maintain their exclusive competence in confronting unemployment and job creation. However, EU governments treat employment policies as a matter of common concern. As a result, joint employment guidelines are published on an annual basis and each Member State submits a National Action Plan (NAP) for employment.

5.4.1.2 Capital

In contrast to labour, capital is very mobile, not only between regions but also between countries. Therefore, the market mechanism works as capital flows (but it flows globally). Governmental and supranational agencies like the EU intervene mainly through financial assistance programmes and regional funds, research and training initiatives – making Europe more and more attractive for internal and external economies of scale on the basis of factor mobility, reinforced flexibility of labour and capital factors, and the highest educational standards recognized EU-wide. The move of the EU economy towards a knowledge-based service economy reinforces these efforts.

The EMU brought about the creation of the ECB. The Maastricht Treaty detailed the role of the Euro-system in defining and implementing monetary policy in the Euro-zone, conducting foreign exchange operations, holding and managing official reserves, promoting the smooth operation of payment systems, and issuing banknotes and coins (Lamfalussy, 1997). A tendency towards monetary integration following the principles of federalism guides the primary objective of the ECB to maintain price stability (Maastricht Treaty). Overall, the EU has successfully centralized its monetary policy and harmonizes interest rates. (Gramlich and Wood, 2000: 19). This topic will be analysed further in Chapter 7.

5.4.2 The competitiveness of European manufacturing and service industries

In 2000, the objective of the EU was proclaimed as being for the Single Market to evolve into 'the most competitive and dynamic knowledge-based economy in the world, capable of sustainable economic growth with more and better jobs and greater social cohesion' (Lisbon Strategy Statement, 2000; Gothenburg Agenda 2001, see European Communities (2000)) by 2010.

Competitiveness is a relative concept that can be defined in several ways: a definition may refer to competitiveness as being industrial, technological or enterprise (Box 24). In all three cases, the term is used relative to several principal factors: price- or non-price (such as high quality, superior design and technical innovation); lower cost; and profitability. Although this approach is used as a basis of most interpretations, literature on the subject may give another set of definitions: the perfect competition concept, as analysed by Kirzner

(1973), emphasizes, for instance, the atomistic structure and product homogeneity as vital determinants; this approach, however, appears to be unrealistic due to the fact that here, 'perfect competition denotes for the price theorist the situation in which every market participant does exactly what everyone else is doing, in which it is utterly pointless to try to achieve something in any way better than what is already being done by others' (Kirzner, 1973: 90). In other words, all competition would be absent in this model.

Box 24   Competition, competitiveness and competitivity

Competition: The act of competing, of engaging in rivalry or in a contest. In business, for example, for markets or customers.

Competitiveness: The ability of a country or region to compete with other countries or regions.

Competitivity: The ability of a sector or industry to compete; the ability to achieve competitive advantage.

Competition refers to the rivalry between independent firms, which is affected by the ability of industry to overtake its foreign and domestic competitors due to design, production and marketing with better price and non-price qualities, mirrored for instance in a country's share in world trade. Hence, a firm is competitive if it is capable of manufacturing products and providing services of superior quality at lower costs than its domestic and international competitors. Competitivity is synonymous with a corporation's *profit performance* in the long run and its ability to reward its employees and distribute high returns to its stakeholders. This concept of competitiveness is in any case relative in terms of measurements used for its assessment. It is a very dynamic concept in terms of the relative position of countries and their firms that is determined continuously by factors like trends, investments, technology and innovation. Note, at this stage, that often the terms competition, competitiveness and competitivity are used interchangeably and their interpretation may overlap.

Non-price factors, such as technology and innovation, are measures of competitiveness often referred to in academic literature. However, there is a wide range of indicators of competitiveness that may give different results depending on which measures are adopted for the assessment. We distinguish quantitative and qualitative indicators (Buckley et al., 1988). *Quantitative* indicators include export market share, market share, export measures, percentage of world manufacturing/GNP, percentage of domestic manufacturers in total output, balance of trade, comparative advantage, cost competitiveness, technology and profitability. *Qualitative* indicators are ownership advantage, marketing aptitude, commitment to international business and globalization, relations with intermediaries, proximity to market, cultural advantages, cross-licensing and acquisition of technology. Buckley et al. (1988) conclude that competitive advantage stems primarily from the ability to reach targets at the least possible cost, defined as efficiency, and secondly to choose the right goals, defined as effectiveness. The achievement of these goals is related to the historical situation, existing competitors, and the existence of a well-defined counter-factual competitiveness. In terms of international competitiveness, these factors will, together with cost and price-developments, either improve or deteriorate the performance of a country or firm.

In this respect, it is essential to define the different levels of competitiveness and its measurement: these are the firm level, the industry level or the national/regional level, which may be analysed on the basis of several market aspects, for example, market structure, organization and performance. Through an analysis of the *market structure*, it is possible to recognize the number of sellers, buyers and suppliers, the nature of the product or service, the amount of knowledge or information at the disposal of the market participants, the mobility of sellers and buyers, *inter alia*. These factors affect the conduct of firms operating in this market, for example, in the field of product differentiation. This analysis of market structures helps industries with the inquiry and acquisition of information and with the evolution of consumer preferences over a period of time in which the data may continuously change. This change of data implies a certain level of uncertainty that is at the heart of a competitive process that is affected by decisionmaking and human, organizational and market behaviour.

Market behaviour and goals are approached by means of strategies, or policies, adopted by the firm. While corporate objectives indicate where the company is aiming to go, the set of policies show, in simple words, how it intends to get there to reach targets set by the objectives. The fundamental policies that emerge from the basic objectives can be divided into marketing and sales, production, financial and personnel policies. They thus concern most the essential competitive determinants of pricing, R&D endeavours, concerted and collusionary actions. The aim is profit maximization, which is the main factor to be satisfied by an enterprise's management on behalf of the owners or shareholders as well as on that of the employees and customers, in the short-, medium- and long-term. Hence, management has to exploit its knowledge of level and the elasticity of demand, production functions and costs. Modifications in objectives and strategies need to be made continuously in accordance with the development of the sector in which the firm operates.

Box 25   Long-term strategies for sustainable competitiveness

- long-term contracts or exclusive distribution agreements,
- an increase in product differentiation,
- technological innovation through R&D,
- concentration by means of merger or take-over,
- globalization by means of investment and acquisition policies,
- establishing or elimination of certain barriers to entry.

The result of this market behaviour and a particular market structure is mirrored in the market *performance* of a company. It can be measured by a firm's profit margins, sustained growth, the degree of capacity utilization as well as product quality. Also, incomes are interpreted as identifications of the degree of competitiveness and the market performance of a company. The aim is to increase incomes as rapidly as one's competitors and to make the investments necessary to remain competitive in the long-term. Income is a good indicator of the competitiveness of a company. However, net income in a pure competitive environment is the last thing to increase in a company. In fact, any profit that a company would make and does not reinvest would weaken its current position relative to the competition. Academics argue that the lower the level of nominal wages, the lower is the external value of the currency and the faster an increase in productivity appears. Consequently, the international competitiveness of the country's industry will be greater.

Following this theory, there are three main options to increase competitiveness:

- low-wage strategy;
- devaluation strategy;
- innovation strategy.

First, the *low-wage strategy*, exercised in the case where nominal wages are decreased while productivity and exchange rate remain at their normal level, will result in higher volume sales without a loss in profit margins and therefore creates an effect equivalent to a direct fall in production costs. However, this strategy would adversely affect the international division of labour and is therefore problematic in terms of international competitiveness.

Secondly, the *devaluation strategy* can be employed; it has experienced major attention in academic literature, particularly in the research on Japanese competitiveness. It has also been used by the French government in the past (Suder, 1994). In general, the devaluation of a country's home currency enables its industry to sell products in foreign markets at lower prices than at home and facilitates the success of domestic sales, because the prices of foreign products in terms of the devalued currency are higher than those of domestic manufacturers. Competitiveness is thus improved at the expense of the country's trading partners, as it is aimed at rendering its products abroad relatively cheaper than in the home market. Devaluation can be achieved either by a formal notice given by the government or by a central bank (in the case of fixed exchange rates) or by some official statement causing the devaluation of the currency in international money markets (in case of flexible exchange rates). This strategy can only be fought on the outside by means of either protectionist measures or devaluation in turn and thus re-establishing the exchange rate.

Thirdly, the *innovation strategy* is a concept that is dependent on a high degree of technological know-how and innovation potential and flexibility and productive efficiency on the part of both the management and the workforce. Innovation takes place in terms of the improvement in quality standards, the development of new products and production processes, and the adoption of modern technology, which is related to the increase of productivity in the country in which incomes grow and stimulate import demand. Thus, trade conditions are improved and benefit the economy as a whole. Designing a particular strategy like this must evolve from the growth of demand in the market concerned, the relevant costs of production as dependent on location, the costs of distribution, marketing and transaction, and the situation of the industry in general. In Europe, these factors are subject to the forces of the single market.

5.5 Competition and the main business-related common policies

Strategy and company policies are not entirely under management control. The dynamic environment of the world economy, for example, preconditions that demand and cost conditions continuously change (Box 26). It is also very important for corporations to monitor the 'uncontrollable' variables of competitiveness, such as the strategies of competitors, and to impose even the marginal adjustments that may be necessary for sustainable competitiveness. This might mean that costs can be cut quickly or resources attributed differently. The enterprise can then keep in close touch with demand conditions, thus keeping ahead of competitors.

Box 26   The First Report on Competition Policy

Competition is the best stimulant of economic activity since it guarantees the widest possible freedom of action. An active competition policy pursued in accordance with the provisions of the treaties establishing the Communities makes it easier for the supply and demand structures to adjust to technological development continually. Through the interplay of decentralized decision-making machinery, competition enables enterprises continuously to improve their efficiency which is the sine qua non for a steady improvement in living standards and employment prospects within the Community. From this point of view, competition policy is an essential means for satisfying to a great extent the individual and collective needs of our society.

Source: © European Communities, 1972: *The First Report on Competition Policy 1972*

The preceding discussion leads to the conclusion that competitivity can be defined simply as the result of a commercialization of a product or service at the right time in the adapted place under the adapted conditions, and is quantifiable through the sustained performance improvement of industry. This depends ultimately on economic choices, financial and market, operational and technological, as well as on human resources and organizational issues.

On a global scale of comparison, European corporations are among the market leaders in the chemicals, pharmaceuticals, electrical engineering, IT, telecoms, food and beverages, metals, motor vehicles, banking, insurance and financial services sectors. Yet, European companies are deeply rooted in their home markets, although transnational companies like Nestlé, Unilever, Philips Electronics, Glaxo-Wellcome and Electrolux are exceptions to that rule. In telecoms and its applications, Europe is highly competitive vis-à-vis its trading partners. The same applies in the field of nanotechnology and biotechnology. The EU is China's biggest trading partner, and benefits from important FDI opportunities there.

EU competitiveness is nevertheless hampered by structural weaknesses that leave the market with high production, capital and labour costs, rigid labour legislation, and heavy social laws that undermine employment flexibility, and R&D spending is relatively low in terms of European GDP compared to that in the USA and Japan. Business is therefore calling upon the EU, as a common European institution, and its members to facilitate and stimulate economic activity by:

- eliminating bureaucracy;
- increasing the efficiency of procurement processes;
- raising the participation of various societal groups in decision processes;
- stimulating education as a key factor to foster information access and content production;
- improving the dissemination of best practices, ultimately leading to better services to citizens and businesses.

Box 27 quotes the Commission.

Box 27   A Council, Parliament and Economic and Social Committee conclusion about Single European Market needs

The debate concluded that the best ways for the improvement of integration would be developed along:

The need to enhance the competitiveness of the European economy as well as to improve the quality of life of European citizens. … Community policies on the environment, economic and social cohesion, health and safety and consumer rights need not only to be coordinated with Internal Market policies but integrated into them, as required by the Treaty.

The need to involve all stakeholders in the continuing development of the Internal Market, be they citizens or business and whatever their location and circumstances.

The need to remove all unjustified barriers to the free movement of goods, services, persons and capital. The new legal framework, created by integrating national markets must function optimally, in order to maximize the benefits to consumers, citizens and business. A proper balance will be sought between legislative and non-legislative activity and between harmonization and mutual recognition.

The need to promote comprehensive structural reform and modernization through the microeconomic strand of the process of trilateral economic surveillance, as established by the Cardiff European Council.

The need to provide an adequate framework to unleash the great potential for the development of the Internal Market for information and communication technologies, including e-commerce.

(Continued)

(Continued)

The need to prepare for the next enlargement of the Union. The accession of ten or more countries represents a major challenge to both current and future Member States. The operation of the existing rules needs to be improved and the candidate countries associated as soon as possible in their practical application.

The need to look beyond the borders of the Union. The internet and e-commerce offer even the smallest of companies the opportunity to trade globally. The Union's experience in creating its Internal Market provides extensive experience on which discussions with its main trading partners can be based.

Source: © European Communities, 1999: The strategy for Europe's Internal Market; Communication from the Commission to the European Parliament and the Council; 1. 1. COM(1999) 464 final. 2. B5-0204/1999, URL: http://europa.eu.int/internal_market/strategy/docs/comstrat_en.pdf

---

Common policies, in supremacy or complements to national policies, were set up by the European treaties to monitor intervention where outcomes may distort Europe-wide benefits. This has been the case in agriculture, transport, social policy and also regional policy since 1987. Also, foreign and security policy are governed under increasing harmonization. This chapter will now analyse competition and commercial policies in more detail due to their essential role for Europeanization.

5.5.1 A common policy to increase competitive market structures

Competition policy has been part of European integration efforts since the Treaty of Paris and the Treaties of Rome. Its aim is to preserve and stimulate efficiencies and effectiveness in the European market.

The CEC is the main institution in charge of anti-trust policy, merger policy and state aid controls. The objectives of competition policy are to:

- promote competitive market structures;
- dissuade anti-competitive behaviour;
- guarantee fair competitive trade in the single market;
- benefit consumers and citizens of the EU.

The conduct of competition policy will help to:

- assure proper application of directives;
- modernize rules, procedures;
- simplify policy processes (transparency).

The tasks undertaken through competition policy are complemented by the ECJ and the Court of First Instance. Also, the Council sets the legislative basis through regulations and decisions that govern the CEC's scope for action. The Common Competition Policy complements national measures that are and were taken by Member States under the principle of supremacy of EU law in case of conflict. Article 81 of the EC Treaty prohibits any agreement as anti-competitive and 'incompatible with the common market' that affects intra-EU trade with an objective to prevent, distort or restrict competition. Collusion is therefore generally impermissible, with a few exceptions of cooperation between corporations where it does not harm consumer welfare. Article 82 prohibits the abuse of dominance, whether by an individual firm or jointly. Mergers and acquisitions are subject to prior clearance under the merger control.

Of major importance also is Article 87 which prohibits state aid that distorts competition, with few exceptions. Reforms between 1997 and 2007, and in particular, reforms in 2004, resulted in a simplification of the rules and an acceleration of procedures. Also, in anti-trust policy, national competences will share more of the EU application of rules. In mergers, the role of Commission investigations was extended beyond that of market dominance towards a focus on the general effect of mergers. The rather limited numbers of staff at the CEC's competition directorate, relative to workloads, means that there is a relatively fragmented control mechanism. Article 81 procedures can be expected to be more frequently applied than those in Article 82, which are particularly burdensome and lengthy. The case of the *Commission* v. *Microsoft* illustrates the difficulties in pursuing this policy, having started in 2003 and run over several years.

These commercial policy areas are underpinned by an industrial policy that in itself is not a 'common' policy per se. The increase in mergers, acquisitions, joint ventures, and other cooperative agreements between firms, identified as cluster building or concentration (Cawson, et al., 1990), as well as the rise in FDI in the single market as part of the globalization of business, underlines the movement towards international economic integration. With this development, European industrial policy shifts the traditional national focus of sponsoring 'sunset' champions with sectoral aid, to an economically more sensitive approach of supporting 'sunrise' innovation with horizontal aid (El-Agraa, 2004). In conclusion, the inherent objective of industrial policy is to increase competitiveness in tandem with the requirements of the market.

Altogether, the European competition policy in itself has as its prime objective the elimination of distortions and the enhancement of the proper functioning of market mechanisms. The main challenge is to avoid 'protectionist' behaviour that would lead to low levels of knowledge and information flows and hinder innovation. It would increase the difficulty of picking champions, and result in retaliation by trade partners. Incentive, R&D-supportive initiatives are, in opposition to this, justified by external factors such as the social returns associated to economic returns. Innovation has become key to European competitiveness. Its promotion typically takes the shape of financial assistance, public contracts, tax incentives, punctual trade barriers in case of unfair competition, and export assistance. Measures of industrial policy are ideally favoured that do not intervene actively and directly, with the exception of punctual action. Rather, measures that stimulate the diffusion of knowledge, innovation and entrepreneurship are to be privileged.

5.5.2 The Common Commercial Policy

Given that EU industrial policy per se does not exist except in action in specific sectors, the Common Commercial Policy (CCP) provides a framework that allows corporations, both domestic and from abroad, to benefit from a single market, rationalization, specialization and internal and external economies of scale.

Both the internal market and the CCP are considered as catalysts that help European business to operate in a healthy competitive environment. The CCP is part of the EU external trade policy and was launched with the Treaty of Rome (Article 113) and further developed through the 1992 Single Market Act, Maastricht and the Treaty of Amsterdam. It allows for a common tariff and a common commercial policy towards non- EU countries. The CCP was completed at the end of the EC's transitional period in 1968; its objective, to create uniform commercial relations of its Member States towards non-EU countries. In reality, note that despite the foundations laid down for a common commercial policy by the Treaty of Rome, some issues in commercial policy remain guarded by national interests.

In December 1968, CEC documents were adopted by the Council in order to establish basic common rules in three commercial fields: trade with state-trading countries, import quotas, and anti-dumping measures. With this, the CCP was to become the first single coherent, common policy of the EU Member States. Today, the CCP allows for the common conclusion of tariff and trade agreements, the negotiation of changes in tariffs, and the achievement of uniformity in measures of liberalization. European export policy and EU-wide trade protection measures, for example, anti-dumping and anti-subsidy measures, are punctually imposed when in the Community's interest (consumer and industry). The application of the CCP therefore necessitates trade policy instruments and trade agreements. Their application regulates and reinforces the opportunities that are provided within the European business environment. Box 28 summarizes the trade instruments that are at the disposition of the EU. Later, in Chapter 10, trade agreements will be discussed further.

Box 28   Trade policy instruments and types of intervention

Balance-of-payment measures, including export rebates (restitutions) refunding the difference calculated by the Commission between EU and world market price, applied foremost in agricultural policy, and restrictions on hire purchase.

Productivity, price and income policies.

Common customs, taxation and tariff instruments, including import quotas, transit duties, preferential duties, anti-dumping duties.

Import monitoring associated with Voluntary Export Restraints (VERs), local content requirements and rules of origin.

Legislation to control not only companies, mergers and restrictive practices within the single market, but also the monitor of illicit action in third countries where EU firms encounter obstacles to market access, through the 1995 trade barriers regulation, leading to negotiation and/or recourse at the WTO if necessary.

Control of scientific research and structural aspects of technology.

Altogether, let us point out that European industry excels in the automotive sector and its components, in engineering and electrical skills, in aerospace, and in the mobile phone industry. LVMH, Armani, Gucci and Dior are leaders in the luxury fashion industry, while Carrefour, H&M, Zara and Metro are highly efficient retailers worldwide (Doz et al., 2001). The Europeanization of the business environment had a largely positive impact on competitiveness and enhances the focus of the market towards specific and functional specializations that enhance effectiveness and efficiency. The financial integration in the shape of a common currency in the Euro-zone stimulates this effect.

5.5.3 Business-related policies: Implications

As noted above the EU is in charge of an important number of common policies. Among them, you can find the CAP, the CFSP, and fisheries, environment and energy, regional, social and employment policies, as well as transport, trade and aid policies. Detailed reviews of each of them can be found in Nello (2005), Baldwin and Wyplosz (2004) and others. For an understanding of these policies' implications, let us look at trade policy in further detail.

In the EU, trade policy links the public and private sector to the WTO and deals with global trade issues, sectoral and horizontal issues, and bilateral agreements with one common approach. At the (WTO), the Member States are represented by the EU. These multilateral negotiations have an important impact on business activity worldwide (see Chapter 10) and these concerns are an integral part of the EU trade policy's tasks. In global trade, the EU supports developing countries in that it assists in their integration of the trading system. The objective is to help these economies mature so as to benefit from liberal trade. The Generalized System of Preference (GSP) runs a system of non-reciprocal tariff advantages for these economies with the EU. In the same logic, the Commission is engaged in sustainable development initiatives and researches the impact of trade negotations on developing countries, on social welfare, the environment, and civil society. The EU concludes bilateral agreements and devises specific trading policies with non-EU countries and regional groupings. These bilateral agreements are legally binding for the partners, for example as custom unions, free trade associations, cooperation or partnerships. At the same time, European trade policy deals with the horizontal and vertical sectoral issues. Horizontal issues may be those of trade and competitiveness, intellectual property, market Access policy, trade and competition, trade facilitation, government procurement – as in the example cited above – and export credits. As an example, export credits that are typically government supported, may create unfair competition: they are used when a foreign buyer of exported goods or services may defer payment. Export credits are hence subject to OECD agreements and understandings and an EC Directive on harmonisation of export credit insurance for transactions with medium- and long-term cover. They are therefore under supervision from the EU for all Member States.

This is why an essential part of European trade policy consists of dispute settlements, trade barrier regulation, anti-dumping, anti-subsidy and safeguard policies, and a range of fair trade defence and monitoring tools. The mechanisms complete the sectoral policies that structure a common market for agriculture, fisheries, services and merchandise. For example, with the EU as the world's largest producer of chemicals, pharmaceuticals and cosmetics (followed by the US and Japan) (CEC, 2006 figures), those firms that export need to overcome a number of obstacles, such as complex standards and technical regulations, intellectual property laws, registration and certification procedures, while those chemical companies that enter the EU market need to be familiar with European regulations such as REACH, the European regulatory framework for the registration, evaluation and authorisation of chemicals for early identification of the properties of chemical substances. The EU, through its trade policy, attempts to facilitate trade in the sector and engages into agreements such as those elaborated under the WTO Chemical Harmonisation Tariff Agreement (CHTA). It hence has an important role to play in the competitiveness of the sector.

Another important example for the implications of common policies on business is the European RTD policy. European centres of excellence are scattered across the continent and need adequate networking. The Commission's directorate-general for research aims to establish a common market for research, the European Research Area. It supports and coordinates research activities and the convergence of research and innovation policies, at national and EU levels. Some main areas of support are mobility and training, women in science, a Community patent policy, and there is also support for SMEs. As an example, the 'Competitiveness and Innovation framework Programme (CIP)', running from 2007 to 2013, with a budget of approximately €3.6 billion, represents a 60 per cent increase in annual spending on actions related to competitiveness and innovation compared to 2006. It pursues the aims of fostering the competitiveness of enterprises, in particular SMEs, promoting all forms of innovation including eco-innovation, and accelerating the development of a sustainable, competitive, innovative and inclusive information society. Finally, the programme supports initiatives in energy efficiency and in new and renewable energy sources in all sectors including transport (more information can be found online at http:// ec.europa. eu/enterprise/enterprise_policy/cip/index_en.htm).

Résumé and conclusion

The Europeanization of the business environment is based on the effects of globalization as well as geo-history and geo-economic evolutions. International trade theory makes a strong case for the internationalization of firms that can obtain important advantages from going abroad. Also, the theories sustain the argument that integration is beneficial for the competitiveness of a nation or, in the case of Europe, a market grouping. The European business environment has been subject to major harmonization, liberalization and deregulation efforts that are illustrated in the common policies that govern important policy areas and their outcome on an EU basis. Nevertheless, income distribution is not equal, and the EU promises huge potential if harmonization efforts continue.

(Continued)

The dynamic though streamlined corporate sectors in the single market prove that Europeanization increases business efficiency and effectiveness. Most governments sustained their 'national champion' expansion with non-tariff trade and investment barriers directed against foreign competitors and strong borders protecting national markets. But these policies failed and caused low growth, unemployment and inflation after the first oil crisis in 1973. The European Commission then decided to work on an integration programme to eradicate the main trade and investment burdens. The single market programme implemented in 1987 had a positive effect, especially from the mid-1990 onwards. The manufacturing industry was the main target of EU initiatives; this focus shifted towards the service industry around 2000. Consequently, 'national champions' and championing governments had to adapt to focus on becoming European leaders. Over the period 1987–97, firms had to adjust, their contribution to the EU production process becoming more important than their contribution to the national; competition became EU-wide. Firms with a high dispersion of their activities at the outset benefited more than others from the single market by rationalizing and concentrating their operations on the EU market. As a result, the competition within the EU has largely enhanced general international competition and competitiveness worldwide (De Voldere et al., 2001).

Competitiveness is a key issue in the EU. This chapter reviewed the main rationale and business-related instruments that drive the common response and support to challenges of market mechanisms. In Europe, there is a tendency to privilege punctual direct intervention that applies in cases of market distortions. In all other cases, the EU role is to monitor and stimulate competition and fair trade. This includes, for example, the fair access to non-EU markets.

Altogether, the globalization phenomenon has evolved in three consecutive steps: first, the internationalization of trade – particularly in the 1950s; secondly, the transnationalization of capital flows – very importantly in the 1980s; and more recently, the globalization of information flows. The development of the information society has become a reality with the installation of global digital networks, in particular throughout the 1990s. Technology developments, especially in communication, have improved the productivity of all sectors of activity in the manufacturing and the services industries. The 2000s add on major developments in innovation and competitiveness convergence through the Lisbon/Gothenburg agenda. The development of multinationals under these market forces enhances competition. An international corporate structure and an externalization of productions are phenomena that are well founded in the evolution of both globalization and Europeanization. The very performance and nature of the business environment constructed in Europe is a motivation to companies worldwide in their call for more regional integration.

Mini case study: When the Volvo Group implements its industrial relocation

---

The Volvo Group is one of the world's leading manufacturers of trucks, buses and construction equipment, drive systems for marine and industrial applications, and aerospace components and services. The Group also provides complete solutions for financing and service. Employing about 82,000 people, it owns production facilities in 25 countries and sells its products in more than 185 markets. Annual sales of the Volvo Group amount to €23 billion. We are dealing here with a publicly held company headquartered in Göteborg, Sweden. Volvo shares are listed on the stock exchanges in Stockholm and on NASDAQ in the USA.

The Volvo Group is relocating its industry in Europe. As a result, manufacture of crankshafts for medium–heavy truck engines is being increased at Villaverde, Spain, while Renault's truck (part of the Volvo group) production is being concentrated in Bourg-en-Bresse in France. The relocation is a consequence of the transition to a greater degree of shared technical architecture for trucks within the Volvo Group. Renault Trucks currently manufactures Kerax trucks and crankshafts for various engines for Renault Trucks at the facility in Villaverde. As a consequence of the transition to a greater degree of shared technical architecture for trucks within the Volvo Group, the truck production in Villaverde is being relocated to Bourg-en-Bresse. The plant in Bourg-en-Bresse is responsible for most of Renault's truck production.

The transfer was completed in 2006. At the same time, the Volvo Group increased its production of crankshafts from 35,000 to 65,000 for the group's medium–heavy engines at new facilities close to Villaverde. Approximately 450 employees were affected by the decision. For them, an extensive package of support measures was developed to facilitate the adjustment process for personnel.

Source: Volvo Company, 2004; AB Volvo, 2006

Mini case questions:

1   Given this case about Volvo, would you agree that Europeanization increases business efficiency and effectiveness?
2   What human resource problems arise with relocation? How would you deal with these problems?

Review questions

1   **Explain** in which cases offshoring is economically sensible.
2   **Explain** the importance of internalization advantages for a Europeanizing firm.

(Continued)

3 **Based** on international trade theory, to what extent can a firm be an instrument of effective production and distribution on a European scale?
4 **Where** can you find trade diversion effects in Europeanization?
5 **Can** market mechanisms combat regional income inequalities?

Assignments

- **Imagine** that you are the manager of a company in the luxury fashion industry. You decide to have your main production transferred to Asia. Why is this subject sensitive? Find a recent example.
- **Compare** income distribution disparities in your home country with that of any (other) EU Member State's. Discuss your findings.
- **Case study assignment:** Read and prepare the EU Transport Policy and the Europeanization of a Business case study in Part IV, and discuss the impact of Europe on the company's operations.
- **Internet exercise:** On the internet, find the main competitiveness charts. Which organizations publish them and based on which criteria? Compare the top rankings for the 20-year period 1985–2005 and interpret your findings.

Web guide

www

http://europa.eu.int/comm/internal_market/score/index_en.htm *Internal Market Scoreboard.*
http://www.europeanbusinessforum.com/home/ebfhome.asp European Business Forum website.
http://www.unctad.org: United Nations Conference on Trade and Development.
http://www.worldbank.org: World Bank website (information on countries).

Note

1 Some parts of this section are based on published material in Suder (2006).

References

Baldwin, R. and Wyplosz, C. (2004) *The Economics of European Integration*. Maidenhead: McGraw-Hill.

Birkinshaw, J. and Hood, N. (1998) 'Multinational subsidiary evolution: Capabilities and charter change in foreign-owned subsidiary companies', *Academy of Management Review*, 23: 773–95.

Bouchet, M.H. (2005) *La Globalisation*, Upper Saddle River, NJ: Pearson Education.

Buckley, P. (2004) 'Cartography and international business', *International Business Review* 13: 239–55.

Buckley, P. and Casson, M. (1988) 'A theory of cooperation in business', in Contractor F.J. and Lorange, P. (eds), *Cooperative Strategies in International Business*. Lanham: Lexington Books, F.J.

Buckley, P.J. and Casson, M.C. (1976) *The Future of the Multinational Enterprise*. New York: Holmes and Meier.

Campbell, J. and Hopenhayn, H. (2002) Market Size matters. *NBER Working Paper* 9113, Cambridge MA.

Cawson, A., Morgan, K., Webber, D., Holmes, P. and Stevens, A. (1990) *Hostile Brothers: Competition and Closure in the European Electronics Industry*. Oxford: Clarendon Press.

CEC (2006) *Europe in figures*. Eurostat year book 2006-07, Catalogue No: KS-CD-06-001-EN-CA Brussels, February 2007.

Commission of the European Communities (1996) *The 1996 Single Market Review: Background Information for the Report to the Council and the European Parliament*, Commission Staff Working Paper, Brussels, URL: http://europa.eu.int/en/update/impact/index.htm

Commission of the European Communities (1999) 'The Competitiveness of European Enterprises in the face of Globalisation – How it can be encouraged', Brussels, 20 January.

Commission of the European Communities (2004) *Internal Market Scoreboard*, Brussels: European Communities.

Czinkota, M., Ronkainen, R. and Moffett, M. (2005) *International Business*, 7th edn. Mason, OH: South-Western Thomson.

De Jong, E. (1988) 'The contribution of the ECU to exchange-rate stability: A reply (with H. Jager)', *Banca Nazionale del Lavoro Quarterly Review*, 166: 331–5.

De Voldere, I., Sleuwaegen, L., Veugelers, R. and Van Pelt, A. (2001) *The Leading Firms in Europe from National Champions to European Leaders*, Vlerick Leuven Gent Management School Working Paper Series 2004/12, Gent.

Dicken, P. (2003) *Global Shift: Reshaping the Global Economic Map in the 21st Century*, 4th edn. London: Sage.

Doz, Y., Santos, J. and Williamson, P. (2001) *From Global to Metanational*. Boston: Harvard Business School Press.

Dunnett, A. (1998) *Understanding the Market*, 3rd edn. Harlow: Longman.

Dunning, J. (1977) 'Trade location of economic activity: a search for an eclectic approach', in B. Ohlin, P. Hesselborn and P. Wijkman (eds), *The International Allocation of Economic Activity*. New York: Holmes and Meier. pp. 395–418.

Dunning, J. (1993) *Multinational Enterprises and the Global Economy*. New York: Addison-Wesley.

El-Agraa, A. (2004) *The European Union, Economics & Policies*, 7th edn. Harlow: FT Prentice Hall.

European Communities (1999) The Strategy for Europe's Internal Market; Communication from the Commission to the European Parliament and the Council; 1. 1. COM(1999) 464 final. 2. B5-0204/1999. URL: http://europa.eu.int/comm/internal_market/en/update/strategy/strat2en.pdf

European Communities (2000) *The Lisbon European Council – an agenda of economic and social renewal for Europe. Contribution of the European Commission to the special European Council in Lisbon*, 23–24 March 2000, DOC/00/7, 28 February.

GATS (2005) Working Party on GATS Rules, Report of the Meeting of 21 September 2005, Note by the Secretariat.

Gramlich, E. and Wood, P. (2000) *Fiscal Federalism and European integration: Implications for fiscal and Monetary policies*, Board of Governors of The Federal Reserve System International Finance Discussion Papers Number 694, December, Washington.

Howell, L. (2001) *The Handbook of Country and Political Risk Analysis*. East Syracuse, NY: The PRS Group.

Inderbrand Corporation (2006) 'The 100 best global brands', *Business Week*, 9–16 August. pp. 58–61.

Johnson, G. and Sholes, K. (2002) *Exploring Corporate Strategy*, 6th edn. Harlow: FT Prentice Hall.

Kirzner, I. (1973) *Competition and Entrepreneurship*. Chicago: University of Chicago Press.

Knickerbocker, F. (1973) *Oligopolistic Reaction and Multinational Enterprise*. Boston: Division of Research, Graduate School of Business Administration, Harvard University.

Kogut, B. and Zander, U. (1993) 'Knowledge of the firm and the evolutionary theory of the multinational corporation', *Journal of International Business Studies*, 24(4): 625–45.

Krugman, P. and Venables, A. (1995) *The Seamless World: A Spatial Model of International Specialization*, CEPR Discussion Papers 1230, C.E.P.R. Discussion Papers.

Lamfalussy, A. (1997) *Address*, President of the European Monetary Institute, to the Euromoney Conference in New York, 30 April 1997.

Nello, S. (2005) *The European Union. Economics, Policies and History*. Maidenhead: McGraw-Hill.

Rugman, A. and Collinson, S. (2006) *International Business*, 4th edn. Harlow: Pearson Education.

Smith, Adam (1776) *Inquiry into the Nature and Causes of the Wealth of Nations*. ed. Edwin Cannan (1904 5th edn) London: Methuen and Co., Ltd

Suder, G. (1994) 'Anti-dumping measures and the politics of EU–Japan create relation in the European consumer electronic sector: the VCR case'; PhD dissertation, University of Bath; Working Paper, Thomson Consumer Electronics external relations department.

Suder, G. (2006) *Corporate Strategies Under International Terrorism and Adversity*. Cheltenham: Edward Elgar.

Vernon, R. (1966) 'International investment and international trade in the product cycle', *Quarterly Journal of Economics*, 80: 190–207.

Volvo Company (2004) Company News Feed (formerly Regulatory News Service), March.

UNCTAD (2005) [1992/(1996] in John M. Letiche (ed.) *International Economic Policies and their Theoretical Foundations*, Toronto: Academic Press, PP. 415–35. *Expected modes of global investments 2005–2006*, Prospect assessment, www.unctad.org/fdiprospects.

6 The Europeanization of Business Management

What you will learn about in this chapter
• The cultural differences and similarities in European management.
• The Europeanization of business management, and the challenges of social and employment policy in this context.
• Does a European strategy make sense?
• The importance of intellectual property rights in Europeanized business.
• Subsidiary management and knowledge transfer issues.

Introduction

Does management Europeanize too? This chapter will inquire into this question through a quest of management styles and cultures. In all EU Member States, distinct management styles, cultures and structures, and resulting management and HR issues can be identified. This chapter will therefore deal with a synthesis of these distinctions and their complementarities for Europeanized business through the examination of key themes. Also, you will learn about some of the main issues that managers have to adapt to in a large marketplace, such as intellectual property rights. Finally, the organizational structures that managers use to adapt, and the particularity of diversity and knowledge management in Europe will be considered.

6.1 Does business management Europeanize?

A World Bank study into certain business operations (presented in Table 16), ranks a set of countries as the best and worst performers in the world. Interestingly, few of them are EU Member States: EU members are in fact situated in the middle. Is this caused by Europeanization? Does a European management exist, on the basis of European competence, culture, identity, and leadership qualities? Does a unique European way make sense in business management? We will now discuss these issues from a cross-cultural management and strategy perspective, while the following chapters will shed light on financial, marketing, regulatory and international challenges to European business performance.

Table 16   A ranking of best performance in various business operation areas

Ease of ...	Economy rank	Best performer	Worst performer
Doing business	3	New Zealand	Democratic Republic of Congo
Starting a business	3	Canada	Angola
Dealing with licences	17	Palau	Tanzania
Hiring and firing	6	Palau	Burkina Faso
Registering property	12	New Zealand	Nigeria
Getting credit	15	United Kingdom	Cambodia
Protecting investors	7	New Zealand	Afghanistan
Paying taxes	30	Maldives	Belarus
Trading across borders	17	Denmark	Iraq
Enforcing contracts	10	Norway	Timor-Leste
Closing a business	17	Japan	West Bank and Gaza

Source: World Bank – Doing Business in 2006, URL: http://www.doingbusiness.org/EconomyRankings/

It can be argued that harmonization, of business opportunities and challenges, is the driving force for coherence or quasi-convergence of European business management: the phenomenon is interesting to European managers and to non-European managers alike as a matter of comprehension of business attitudes.

6.2 Intercultural management in Europe

With its conception of unity, Europe constitutes in reality a microcosm of *diversity* that experiences convergence around certain common interests. In the increasingly global and multicultural world of European business, managers hence need to understand how people act and react in national, international and even locally based organizations. Even more importantly, any company seeking to do business outside the comfortable base of its own culture is dependent on a sound comprehension of *mindsets*. This comprehension, or expertise, facilitates relations to customers and clients, suppliers, intermediates, distributors or agents, and also to those public officials whose backgrounds and cultural expectations may be quite different from one's own. Moreover the *culture of an organization* is not expressed in a singular and unique trait, but by its diverse and ever-changing management process.

The culture of a company depends on sector(s), professions, goods and/or services, diversity of employees' and employers' backgrounds, its origin and the markets that the company operates in. Much value is created by business management that is capable to adapt to an environment that is intrinsically and inevitably multicultural.

Increasingly, the same is true of organizations that function in a purely 'national' context, because diversity is the norm in Europe. Corporate Europe is reflected not only in a broad, multicultural customer base, fast communication between people and organizations, strong corporate power, but also in environmental pressure and turbulence stemming from different points of view and perspectives. These pressures must find their answer in efficient diversity management.

Europeans share an increasing set of common traits. For example, cross-border preoccupations focus upon the impact of such issue as environmental hazards, natural disasters, poverty in the world, global warming and rising sea levels, the Kondratieff cycle, epidemic diseases, civil destabilization and global conflict and terrorism. Many of these preoccupations are based on historical experiences, and Europeans look out for peace through multilateral coordination and try to understand the impact of risks and conflicts so as to deal with them better. The desire for steady growth, open boundaries and a cosmopolitan community are based on this.

At the same time, Europeans have a historico-cultural tendency to fear nationalism, war and military conflict, but also a crisis of the welfare systems through demographic changes, an increase of unemployment, and inequalities. The notion of Europe therefore encompasses a strong psychic dimension, of shared fears and of confidence in a better management of those challenges together, rather than separately.

6.3 A management definition of culture

For business management, the focus on culture necessitates the study of:

- systems of shared ideas;
- the value of diversity;
- conceptual designs supporting learned behaviours;
- beliefs, values, norms;
- patterns of symbols and artifacts;
- the sum total of all of these in relation to the specific corporate culture of one's firm.

Efficient European business management is prepared to cope with various languages (verbal and non-verbal). The challenge is to always find a solution in a multi-language environment, and to make sure that a common language is found for negotiation. Sound language skills help significantly for information-gathering and evaluation. Language provides access to local societies, ensures that company communication is efficient, communicates in the right way, and reduces the risk of cross-cultural misunderstanding – and thus of corporate disaster. A general recommendation is to speak and write at least three languages that give essential access to communications in Europe, that is, German, French and English. Interestingly, these three languages are also the three relay languages at the EU institutions' language centres, that is, the languages that permit translation between two other languages.

In the spoken language, the interpretation of contexts that influence business operations also includes non-verbal signals: this includes mainly an interpretation of time, space, body and facial expressions, social patterns and behaviours, and agreements. The analysis of any announced message therefore includes various criteria that influences the reaction of the receiving party. The criteria are:

- pronunciation;
- speech rate;
- message content;
- code-competence and code-switching competence.

Humour, in the context of business management, can be important in some cultures more than in others. Some companies may even be a victim of such humour, as illustrated in Box 29 with examples from Galicia in Spain.

Box 29   Cross-cultural complexity: jokes

Humour is an excellent tool that helps us to understand cultures. In addition, laughter breaks down possible cross-cultural frontiers. Here are some examples from Spain:

Porqué los gallegos cuando se ponen crema en la cara, cierran los ojos ? Porque la crema dice <<Nivea>>. = Why do Galicians close their eyes when applying facial cream? Because it may be the facial cream marked 'Nivea' (Don't look).

Porqué cuando los Gallegos se lavan los dientes, se cuelgan? Porque en la pasta dice <<Colgate>>. = Why would Galicians hang themselves when they brush their teeth? Because the toothpaste is called 'Colgate' (Hang yourself).

A given culture is certainly evident to you if you are inside and part of it, but it may be baffling if you're outside. You may consider it strange, threatening, or exotic; it may be acquired with difficulty, and it may not readily change from outside influences. This is often so when one thinks of other religions, customs, and the variables that give a certain identity to individuals and groups. Such variables, on which cultural traits depend in that they both characterize and reinforce one's community adherence include:

- religion;
- values and attitudes;
- manners and customs;
- material elements;
- aesthetics;
- education;
- social institutions.

From the list above, for example, education – that from parents, institutions, media and publications we choose to look at, travel and our surroundings as a whole – shapes our mindsets and our way of thinking and behaving in a particular situation.

Another illustrative example is that of time, that is, a notion that becomes relative and situation-dependent, but its interpretation mainly depends on cultural contexts. Manners related to time are learned from the social environment, from institutions, and from educational contexts at any given moment in life; attitudes towards time shift when one changes any of these three variables over a longer period. This goes further than punctuality. In negotiations in southern Europe, for instance, the first meeting may be just to get to know one another and it can well take several meetings to get to the business. In northern Europe, the first meeting is about business immediately. Hall and Hall (1990: 15) also analysed time in terms of *monochronic* and *polychronic* commitments. *Monochronicity* translates into dealing with one issue at a time, along deadlines, with high focus on the job, on short-term relationships, low contexts, and a need for information inputs to enable this promptness. *Polychronicity* is characterized by dealing with several issues at a time, with flexible timeframes and roles, a focus on high contexts (attention to the unspoken), and a dedication to long-term relations that share information.

The challenge for companies that work across borders and across cultures is to reduce the gap that employees perceive between encountered cultures and their own, and to help them deal with this. This is to shorten the period of time that it takes employees to understand different ways of doing, of working and of knowledge, so that efficiency is maintained or increased rather than (even if only temporarily) lost because of 'culture shocks'.

Systems of shared ideas in one culture are, more often than not, not the same in another. They may appear complex, interpersonal, process-oriented or not, relational or contradictory. Many of these tensions are antithetical to our taught ways of doing things and to apprehending reality, especially in a 'scientific' context. So how can one survive in this 'jungle' of cultures? Is there *the* right way to communicate and to negotiate in a multicultural environment such as that in Europe? What will one need to expect as an 'expatriate' within Europe? How does one best prepare to deal with your partners or subsidiaries across Europe?

Carey (1989) developed communication models that explain the 'symbolic process whereby reality is produced, maintained, repaired and transformed'. Herein, communication is based on:

- the transmission of a given message;
- its translation;
- its interpretation.

These three stages take place, ideally, within an effort for reality-sharing, because the emitter/sender needs to ensure that the message is well understood. The message is only well understood when intentions, behaviours and interpretations surrounding the message are jointly believed to be viable, that is, when a certain level of *synergy* or *convergence* can be achieved between the communicator on the one hand, with one cultural background, and the receptor on the other, with possibly another background. For example, in recent times, sustainable development has become a focus for managers in very different countries, and messages about the business impact in this matter are convergent. With this, knowledge is transmitted more easily from one actor to another, and can be translated into different cultures, or even into common shared legislation, and the protection of ideas and concepts.

Synergy is, in most cases, partially obtainable only: it is situation-dependent. However, following the argument that diversity adds value, any complete and entire synergy would kill that value of diversity, and hence be negative for a corporation, because it would be common to others (if not all). A speaker with a banking background from London expects an audience with a banking background in Frankfurt to have 'appropriate' synergy originating from competence and from appropriate norms for language use. However, the speaker is deceived if perspectives on banking issues do not diverge because of the 'brainstorming' effect that these divergences have. If the speaker does not make any effort to seek the values of synergy and from diversity, this will normally be perceived as negative, even more than is incompetence (Giles and Noels, 2002; see also their other numerous publications in the field). Hasn't the different eating culture of Europeans helped McDonald's improve its customer services and product lines (Grant, 2006)? Haven't country cultures that are supportive of innovation, R&D and technologies (such as Sweden, the UK and the Netherlands) changed the EU-wide (sometimes skeptical) acknowledgement of the economic potential of GM (genetically modified) crops for farmers, the food industry and European economic development?

For companies, culture also has a direct impact on negotiations. Negotiation may well be easier with similar counterparts abroad (not sharing the same common national or regional culture) than with unsimilar counterparts at home (sharing that culture but not sharing that of professions or of complementarities): when doing business across borders, it would be easiest to start with firms that are similar in terms of ownership and organization (Sparrow et al., 2004), because of comparable business and sector cultures. In this case, *business and sector culture advantages opposed to national and regional cultural divergence* grant a higher probability of return on investment in the negotiation and operation phases than *common national and regional cultural traits and advantages of similarity opposed to business and sector divergence*. For example, it may be easier for an Italian textile producer to handle negotiations with a Polish or Russian counterpart in the same or complimentary sector, than to negotiate with a Spanish banker about the funding of the operation.

Also, human resources management is directly affected by cultures. National institutional contexts are rather predominant in this field, that is, in Europe, subject to EU efforts to complement or – in the long run – substitute certain sets of national legislation (through, for example, the part- and fixed time directives of 1999 for equal employment protection for both status). Earlier examples are the Regulation 1408/71 of 1971 that was to facilitate mobility within Europe by offering the possibility to the secondees to remain in their previous social security scheme, given the diversity of social security systems in Europe. It applies for limited periods (1 + 1 years) only, with an extension up to five years, but, again due to the differences in systems, is technically very complex to implement.

Furthermore, the field of information and consultation of employee representatives is regulated at European level, starting with the 1994 European Directive introducing European Works Councils (Council Directive 94/45/EC of 22 September 1994). The broad-scale use of contingent employment practices (that is, 'the ability to adapt without undue pain or cost to the requirements of the market' – Tregariskis and Brewster, 2006: 112) through different types of employment contract is facilitated, in some Member States more than in others, by social security, trade union support and employment protection (Koene et al., 2004)

The EU thus aims to encourage companies in specific areas to facilitate mobility in order to avoid classical lay-offs as far as possible, and to provide subsidies for mobility and training. The ESF launched actions to fight against some potential discrimination: The Quinqua

Competencies Project is an example of this: it analyses the impact of the ageing of salaried employees on cross- border companies; the Franco-German–Spanish helicopter company Eurocopter was acting as one pilot company for this project. The challenge in this context is to adapt and explain retirement policies according to the evolution of legislation, the social rules and conventions; manage the transfer of competencies between generations; enhance and manage the ends of careers along adapted remuneration and recognition criteria; and define organization and working hours (that is, flexible time, part-time, full-time). Part of this involves the adaptation of workstations and their environment to the challenges of European human resources (HR) policies in response to demographic and economic necessities (ageing workforce, equality, etc.).

Of course, diversity management across borders and cultures is a highly complex matter. Comparative research into management styles and norms reveal, however, that in similar institutional and cultural contexts, one can expect similar systems, for example in HR policies. Predominantly, the separation is made between the Anglo-Saxon cluster and the Rhineland cluster in Europe, though hybrid systems exist (Koen, 2005). Table 17 compares the two.

Table 17   A tentative comparison of two selected HR models in Europe

The Anglo-Saxon model	The so-called Rhineland model
Short-term benefits (contracts; recruitment based on technical or experience match; high wage disparencies; profit-sharing or reward upon individual merit and position)	Long-term orientations (contacts; recruitment policies based on complete reviews of files, interviews, references, aptitude testing; performance-related reward for group)
A highly flexible and fluid labor market (few in-house promotions, hire and fire)	Low degrees of flexibility of labour markets (dismissal complex)
Generalist management training (business-school type)	Specialist management education (engineering, sciences, law, etc.) and in-house training
Low degree of vocational training	Close industrial relations (important union and bargaining structures)
High degree of specialization of staff	Low staff specialization (in-house mobility)

Source: adapted from Koen, 2005; 198–243

Not only HR management, but every level of the corporate value chain (most commonly studied alongside Porter, 1987, as explained in Chapter 5) is affected by cultures, ideally by the search for useful synergies. This allows business to preserve the benefits of diversity. In HR, different backgrounds allow for a range of perspectives that are useful with staff that travels, works, and/or lives across borders, but also, technological development benefits from a diversity of education, conceptual thinking, preferences in design, and an understanding of consumer needs and desires. In procurement, cultural diversity helps by giving a wider perspective to what is happening in the field and where opportunities lie; in logistics and in operations, value is added when execution excels through transnational knowledge, which is a key to marketing, sales and service efficiencies and effectiveness across Europe (Schueffel and Istria, 2006).

6.4 Crucial cross-cultural and convergence management methodology

Management across borders necessitates an expertise of cross-cultural management methodology that can be acquired through training or experience. On the one hand, the advantage of training is that trainees show a fast learning curve in regard to reference points that are useful when facing particular situations. On the other hand, nothing can replace real experience, because training always *stereotypes* to some extent. Also, monocultural staff may experience subconscious barriers to the penetration of other cultures and therefore, if selected for an international assignment because of rare professional competence in the firm, need particular attention. The selection of adapted staff is hence key to cross-border efficiency, as detailed in Box 30.

Box 30   The value added when joining the two methodologies of training and experience

- the level and frequency of cross-cultural clashes are reduced;
- the adaptation phase to foreign cultures is shortened;
- the efficiency of managers in a foreign environment is immediate.

This efficiency is strongly influenced by what can be called the 'life cycle of adaptation' that the international manager is living. Danckwortt (1959) is one of the precursors of this life cycle, and separated the cultural adaptation process into the four main periods of observation, interpretative and consolidation phase, and the leaving phase. The key to multicultural management is the creation of trust and confidence between cultures. Though European cultures are relatively similar, each of them has a particular way of achieving this feeling of *security* that:

- drives common achievements on business operations level;
- motivates people;
- enhances efficient communication.

While each business case is different, common models and concepts help calculate potential options to exploit and traps to avoid. Hofstede's five fundamental cultural dimensions (see Box 31), researched across a sample of 55 countries, offer this kind of help. An early acquisition of expertise about a host country's cultural dimension, set in relation to its own culture, reduces the country-of-origin effects of cross-cultural management: this is the reason why we will also now structure our discussion along Hofstede's principles.

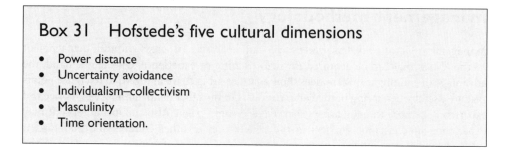

Box 31   Hofstede's five cultural dimensions

- Power distance
- Uncertainty avoidance
- Individualism–collectivism
- Masculinity
- Time orientation.

6.4.1 Large or small power-distance culture

Power distance highlights the way in which less powerful members of a society accept that power is distributed unequally. In large power-distance cultures, such as in Belgium, France, Poland and Portugal, everybody has his or her place in a hierarchy. In the UK, Germany, the Netherlands and Scandinavia, this idea of hierarchy is less important and more transparent. These countries are said to be in cultures of small power distance. Hierarchies are rather flat in these societies, and the focus on collaboration of different power levels is higher. Management decisions, negotiations, HR policies and business–government relations are influenced by the power-distance culture.

6.4.2 Individualist or collectivist culture

In individualist cultures people emphasize their own concerns, even those of their own family, and want to differentiate themselves from others. In collectivist cultures people belong to in-groups, which support them in exchange for loyalty, and are preoccupied with a common goal rather than an individual one. In collectivist cultures, the need for harmony may translate into higher degrees of conformity and acceptance of challenges. Northern Europeans are typically considered as tending towards individualism, and the south of Europe as rather collectivist. The goals of your staff, management and corporate culture are mainly influenced by this culture; for example, your reward policy may need to vary from one geographically based business unit to another. Also, we can argue that a public sector entity is by nature one that is driven by collectivist goals, though that does not imply that all individuals herein are driven by collectivism in their career management. This leads us to the awareness that culture is not only linked to nationality but also to industries, sectors, professions, and other factors.

6.4.3 Masculine or feminine culture

In masculine cultures, the dominant values are achievement and success. The dominant values in feminine cultures include care for others and quality of life, the focus on performance and achievement is less important while key for pride in masculine cultures. In addition, status is not interpreted equally in the two approaches. In Europe, a tendency towards masculinity can be found in the cultures of the UK and Italy. Examples of feminine cultures are the Netherlands, and the Scandinavian countries. Depending on the origin of your company, the origin of its executives or that of the majority of its employees, the Europeanized enterprise will tend to satisfy more than one or the other culture. For example, employees may push for involvement in social and humanitarian initiatives that stimulate the corporate culture through ethical standards and stakeholder satisfaction. Conversely, a company may focus its corporate governance on shareholder satisfaction and translate this into an essentially Milton Friedman-type of profit focus. Friedman, the recipient of the 1976 Nobel Memorial Prize for economic science, forwarded in *Capitalism and Freedom* (1962), that corporate social responsibility (CSR) is a 'fundamentally subversive doctrine' in a free society, and that in such a society, 'there is one and only one social responsibility of business – to use its resources and engage in activities designed to increase its profits so long as it stays within the rules of the game, which is to say, engages in open and free competition without deception or fraud'. We can then assume that its CSR initiatives are driven by marketing and communication objectives rather than deep long-term moral and resource-related investments. This does not necessarily connect to the individualism or collectivism measures.

6.4.4 High or low uncertainty avoidance

Uncertainty avoidance is the extent to which people feel threatened by uncertainty and ambiguity, and hence try to avoid these scenarios. In cultures of strong uncertainty avoidance, rules and formality provide for a feeling of structure and security. In weak uncertainty avoidance cultures people tend to be more innovative and entrepreneurial, in other words more risk-taking. The countries of south and east Europe score highly on uncertainty avoidance, England and Scandinavia lower.

Hofstede's dimensions (Box 31), though accused of a certain rigidity by some, allow for helpful insights into the way in which both HR management and business negotiations need to be ruled by flexibility and understanding of diversities. Aviat et al. (2007) demonstrate that, on the basis of a gravity equation model, countries with common borders trade more with each other than others. Frankel and Rose (2002) illustrated earlier that market integration stimulates trade, being linked to factors such as informational content of international trade costs: 'Trade between people who know each other is less costly and as a consequence people who belong to the same social networks trade more' (Aviat et al., 2007; 6). This increases the probability that business in Europe encounters multicultural issues and complexities. Historico-anthropologically speaking, the precondition of any intercultural value is positioned in social links between societies or groups of a society.

Any lack or loss of unity and trust potentially leads to the risk that a society or organisation may be divided or destroyed.

The European cultures have increased its peoples' common economic, societal and even political links; this provides a feeling of belonging to a shared cultural space that underlies social, economic and political cohesion – and hence a prosperous breeding ground for transnationality of business. The feelings that define this cohesion, that is, the identity of the European people, is based on the identification of what is shared ('us') and what is different ('the other'). Only this in- and out-group identification (subconsciously often more than consciously) enables the construction of a true European identity (Box 32). On the one hand, the sussessful construction of European relations over old fractures is in itself a shared 'us' – a characteristic that (situated in time rather than in space) separates contemporary Europeans from 'the other', that is, the past wars and conflict. Demorgon (2005), particularly, stresses this basis of a European culture in that antagonisms can, by use of adaptive mechanisms that benefit from the overlaps that always exist, turn from hostility to emotive and cognitive conditions for intercultural comprehension. On the other hand, economic competition helps identify the 'other' in terms of space (markets), GDP, corporate revenue and similar characteristics.

Box 32   A 'European tribe'?

Feeling excluded from the 'European tribe', Caryl Philips stated that '… a large part of finding out who I was, and what I was doing here, would inevitably mean having to understand Europeans … They all seemed to share a common and mutually inclusive, but culturally exclusive culture.'

Source: Phillips, a British national of African–Carribean descent (1987)

European management needs to be responsive, proactive, flexible and information-based in order to make it through the European complexity of cultures. Qualifications for managers that work across borders clearly are different to those that are recruited for local assignments only. Also, for those working in local firms but relating to non-local customers, distributors, suppliers and partners need to be caies (ageing workforce, equality, etc.).

Of course, diversity management across borders and cultures is a highly complex matter. Comparative research into management styles andEffective and efficient business is optimal in the case of information convergence from different people, cultures and markets, such as that found in intellectual property (IP) rights, which is the issue of international multicultural perceptions about property. While we can expect that cultures shape attitudes in regard to the importance and economic sense of IP rights, they are a splendid example of converging norms and values across diverse markets, and their importance.

6.5 Intellectual property: A case for convergence

A recent study of culture, work dependence and local embeddedness (Newburry and Yakova, 2006) demonstrates clearly that, on the basis of sound research data from the public relations sector, employees from high power distance, high uncertainty avoidance and high-context cultures are more likely to favour standardization. In marketing, factors resulting in standardization preferences have also been studied (Laroche et al., 2001). In these studies, standardization is recognized to have an effect on cost-saving, coherency-raising, improved planning and control, and greater ease to exploit ideas (Buzzel, 1968). This leads directly to a reflection upon the utility of IP protection as a case of convergence and synergy. You will note that Europeanization of IP is very much dependent on international synergies and regulations based upon these.

IP refers to creations of the mind: inventions, literary and artistic works, and symbols, names, images, and designs used in commerce. In Europe, as much as in international business in general, IP is important to preserve and costly to lose for a business. As we will see in this section, it is well protected in Europe.

Areas that IP covers, include:

- Patents
- Trade marks
- Industrial designs
- Geographic source designations
- Copyright.

It is divided into two categories: *industrial property*, which includes inventions (patents), trade marks, industrial designs, and geographic source designations; and *copyright*, including literary and artistic works (such as novels, poems and plays), films, musical works, and other artistic works (such as drawings, paintings, photographs and sculptures), and architectural designs. Those rights encompass artists' performances, producers' recordings, and broadcasters' radio and television programmes.

By definition, a *patent* is an exclusive right granted for an *invention*, that is, a product or process that provides a new way of doing something, or offers a new technical solution to a problem. But does an invention differ from an idea, and when is it named an innovation? An invention can be considered as the creation of an *idea*, while an innovation is its adoption (Rogers, 1995). For an idea to be adopted, and hence to turn into an innovation in the long-term, it must be shaped so that it can be understood by a recipient. This requires that the idea takes a form that is compatible with the norms and beliefs (the culture) held by the recipient of the idea. The process of turning an invention into an innovation is therefore *culturally biased* and the impact of a given innovation on a foreign culture cannot be anticipated using cultural traits other than those of the receiving culture.

An interpretive process (Strang and Soule, 1998; 276) is, then, a prerequisite in the diffusion of ideas. The recipient understands the innovation through the perspective of their own cultural norms and beliefs. Lillrank (in Rogers, 1995) suggested that ideas have to be put in an abstract form for 'export' (Suder and Lefevre, 2006). Ideally, these abstract forms are then reinterpreted into another culture and adapted accordingly. According to diffusion theory, ideas that are easy to understand in this abstract form spread rapidly and widely, while those difficult to understand or in conflict with a given culture are abandoned. People and cultures, and their management as recipient or source of a message are hence crucial to business management in a complex environment such as the European one. Remember our jokes (see Box 29) that illustrate how different receivers of a same message can (mis-)interpret it.

Well defined, their proper identification and protection as your *property* is also crucial. Once you are awarded the patent, protection for an invention to the owner of the patent is granted for a limited period of time that generally covers 20 years. This patent protection excludes the invention's commercial make, use, distribution or sale without the patent owner's consent. As the patent owner, you may give permission to, or license, other parties to use the invention on mutually agreed terms. You may also decide to sell the right to the invention to someone else, who will then become the new owner of the patent. Infringement of these patent rights is judged in court, and a court can also declare a patent invalid. For example, after the communication about an invention, the right to claim it as a patent may have been lost or the innovation may not be unique. Patents provide incentives to individuals by offering them recognition for their creativity and material reward for their marketable inventions. These incentives encourage innovation, which assures that the quality of human life is continuously enhanced. Patented inventions can be found from electric lighting (patents held by Edison and Swan) and plastic (patents held by Baekeland), to ballpoint pens (patents held by Biro) and microprocessors (patents held by Intel, for example). All patent owners are obliged, in return for patent protection, to publicly disclose information on their invention in order to enrich the total body of technical knowledge in the world. Such a seemingly unlimited pool of public knowledge promotes further creativity and innovation in others.

The first step in securing a *patent* is the filing of a patent application. The patent application generally contains the title of the invention, as well as an indication of its technical field; it must include the background and a description of the invention in clear language and in enough detail so that an individual with an average understanding of the field could use or reproduce the invention. Visual materials such as drawings, plans or diagrams accompany the file to illustrate the invention. The application also contains various 'claims', that is, information which determines the extent of protection granted by the patent. An invention must, in general, fulfil the certain specific conditions to be protected by a patent, in that it must be of practical use and show an element of novelty, to add on the body of existing knowledge, called 'prior art'. Also, it must be considered as 'patentable' under law, and you must be the 'first to file'. If these conditions are satisfied, the patent is then granted by a national patent office or by a regional office that does the work for a number of countries, such as the European Patent Office (www.european-patent-office.org) if you chose to cover the single market area. However, going past European frontiers, the World Intellectual Property Organization (WIPO)-administered Patent Cooperation Treaty (PCT) allows for the filing of a single international patent application with the same effect as national applications that would be filed in the designated countries (Box 33). With one application, you may request protection in as many signatory states as necessary. Consequently, your invention cannot be commercially made, used, distributed or sold without the patent owner's agreement. A court can ensure the patent owner's rights in case of infringement, or also declare a patent invalid due the rightful recourse by a third party. For comparison, in the US you will be subject to the 'first to invent' (instead of the 'first to file') principle, in which the patent is attributed to a name of inventor (individual or group); in this market, it is easier to risk communication about an invention because the law allows for a one-year period after the first communication to ask and obtain the patent (www.uspto.com)

Box 33   Main treaties governing patent law in Europe and internationally

The Paris Convention; signed by 164 states, grants (1) a one-year priority, from your national deposit onwards, for international filing; and (2) that communication about the innovation does not inhibit your patent rights.

The Patent Cooperation Treaty (Treaty of Washington, 19 June 1970); provides the possibility to deposit the same patent in 121 countries simultaneously.

The Munich Convention on European patents (5 October 1973); helps to obtain the European patent, which has the same characteristics as the national patent, covering 27 countries.

Cooperation and European patents can be obtained from national IP agencies (such as the French 'Institut National de la Propriété Industrielle'; www.inpi.fr)

What is the difference with a trade mark? A *trade mark*, a distinctive sign, serves to identify goods or services as those produced or provided by a certain person or enterprise only. The first objective of trade marks is to make sure that consumers identify and purchase a product or service with a specific image, reputation, nature and/or quality through words, letters, and numerals, or other signs. Simultaneously, the owner of the trade mark enjoys exclusive use of its rights, or can authorize others to use these rights in return for payment. Therefore, trade marks foster recognition and financial profit. Renewed simply via the payment of additional fees, trade marks can be held for as long as judged necessary. Again, protection is enforced by the courts against counterfeiters who could potentially use similar marks to market inferior or different products or services.

The registration of a trade mark requires an application to an appropriate national or regional trade mark office. A reproduction of the sign filed for registration, including any colours, forms, or three-dimensional features is needed, and a list of goods or services to which the sign would apply. The applicant must demonstrate that the sign is sufficiently distinctive, so that consumers identify it as a particular product or service clearly separate from other existing trade marks. Most countries in the world register and protect trade marks, with offices that maintain a Register of Trade marks that contains all application information on registrations and renewals. WIPO again allows for international registration of marks, on the basis of the Madrid Agreement Concerning the International Registration of Marks and the Madrid Protocol, cover over 60 countries.

Industrial designs help protect a very large array of industrial and handicraft products, including, for instance, electrical appliances and textile designs. The design must be recognizable from an aesthetic viewpoint, but the protection does not cover its technical features; the first objective here is the marketability of the product. The protection against unauthorized copying or imitation of the design by third parties is meant to encourage creativity, and also to preserve and boost traditional arts and crafts. A new industrial design must be registered in order to be protected under industrial design law, but this is generally inexpensive. The registration certificate issued grants a term of protection of mostly five years, but can often be extended to 15 years. Generally, industrial design protection is limited to the country in which protection is granted. Under the Hague Agreement Concerning the International Deposit of Industrial Designs, another WIPO-administered treaty, a procedure for an international registration is possible.

Geographical source indications are signs used on goods that have a specific geographical origin relating the product or service characteristics to those created in that place of origin. A place name, for example, may be that of perfume from Paris, English tea or Belgian chocolate. The efficiency of such signs in terms of market share or financial profits depends on national law and consumer perception. However, in the EU, geographical source indications are required by law, and protected under European regulation. An appellation of origin is a particular case for products that have a certifiable exclusivity quality, or one that is substantially due to the geographically dependent climate, resources, or handicrafts. In contrast to a trade mark, the geographical source indications may be used by all producers who make their products in the place designated by a geographical indication and whose products share typical qualities.

The *laws against unfair competition, consumer protection laws, laws for the protection of certification marks* or *special laws for the protection of geographical indications* or *appellations of origin* give the basis for this protection. From national to regional to international agreements, the WIPO again provides protection, this time mainly based on the negotiations at the Paris Convention for the Protection of Industrial Property of 1883, and the Lisbon Agreement for the Protection of Appellations of Origin and International Registration. Also, the Agreement on Trade-Related Aspects of Intellectual Property Rights (TRIPS) covers the matter, this time within the framework of the WTO. In some countries where protection extends over a lengthy period of time, consumers transpose geographical terms, for example Dijon mustard, a style of mustard originally from the French town of Dijon, to a type of product, even if not produced at the location. The same may happen to trade marks of specific companies, such as Scotch and Tesafilm for adhesive tape.

A different case of protection is that of *copyright*, in which rights protect creators for their literary and artistic works. This applies to works such as novels, poems, plays, reference works, newspapers and computer programs; databases; films, musical compositions, and choreography; artistic works such as paintings, drawings, photographs and sculpture; architecture; and advertisements, maps and technical drawings. The rights protect the original creators of works protected by copyright, and their heirs who hold exclusive right for their use – prohibiting or granting to a third party the reproduction, public performance, recording, broadcasting, translation or adaptation within a time-limit (under WIPO legislation, this is 50 years after the creator's death). Interestingly, filing for national law protection may establish longer time-limits than these. No official filing is necessary for copyrights because the works pure existence is protected at once, as explained in the Berne Convention for the Protection of Literary and Artistic Works, for example. Copyright offices and laws, however, help identify works that can be useful in case of infringements On the Internet, the 1996 WIPO treaties protect authors of literary and artistic works, such as writings and computer programs; original databases; musical works; audio-visual works; works of fine art and photographs. In addition, the WIPO Performances and Phonograms Treaty (WPPT), protects certain rights of performers and producers of recordings.

IP protection in Europe, if not filed under WIPO, does not cover the US or other third party markets. In manufacture, in services or in capital markets, successful companies protect innovations that may relate to sales; for example outsourcing, with or without technology transfer, through the Contract Research Organization (CRO) and the Contract Manufacturing Organizations (CMO). For the company that works across borders, national protection does not suffice because it most often engages in the transfer of know-how, programmes, license-in or license-out for specific periods, or the transfer of patents if the innovation is to be sold or joint ventured.

IP laws preserve the values and ethical basis of business management in different societies with regard to creativity, knowledge and innovation, which are the underlying elements for a sound corporate culture. The satisfaction of stake- and shareholders depends on these values; harmonization of European and international norms is essential for this type of return on investment: through convergence of principles and behaviours.

6.6 Commonalities about equality?

IP is a clear case for convergence at the European level for enhanced innovation across a highly diverse and culturally promising market. A different scenario can be observed when it comes to equality issues. This area in particular shows how difficult the path to common laws and standards is in many other fields that are directly or indirectly linked to efficient business management.

Women are better educated and hold more jobs worldwide than ever before. However, most women continue suffering from occupational segregation in the workplace and rarely break through the 'glass ceiling' separating them from top-level managerial positions. The term 'glass ceiling' is used to describe the invisible barriers (prejudices, social attitudes, cultural biases) barring women from top executive jobs. The International Labor Organization (ILO) reports that despite progress in closing the gender gap in managerial jobs, the glass ceiling is still relatively intact. For example, women hold less than 5 per cent of the top jobs in corporations even though they represent more then 40 per cent of the world labour force. Statistics and international surveys have also shown that even when women achieve high-level positions, these are restricted to areas considered less strategic for the company, and they nearly always earn less than men, although Treaties of Rome Article 119 stipulates 'equal pay for equal work'. Note also that among Community initiatives we can find *equal* ways of promoting equality of opportunities for both genders and disadvantaged groups, within a multifund system financing initiatives and projects in that area.

There has been increasing interest from enterprises recently in attracting qualified and talented women, and in addition, governments and enterprises have committed themselves to policies and programmes to enhance women in top management. We can see the gradual emergence of women to positions of power and some now hold the most important positions in their corporations, such as the CEO of Hewlett Packard in Singapore. In Europe, the most successful business women are ranked by publications such as the *Financial Times* (see 'Women in Business: Europe's Top 25', *Financial Times*, p. 18, 15 October 2005; *Financial Times Magazine*, 7 October 2006) and *The Wall Street Journal*'s '50 Women to Watch' list.

On the other hand, only 16 companies in the Fortune 100 are run by women. With this data it is evident that the share of management positions remains very low indeed. Equality between women and men has been one of the fundamental principles of the EU since the very beginning, and equal treatment legislation has continued to grow, while new programmes and policies have been developed. However, it is a fact that women and men do not enjoy equal rights in practice.

The legal base of the EU's gender mainstreaming is found in Articles 2, 3 and 23 of the EC Treaty, establishing that the promotion of equality is a task of the EC, that it shall aim to eliminate inequalities between women and men and that equality must be ensured in all areas. This communication confirms the Commission's present and future strategy on gender equality. Its purpose is to establish a framework for action within which all Community activities can contribute to attain the goal of eliminating inequalities and promoting equality between women and men. It actually works hand in hand with gender mainstreaming, thus making objectives easily met by the EU. One of the objectives of this framework strategy is to promote gender equality in economic life by strengthening the gender dimension in the European strategy, improving the use of the structural funds for the promotion of gender equality or developing strategies to encourage gender mainstreaming in all policies that have an impact on the place of women in the economy. This means focus on the adjustment of policies and/or the implementation of concrete actions designed to improve the situation of women in society. Inequality between women and men is a multidimensional phenomenon that has to be tackled by a comprehensive mix of policy measures. The challenge is to ensure policies that support equal opportunities for women and men in education, employment and career development, equal pay for equal work and balanced participation in decision making. The promotion of equality must not be confused with the simple objective of balancing the statistics; it is a question of promoting long-lasting changes and excelling in diversity management: the capitalization on personal diversity in a corporation's personnel, based on obvious (gender, skin colour, etc.) and non-obvious (ways of thinking and doing) characteristics of individuals or groups of individuals. The recognition and utilization of diversity in a firm then drives its flexibility and adaptation to the challenges of international competitiveness.

The agendas not only of the equality of gender but also of the equality of chances are continuously evolving through advances in cross-cultural convergence at the regulatory as well as corporate level. When cultures are shared and overlap increasingly (as pointed out above) and when the legislation allows its norms and values to reach the status of common sets of rules (as demonstrated with the IP example), then we can rightly argue that the equality issues will find increasing convergence too, and allow the European economy to benefit fully from equal chances, translating into rising household incomes, purchasing power, spending and, hence, economic growth.

Further convergence is also dependent on *trust* in values shared at the cross-border level, between countries and between corporations and their units. In the corporation, this is reinforced by the leadership qualities of a firm's management which, again, vary between one culture and another. This is what gives importance to the structure of the organization and to the factors in the business environment that help or hinder the manager in the area of subsidiary management that you will study in the following section.

6.7 The role of subsidiary management

The most common cross-border structures in Europe are functional structures, international divisional structures and products structures. Functional structures are usually used in the early stages of a company going European, since no international specialists are in place and only a few numbers of products are positioned in a limited number of cross-border market segments. When growing, the international divisional structure serves the company when it opts for standardized production or servicing in response to European consumer needs. In this structure, one particular division of the firm deals with all international business activities. Product structures are usually used in corporations that have acquired significant international experience. In this structure, each product or service division is in charge of its own R&D, production, marketing and sales departments. Many food, beverage, car and pharmaceutical companies in particular use a geographical structure in addition to the functional one, well adapted to a relatively homogeneous range of products that require a fast and efficient distribution channel. In this structure, each country department has its own production, marketing and financial services. Close to this is the matrix structure, organized under a two-dimension basis that emphasizes product and geographical areas, often all of Europe or as an EMEA region (Europe – Middle East – Africa). This structure is widely adopted in MNEs that have large ranges of product to sell in a geographically widespread market. Each subsidiary management depends on the firms' particular knowledge of the market, and the level and share of cross-border activity of the company. Stopford and Wells (1972) demonstrated that foreign product diversity and sales as a proportion of total sales encourages the turn to a matrix structure with geographical extended product divisions or area structures.

Hence, corporations change structure as they grow (Daniels et al., 1984, among others), and respond in this manner to the competing forces of local responsiveness and global integration (Bartlett and Goshal 1988; Prahalad and Doz, 1987; Rosenzweig and Singh 1991, among others). Some indications were found by Brock et al. (1999b) that those firms which use the highest integrative structures globally are less effective then those with relatively lower integration structures, arguing that going straight to standardized global structures hurts effectiveness; regional structures based on diversity values may hence be considered more efficient than (a) firms structured with low degrees of integration, that is, favouring locality or (b) highly globalized firms. The structures described above increase the involvement of business management at different degrees of cross-border activity if well adapted to localities only. We can argue that the more business management engages in Europeanization, the faster it climbs up structures that we can call the 'subsidiary management ladder'.

Indeed, a study published by the European Commission in the mid-2000s and realized by EOS Gallup Europe, based on the response of 200 companies, shows that the strengthening of organizational and human capital represents key assets to establish competitive advantage. This suggests that managing diversity has a real business asset which delivers long-term benefits. **Thanks to a multicultural Europe and an economic vitality of the European market place, European companies are well positioned to turn diversity into a source of growth and of motivation for its employees – and to structure its subsidiary management efficiently.** Companies know how to deal with local standards, adopt responsiveness and innovate accordingly. This may be very costly for SMEs in particular, but is a main key to survival. For MNEs, the advantages of a Europeanized business environment are easier to exploit, marrying responsiveness to innovative efforts. For instance, ST Microelectronics is continuously ranked number four in the world semiconductor industry because it continues to adopt a 'system on a chip' strategy by accessing and combining European knowledge. In the European companies that gained worldwide market share, we can note a successful management of corporate development by stimulating innovation and by sharing cross-European knowledge of different environments, socio-political institutions and cultures. European companies attain a learning curve of diversity that provides business with a diversity of knowledge applicable in the US and Asian markets. It was found that rapid growth of American companies in the EU is also due to this strategic orientation: Starbucks, for example, pays great attention to European behaviour, tastes and coffee cultures. This means that the described effects apply for European firms as much as they do for companies from non-EU countries that operate intensively and efficiently in the European market.

Early and rapidly internationalized structures can be found in *Born Globals*, that is, firms that are international by 'birth', such as global start-ups, instant globalization of high-technology firms, online services, IT (information technology) security solutions. These corporations, often of SME size, rely heavily on their network structure and the diversity of the value-added of each component of this structure: the advantages in the use of resources, procurement, distribution and cross-border sales characterize this form of diversification and corporate risk-reduction. At the same time, *Born Globals* need to be run with a global vision and a network relying on the know your customer, your supplier and your distributor principles more than traditionally internationalizing firms. In Europe, start-ups are increasingly *Born Europeans* given entrepreneurs' increasing awareness about the value creation that is possible through harmonized networks of transportation and communications, of market expertise through the proximity of European markets, and cross-cultural competences.

Subsidiaries are sometimes competing amongst each other and with local firms. The challenge is to use the best available structure so as to link knowledge retained in these subsidiaries to that relevant for efficient cross-border management (Brock et al., 1999a). The relatively low level of risk in Europe, coupled with resulting relatively high trust levels that issue from European integration on various levels reinforce a unique feature of internationalization: **European firms tend to move up the subsidiary ladder of structures in Europe faster and more voluntarily than when it comes to the internationalization of non-EU countries.**

The differences across Europe in culture and behaviour, in management styles, in factor efficiency, and in price competitiveness are responsible for cost and price differentials that do not quickly vanish despite a high degree of market harmonization efforts. They will, rather, lead to the rationalization and streamlining of an organization. Efforts to reduce costs include diversity management and the search for cost-beneficial overlap that are necessarily good for international competitiveness, and bad for those firms that do not succeed in coping. The structure of the organization helps or hinders the manager, and so does his or her ability to lead the organization efficiently.

6.8 The role of a leader

The necessary charisma and qualities of leadership and management constitute a set of features which vary between one culture and another. Recent studies (Fendt, 2005, a.o.) demonstrate that some overlap can be found that helps us characterize a successful European leader. A convincing leadership is a key competitive resource in cross-border structures and markets, and therefore essential in European business.

Because three-quarters of all international business assignments are connected with the transfer of knowledge (Weir, 2004), and because intercultural communication is an elementary skill area in these transactions, the leadership of a corporation can be characterized ideally by a profile that knows how to:

- involve and listen to people (motivate and stimulate effective interaction);
- work multiculturally (in terms of countries, cultures, sectors and professions);
- recognize value diversity (flexible, intuitive, based on a broad vision);
- converge and protect value (human resources', negotiations' and IP skills)
  (adapted from Calori and de Woot, 1994; 237, and Paulson et al., 2002; 410–11).

European business management is relationship-based, and engages economic determinism towards inescapable cultural convergence, with its leads and lags. While the role of managers consists essentially in rationality, control and problem-solving, the role of a leader reaches much further. Leadership in Europe is the art of recognizing the meaning of decisions and actions to a set of highly diversified people that are to share a common goal. The instrument for it is the recognition of what is shared and what can be shared by these people as individuals and collectively. Leadership is the power exerted 'in altering moods, evoking images and expectations, and in establishing specific desires and objectives, it determines the direction a business takes' (Zaleznik, 1992: 128).

The locus and transfer of knowledge management in the European single market is best distributed through the use of writings (texts, books, e-mails), training, (best) practices, and in particular through individuals that have expertise and that can be observed, asked and listened to – the latter being identified as a crucial element for efficient management and leadership. Suitable knowledge for a diversified European market is scientific, positivistic, or causal; it may be quantitative, linear, context-free, or public. Alternatively, it may be lay, narrative, exemplary, qualitative, recursive, and is surely context-bound and idiosyncratic. Its transfer, and hence its convergence at company level across borders, is largely dependent on trust; a sentiment that can be fostered by efficient leadership.

Box 34   What are the skills that a global manager should have? A European opinion

For me, a global manager knows how to coach a diverse array of people. This is a person who has good relations with people and is characterized by loyalty, people assets, and so on – a person who is willing to take chances, and work them through within a long-term approach. It is a listener who is careful to approach a decision. (Jean-Philippe Courtois, CEO Microsoft International, formerly CEO Microsoft EMEA)

Source: Suder, 2005

6.9 Trust and diversity

A 'diverse workforce … will increase organizational effectiveness. It will lift morale, bring greater access to new segments of the marketplace, and enhance productivity' (Thomas and Ely, 1996). This statement comes from an article entitled 'Making differences matter', diversity being the main research topic of Thomas and Ely in the *Harvard Business Review*, which reviews the topic (or similar ones) regularly: thinking of diversity management in a holistic manner is based on a feeling of trust that may foster or hinder knowledge transfer across cultures, along the paradigms (Thomas and Ely, 1996) of:

- discrimination and fairness: in HR management;
- access and legitimacy: in marketing and internationalization;
- learning and effectiveness: in knowledge management.

In academic literature, trust is typically classified as etic, that is, general or universal, or as emic, that is, culture-specific: these two notions help understand trust in cross-cultural business. They help understand which conditions, strategies and structures of a firm generate symmetries or asymmetries of trust. For example, what types of relation (communication tools, knowledge transfer tools ...) generate trust between subsidiaries, and, by consequence, may be acceptable to all or may be limited only to few individuals or units? In an alliance, what are the best available patterns of ownership and distribution of resources?

Lane (1977), in an analysis of the foundations of trust along cultures, found that they differ significantly in terms of the meaning and significance of trust and the manner in which it can be obtained. These conditions depend, in particular, on social and institutional characteristics of cultures. For example, in Germany technical expertise is one main precondition in the acknowledgement of managerial power, and in trust in managerial capabilities. However, personal relationships are predominant in trust-creation in Latin cultures. Stereotypes, though useful reference points for cross-cultural relations, may reduce trust-creation between partners in foreign countries (Zaheer and Zaheer 2006; Arino et al., 2001). Consequently, motivations and expectations are preconditioned by trust patterns and influence cross-border partnerships and operations in terms of investment volumes and investment modes, institutionalization of relations, internalization and knowledge transfer, monitoring and controlling (Zaheer and Zaheer, 2006).

Any culture-, gender-, or colour-blindness is detrimental to the values that originate in diversity. If the knowledge of any of a company's cultures (in headquarters and subsidiaries or at agents) is not fully taken into account, knowledge is not at its best.

The Europeanization of the business environment of more than 27 countries is a unique chance for corporations. In terms of business management, strategy, and knowledge management conditions, a firm has the opportunity to benefit from shared cultural, social, economic and business conditions that converge at a fast pace. In terms of the constant strive for competitive advantage, the Europeanization of this business environment underlies corporations' capabilities 'to integrate, build and reconfigure internal and external competences to address rapidly changing environments' (Teece et al., 1997). Its diversity makes organizations capable of identifying the most valid and promising conditions.

Résumé and conclusions

This chapter positioned Europeanization issues in the area of business management. It offered the chance to learn about the cultural differences and similarities in European management; and to reflect on the question of whether a European strategy makes sense, and whether that concerns the HR management or any other stages of the value chain that are influenced by diversity. We learned that diversity can be of great competitive advantage to corporations in many different fields. But also a certain convergence of interests, values and priorities in business helps it to

(Continued)

(Continued)

remain on top of the competition. The use of synergies and convergence facilitates the efficient application of resources and the protection of ideas and inventions. International property rights were the main example when studying convergence, but we also looked at equality issues, given their significance for economic growth and diversity value creation. The same phenomena of diversity and synergy were found in subsidiary management, across the value chain of business in Europe, and underline the utility of knowledge transfer.

Cultures, structures, roles and behaviour are ongoing but ever-changing challenges for the European firm, from the inside and the outside; they are essential to the evolution of a European self-concept and identity with its particular contexts, situations, personalities and leaders, literatures and emotions.

The knowledge and expertise of multiculturalism is a key competitive resource in global markets that is acquired day after day in the European business management. The following chapters shed light on those particular stages of the value chain and competitive edging that are crucially influenced by European diversity and convergence phenomena.

Mini case study: Consulting in Estonia with East Partners – bridging East and West

I still clearly remember the first time I was in Latvia. The year was 2000. I had been selected for a consulting project at very short notice, and flew to the capital Riga the next day. At the time I had been a management consultant in Helsinki, Finland, for only a year, and the Latvian assignment was one of the first projects where my role was more central. Our Latvian client was a large former state-owned monopoly, whose management was still very heavily politically connected.

For a young Finnish consultant everything about Latvia seemed different. Big companies placed guards (in dark green army uniforms) by all entrances, and all the buildings seemed to have an 'old world' feeling to them. As we approached the large oak doors of the company's headquarters, our project manager (who had some experience of doing business in Latvia) gave us some final advice: 'First, these people really value decades of experience, so don't bring up your age or limited time with our company. Second, you should know that in this country men don't shake hands with women.' A few seconds after these words the large oak doors were opened, and we proceeded to meet the management of the company in a large and gloomy hall-like room. And indeed, following what I later learned was commonly accepted business behaviour in Latvia at the time, the women in the room did not make any effort to shake our hands.

(Continued)

After that initial trip to Latvia I ended up returning there about 40 times during the next three years. I began to understand the Latvian mentality and all the challenges and opportunities linked with an economy in violent transition. Although the people and the culture could have been described as very different from a Nordic or western perspective, I realized that these differences were mostly about people adapting to the economic environment; in private, people had basically the same sources of joy and sorrow as anywhere else in the world. Perhaps the biggest differences I experienced in Latvia compared to the Nordic countries, were related to a male-dominated culture and a lack of trust in business relations.

After finalizing my last project in Latvia, my career headed more westwards, with work in Sweden, the UK and France. Even though these working environments were much closer to 'home', I couldn't help feeling that something was missing. In Western Europe people seem to be more satisfied with their standard of living and this, in my view, results in a sort of lack of inspiration. What I had instead experienced in Latvia was a sort of unbiased energy, which could be felt among the young, local managers (although less so among the politically elected 'old dinosaurs'), and which gave an edge to all business transactions.

This energy and the great opportunities in Eastern Europe were the most important drivers behind my decision to join some of my old colleagues to form the company East Partners.

My involvement with East Partners began in May 2005, when I happened to have an internet chat with one of my former colleagues, Antti Saarnio, who was just setting up the company in Estonia. Like me, he had previously worked in Latvia and had been impressed by the energy and opportunities of Eastern Europe. A few years earlier, Antti had met an Estonian businessman, Eero Erastus, who had had a successful career within a Finnish company, practically building up the company's operations in Eastern Europe from scratch. During the 15 years he worked for the company he had built a vast network of contacts, something Antti instantly realized the value of. After only a couple of discussions the two men decided to look into the possibility of cooperation more closely. Six months later they decided to create East Partners.

East Partners currently has offices in Estonia, Ukraine and Romania and, in addition, has operations in the other Baltic countries and Russia. The company has managed to attract an international clientele, with its simple value proposition: 'To help western companies and investors succeed in Eastern Europe'. The rapid growth of East Partners has in essence been the result of two factors.

First, the growth has been the derivative of the large economical gap that exists between East and West. The average GDP per capita for the EU15 countries was € 24.1 in 2004 with hardly any growth. The same figures for Ukraine and Romania

(Continued)

(Continued)

were € 5000 and € 6200 respectively, with an annual growth of between 5 and 10 per cent during the last five years. You hardly have to be an economist to guess what happens when an area with such wealth is located next to an area which such investment potential.

The second factor, which is essential to companies like East Partners, is the understanding of cultural differences. Even though companies are increasingly operating on a pan-European and global basis, one cannot underestimate the value of understanding people in different cultures, and how they feel comfortable in doing business. This is also precisely the idea of East Partners; western companies are dealing with people they know and trust, while the same is true for companies in the East. Following this, there will be a minimum amount of awkwardness and friction related to knowing whose hands to shake and whether you can trust your counterpart or not, not to mention getting access to the right people in the first place.

All in all, my experience is that Western Europe has very exciting neighbours in the East. It is a historic time, and we should take the opportunity to benefit from this development, both economically and culturally. At least, for me, what started in those gloomy Latvian halls some five years ago, has led me to many experiences I would not have dreamed of having otherwise. I hope the coming years will bring more of these adventures and opportunities as European integration continues.

Source: Dr Martin Seppälä, East Partners and Hanken Swedish School of Economics and Business Administration

Mini case questions:

1   How did Martin's perception of cultural difference evolve over time?
2   Why is this evolution key to his consulting activity in Europe?

Review questions

1   **Explain** the difference between business cultures and national cultures.
2   **Why** does the EU strive to complement national rules affecting human resources management?
3   **To what extent** does the European social agenda influence business management?
4   **Does** Europeanization phase out and equalize cultures, norms and behaviour?
5   **To what extent** does the valuation of diversity sustain or even increase the competitive edge of European corporations?

Assignments

- **Imagine** that you are the operations manager of an English company. You are being relocated to Austria. How will you go about obtaining the trust and confidence of your staff in a location that is new to you?
- **Compare** the threats and opportunities that innovative companies face: Are international property rights really useful?
- **Case study assignment**: Read and prepare the European Chief Executives in the Merger Maze case study in Part IV, and discuss the impact of European mergers on management styles.
- **Internet exercise**: Compare the social security systems of three EU states of your choice. Discuss your findings, and their significance to a firm with staff working across these three countries.

Web guide

W W W

http://www.europa.eu.int/comm/employment_social/gender_equality/ The EU's official site with links to employment, social policy and other fields.

http://www.coe.int Council of Europe site with information about European identity, human rights, social cohesion, education, culture and heritage, youth and sport, of 46 nations.

http://www.unece.og United Nations Economic Commission for Europe site illustrating the values that are important to the European economic sector and link to populations activities unit working on gender, ageing and generation issues.

http://www.osce.org/regions/ The Organization for Security and Cooperation in Europe's 55-country activities in Western Europe, including women, children, security, preventive diplomacy.

http://www.european-patent-office.org The site of the European intellectual property authority and watchdog.

http://www.uspto.gov US Patent and Trademark Office site.

http://www.usgovinfo.about.com Functions and history of US patents and trade marks.

http://www.patent.gov.uk; www.hpo.hu Examples of national European IP offices (UK and Hungary).

http://:www.wipo.int The WIPO's 183 nations' resources.

http://www.crseurope.org Corporate social responsibility network for sustainable development in Europe, with information about business leaders and campaigns.

http://www.ebsummit.org Site of the European Business summit, network of business leaders and policymakers.

References

Arino, A. Torre, S.D.L and Ring, P.S (2001) 'Relational quality: Managing trust in corporate alliances', *California Management Review* 44: 1.

Aviat, A. and Coeurdacier, N. (2007) *The Geography of Trade in Goods and Asset Holdings, Journal of International Economics* 71 (March): 22–51.

Bartlett, C. and Goshal, S. (1988) 'Organizing for worldwide effectiveness: the transnational solution', *California Management Review*, 31 (1): 54–74.

Beeth, G. (1997) 'Multicultural managers wanted', *Management Review*, American Management Association, May: 17–21.

Brewster, C. and Hegewisch, A. (ed.) (1994) *Policy and Practice in European Human Resources Management*. London: Routledge.

Brock D., Powell M. and Hinings, C.R. (1999a) *Restructuring the Professional Organization: Accounting, Health Care and Law*. London: Routledge.

Brock, D., Siscovick, I., Thomas, D. and Burg, J. (1999b) *Global Integration and Local Responsiveness in Multinational Subsidiaries: Some Strategy, Structure and Effectiveness Contingencies*. World at Work Paper, Watson Wyatt.

Buzzel, R. (1968) 'Can you standardize multinational marketing?', *Harvard Business Review*, 46 (November–December): 102–13.

Calori, R. and De Woot, P. (eds) (1994) *A European Model of Management: Beyond Diversity*. London: Prentice Hall.

Carey, J. (1989) *A Cultural Approach To Communication*. New York: Routledge.

Chandler, A. (1966) *Strategy and Structure*, Anchor Books edn, New York: Doubleday.

Claus, E. (2003) 'Similarities and differences in human resources management in the European Union', *Thunderbird International Business Review*, 45 (6), November–December: 729–56.

Commission of the European Communities (1999) *Employment and Social affairs*. Luxembourg: Office for Official Publications of the European Communities; Council Directive 94/45/EC of 22 September 1994.

Danckwortt (1959) *Internationaler Jugendaustausch*. Bad Neuenahr: Juventus.

Daniels, J., Pitts, R. and Trotter, M. (1984) 'Strategy and structure of US multinationals: an explanatory study', *Academy of Management Journal*, 27 (2): 223–307.

Demorgon J. (2005) *Critique de l'interculturel*. Paris: Economica.

Egan, M.L. and Bendick, M. (2003) Workforce diversity initiatives of U.S. multinational corporations in Europe, *Thunderbird International Business Review*, 45 (6), November–December: 701–27.

European Commission and EOS Gallup (2003) *Flash Eurobarometer 151b 'Globalization'* (realized by EOS Gallup Europe upon the request of the European Commission (Directorate-General 'Press and Communication')): Survey organized and managed by Directorate-General 'Press and Communication' (opinion polls, press reviews, Europe direct), URL: http://ec.europa.eu/public_opinion/archives/flash_arch_fr.htm

Fendt, J. (2005) *The CEO in Post-Merger Situations: An Emerging Theory on the Management of Multiple Realities*. Delft: Eburon Academic Publishers.

Festing, M., Kabst, R. and Weber, W. (2003) 'Personal', in W. Breuer and M. Gürtler (eds), *Internationales Management*. Wiesbaden: Gabler.

Frankel, J. and Rose, A. (2002) 'An estimate of the effect of common currencies on trade and income', *The Quarterly Journal of Economics*, 117 (2), May: 437–66.

Friedman, M. (1962) *Capitalism and Freedom*. Chicago: University of Chicago Press.

Gallois, C. and Callan, V. (1997) *Communication and Culture: A Guidebook for Practice*. London: John Wiley & Sons.

Gannon, M. (2001a) *Cultural Metaphors: Readings, Research Translations, and Commentary*. Thousand Oaks, CA: Sage.

Gannon, M. (2001b) *Working Across Cultures. Applications and Exercises*. Thousand Oaks, CA: Sage.

Giles, H., and Noels, K.A. (2002) 'Communication accommodation in intercultural encounters', in J.N. Martin, T.K. Nakayama and L.A. Flores (eds), *Readings in Cultural Contexts: Experiences and Contexts*, 2nd edn. Boston: McGraw-Hill. pp. 117–26.

Grant, Jeremy (2006) 'Golden Arches bridge local tastes REGIONAL STRATEGY', *Financial Times*, London edn. Business life, 9 February, p. 9.

Hall, E. and Hall, M. (1990) *Understanding Cultural Differences*. Yarmouth: Intercultural Press.

Hampden-Turner C. and Trompenaars, A. (1994) *The Seven Cultures of Capitalism: Value Systems for Creating Wealth in the United States, Japan, Germany, France, Britain, Sweden, and the Netherlands*. London: Piatkus.

Hampden-Turner, C. and Trompenaars, F. (2002) *Building Cross-Cultural Competence*. London: John Wiley & Sons.

Hickson, D. (ed.) (1993) *Management in Western Europe: Society, Culture and Organization in Twelve Nations*. Berlin: De Gruyter.

Hofstede, G. (1980) *Cultures's Consequences*. Thousand Oaks, CA: Sage.

Hofstede, G. (1991) *Cultures and Organizations: Software of the Mind*. New York: McGraw–Hill.

Holden, N. (2002) *Cross-Cultural Management: A Knowledge Management Perspective*. London: FT Prentice Hall.

Karra, N. and Phillips, N. (2004) 'Entrepreneurship goes global', *Ivey Business Journal*, November/December: pp. 1–6.

Koen, C. (2005) *Comparative International Management*. Maidenhead: McGraw–Hill.

Koene, B., Paauwe, J. and Groenewegen, J. (2004) 'Understanding the development of temporary agency work in Europe', *Human Resources Management Journal*, 14 (3): 53–73.

Lane, C. and Bachmann, R. (eds) (1998) *Trust Within and Between Organizations*. Oxford: Oxford University Press.

Laroche, M., Kirpalani, V., Pons, F. and Zhou, L. (2001) 'A model of advertising standardization in multinational corporations', *Journal of International Business Studies*, 32: 249–66.

Ledent, B. (2002) *Caryl Philips*, Contemporary World Writers Series, Manchester: Manchester University Press.

Maalouf, A. (1998) *Les Identités Meurtrières*. Paris: Editions Bertrand Grasset. (Published in English as *On Identity*. London: The Harvill Press, 2000).

Morosini, P. (1998) *Managing Cultural Differences: Effective Strategy and Execution Across Cultures in Global Corporate Alliances*. Oxford: Pergamon Press.

Newburry, W. and Yakova, N. (2006) 'Standadization preferences: a function of national culture, work interdependence and local embeddedness', *Journal of International Business Studies*, 37: 44–60.

Paulson, S., Steagall, J., Leonard, T. and Woods, L. (2002) 'Management trends in the EU: three case studies', *European Business Review*, 14 (6): 409–15(7).

Phillips, C. (1987) *The European Tribe*. New York: Farrar, Straus and Giroux.

Pitts, R. (1980) 'Towards a contingency theory of multi-business organizational design', *Academy of Management Review*, 5 (2): 203–10.

Porter, M. (1987) 'The State of Strategic Thinking', *The Economist*, No. 23, May.

Prahalad, C. and Doz, Y. (1987) *The Multinational Mission: Balancing Local Demands and Global Vision*. New York: Free Press.

Redding, G. (ed.) (1995) *International Cultural Differences*. Aldershot: Dartmouth.

Rogers, E. (1995) *Diffusion of Innovations*, 4th edn. New York: The Free Press Division of Simon & Schuster.

Rosenzweig, P. and Singh, J. (1991) 'Organizational environments and the multinational enterprise', *Academy of Management Review*, 16 (2): 340–61.

Schueffel, P. and Istria, C. (2006) 'Winning through diversity', *European Business Forum*, 21, Winter 2005/2006: 41–4.

Sparrow P., Brewster C. and Harris, H. (2004) *Globalizing Human Resource Management*. London: Routledge.

Stopford, J. and Wells, L. (1972) *Managing the Multinational Enterprise*. New York: Basic Books.

Strang, D. and Soule, S. (1998) 'Diffusion in organizations and social movements: From hybrid corn to poison pills', *Annuel Revue Sociologique*, 24: 265–90.

Suder, G. (2005) 'The CEO interview: Jean-Philippe Courtois, CEO Microsoft EMEA', *Thunderbird International Business Review*, 47 (2), March–April: 153–161.

Suder G. and Lefevre, J. (2006) *The Diffusion of Corporate Governance Paradigms: The Role of Sustainable Development in the Shareholder and Stakeholder Model*. Paper presented at the Research Colloquium on Sustainable Development as a Tool of Competitiveness in the Multinational Enterprise, Georgia Tech, Atlanta, October.

Tayeb, M. (2000) *International Business*. London: Prentice-Hall/Pearson Education.

Teece, D., Pisano, G. and Shuen, A. (1997) 'Dynamic capabilities and strategic management', *Strategic Management Journal*, 18 (7): 509–33.

Thomas, D. and Ely, R. (1996) 'Making differences matter: A new paradigm for managing diversity', *Harvard Business Review*, 96510, September–October: 70–90.

Tregariskis, O. and Brewster, C. (2006) 'Converging or diverging? A comparative analysis of trends in contingent employment practice in Europe over a decade', *Journal of International Business Studies*, 37: 111–26.

Warner, M. (2000) *Management in Emerging Countries*. London: Thomson Learning.

Warner, M. and Joynt, P. (2002) *Managing Across Cultures*. London: Thomson Learning.

Weir D. (2004) *Teaching material*. Sophia Antipolis: CERAM.

Zaheer, S. and Zaheer, A. (2006) 'Trust across borders', *Journal of International Business*, Commentary, 37 (1), January: 21–9.

Zaleznik, A. (1992) 'Managers and leaders: Are they different?', *Harvard Business Review*, March–April: 126–44.

Other web sources:

Report on Equality between women and men 2004, URL: http://europa.eu.int/comm/emplyment_social

Gender Mainstreaming, URL: http://europa.eu.int

Women in political decision making; Facts and Figures, URL: http://www.onlinewomeninpolitics.org/beijing12/women-decision-making.pdf

WIDNET (Women in development network) Statistics – Europe, URL: http://WIDstat Women In Development – Statistics – Europe – Power.htm

Online Women in Politics. Org. Economic decision-making facts and figures, URL: http://www.onlinewomeninpolitics.org/statistics.htm#wlp

'Will the glass ceiling ever be broken?', *ILO Magazine. World of Work*, URL: http://www.ilo.org

The top five women in business, URL: http://www.fortune.com/fortune/powerwomen

Women in leadership, URL: http://education.guardian.co.uk/egweekly/story/0,,1485026.00.html

Part III

BUSINESS ACTIVITY FUNCTIONS IN THE EUROPEAN ENVIRONMENT

7 European Economics and Finance

What you will learn about in this chapter

- How Europe attempts to master macroeconomic fluctuations.
- The uniqueness of a single currency within a market grouping.
- How to obtain capital funding.
- Selected analyses of other harmonization and convergence efforts.
- The consolidation of the European financial markets.

First, you will obtain an insight into macroeconomic fluctuations that the EU attempts to regulate through harmonization efforts and the unique single currency that the majority of EU members have joined. Moving from the macro- to the micro- level, we then shed light on the opportunities for firms to raise funds in Europe. Finally, you will learn about crucial convergence efforts in the field, that go hand in hand with the region's larger specificities (ageing, retirement, taxation, accounting and stock market consolidation efforts).

Introduction

European economics are characterized by the harmonization of rules that attempt to maximize the benefit gained from trade and financial integration through risk-sharing (the main traditional argument for cross-border asset trade), spill-over of macroeconomic fluctuations and product and consumption co-movements. A main step towards common measures was the introduction of the single currency in 1999, which provided the Eurozone members with a unique chance for economic cohesion. Also, it stimulated financial flows in an unprecedented manner.

In regard to cross-border equity flows, Portes and Rey (2005) demonstrated that geographical proximity is a strong stimulation factor, increasing flows even if informational asymmetries may increase transaction costs, and vice versa. This research has been further confirmed (Aviat and Coeurdacier 2004) by means of evidence from data on bilateral tax treaties and institutional proximity variables, linking trade in goods (based on geographical determinants and transportation costs) to bilateral financial claims. Distance may be geographic but also institutional: proximity was found to affect asset holdings across borders, because trade in goods has a significant impact on asset portfolios, and stimulate their engagement. This confirms that institutional and cultural proximity, as noted in Chapter 6, affect cross-border bilateral asset holdings positively. It appears therefore that financial Europeanization and globalization 'has gone much further on the financial side than on the real side' (Aviat et al., 2007: 5).

7.1 Mastering macroeconomic fluctuations?

7.1.1 The euro

The euro was introduced on 1 January 2002 as the new currency of 12 of the 15 EU Member States: Austria, Belgium, Finland, France, Germany, Greece, Italy, Ireland, Luxembourg, The Netherlands, Spain and Portugal. It was the culmination of the EU's plan for Economic and Monetary Union (EMU). The precursor and foundation of the euro, the ECU, was the official currency of the EC. Its value was defined in terms of a 'basket' of all of the Community member states' currency (The ECU, European Documentation Series, 1987). The basket was composed of fixed proportions of Community currencies. The ECU had no independent value on its own, but its value was calculated from the value of all 12 currencies, each reflecting its economic and financial strength and the relative economic importance of each Member State within the Community. The value of the ECU was revised every five years or on request if the external value of a currency had changed by 25 per cent in accordance with Section 2.3 of the European Council Resolution of 5 December 1978.

Since the ECU was based on a mixture of currencies the value of the ECU against any particular EU currency did not alter much over time. The Maastricht Treaty did not allow any new currency in Europe, even if the EU was enlarged. This explains why, for example, the Austrian, Finnish and Swedish currencies could not be included.

The ECU was used for no-cash transactions, such as cheque or bank transfers, for deposits on savings accounts, the purchase of bonds or other forms of investment. It was used mainly for loan issues on the international capital market by the Community institutions. The EC budget was drawn up in ECUs and all accounts were in ECUs, and financial aid and Community loans were also expressed in ECUs. The Commission used the ECU for billing and as an instrument of payment (El Kahal, 1998). Given its importance, it is necessary to understand its foundation.

7.1.1.1 A brief history of the euro

On 2 December 1969, The Hague Summit of Heads of State and Government decided to make EMU a main goal of the Community. The EU's history of monetary integration effectively began with the organization of a series of formal financial instruments designed to limit exchange rate volatility in the EEC markets of the 1970s. The Summit ended by signing to create the EMU: European leaders had begun to realize that the Bretton Woods system was deteriorating in the late 1960s and they considered that it may be time to seriously weigh up the benefits of exchange rate coordination and the possibility of establishing a true European monetary union. The main aim was to limit exchange rate volatility.

As a result, the Economic and Finance Committee (ECONFIN) established the Werner Committee, which proposed the management of a three-stage currency arrangement to facilitate the establishment of a full EMU within the following 10 years. In August 1971, the Bretton Woods system effectively collapsed when the US president, Richard Nixon, unexpectedly announced that the USA would discontinue the convertibility of the US dollar to gold. Given the shock that this caused on the financial markets, it was decided to put EMU on hold. On 24 April 1972, the six founding Member States set up a 'snake in the tunnel' mechanism that floated the European currencies within set limits (the tunnel) against the US dollar. The oil crises, however, put the system under harsh pressure and it was soon abandoned.

In 1978, the EC finally decided to relaunch the process of monetary integration at the Brussels European Summit through the creation of a European Monetary System (EMS), that entered into force in 1979. Its main goal was to initiate monetary integration and, through the introduction of a currency basket (with the ECU), a monetary stabilization mechanism, the Exchange Rate Mechanism (ERM) and a mechanism to finance monetary interventions, the European Monetary Fund (FECOM). On 28 February 1986, the SEA was signed to modify the Treaty of Rome. It significantly reinforced the free movement of capital in the EU, among its other provisions. On the basis of further advances in the field, on 7 February 1992 the Treaty of Maastricht smoothed the way for European monetary integration by installing a union, and stipulated the following conditions that would later allow Member States to join the Euro-zone:

- A country's inflation rate: no more than 1.5 per cent higher than the average of the rate in the three countries with the lowest inflation rate.
- A country's budget deficit: no more than 3 per cent of GDP and its national debt no more than 60 per cent of GDP.
- A country's long-term interest rate: no more than 2 per cent of the average of the rate in the three countries with the lowest interest rates.
- A country's currency: not devalued against any other Member States' for at least two years prior to monetary union.

At the beginning of the 1990s public debt had reached its highest level ever in several European countries and it could not be reduced during the resulting recession. With this experience, EU Member States agreed to diminish the ratio of deficits and debt to GDP for the good of the introduction of a single currency, with a pact that was to dramatically reduce if not eliminate the phenomenon in the future.

At the Dublin Summit of December 1996, Euro-zone members established the *Stability and Growth Pact,* which set rules for Euro-zone members. The pact, confirmed at the Amsterdam Summit in 1997, determined that government debt and deficit levels should be mastered over the long-term at/or below the EMU ratios (60 per cent and 3 per cent of GDP respectively). The pact also served to protect from individual Member State's forcing interest rates to increase for all other members. At the same time and primarily, the Stability and Growth Pact strove to create a stable economic environment at its best, despite national difficulties to implement and maintain its obligations. During times of economic growth in the markets, the pact is useful to restrict the members' budgetary policy to avoid inefficient expenditures and increasing deficit. However, in times of recession, some flexibility in budgetary policy may well need to be necessary to enable financing of social help and restructuring.

From 1 January 1999 onwards, the Euro-zone experienced a transition period with the introduction of the euro, which was essential for accounting purposes. Restating all existing financial contracts (bond issues etc.) in the euro was a huge and complicated process. With this development, companies succeeded in significantly reducing intra-European exchange risk. On 1 January 2002, the euro became the official currency of the EU under the control of the ECB, and a reality for all financial interactions at every level in the Eurozone.

7.1.1.2 The benefits and consequences of the euro
Lower transaction costs

The euro is the natural progression towards a complete economic union. Companies do not have to deal with foreign exchange risk costs. Therefore, they reduce cross-border payment costs, they improve the management of their payment mechanisms and of the hedging costs of many currency accounts (such as the risk of one currency devaluing against another). There is also a greater liquidity in financial instruments. Since the introduction of the euro, countries that participate in EMU have saved an estimated $30 billion per year in the reduction of such costs ('The Euro', *The European*, 2004: 154). A decrease in currency risk decreases a country's risk premium, which then makes the single European market much more attractive to foreign investors.

Macroeconomic stability and growth

The primary goal of EMU, and the subsequent introduction of the euro, served two objectives; on the one hand, to ensure inflationary and employment stability and on the other hand, to enable EU members to remain competitive in a globalized market.

In terms of economic stability for a stable economy and further economic prosperity, the Eurozone saw tremendous economic growth between 1998 and 2001, characterized by increasing levels of FDI; the worldwide economic slowdown then led to a subsequent decrease in FDI influxes into the EU. It is noteworthy that the lesser developed countries enjoy an increase in FDI from the stronger EU economies, while the stronger EU economies are the main FDI recipients and donors with non-EU states.

Efficient capital markets

The euro and the single European market facilitate financiers', borrowers', and consumers' access to capital markets. Even though the emerging markets in India and Asia are very

Table 18   Price comparison in the EU at the launch of the euro: examples

City	1 litre of milk	Music CD
Madrid	€0.90	€18.60
Berlin	€0.60	€20.43
Paris	€1.06	€18.24

competitive, the emerging economies in Eastern Europe provide investors with the low-cost benefits associated with a developing economy that has the stability of a single European currency (Brenneman, 2004).

Within the European market for consumers and corporations (Table 18), the euro allows for a price and purchase transparency for goods and services. Combined with the accessibility of the Internet, the European market has become more liquid. Capital, from either domestic or foreign investors, is accessible on a European scale. With a European market being one's domestic hunting ground, obtaining capital is simpler, but also, if capital markets concentrate, prices rise.

For corporations, the European market is at the origin of strong competition between all levels of the value chain, with free information flows that confront prices and intra-EU transfers of goods, services and capital.

Transparency, discipline and competition

One major benefit of a single currency and market is a homogenized monetary policy that expects full financial transparency from each Member State. Some challenges have appeared since the introduction of the euro. Greece's budgetary deficits, the legitimacy of budgetary statistics, and the problems of Germany to keep inside the pact's obligations are examples (see, for example, www.EUobserver.com).

As a result of the pact, the Euro-zone Member States' finances need to be transparent, leading in principle to a coherent budgetary discipline. This is to instill consumer confidence as well as economic stability and growth. The advantages of the single currency encompass stable cross-border trade and ease the movement of people, goods, services and capital. The disadvantages, which are less important than the advantages, include increased cross-border competition, squeezed margins and a more complex management of European economies: the ECB must set common interest rates that are adapted to rural as much as urban regions, and for more or less advanced economies. Note that thanks to the euro and the Stability and Growth Pact, the EU has improved significantly the inflation record of the EU economies.

Single European policy and the loss of autonomy by individual states

The loss of autonomy incurred by adhering to the single currency means that countries are not able to use monetary policy as a fix. For example, lowering interest rates when Ireland is booming could cause the Irish economy to overheat, as the added liquidity will spill into worse investments and lead to inflation. An opposite example is increasing interest rates when southern Italy is in a near recession. This does not stimulate growth and consumption, but leads deeper into a recession than would have been done with a looser economic policy. It can be assumed that the larger countries such as Germany and France have more of a say in the direction that the policy takes.

Whether regional, or country monetary policy independence is worth having or not is debatable. Indeed, in the highly integrated European markets fiscal policy is potentially more effective than monetary policy. So, forgoing this advantage might not be such a tremendous loss after all. However, the Stability and Growth pact also puts limits to the extent that fiscal policy can be used to stimulate an economy. The aim of this policy is to 'strengthen the conditions for price stability and for strong sustainable growth conducive to employment creation' (Lord Currie, 1999). This is achieved through keeping government deficit under 3 per cent and national debt under 60 per cent. The implications of this pact are particularly apparent at those moments when economies suffer from economic downturn and use fiscal policy to stimulate their economies, such as happened in France and Germany in the 2005–6 period. This high government deficit led to a review of the pact, in itself showing signs of weak political integration as some Member States breached the pact.

All Member States that are part of the Euro-zone had to give up some cherished symbols of identity and nationhood when adopting the common coins and notes. The Greek drachma, for example, had originated in the times of Alexander the Great, while the Deutschmark was a sign of post-World War II recovery and economic strength throughout a region further than Germany, into Eastern and Central Europe (you can find information about this, for example, in *Time*, 14 January 2002, and in other media of this period). They were given up to be replaced by the euro, with each nation's main symbols on one side of its coins, circulating throughout Europe.

Different business cycles

Within Europe, monetary and fiscal policy freedom has been restricted. The implications of this can be even more tremendous when one takes differing business cycles into account. It is true that the difference in cycles calls for different policies that individual countries are not able to set; however, in the case of differing cycles, economic shocks can be smoothed by absorbing them throughout the Euro-zone. On the other hand, if business cycles are synchronized, then big economic shocks that are incurred by the driver countries will tend to extend to other countries through spill-over effects, thus worsening the situation in times of downturn. An optimum currency area (OCA) is defined by Mundel (1961), one of its founding fathers, as a currency area for which the costs of relinquishing the exchange rate as an internal instrument of adjustment (that is, within the area) are outweighed by the benefits of adopting a single currency or a fixed exchange rate regime. This implies that factor mobility, in particular in labour, throughout Europe is sufficiently large and highly reactant. Unfortunately, there are many barriers to the various forms of mobility. European countries vary in culture; the main difference being that of language. It is unthinkable for a German factory worker to leave his country to go to France or Italy in search of a new job. It is true that more service-based and international jobs, such as consulting, require and enable factor mobility thanks to a common business language. But the assumption of human mobility in Europe is still unreasonable. This means that the increased factor mobility must be found elsewhere. One could argue that mobility is felt on wages. Indeed, price rises accompanied with no wage increase are a form of mobility. Instead of companies moving to countries with cheaper labour, the harmonization of prices through Europe is the mobile factor. Increasing prices with no wage increase is equal to a discrete reduction of salary. Furthermore, past events in Germany are proof of the existence of wage mobility in the Euro-zone. The fact that workers have agreed to lower wages in order to remain competitive is the first sign of an adjustment to larger international trends by the German workforce. One can notice that since the integration of 10 new countries, and even before, companies have started to move to benefit from cheaper labour. This is amplified by tax differentials in Europe. It is true that companies are not going to constantly move from place to place to benefit from lower taxes. But the decision to base somewhere might be influenced by these differences. Ireland, for example, has run a 12.5 per cent tax rate for corporations. Furthermore, it is planned to harmonize all VAT over the Union.

Changeover costs: prices, money, machinery

There are many costs associated with the transition into a single currency. Gathering the old money and destroying it, printing the new money, changing accounting systems to deal with the euro, etc. Many of the 'menu costs' have increased. According to the British Retail Consortium, the transition costs for the retail industry alone in the UK have been put at £3.5 billion, although Britain did not participate. This would amount to approximately 3 per cent of turnover for small businesses. These include training personnel and changing machinery and price tags. Another significant difference is with people. Many argue that changing from one currency to another can be confusing, especially if one is still counting in the 'old' currency as well. The transition into a single currency has led to very specific costs for businesses within Europe as well as abroad. As mentioned earlier, menu costs have increased. A dual pricing system was implemented by all the big retailers and most companies during the transition. This is still visible today. The European Commission has recommended that retailers swap from the dual pricing system to a single pricing system as soon as possible, in order to get people used to the euro. According to Barysch (2005), this is a method that is doomed to fail and will only result in added costs. Also, the cost of changing IT systems and accounting procedures is not to be neglected. Estimates show that the cost associated with IT changeover can reach between 0.25 per cent and 1.25 per cent of turnover. During the transition process, accounting in two currencies increased the difficulty of coping.

Although people gradually adapt, the changeover comes with a certain cost. In Germany and Greece, for example, many consumers have felt ripped off by the conversion (Barysch, 2005). It was the same in France and Italy. People have often blamed businesses for using the euro in order to increase prices. This resulted in a four-day boycott in Greece, and specific consumer organizations being created to monitor prices.

7.1.2 The European Central Bank

The ECB was set up in June 1998 under the Maastricht Treaty. From its location in Frankfurt, Germany, the ECB began operations in January 1999, to introduce and manage a new currency, conduct foreign exchange operations and ensure the smooth operation of payment systems by focusing on price stability and keeping inflation lower than 2 per cent within the Euro-zone. In order to do this, the ECB may cut or raise interest rates. The ECB is responsible for the holding and management of the official foreign reserves of the euro area countries (portfolio management). The bank has exclusive right to authorize the issue of banknotes within the Euro-zone, and collects the necessary statistical information, either from national authorities or directly from economic agents.

At the same time, its main responsibility is to frame and implement the Euro-zone economic and monetary policy. Therefore, the Bank works closely with the *European System of Central Banks* (ESCB) that associates the central banks of all EU Member States. The institution is governed by a board of directors, headed by a president and a board of governors. Within this structure, only governors from national banks that belong to the Euro-zone are involved and are responsible for the decision process. In its relations, the EU institutions and the European Member State governments must respect the independency principle of the ECB.

On the one hand, critics argue that the ECB sets interest rates with a view to controlling inflation, but does not necessarily take into account objectives such as employment and sound exchange rate stability. The complexity of its tasks seem particularly challenging, and the analysis of the collected data relies on the accuracy of its sources. On the other hand, the ECB works in relation with and taking account of other main international financial institutions, and needs to adapt accordingly.

7.1.3 The European Investment Bank and other sources of capital

The EIB was set up by the Treaty of Rome, and is the main financing institution of the EU. It is owned by the EU's sovereign Member States, and has a subscribed capital of around €165 billion (statutory lending goes up to 250 per cent of this capital). Its Eurobonds are listed mainly on Euronext and the London Stock Exchange, and price quotations can be found best on Reuters and Bloomberg systems.

In accordance with the EU institution's political and economic objectives, the EBI focuses on raising very significant volumes of funds that are used for the financing of capital projects, on very favourable terms, inside the EU and also in components of development aid and cooperation projects in non-EU countries. The objectives that need to be satisfied for EIB loans have to serve the EU's economic development, competitiveness, human capital, ICT networks, R&D and innovation, transport, telecommunications and trans-European networks (TENs), as well as the environment, SME development, and critical infrastructures in the EU. Projects of non-EU countries are dealt with in two categories: accession countries and other non-EU countries. In accession country projects, the focus remains on the transfer of EU expertise and legislation, and the development of infrastructural and other economic activities. For the projects of other non-EU countries, initiatives, such as the 2012 Euro-Mediterranean Partnership of a Customs Union, link the EU to non-EU Mediterranean countries with the same perspective (compare the Airbus case study on p. 376–92), to African, Caribbean and Pacific (ACP) countries, to Asia and Latin America in terms of mutual interests, and to the Balkans regarding the Stability and Growth Pact for the reconstruction of infrastructures and regional development (EIB, 2001; Annex). The AAA-rated bank is, for example, involved in the financing of the EuroMena fund in Beirut, Lebanon, of the infrastructure development project in Medina, and the modernization of Budapest's healthcare system.

The projects are submitted officially or informally via potential promoters (such as companies), or commercial banks, or public authorities, or international or national development finance institutions (cf. 'The Project Cycle', EIB, 2001); those that are eligible to benefit from the EIB's financing facilities will have been scrutinized in terms of economic, technical, environmental and financial viability in accordance with EU objectives, and get accepted in terms of a sound evaluation of risks and benefits. Since 2001, the projects are publicly listed at an advanced stage on the Bank's website.

The EIB grants long-term loans in support of projects that demonstrate a direct link to the EU market, and that cope well with an analysis of its contents, of the borrowers and of the guarantees, which complement other sources of finance.

The bank's *global loans* are credit lines made available for the funding of small and medium-sized projects (ventures of SMEs or infrastructure schemes) through intermediary banks; these are projects that are not big enough for direct EIB funding. *Aid and assistance* is granted to EU development aid and initiatives such as operations under the Lomé Convention and the Cotonou Agreement with ACP countries. Altogether, EIB is the world's largest borrower on the capital markets, with the issue of large, liquid benchmarks in the main currencies (euro, British pound and US dollar), and specific securities in up to 15 currencies.

7.1.4 Venture capital and private equity

Venture capital (VC) and business angels are an important alternative financial source in the EU. Venture capitalists appeared tentatively in the EU around 1997, but were showing a strong presence by 2000. It is a phenomenon that, along with business angels, is widespread in the USA and has been for a long time. The adoption of private equity as a means of business funding started in the UK, and made its way rapidly into the other EU Member States. Amounts invested in this manner are at historic levels in Europe. In Germany, the share of investments into start-ups by this means is particularly significant with approximately 20 per cent of investment capital dedicated.

Many small internet entrepreneurs, however, prefer to operate without VC so as to remain independent from VC returns, and to sell off activity before growing becomes costly. Lower fixed costs for servers, storage and software, as reports the *Financial Times* (13 April 2006: 10), then in the 1990s, self-funded micro enterprises can deal with costs for much longer, and exploit ICT evolutions. Web design and programming are often outsourced for cost efficiency. However, semiconductor and mobile technologies do rely on higher, mainly external, funds.

Additionally, the European Investment Fund (EIF) is one the EU's main instruments to stimulate innovation through VC funding for SMEs and entrepreneurship. Its funds are dedicated mainly to the early stages of development of technology-oriented ventures, with a portfolio of over €2.2 billion. This fund relies on capital from the group that includes the EIB and the EIF. Within its mandate, the EIF also manages resources of the EIB. In addition, capital from the CEC is allocated through the ETF Start-up Facility and Seep Capital Action to investing in new funds. These two actions are part of the Multiannual Programme for enterprise and entrepreneurship, and covers Member States; accession states; and EFTA countries Norway, Iceland and Liechtenstein as eligible participants.

The EIF is a tripartite shareholding consisting of the EIB (its main shareholder), the CEC and the EU, as well as public and private banks and financial institutions that receive returns. Among these public and private institutions are Bank Austria Creditanstalt AG, Encouragement Bank AD of Bulgaria, Vaekstfonden of Denmark, BGL Investment Partners SA of Luxembourg and NIBC of the Netherlands. It is managed by a chief executive, a board of directors and an audit board, holds an annual general meeting, and is monitored by a range of authorities.

Direct investments in SMEs are excluded from the EIF scope of action. Rather, working under market conditions, the Fund supplies SME financial guarantees to facilitate access to debt finance, and acts through intermediaries for its VC.

7.1.5 Business angels

Business angel investment is the most significant source of external equity finance for young companies. About 75 per cent of this money is invested in businesses at an early stage of development. With straightforward deals, and staying with the investment for longer than more traditional sources of capital investment, business angels also provide knowledge, expertise and business contacts because they only invest in projects or firms that they feel an affinity for.

Although some deals are put together by groups of investors, the majority of business angels are individuals with widely different preferences and styles who make infrequent investments, maybe every three or four years, and are rarely actually searching for investment opportunities. Typically, they are top executives of companies, high-level managers or wealthy people who feel a passion for their work or a particular business sector, and they tend to be between 35 and 65 years old. With the passion and the capital that business angels provide, they generally want to be involved in the companies they support, which makes the relationship between the investors and the companies rather close. Indeed, investment takes place in the shape of direct capital, and not as a loan. Rather, this is a 'patient' investment, in which capital stays in the company for at least three years. A benefit for the business angel is thus generated from selling shares at the moment of early maturity of the business. In most EU countries, sums invested are usually between around, €25, 000 and €250, 000.

The main interest for this type of investment will be found during the first stages of a company's development, during the development of a prototype, or during a diversification of activities such as internationalization efforts. Through taking the risk to invest early, business angels hope that the success of the company will be highly beneficial to them.

Business angels invest in all the sectors. However, they invest rarely in social projects or in order to acquire recognition from the community. Rather, the 'business passion' is enflamed by the belief in the competitive advantage of the product or service commercialized by the company and its potential for growth. Where traditional funds are less accessible or expensive, business angels can step in and often operate at smaller levels than venture capitalists. But while business angels are less demanding than other sources of equity finance, such as the public sector or venture capitalists, they will always make sure that the business plan is convincing, that the risk suits the potential return, and that the information supplied is accurate. Confidence and interpersonal affinity is key here: the more the angels know about the entrepreneur seeking investment, the more likely they are to invest.

7.1.5.1 Searching for an angel?

Business angels are looking for investments capable of achieving a return of 20 per cent or more. To avoid wasting time chasing investors, it is important to make sure that this condition can be satisfied. Also, this type of investor typically invests locally, nationally or on a well-defined level such as that of the EU. The most likely place to find an angel is within the region around your main business premises. In terms of numbers, for example, there are around 1500 active business angels in Scotland, but the number of potential investors is likely to be much larger (see www.businessangels.com). However, they are less easy to recognize than venture capitalists or other sources of funding.

The search for such investment mainly concentrates on the contacting of successful and leading individuals within the same or a similar sector or industry, because business angels provide not only capital but also advice, and thus look for investments in areas that they possess important expertise in. Given the certain informality in this approach, the first meeting is particularly important because business angels invest along the lines of their passions and affinities, and hence tend to place emphasis on the human relations with the entrepreneur and management team. Networking and listing one's contacts who are or have been in the same business sector or industry is essential, as is mixing with them (through making direct contact or at business events); this helps in spreading the word about your activities and your search for investors. In general, business angels who are contacted but not active in your sector will be happy to refer you to someone more suitable.

The CEC financially supports the European Association of Business Angels (EBAN).

7.1.6 More sources of capital for established corporations

European funding is not only a source of capital but also a proof of the validity and financial health of one's business project, and of its coherence with the EU objectives and evolution. Hence, it is of great interest to apply also for funding stemming from specific EU programmes. These programmes are not exclusively destined for companies, are very precise and detailed, and are regularly monitored.

Generally, corporations already established are eligible for these programmes, as only this type of company satisfies the conditions. However, some indirect mechanisms can allow start-ups to obtain support, and benefit from funded actions such as conferences at universities and business schools. Gate2Growth offers individual financial counsel for high-tech projects, and is a partner for actions of the EU. Also, Business and Innovation

Centres (BICs) help business creation (www.ebn.be, for example), and regions co-finance certain initiatives (see EuroInfoCenters and your local Chamber of Commerce and Industry). Some regions in particular are supported by the European regional policy, and business is well advised to refer to the information provided in DOCUP, the programme documentation, that states the main objectives of funding, and to know that these funds are allocated as an integral part of local aid complemented by regional funds.

The EU does not provide any direct funds for exports, for employment, or for specific corporate development. Rather, support is indirect in the form of:

- investment aid (structural, non-reimbursable funds);
- co-financing (non-reimbursable);
- loan or bank guarantee (by EIB and EIF);
- participation (VC through intermediaries);
- non-financial aid (technical tools such as Ecolabel, or information);
- payment of service or purchase (calls for tender in case of programmes with non-EU countries).

It is important to note that initiatives that focused on the creation of joint business ventures between firms in Member States with firms in accession countries or Asian and Latin American countries do not function anymore, nor does the programme supporting the creation of joint ventures between European SMEs.

In addition to its legislative tools (mainly directives and rules) that open up possibilities for funding, the EU defines technical programmes that specify objectives, requirements and budget lines. In this context, the 7th Framework Programme (FP7) is the EU's main instrument for funding research and development. Framework Programmes are proposed by the European Commission and adopted by the Council and the Parliament following a co-decision procedure. The Programmes were first implemented in 1984 and cover generally a period of five years, with the last year of one Programme and the first year of the next overlapping. FP6 was running up to the end of 2006, when it was replaced by FP7, which runs for seven years to ensure consistency and economic convergence. It has been fully operational since 1 January 2007 and expires in 2013 when FP8 is defined and launched.

FP7 is designed to build on the achievements of its predecessor towards the creation of the European Research Area, and carry it further towards the development of the knowledge economy and society in Europe. With over €70,000 million for the period 2007–13, FP7 focuses on cooperation, convergence, knowledge sharing, international research (with the establishment of the European Research Council) and a simplification of operations internally. This field refers to gaining leadership in key scientific and technology areas by supporting cooperation between universities, industry, research centres and public authorities across the EU and with the rest of the world. Transnational cooperation is the main instrument for carrying out research activities. This programme is organised into nine sub-programmes with nine different thematic research areas in which Community support can be obtained (the so-called thematic priority areas). FP6 thematic priorities continue to be supported in FP7. Only one new priority, 'space and security', has been added to the previous set of themes. Joint, cross-thematic approaches to research subjects of common interest are also encouraged. Thematic programmes include eContent, to make digital content more accessible, usable and exploitable, through best practice, cooperation and awareness, SaferInternet Plus (to combat illegal e-content) and also IDABC (Interoperable Delivery of European eGovernment Services to Public Administration, Business and Citizens), TENs (trans-European networks), and LIFE + (natural habitat improvement), among others. CIP (Competitiveness and Innovation Framework, with €4.21 billion to 2013, is a new programme in FP7.

When applying for EU funding, it is of primary importance that you satisfy not only the expectations and objectives of the EU, but also the specific file components and the information criteria (compare Box 35). For any DG grant programme, an information unit of the relevant DG can be contacted for advice. In the starting phase of a project proposal for funding at the EU, the sound distribution of tasks and finance among partners, and the arrangement of intellectual property rights between them, is vital. Who are the organisations involved, who is the legal representative, who is the project leader, and who is the contact person for your project? Also, the organization's usual sources of finance are important, as the EU usually only co-finances projects.

A steering committee for intermediate and final reports needs to ensure the liaison with the EU at all relevant stages and during auditing. Outcomes of the project must be well defined, for example in the shape of business plans, databases and web-supported dissemination of findings, reports, conferences and publications.

Box 35   The crucial parts of a submission after call for tendering of the EU consist of the specific and correct application

☐   Application form (acknowledgement; the receipt proves registration of your file at the EU).

☐   Budget form (total budget estimation with all sources of funding, quantitative measures and expected revenues).

☐   Checklist.

☐   Compulsory Appendices.

☐   Possible Appendices: MEP's (of the right working groups) or local representative's letters of support or other; details on aspects, information on subcontractors, on methods of calculations.

Any application needs to state precisely the objectives, the duration of activities, and the methodology of the project. What is the rationale, problems identified, match with programme and EU objectives? Is your project innovative, and how will its results make a difference that is beneficial to all partners and the Community?

Calls for tender are top-down calls in which the EU pre-defines needs that companies may answer to and execute if selected. Sometimes, these calls are restricted to certain organizations or to actors that had already submitted to calls for interest. In Calls for Proposals, a bottom-up strategy, the EU asks for creative promotion of its objectives by projects defined by the applicant along guidelines.

In terms of budget, an application is sound when it shows a balance of expenditure and revenue, in euros, in respect of financial conditions set out clearly in the call for proposals published by the EU in its *Official Journal* (C and S) and on its website (http://ted.europa.eu). This includes realistic costs/prices that can be found through benchmarking, analytical accountancy, and record calculation methods for possible later audits, and should take into account that organizations privilege low translation costs, travel costs (rather using ICT, see EU objectives), staff costs, and subcontracting costs that should be limited. For example, the cost of equipment (first-, second-hand or renting), stated at the depreciation rate – usually 10 years for electronic equipment – and only for the period of time calculated for the project, supplies, consumable goods, services and (limited) subcontracting, and those linked to dissemination (printing, photocopying, communication, etc.). For staff costs, ISCO international standards can be applied but are not compulsory because of wages varying between EU countries. You may use rates of the specific markets, but may want to explain them. Staff costs (excluding incentives; day rate x no. of days) exclude secretarial tasks that are part of usual job tasks, but can be included for placements, or if the precise job tasks are exclusively dedicated to the project to a percentage, for example 10 per cent. For travelling, private car use is calculated as first-class train fare, while air fare is always benchmarked on economy rates. Once the project is running, all reservation details and boarding cards are proofs for evaluation and audit by the EU. For subsistence allowance, the calculation is made for two meals, accommodation, local travel and other necessities on travel (per diem rates or real costs). Other eligible direct costs on your budget may include particular financial services (financial guarantee if necessary, costs for specific bank account), and those stated on the call for proposal. Indirect, overhead costs can be stated but must be limited to 7 per cent of eligible direct costs. Any expenses that concern, for example, interest paid, exchange losses, unestimated costs, provisions, or representation costs, or VAT (except for organizations that pay VAT and cannot recover it) are excluded (*Information & Enterprise*, 1992; in Suder, 1994; Welcome Europe 2004; ETI, 2006; interviews at CEC).

The only revenues that are eligible are those generated by your project, financial contributions by the applicant and partners, grants, and certain other contributions. Contributions-in-kind are non-eligible costs, that is, part of the total budget but not of the funding budget. They are revenues on the total budget, not on the funding budget.

In addition to the qualitative and quantitative soundness of the application, some details enhance the probability of being in line with the institution's ways of working. For the papers themselves, staples are not recommended, signatures should be in blue (not black) ink, and plastic covers (in open folders) make it easier for papers to be extracted and make the life of your evaluators easier. A good acronym for the title of your project helps its understanding and dissemination, and English is often the main language when filling in the forms because it is read by the majority of evaluators. Early and continuous contact with the Commission is useful; it helps to ensure that your project is in line with those of the EU in the programme. While consultants and advisors can help you fill in your application, make sure that the main actors of the project are an integral part of the formulation of the contents to ensure coherence. All funding by the EU is subject to specific reports. The granting of the funds is subject to a highly competitive evaluation procedure. The funds may attribute very important support to projects. Information can be obtained on www.cordis.lu/ and also from Heads of Unit. Chapters 3 and 9 are also useful for information on funding, opportunities with enlargement and the importance and techniques of public affairs management.

We will now turn to study a different set of conditions in European finance and economics that are equally relevant for doing business in Europe.

7.2 European harmonization efforts

While not exhaustive, due to the ever-changing EU financial and economic regulatory framework, this section presents the most revelant developments in selected harmonization efforts that influence corporate activity. It reviews the most challenging of economic and financial issues that the modern EU is facing. Box 36 examines retirement and pension funds.

Box 36   Retirement and pension fund industry: current challenges in Europe

The EU is often considered to be the realm of the national 'pay as you go' retirement system. This traditional approach is no longer suitable at the time of globalized competition, unequal wealth diffusion and mutualized welfare beyond frontiers.

   The UK, the Scandinavian countries and the Netherlands are already relying substantially on funded pension schemes, on a defined benefit (DB) or defined contribution (DC) basis, the second solution being currently preferred by transnational companies in order to avoid long-term liabilities. EU pension funds manage one-third of the €15 trillions of assets – at market value – owned by occupational schemes worldwide, Japan and the US representing two-thirds, mainly invested in equities. The bursting of the 2001 bubble has deeply affected the financial health of these pension funds. According to the UN's conceptual framework, occupational retirement schemes encompass three pillars:

First pillar: basic compulsory 'pay as you go' systems (for instance, state basic pension in the UK). The global return of these schemes depends on various criteria, such as national rate of employment, salary levels and life expectancy. They should provide minimum pension income, for everybody, even in cases of unemployment.

Second pillar: additional compulsory 'pay as you go systems' (such as state second tier pension in the UK) that have been implemented, after political debates about

(Continued)

(Continued)

an awaited pension gap. Additional costs linked to the first and second pillars are today considered as a major delocalisation factor by many companies, which are reluctant to pay an increasing price for employee pensions, especially in continental Europe.

Third pillar: additional 'funded' pension schemes, mostly designed, at least in the beginning, for top management of transnational companies.

Studies about two new pillars are being discussed at UN level, in order to provide a minimum level of state pensions for people without revenues, on the one hand, and personal long-term savings schemes for wealthy independent professionals, on the other. In most European countries, new reforms have projected, or already introduced, the third pillar for all categories of the active population: employees, professionals and independent workers (Fillon in France, Riester in Germany, Amato and Dini in Italy). At the same time, new 'directives' regarding pension funds' solvency, asset management and governance are currently implemented in the EU. IAS (International Accounting Standards)19: long-term benefits and its US counterpart FASB 87 have had to be promptly adjusted to the global economy and the regulation of international financial markets. In the UK, the 2004 Pensions Act has boosted pension schemes' rights to become effectively a more 'global secured creditor'. 'International benefits guidelines' are becoming common practice for 'remuneration committees' of most transnational companies. Some countries praise pension funds as being an effective tool for preventing unwanted takeovers and as being a powerful driving force promoting financial stability in the long-term. Unfortunately, claims for higher returns are not satisfied, at least through long-term indexed bonds, leading to the search by asset managers for riskier investment vehicles such as hedge or venture funds, under the governance of trustees. Recommendation by specialised advisors (actuaries, lawyers, etc.) yield a specific influence on the quality of that social governance.

The success of these ambitious European reforms relies mainly on the good practice of LDI (liabilities driven investments) and social governance: the returns on assets have to compensate, in the long-term, the costs induced by a better life expectancy, under the monitoring of involved stakeholders, including competent and available and accountable trustees. Claims for higher returns on all classes of assets (bonds, equities, real estate, etc.), at an accepted level of risk, are clearly influenced by the pension funds' adequate investment strategies. Balance of power between stakeholders and effective transnational mutualization of benefits are regarded as the main challenges for the future. Underfunding of pensions remains, a threat, however, and is a key issue for sponsoring companies, through DB schemes. Rating agencies are now assessing more precisely these new 'conditional' liabilities, notably in the UK and the Netherlands. The Pensions Protection Fund (PPF), a safety net set up by the UK government, was solicited by more than 40 companies in 2005, and

(Continued)

63 applicants were in the assessment period by the end of 2005. Actuarial practices evaluate average underfunding of UK pension funds between 10 and 15 per cent of their liabilities, according to the discounting rate, and the 'fair value' of assets. Interestingly, new economies, like Ireland, are enjoying a much better financial position, due to the overall organization of its pension schemes, the demographic structure of its population and the sustainable dynamic of its business environment.

Source: Professor Dr Gerard Valin, CERAM Sophia Antipolis and ASTCF

7.2.1 VAT harmonization within the European Union

European Member States mainly control all sales taxes, excise duties, income and corporate taxes to date, but increasing efforts are being made to obtain at least partial harmonization, such as that of VAT. In the field, the unanimous approval of all Member States is required. Hence, a common European tax regime is currently unlikely. However, certain rules and legislation stimulates tax convergence, such as those on state aid. Corporations are not necessarily striving for fiscal harmonization in Europe, because its divergence helps business benefit from the tax regime that may be the best adapted to its activity or organization. Also, elected politicians tend to avoid potentially unattractive tax reforms.

In the late 1990s, most European governments engaged in a process of tax reforms in all the main areas of taxation so that corporate cross-border activities and price convergence would be facilitated. The trade, capital flows and monetary policy that interlink EU Member States cause negative externalities that are the issue of singular tax reforms in those States, and could be eliminated through effective tax harmonization. Indeed, specifically cutting taxes in one country raises the competitiveness and/or attractiveness of this country relative to others (so did the process of currency devaluation in the past), and those that are substituted through tax arbitrage.

In the area of VAT, which is mainly a tax on the supply of goods and services, the EU first decided upon a Europe-wide VAT information service in 1979. The removal of tax borders between EU Member States became a reality in 1993, with the implementation of the VAT Information Exchange System (VIES) that links EU members' national VAT databases. With this, corporations can also check the validity of their contracting parties' VAT data. The EU has also conducted an anti-fraud strategy due to the increase in international fraud in the field.

The EU has a certain say in fixing rates and bases of indirect taxes. VAT is one example of many illustrating the need for further harmonization. In direct taxes, the situation is difficult, and any implementation of a European fiscal policy altogether requires the coordination of each national fiscal policy. This is because a Member State's fiscal policy actions spill-over to its European partners on income and spending, inflation, and borrowing costs. Given that a divergence in fiscal conditions may be beneficial for governments for very different reasons (on the one hand, for state income, on the other, however, to attract investment), negotiations are long and complex, and compromises hard to find: As we learned in Chapter 4, unanimity is needed for this type of harmonization.

In corporate taxes, therefore, the low flat tax rate of some European countries, in particular in recent members (for example Estonia and Slovakia), installs worries about a downward spiral across Europe that could lead to lower state revenue and hence endanger social networks. However, others believe that they lead to better tax utilization and more dynamic growth (*Financial Times* 24 November 2005)

7.2.2 International accounting standards

The evolution of IAS also has an impact on European business activities. The EU harmonizes rules governing financial statements in order to guarantee the protection of investors. The main objectives are a better integration of financial markets and activities, and easier cross-border and international securities trading. This then improves the element of trust between companies working together in the international value chain, in which the Know your customer principle is key to risk reductions. The IAS are now International Accounting or Financial Reporting Standard (IFRS) as well as the similarly structured (Generally Accepted Accounting Principles (US-GAAP)) that are accepted throughout the world, and adopted in the EU, to improve the credibility of European corporations towards the non-EU countries and vice versa. EU Member States were free to adopt the standards until the final implementation in the middle of 2007. Within these countries, listed companies (including banks and insurance companies) prepare consolidated accounts in accordance with ISA that facilitate the marketability of securities, cross-border mergers and acquisitions, and the raising of finance. The mini case study for this chapter examines IAS and their impact further. It appears less and less acceptable and feasible that investors still do not compare the like, and obtain information, say interim information, about costs of goods, when costs of raw materials, packaging or transport, for example, are volatile. Harmonization is to provide transparency for investors, analysts, bankers and other actors in the field.

7.2.3 Stock exchange consolidation

The introduction of the single European currency, the euro, has enhanced the transparency and eased profit-making opportunities on the European stock exchanges. The consolidation of these stock exchanges constitutes an essential step towards the harmonization of capital market conditions for corporate benefit. In this type of convergence, costs are reduced and cross-border trading is facilitated. Steil (2001) demonstrates that exchange places would make economies of scale both in operations and in trading. As a result, market liquidity increases, market fragmentation is reduced, investment and performance ratios of capital assets in Europe increase (McAndrews and Stefanadis, 2002).

Investors hold more assets from countries whose returns are positively correlated with their own stock market (Aviat and Coeurdacier, 2004). The degree to which capital moves freely through the EU is critical to its Member States' balance of payments. The sound integration of the appropriate measures, on the economic and the political side, can dramatically reduce capital flight – the sudden outflow of capital from the economy that indicates forthcoming crises (political, economic, financial, etc.) – that was significant before the Asian crisis in the late 1990s, and in Argentina and Turkey in 2000/1 for example. In those crises, the main causes of instability were linked to corporate governance issues, bank liquidity and capital management.

Typically, stock exchanges in Europe are national institutions that trade on a national or restricted cross-European level. However, developments can be noted in this area, such as an increasing number of stock exchanges that attempt to operate on a wider European level. A full-scale consolidation of European stock exchanges could be a long process since regulatory, legal, and economic barriers and national interests may hamper the process on a large scale and for a long time to come. As an example, let us analyse the ongoing consolidation and takeover speculations by Deutsche Börse of the London Stock Exchange. On 3 May 2000, Deutsche Börse, the sixth largest stock exchange in the world at the time, announced its interest to merge with the London Stock Exchange, number three worldwide with 5169 US$ of shares traded. It would have created the second largest exchange after New York and thereby consolidated the European stock exchange market to a degree as yet unknown. Werner Seiffert, chief executive of Deutsche Börse, offered 530p a share, or £1.3 billion, for the London Stock Exchange; the bid was rejected. Nevertheless, Deutsche Börse submitted another bid at the same price in January 2005; this was also rejected.

The rejections reflected not only the fact that the London Stock Exchange considered itself to be undervalued, but also the difficulty when it comes to playing one's hand at management control. It also appeared that the main shareholders of Deutsche Börse (TCI and Atticus) tended more towards continuous dividends rather than investment in another stock market, and emphasized this interest through a shareholder petition that was reported to have ultimately removed Seiffert from his position. Deutsche Börse, however, did reserve the right to return as a bidder if Euronext made an offer.

Euronext, then, also showed interest in the London Stock Exchange and was seen as being more knowledgeable about the management of multinational exchange, for example with the London Future Exchange (Liffe). However, Euronext made no formal offer at the time.

The London Stock Exchange continues to be a target of takeover speculations and investors from the European continent and non-EU countries, such as the Macquarie Bank, an Australian bank that has little experience with financial exchanges, preferring to invest in roads, airports and property. The European competition authorities investigated the potential consequences of a monopoly status of the European stock exchange. The interest in the Stock Exchange led to a significant rise of stocks and the FTSE 100 was able to double its gains in 2004.

In 2007, neither of the two European groups, Deutsche Börse and Euronext, had abandoned its interest. Before any further formal bidding, both need to cope with the British national authorities' requirement to reduce their stakes in clearing and settlement operations. Nasdaq Stock Market Inc. of the US approached the London Stock Exchange unsuccessfully in 2006. In the same year, Deutsche Börse and Euronext shareholders looked into a merger between the two. In the long-term, consolidation will allow for greater economies of scale and a move into new trading products: this is the reason why consolidation efforts in Europe continue (*Deutsche Welle*, 2004; *Daily Telegraph*, 2005; *Herald Tribune*, 30 September 2005; *AFX News*, *The Economist*, 17 December 2005; www.bseindia.com: Consolidation of Stock Exchanges 2006; *The Wall Street Journal*, 4 April 2006).

We saw in Chapter 5 that in Lisbon the European Council set the ambitious goal to become the most competitive economy worldwide within a decade. To achieve this objective, the EU must accelerate the integration of the European financial market, through the completion of the Financial Services Action Plan. The Committee of Wise Men proposed a four–level approach to European securities regulation, with the creation of two new committees, the European Securities Committee and the Committee of European Securities Regulators. The four levels consist of legislative acts that make progress in implementing adapted and uniform measures.

Résumé and conclusion

This chapter has reviewed the most important features of convergence and divergence of European finance, emphasizing those features that have a significant impact on the economy and corporate activity. Following the argument that investments and movements of financial assets are more frequent and intense when conditions of economic and political proximity grant stability, we have been able to observe two main phenomena. On the one hand, national interests, of governmental income, of electorate considerations, and of social policy have a significant impact on the willingness to negotiate the consolidation of financial markets and harmonized market conditions. On the other hand, public and private initiatives and interests across Europe drive a Europeanization for compatibilities that increase BOP stability; it enhances the liquidity of financial markets in Europe. Also, a European approach in monetary, fiscal and financial policy altogether can hamper economic and financial crises, under the condition that it preserves the flexibility necessary in times of recession. In the following chapter we will look at the way in which the single currency, harmonization and convergence efforts, and diversity influence the purchase and sales of products and services in Europe. Consequently, the next chapter focuses on marketing.

Mini case study: Auditing in Europe

Where does auditing come from? As a reaction to the collapse of the New York Stock Exchange in 1929 and the following world economic crisis, the 1934 Securities and Exchange Act required all publicly traded companies to disclose certain financial

(Continued)

information. This financial information has to be viewed by an auditor as an independent and qualified party. The general focus is to assure the shareholders and other stakeholders that the reported financial statements represent a true and fair reflection of the company's financial status.

Since that time most countries oblige companies to audit their financial statements by certified auditors. Clients and public are dependent on the reliability of the auditor. Therefore the legislator, as well as the auditing profession itself, have written out professional duties and general standards of auditing over the years. Some of the spectacular accounting affairs like ENRON, WorldCom or Parmalat have shown in the past that a good accounting policy is an indispensable precondition for cross-border capital markets.

How about a harmonization of accounting and auditing then? Global companies are competitors on the global capital markets. To get access to these markets, companies need comparable financial statements, so that investors get comparable financial information about all participants. This is one of the most important issues and the main reason for the necessary harmonization of accounting and auditing worldwide and especially in the EU. The main assumption for the harmonization of the economic audit service is the creation of consistent accounting principles and adaptation of supervisory authority in the EU.

The harmonization of accounting principles in the EU is one of the basic elements of the harmonization of European corporate law and for that, the formation and the embodiment of a European domestic market of financial services. A bare unification of accounting principles is not the main ambition and because of the differences in 'accounting traditions' not realizable. Growing pressure on the part of capital markets led to a ratification of accounting guidelines that resulted in a noticeable convergence of various traditions. Instead of developing its own accounting principles, existing standards (IAS) were imported. These former IAS are now called IFRS, as well as the similarly structured US-GAAP (Generally Accepted Accounting Principles) accepted throughout the world. While US-GAAP are used mainly in the USA for SEC-listed companies, IFRS is common in the UK. There are some main differences to the use of rules in continental Europe today (the German 'HGB-Rules').

The IAS/IFRS were permanently modified in the 1990s. They are becoming more and more relevant. Importantly, the IFRS also contains most of the core statement of US-GAAP. The simple absorption of the IFRS would cause miscellaneous problems regarding accounting, taxation and also in terms of guidelines of assessment, publicity requirements and facilities for SMEs. Given its cross-border dimension, the European Commission is the authority to ratify the IFRS as guidelines for its Member States. In addition to the guidelines of assessment and disclosure, the EU guidelines include the responsibilities of independency and the professional principles of the auditor. In cases of external quality control (peer review), the guidelines

(Continued)

(Continued)

guarantee a supervision of the auditor and enhance cooperation of the different supervisors in the EU.

The different national professions of auditors founded international organizations to accomplish exchange of information, transparency, conception and implementation of standards. The International Federation of Accountants (IFAC) aims at a worldwide harmonization of accountancy professions. Also, the IAS Board (IASB) was founded to develop accounting standards for the public benefit and to enhance their acceptance as well as their compliance. The IASB is committed to improving and harmonizing cross-border accounting principles, and therefore is an essential component to their convergence. On a European level, the Fédération d'Experts Comptables Européens (FEE) represents the interests of auditors. It comprises 44 professional associations from 32 countries including all Member States of the European economic area. Altogether the federation has 400,000 members, of whom approximately 95 per cent come from EU countries. In the course of the progressive adjustment of the accounting standards and their implementation in Europe, other committees were founded: the purposes of the Contact Committee, the European Financial Reporting Advisory Group and the Accounting Regulatory Committee consist primarily in their consultation and advice to the European Commission regarding the extension of and changes to the guidelines and the standards. The long-term objective of the European Commission is hence to efficiently and effectively establish uniform professional auditing and standards of accounting and auditing across its Member States.

Source: Dirk Feldhausen, auditor and tax advisor, BDO Deutsche Warentreuhand AG, Germany

Mini case questions:

1   Why does the EU aim for the adoption of uniform accounting standards by all of its Member States?
2   What role can accountants play in these harmonization efforts?

Review questions

1   **Explain** why the single currency helps to master macroeconomic fluctuations.
2   **Why** (and in which case) may it be crucial to approach business angels?
3   **To what extent** do consolidated accounts along IAS/IFRS facilitate corporate cross-border activity?
4   **Does** the Stability and Growth Pact guarantee European growth?
5   **To what extent** do stock market consolidation efforts enhance the liquidity of capital markets in Europe?

Assignments

- **Imagine** that you are a new financial auditor in Europe. How will you go about obtaining the relevant information about EU standards?
- **Compare** the advantages and disadvantages that companies may encounter due to corporate tax divergence in European Member States.
- **Case study assignment**: Read and prepare the case study A Corporate Challenge Resulting from the Introduction of the Euro in Part IV, and discuss the impact of the European currency on corporate financial management.
- **Internet exercise:** Compare the price of fixed phone services in three EU Member States of your choice. Discuss your findings, and the impact of the Euro for business opportunities across the European market in this context.

Web guide

www

http://www.europarl.eu.int/facts/5_5_0_en.htm Fiscal policy in European countries.
http://europa.eu.int/scadplus/leg/en/lvb/l26040.htm IAS.
http://europa.eu.int/scadplus/leg/en/s27000.htm European budget legislation.
http://www.ecb.int/home/html/index.en.html ECB website.
http://eib.eu.int/ EIB website.
http://www.eif.org/venture EIF and VC information.
http://www.europeanvc.com VC in Europe.
http://europa.eu.int/scadplus/leg/en/s01040.htm Stability and Growth Pact and economic policy coordination of the EU.
http://europa.eu.int/scadplus/leg/en/s70001.htm Free Circulation of capital in the EU.
http://europa.eu.int/scadplus/leg/en/s08000.htm Financial service information of the EU.
http://europa.eu.int/scadplus/leg/en/s10000.htm Taxation in the EU.

References

Aviat, A. and Coeurdacier, N. (2007) *The Geography of Trade in Goods and Asset Holdings, Journal of International Economics,* March, 71: 22–51.

Baldwin, R. and Wyplosz, C. (2004) *The Economics of European Integration,* Maidenhead: McGraw-Hill Education.

Barysch, K. (2005) 'East versus West? The European economic and social model after enlargement', Essay, Centre for Economic Reform, URL: http://www.cer.org.uk

Brenneman, D. (2004) *The Role of Regional Integration in the Development of Security Markets* Paper presented at Professors Jackson and Scott's International Finance Seminar, Harvard University, April.

Deppler, M. and Decressin, J. (2004) 'How to Help European Fiscal Policy: A Commentary' by Deputy Division Chief, EU Policies Division, European Department, International Monetary Fund, *Financial Times*, 15 February.

El Kahal, S. (1998) *Business in Europe*. Maidenhead: McGraw-Hill International.

European Central Bank (2002) *Evolution of the exchange rate between $US and the Euro from January 1999 to July 2005*. Frankfurt: ECB.

European Communities (2000) '*International exchange of VAT information within the EU*', Donato Raponi, DG Taxud, Head of the Unit, URL: www.itdweb.org/VATConference/Documents

European Communities (2001) *The Reform of Taxation in EU Member States, Final Report for the European Parliament*, Report for the European Parliament, Tender N° IV/2000/05/04, Final Version, 9 May 2001.

European Communities (2005) *Framework for fiscal policies*, European Parliament Fact Sheets, URL: http://www.europarl.eu.int/facts/5_5_0_en.htm

European Investment Bank (2001) 'The Project Life Cycle at the European Investment Bank', 12 July 2001, URL: www.eib.org

European Documentation Series (1987) The ECU, 2nd edition European Documentation 5/87, Luxembourg.

Government of Australia (2005) *Export EU – A guide to the European Union for Australian Business*, URL: http://www.dfat.gov.au/publications/eu_exports/exporteu_2005.pdf

Government of the United Kingdom of Great Britain (1997) *Fiscal Policy*, URL: image.guardian. co.uk/sys-files/Guardian/documents/2003/06/09/policyframeworks2.pdf

Inforeg (2004) *Guide des Financements européennes pour les enterprises. Tout savoir sur les mechanismes des aides européennes*. Paris: Gualino Editors, EJA, CCI Paris, Euro Info Center.

Lord Currie of Marylebone, D. (1998) *Will the Euro Work? The Ins and Outs of EMU*. London: Economist Intelligence Unit.

Lord Currie of Marylebone D. (1999) 'EMU: Threats and opportunities for companies and national economies', in M. Baimbridge, B. Burkitt, and P. Whyman, *A Single Currency for Europe*. Basingstoke: Palgrave Macmillan.

McAndrews, J. and Stefanadis, C. (2002) 'The consolidation of European Stock Exchange, June 2002, Vol 8 No 6, *Current Issues in Economics and Finance*, Federal Reserve Bank of New York, http://www. newyorkfed.org/research/current_issues/ci8-6/ci8-6.html

Mercado, S., Welford, R. and Prescott, K. (2001) *European Business*. Upper Saddle River, NJ: Prentice Hall.

Mundel, R. (1961) 'A theory of optimum currency area', *American Economic Review*, 51: 657–65.

Pagano, M. (1998) *The Changing Microstructure of European Equity Markets*, CSEF Working Papers 04: Salerno: Centre for Studies in Economics and Finance (CSEF), University of Salerno.

Portes, R. and Rey, H. (2005) 'The determinants of cross-border equity flows', *Journal of International Economics*, 65(2): 269–96, March.

Suder, G. (1994) 'Anti-dumping measures and the politics of EU Japan create relation in the European consumer electronic sector: the VCR case': PhD Dissertation, University of Bath, working paper, Thomson Consumer Electronics external relations department.

Steil, B. (2001) *Borderless Trading and Developing Securities Markets*. Paper presented at the World Bank, International Monetary Fund, and Brookings Institution Third Annual Financial Markets and Development Conference, Washington DC, April.

WelcomEurope (2005) *Eurofounding – Complete Guide*, 7th edn. Paris: WelcomEurope.

Wildavsky, A. and Zapico-Goni, E. (eds) (1993) *The Role of Budgeting Procedures for Improving the Fiscal Performance of the Member States of the EC, National Budgeting for Economic and Monetary Union*. Boston and London: EIPA/Martinus Nijhoff.

Other web and media sources:

AFX News
Daily Telegraph, 2005
Deutsche Welle, 2004
The Economist, 17 December 2005
The European, 2004
The Financial Times, 24 November 2005, 13 April 2006
Herald Tribune, 30 September 2005
Time, 14 January 2002
The Wall Street Journal, 4 April 2006
www.bseindia.com
www.businessangels.com
www.EUobserver.com

8 Marketing in Europe

What you will learn about in this chapter

- European marketing diversity and points of convergence.
- The dos and don'ts in European marketing.
- The future of the marketing mix in Europe.
- Opportunities and challenges for the marketer in Europe and also for the European marketer.

Introduction

The introduction of the single currency and the relative harmonization of financial management tools illustrate an increasingly competitive EU market. Transparencies, thanks to easier price comparisons, have more and more impact on pricing strategies and marketing investment. The need to excel through innovation and creativity, in order to differentiate your product, is a determinant force of marketers in Europe. It is reflected in communication and brand-building strategies.

Indeed, harmonization and diversity in Europe establish paradigms in marketing that are shaped on the basis of a *European-wide* strategy and on the opportunities of standardization versus niche positions. These strategies depend, in a similar fashion as in international marketing, on the definition of the product, the market and the timing.

But European marketing has been recognized as different to the typical 'international marketing' theory. Marketers are positioning their product or service into a highly integrated market, facing European-wide high levels of competition. All developments in the political economy and in the frame of business transactions and relationships in the market have a direct consequence on the work of marketers. This concerns marketing departments, advertising agencies and market-research companies on a level that encompasses all EEA countries, whether the concerned firms or products be of European origin or not. European marketing translates into far-ranging, long-term marketing strategies in which diversity management and strategic partner relationships are key. Also, the high rates of adoption of new communication technologies in Europe force the marketing manager to reinvent or readapt strategies in accordance with European-wide adoptions. For example, the Internet and third generation telephoning have significantly altered the panoply of marketers' tools in advertising and promotion, and also for the management of commercial transactions.

The main question that is asked in the context of how European marketing deals with the approach towards the consumer is: Does the ongoing progress in European integration allow the company as a whole, and the marketer in particular, to deal with one single market approach, that is, standardization? On the one hand, consumers are more numerous than those in the US, with comparable purchasing powers in certain regions, and are situated in one single market almost comparable to that of the American market. On the other hand, Europe is more diverse in terms of cultural interrelation, distinct local and regional long-lasting roots and attachments, and a motivation to work together that is founded in European history. Can we talk of a convergence of the European consumer? Can European-wide business act as a change agent to 'standardize' the European consumer, hence facilitating the work of European marketers?

The business reality shows that, for example, Europeans show similar behaviour towards low-cost air carriers, but differ considerably when it comes to the purchase of meals on these flights. German and Dutch clients show a tendency to bring along their own food. French and Spanish clients will want to purchase their meal in-flight.

This chapter reviews the main concepts that characterize European marketing activity and its realities. The chapter does not attempt to replace a marketing course but rather builds on it. It provides you with the distinctive knowledge and tools for marketing in Europe.

The loss of barriers, the increasing harmonization of educational standards, the continuous evolution of financial-product ownership on a scale wider than national and the emergence of pan-European media enhances the feeling among consumers and marketers that Europe is one entity. Nevertheless, we will see in this chapter that the more the market converges, the more the consumer likes to be considered as unique and locally rooted.

The view of Europe as a homogeneous market is erroneous and this view can only be considered appropriate for strongly branded products. This approach is interesting in terms of economies of scale, but for most markets market heterogeneity reigns in Europe. In a context of cultural, linguistic and remaining regulation differences between European countries, it is a mistake to think of Europe in terms of standardization. Rather, it is important to know how to adapt your marketing approaches and strategies to customers in their context. Economies of scale can apply to some contexts but not to others.

A European firm, or non-European firm that effectively benefits from the single market, typically pursues European-wide strategies, rather than local or regional-based marketing for several explicit reasons that are similar to those that we found in Europeanization. These reasons centre around the issues of potential convergence or divergence of demand and potential efficiencies on the supply side, such as:

- advantages from wider business volume on an incremental basis;
- expansion of life cycles when the domestic market has reached a certain level of maturity;
- with fixed costs being committed, achievement of economies of scale;
- high sales figures obtain high additional volume;

- first-mover advantages or advantages in following competitors, or following clients, for example in financial services or specific components supply;
- defence or anticipation of potentially growing European and international competition towards the local, regional or European market;
- streamlining of marketing services in terms of return of investment, risk diversification, account-ability for efficiency, speed and quality in creativity.

From earlier chapters, we have acquired a sound knowledge of the European market. For example, it has become important for us that a single market has the particular advantage that import duties from non-EU imports and supplies are payable only at one given point of entry into the EU, and not again upon transportation of the product within the EU. Nevertheless, we also learned that the harmonization of the European market does not eliminate the diversity of micro-indicators that analyse the potential acceptance of the product or service. For instance, factors of great variance in the different Member States encompass the rate of, say, coffee consumption, or of tourism, or of the number of farms or 3G or 4G telephones. This is essential knowledge, but that is not sufficient for doing business in Europe. We will now need to study the way in which market research is conducted in Europe. Understanding consumer behaviour is the prevailing preoccupation for any firm.

8.1 Understanding consumer behaviour

The basis of successful marketing is the screening and assessment of opportunities: the screening process typically reviews specific selection data that include size and growth of the market, political and social conditions, competition, and market similarities. Since 9/11 and the following awareness-building that a new global risk of international terrorism had developed, marketers increasingly also look at potential shifts in consumer behaviour due to threatened or experienced violence. Risk diversification has been given more thought in investment and in marketing. A stable business environment such as that of the EU is hence of vital importance as a basis for international operations because it challenges the marketer as a microcosm of reactions and reactivity.

Macro-level data help select a general market potential that is then considered by relating the specific product or service. This market-level screening helps to obtain answers to the most important market condition inquiries (see Box 37).

Box 37   Market conditions

- existence and evaluation of similar existing products/services or substitutes for it;
- likelihood of cultural adaptation;
- market size;
- taxes and duties;
- stages of development.

The availability of data in the EU underpins the advantages that can be obtained from a single market strategy in marketing, but also allows you to learn about the cultural, linguistic, geographical and social differences.

As a market grouping, the EU is the most advanced entity in the world and *proxy variables* in the research of market potential, that is, studying a similar or related product or service for indication purposes, becomes a particularly powerful tool. Methodologically, marketing studies traditionally use four types of research tool:

- qualitative marketing research;
- quantitative marketing research;
- observational tools;
- experimental tools.
- we add also the much more recent addition of Six Sigma analysis.

The research tools necessary for our purposes can be found in the classical market research toolbox of international marketing (see Box 39, p. 202), but differ in terms of the availability of data, their source and the diversity of findings for any Europe-wide approach.

Qualitative marketing research is generally used for exploratory purposes, in which the perception of a small number of respondents to your product or service is analysed. The study is not made to be generalized to the whole population, and is typically already based on a sound knowledge of the type of customer that you are targeting. Qualitative marketing research has a statistical significance and confidence not calculated; rather, you are looking into the needs, desires and availabilities of purchase of a given focus group, using in-depth interviews and projective techniques. This tool may help you study the commonalities or divergence between consumers of, say, the same level of education and professional background but from different cultures, so as to well position e-learning tools or e-government initiatives for a specific clientele.

Quantitative marketing research allows you to draw conclusions in regard to a specific hypothesis, rather than few specific insights. This tool typically requires the use of random sampling techniques and involves a large number of respondents from many different backgrounds answering through surveys and questionnaires. This is a common marketing research tool for consumer products, such as dairy products, but is being used more and more for commodities such as gas and electricity.

Observational tools demand a direct involvement of the researcher in terms of an observation of social phenomena in everyday routines. These observations may well occur on a cross-sectional basis, with a number of observations made at one single moment in time. Another approach is longitudinal, that is, few observations are confirmed throughout several time periods. Examples include product-use analysis and computer cookie traces.

Experiments may then follow, complement or stand alone in market research. Experimental tools create a quasi-artificial environment that excludes non-controllable forces as much as possible, then manipulate at least one of the variables in the environment, for example in test markets. This is of major significance for service marketing in which the consumer not only receives but also interacts, and is hence involved in the consumption, that is, in the process more than an outcome (Hollensen, 2004: 73). None of these tools a guarantees the

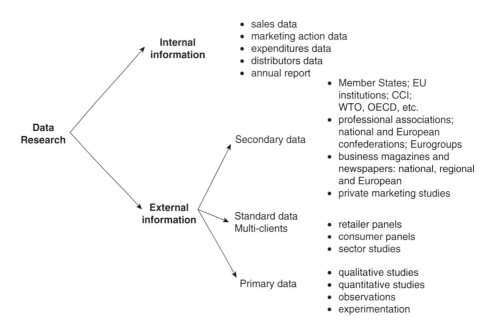

Figure 9   Information research for European marketers

success of a marketing operation; normally you will use more than one of the above tools based on secondary research that is only at a second stage complemented and refined by this primary data. The secondary data is best obtained covering the national, regional and European level, adding up complementary sources that convert a puzzle into a comprehensive picture. Figure 9 illustrates the main sources available for this research of external information, which needs matching with the internal information to evaluate whether the pieces of the puzzle actually fit together – whether your product or service fits with the market targeted, and whether you may envisage a Europe-wide or segmented market strategy in the EU.

Marketing research is, at its best, a long-term exercise in which a consumer database is continuously updating the corporate understanding of consumers, their purchasing behaviour and the risk factors that may lead to changes in this behaviour.

Altogether, the market study helps define a commercial strategy that is based on the highlighting of strengths and weaknesses of the firm compared to the competitor's. Then only the firm chooses its commercial actions. Internally, the validation of appropriate marketing strategies can be based on techniques such as the *Six Sigma* quality-control concepts that became famous through Jack Welch at GE, and have great potential in terms of process discipline and performance value in marketing: Quelch and Harris (2005: 33–5) discuss successful experiences made by senior management trained to use Six Sigma in this sense. The experiments focused on the enhancement of criteria in marketing that is generally known to quality management as follows:

- applicability
- visibility
- manageability
- replicability
- receptivity
- profitability.
- the criteria of sigma techniques such as value mapping.

These techniques then lead to best practices that may be replicated in the European, and later, in the international market. Therefore, the techniques are particularly well adapted for vast and complex markets in which the marketing research and practice may cause high costs and encounter diverse levels of performance due to diverse requirements of markets. The evaluations made on the basis of the marketing study, return on investment and quality criterion of your specific product or service defines the marketing approach that will best apply in the European environment, either as a market grouping, or by consideration of specific Member States or regions. The process followed for market segmentation is illustrated by Figure 10. Market segmentation into single Member States or into regions of the EU can only be pursued on the basis of the micro- and macro-conditions that define your task as a marketer. Getting there requires assessing the product or service and the targeted business environment.

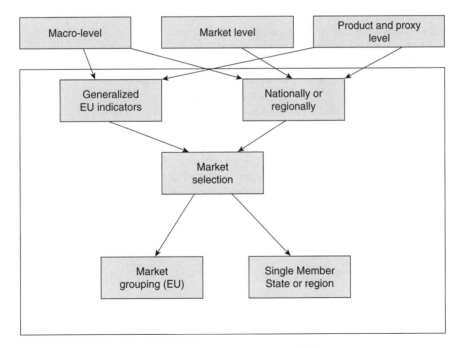

Figure 10   A fundamental market selection process in Europe

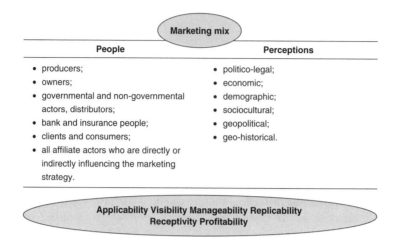

Figure 11   People and perceptions for a Marketing Mix

8.2 Assessing the product or service and the targeted environment

The traditional approach to international marketing focuses on the definition of the most adapted marketing mix, based on the work of Kotler. This marketing mix includes the right product, at the right price, known through the right promotion, and available at the right place (the 4Ps). The *best product scenario* is that in which the quality, features, options, style, brand name, packaging, sizes, services, warranties and returns are ideally adapted and adaptable to the price, promotion and place-conditions. The *best price scenario* balances the list price, discounts, allowances, and payment, period and credit terms with the product, its promotion, and the place where it will be available. The *best promotion scenario* deals with the adaptation of advertising, personal sales, promotion and publicity to the product, price and place where will be sold. Finally, the *best place scenario* defines the channels, geographical coverage, locations, inventory and transport conditions for the product, at its price, and in accordance with its promotion (cf. Kotler and Armstrong, 1991; 41). The 4Ps provide us with a wonderful tool that deals primarily with the micro-level of marketing decisions; therefore, the marketer in a complex marketplace needs to recognize that the 4Ps bathe within a diversity of perceptions of very diverse people – and deal with this accordingly. Figure 11 provides the main criteria that are needed to gear to a strategy in the search for Six Sigma.

8.2.1 Segmentation in Europe: targeting similarities

Segmentation aims at identifying distinct groups of consumers whose purchasing behaviour differs from others significantly by subdividing a market into distinct subsets of customers that behave in the same way or have similar needs. Several segmentations can be used and combined by marketers. Usually marketers identify niches, which are narrower defined groups seeking a mix of benefits, by dividing a segment into subsegments. Types of

Table 19   A general European segmentation table for adaptation

EU member	Perception lines
Spain and Portugal, southern Germany, northern Italy, south-eastern France	West Mediterranean
South Italy, Greece, Malta, Turkey	Eastern Mediterranean European
UK and Ireland	Anglo-Saxon
Central and northern France, south Belgium, central Germany, Luxembourg and Austria	Centre
Northern Germany, the Netherlands, northern Belgium, Iceland, Norway, Finland and Denmark	Northern
Eastern and Central European countries	Eastern, Central or Baltic

Source: adapted from VanderMerwe and L'Huillier, 1989, Harris, 2004, and others

segmentation are unlimited ranking from geographical bases to psychosocial and behaviour. The ultimate segmentation is one based upon the benefits sought by customers for the product or service in question.

Nevertheless not all segmentations are useful. A segment has to be at least measurable and differentiable – the marketing-mix elements and programmes are distinct from a segment to another – and reachable.

The conditions outlined above lead the marketer to search for similarities in accordance with the perception of the product or service that is to be positioned. On a purely sociocultural basis, a separation of Europe into the following segments or perception lines, similar but not identical, is sensible for a start. Table 19 illustrates possible distinctions.

A similar table needs to be drawn in terms of economic, demographic, sociocultural, geopolitical and geo-historical conditions, while the main politico-legal and economic cross-border conditions in Europe are highly integrated. A comparison on the basis of these analyses creates the mapping of opportunities on the grounds of segmentation, in response to the European market diversities and the advantages stemming from the single market. The standard socio-economic group segmentation that is often applied in national markets, however, may not provide sufficient definition because of the differences of purchasing power, national and personal income levels, attitudes to savings, and lifestyles across Europe. To date, only a few products have become relatively homogeneous. These include household cleaning products, soft drinks and cigarettes, as well as computers, computer applications and Internet services. All of these had been dominated by American or British brands at the beginning of European single market opportunities, and have been marketed with a European-wide standardization strategy.

Clearly, only a sound assessment of the business environment can allow a company to best price, promote and locate a product or service in a market that is as complex as the European one. We will now study some more of those particularities in the European market.

8.2.2 Political and legal conditions

Political and legal conditions within European countries are only partially harmonized, and allow the marketer to include various crucial criteria in the evaluation of the marketing mix. The existence, non-existence or level of trade barriers, the taxation rates and restrictions on foreign ownership or assembly operations, the rules of origin, the repartitions of profits on capital movements, the protection of intellectual property, labour laws and other aspects of business law are essential to the definition of the product or service's price, promotion and place potential.

The degree to which European countries adopt EU legislation and opt for integration, for example into the Euro-zone, defines the degree of harmonization of politico-legal factor advantages. A homogeneous political and legal framework does not exclude significant differences in taxation rates in the EU.

Administrative differences between European countries can hence be a hurdle for trade and marketer: in agricultural goods, for example, European law on food traceability can hamper marketers. However, in advertising, the EU is setting standardized regulation for the harmonization of communications legislation, to ease and make marketing action cheaper for Europe-wide advertising campaigns. European legislation also stipulates conditions that apply to packaging, for example in language requirements.

A non-exhaustive list provided in Box 38 summarizes the main politico-legal challenges that may hinder corporate marketing across borders. Stimuli are also available through governmental policy; for instance, the EU smoothes the technological and digital business conditions across the single market so as to enhance knowledge transfer, innovation, and competitiveness. Some of the disadvantages of politico-legal intervention are relatively unimportant for business within Europe; others may serve as non-tariff barriers at particular moments in time. For example, the EU may well use custom and entry procedures as non-tariff barriers to entrance. In 1986, France insisted that all EU imports of video recorders came through one particular small customs point in Poitiers causing delays and a logjam, in particular for Christmas sales (Suder, 1994). In quotas (quantitative restrictions), the Japanese car industry faced particular quotas in Europe a few years ago; in consumer electronics and semi-conductors, the use of anti-dumping policy can be observed as a means of punctual intervention.

Box 38   The impact of politico-legal frameworks: administrative risks

→   Administrative guidance
→   Subsidies
→   Government procurement and state trading.

(Continued)

- **Customs and entry procedure:**

  → Product classification
  → Product valuation
  → Documentation
  → License to permit
  → Inspection
  → Health and safety regulations.

- **Product requirements:**

  → Product standards
  → Packing, labelling and marking
  → Product testing
  → Product specifications.

- **Quotas: export and import**

  → Absolute
  → Tariff
  → Voluntary.

- **Financial control:**

  → Exchange control
  → Multiple exchange rates
  → Prior import deposits
  → Credit restrictions
  → Profit remittance restrictions.

- **Other policies and requirements:**

  → Market reserve policy
  → Performance requirements.

Source: adapted from Onkvisit and Shaw, 1988

For the 4Ps, in terms of place, specific locations give you access to particular conditions in price, product, and promotion or image. While London gives you an image important in financial services, but is costly in terms of location, the Baltic countries allow you cost-savings in production and have the highest IT skills, though links with the rest of the region need to be improved. Visa laws in Sweden are relatively harsher than those in Greece, and may define your location of HR. Also, advertising is strictly regulated there, in particular at times when children watch TV. On the other hand, the politico-social stability and quality of life may be interesting depending on the product or service to be marketed. The Czech

Republic is used by Lufthansa, the German airline, for example, for data-processing operations because of a stable politico-legal environment, while Zara, the Spanish fashion store, produces most of its materials in Europe and opened its first non-Iberian store in Paris. Li & Fung, an important Hong Kong-based trading company, operates in Europe from two Eastern European Member States.

8.2.3 Economic conditions, national income and quality of life

For successful marketing, it is best to have stable economic conditions. Economic instability results in risks associated with inflation rates, balance of payments, exchange rate stability, government budgets and growth. Within the Euro-zone in particular, these indicators are likely to present similar macroeconomic trends. However, the more members there are, the more imbalances are likely to exist. These imbalances can be counterbalanced by fostering strong competitiveness of the single market through EU-wide initiatives. The countries that subscribe the most to these initiatives are likely to be those that are economically best performing in the long run, and are most suitable for the constitution of a whole market segment. A measure for this is the annual report of Eurostat that rates Member States' adoption of EU legislation. This information is easily accessible on the Europa website.

Economic conditions have a strong impact on consumer behaviour. During recessions consumers prefer to save money; in times of economic risk and crisis, they will invest differently. In periods of growth, consumers have a tendency to spend more and more loans. National income usually explains some of the EU-wide differences of consumption, but in a more homogeneous economical, legal and technical environment such as the European market, how does consumption differ? In Europe, variations in income can explain a lack of convergence between the Euro-zone countries and the others. Where we find similar economic and politico-legal conditions, some product and service consumption tends to converge at first, and is then followed by divergence. For example, new technology converges at macro-level, but differs at the micro-level. National income gaps typically exist between new entrant countries, and even more with Bulgaria and Romania (the newest members, in 2007) and candidate countries including Albania, Bosnia-Herzegovina, Croatia, Macedonia, Serbia and Montenegro, and Turkey.

In addition, personal income (discussed in Chapter 5) and the quality of life of Europeans will influence the marketing mix. The 15 'older' European members are more intensively exposed to the marketing mix and its influences than newer European Member States. This means that the product or service may need to be more innovative and promoted differently in older Member States. Consumers may be less sensitive to price issues, and have reached a higher level of consumption saturation. Marketers need to think in terms of questions similar to the following: Why buy another car if you already own two? What would motivate your client to purchase another or different mobile phone if everyone in the household and workplace already owns one or more? For new members or applicants, what fashions lead consumers to purchase your goods or services? Is there a desire to resemble Europeans, and do consumers wish to obtain the same or a superior quality of life?

8.2.4 Demographic conditions

Demographic variations can also have a significant impact on the assessment of the EU market and its opportunities to the marketer, as do disposable incomes per head. We can estimate the levels of demand, size and development of the market, its regions or single Member States via information about demographic movements. Also, price movements in these markets, the level of development of financial, physical and supporting HR infrastructures are influenced by demography. The analysis of similar or supplementary products or services assesses the conditions of marketing in a very precise manner. While the size of the population in a given market is important, its characteristics are more crucial in relation to the product or service. The identification of the right clientele, a reliable population with similar behaviour and attitudes, can be pursued by means of countries, reports, sector analysis provided by EU and international institutions such as the OECD, or market studies. The sources obtainable from governmental and non-governmental agencies are most useful for SMEs that do not necessarily have their own departments dedicated to this exercise, in contrast to large or highly resourced enterprises. The latter typically, though not systematically, attempt to stay close to the information of the market through their own researchers and consultants.

Market segmentation will take demography into account because it involves aggregating prospective buyers into groups that not only share common needs or desires, but will respond similarly to the marketing action. Communities are sought in opposition to individuals, though the promotion exercise answers to the desire of Europeans to be individual and unique. This desire is noticeable towards the northern countries.

Segments must be measurable in purchasing power and size. This means that marketers must be able to promote effectively and to serve the segment. The segment must be sufficiently large for sound profit potential, and also must match the corporation's marketing capabilities. Age defines some segments, for example, reaching from the teenager segment (12–19 years) to the senior citizen segment (from 70 onwards). In the ageing populations of Europe, these two segments are most interesting because the first has a growing (relative) purchasing power and decision impact in the buying process, while the latter segment is increasingly large. Both segments also exhibit very similar needs or behaviour across borders, and are part of the most important subcultures in Europe. However, the purchasing power does vary between the segments. Both segments require that the corporate sector provides specifically adapted products and services in terms of comfort and lifestyle. Since 1999, the EU population has fewer children but is living longer than two generations ago. Eurostat figures show that between 1997 and 2007, only Ireland experienced a baby boom.

A demographic segmentation by gender may be useful, knowing that women's equal rights are protected by EU legislation and women's equality in the society and the workplace is more prominent the more the society is situated in the north of the EU: the participation of women in the economic, social, political and civic components of society, as well as equal treatment on pay, desegregation, family and working life provides households with additional purchasing power and evolving preferences on an individual and family level.

Marketing needs to recognize that European society faces important demographic challenges that may have positive or negative impacts on its activities. These changes open up opportunities for adapted products and services: European societies, for examples, necessarily have to find solutions for pensions, healthcare and welfare through such measures as raising the retirement age, increasing taxes or cutting benefits (or a mix), or immigration. Europe's demographic problem of a large elderly population is a challenge to pension funds and other financial organizations in this sector. At EU level, a pension forum exists which improves collaboration between the Member States, aligns their different points of view, solves issues, and proposes solutions to pension management in consultation with the private sector. The forum also aims to agree a general strategy on the pension programme that the member countries will be satisfied with.

Indeed, the absence of a common regulatory framework for pension rights still leaves barriers to the free movement of workers, which is a difficult situation for social policies and labour needs. At the same time, immigration from other continents brings in a temporary and permanent workforce between the two sides of the international division of labour: On the one side, guest workers often arrive under substandard conditions as a result in a shift of labour resources away from underdeveloped countries. Refugees and asylum seekers avoid persecution coming into the most liberal countries of the EU; for example, in the UK, where the administrative requirements for the job market are less strict than in other EU countries. On the other side, highly educated migrants from non-EU countries come to Europe as part of a so-called brain drain in order to earn higher occidental salaries and to experience more liberal attitudes. This phenomenon attracts a niche customer base that is quite different, in its first generation, from the traditional 'European' clientele, with cultural and societal behaviour and preferences that the marketer can be interested in. The second generation is normally a segment that desires a fast integration into the society while being soundly rooted into the parent's identity. Again, this is a segment for the marketer: one that is comparable to that of the segments in future candidate countries.

Europe needs cheap labour in order to keep its industry and competitive edge vis-à-vis low-cost competition from all over the world (this will be studied further in Chapter 10). In France, immigration flows in mainly from the Maghreb (North African Mediterranean countries), in the UK from India and Pakistan, in Germany from Ukraine and Eastern Europe, and formerly from Turkey, in Poland from Russia, in Italy from Albania and other countries from this region; with people coming in legally or illegally.

8.2.5 The social agenda and sustainability

The sustainability of marketing in Europe is dependent on issues that directly flow from the conditions developed in the analysis above. This sustainability is profoundly influenced by the EU's vital interest in economic growth and welfare. The current challenges are defined by an analysis of the unemployment deficit, through the European Commission, forwarding crucial factor disadvantages as stemming from:

- A services gap: employment in the services sector is much smaller in the EU than in the US.
- A gender gap: only about half of European women are part of the workforce compared to two-thirds in the US.

- An age gap: the rate of unemployment in the 55–65 age group is high.
- A skills gap: skill requirements in the EU are not matched by supply, particularly in the IT sector.
- Long-term structural unemployment: about half of those out of work have been so for over a year (Social Policy Agenda, EU).

As a solution to these issues, demographic evolution and education are key to the EU socio-economic agenda. Demographic developments are accompanied by social issues and particular challenges to (or from) minorities. An illustration for this was the rioting in French and other European suburbs in 2005/6. With the support of European institutions, various organizations exist that aim to combat discrimination against minorities, and equal rights and opportunities. Institutions include AGE (European Older People's Platform), ILGA Europe (International Lesbian and Gay Association – Europe), ENAR (European Network against Racism), and the EDF (European Disability Forum) (more information can be accessed online at http://europa.eu.int/comm/development). These are anti-discriminatory organizations among the community that attempt to decrease the discrimination against old people, women, people with disabilities, poor people, people of varying origins, cultures, and personal sexual preferences. Engaging in these anti-discriminatory or humanitarian initiatives, as well as in conflict prevention, raises the image and brand reputation of firms. In Europe – again more in the north than towards the south – corporate social responsibility is a clear necessity and at the same time a value-added to marketing efforts. The main parties that interact in the corporate social responsibility are the business, workers, investors and consumers (Monks, 2004). All stakeholders are concerned with ethical labour standards, which should conform to the standards set by European institutions for working conditions, child labour, forced labour and pension systems. Also, sustainable development is at the top of the agenda in this context.

Yet another, new social phenomenon is detectable for the attentive marketer, in Europe and in all rich economies, caused by commercial and industrial changes due to technology. The developments in this field cause an individualization and intensification of work, which results in increasing stress and work accidents. The concept of 'wellness' has become important in marketing in Germany, and it has a great marketing potential.

A firm cannot pretend to be something or believe in an action; it has to show that that very something is part of the corporate reality. The transparency installed within Europeanization and globalization ensures that image can only be created from real actions, or else, a boomerang effect leads to corporate disaster in terms of marketing.

Efficient marketing takes account of these different phenomena and adapts to them in the quest for message sustainability. Some of the phenomenon that we have studied are similar among EU Member States and may invite an EU-wide marketing approach. Others are more diverse from one country or region to another and may ask the marketer for further segmentation. The sociocultural conditions of the European environment will provide further insights.

8.2.6 Socio-cultural Conditions

The understanding of cultures is crucial for marketing across borders because it defines norms and values, behaviours and perceptions, as well as preferences of the consumer.

Therefore you have to be able not only to know cultures but, even more, to adapt to cultures. Chapter 6 has exposed the fact that this includes national or regional, professional, industrial and functional, and company cultures (Schneider and Barsoux, 2003). All of them shape how the firm markets and how the consumer acts and reacts.

The temptation to over-generalize stereotypes is strong for marketers since culture conveys basic values, consumer's perceptions, wants and behaviour of individuals in every society. Although consumer's needs and perceptions may vary from one region to another within the same country, consumers from different bordering countries may share common values, attitudes and behaviour. A response to the unique needs of consumers in more than one market requires most of the time a customized process, in order to fully satisfy consumer's local needs or specificities. On the other hand, standardizing a product or service reduces expenditures, and allows for economies of scale. How can one expect which client to act and react in a given cultural context?

Some basic cultural information about European countries is most useful for understanding the European market. While direct exposure to different cultures is the very best way of learning about them, and how to adapt, this is only possible for some countries. It is barely possible to go and live in every single market that is targeted across Europe. That means that tools are needed that allow recognition of marketing opportunities and threats based on certain cultural traits. Understanding cultures (see Box 39) and showing adaptability to different contexts is key to marketing in Europe.

Box 39   The marketer's sociocultural understanding focus

- different ways of thinking and behaving;
- different tastes and preferences (aesthetics, religions, personal choices);
- different lifestyles (brand images, signs and values, family);
- different priorities (individualist versus collectivist, dedication to work, family, leisure, attitude to change).

By identifying difficulties in intercultural relations, the marketer comes to relativize 'different' or 'disadvantageous' elements in another culture by comparing these to similar situations already encountered in a similar context. An example is how important it is to know about the acceptance of foreign languages in the media: in Germany, for instance, English words are regularly adapted to the German context, and this is considered as normal, modern and a sign of openness to others (an interesting illustration is that in Germany, the mobile phone is called a 'Handy', which leaves Anglophone visitors stunned). In France, any English wording in a product or service promotion needs translating and is restricted in number (the Académie Française controls the proper preservation of the French language); in Sweden and Finland, most TV programmes are shown in the original language, often in English, and the consumer is used to that. This is the reason why case studies are excellent tools for this exercise. They can show you failures and successes in translations for example, such as that of Carrefour (see the case study at the end of Chapter 3). When self-acquired, first-hand information is missing or incomplete, commercial sections of embassies and consulates, or academic and consultancy services in the targeted cultures can help avoid making marketing mistakes.

On the basis of comparison and analysis, the marketing of a good or service can be based on the transmission of a better understanding of the customer. Consequently, the product and the price can be adapted and a sound basis for communication can be founded through promotion. The study of consumer behaviour in relation to culture provides determinant information to firms and organizations. In what Kotler named core cultural values (1988: 160), certain beliefs and values persist over a long time and the firm needs to adapt to these. In Europe, people believe in freedom, in particular that of expression, in equality of people and chances, in the benefit of democracy, in social networks, to mention just a few commonalities. In what Kotler (1988) calls secondary beliefs and values, that may change at a much faster pace, Europeans generally accept that marriage or partnerships may be hetero- or homosexual, that monoparental families are relatively frequent nowadays, and that the social security networks and pension policies need to be adapted to demographic necessities and to survive these challenges so as to maintain an appropriate quality of life for all.

Most of these values are clearly rooted in religious ideas or a societal history. In Europe, Christianity is the most represented religion and has been for centuries. Mainly, you will expect to encounter Catholics, Protestants and Orthodox Christians, a result of the religious division of the eleventh century. In 1904 German sociologist, Max Weber, made a famous connection between Protestant ethics and 'the spirit of capitalism' that had many repercussions in the Anglo-Saxon world – and for the economists influenced by this school of thought – because it was in opposition to Catholic doctrine that salvation arrives in life after death, and is not connected to wealth. The Islamic religion is becoming increasingly represented in Europe due to immigration, and this phenomenon plays yet another role in the consumer behaviour of Europeans.

This perception of religions may lead to stereotypes that are too harsh to be true. Nevertheless, any classification or segmentation is subject to a certain tendency to stereotype, which is not necessarily bad if used as a reference point. If you leave this reference point and then adapt it to lived realities, the stereotype will have had a positive role to play.

Stereotypes may be enhanced through differences in interpersonal communication, either more expressive (in the south) or rather reserved (towards the north), or with a variable expressive culture (Eastern Europe). Verbal communication has to do with words and the meaning of words. Para-verbal language refers to how loudly we speak those words, the meaning of silence and the significance of conversational overlap. With non-verbal communication (also called body language) we communicate without using any words at all. For example, in Estonia, women do not shake men's hands in business when greeting each other. In France, you may be greeted by being embraced and kissed on the cheeks (with two, three or four kisses depending on the regional culture), and this may also happen in Spain; in Germany and Austria, greeting someone means shaking their hand. Body language can also be different from one culture to an other; so is the perception of space and intimacy – again, while there is much diversity, certain similarities can be found. In northern European countries, priority is given to work, and behaviour reflects this in the lifestyle; in the Latin and Mediterranean cultures, people say that 'there is life after work', and give a relatively high priority to personal relationships. There, communication is more dynamic and warm-hearted. A business meeting may well start with a discussion about one's children. The presentation and discussion of your marketing report may extensively include the personal perceptions of those colleagues invited to the meeting. Again, similarities may be found in several countries or regions. Testimony 2 illustrates the necessity for adaptation with the example of Euro RSCG's activities in southern Europe.

Testimony 2   Ricardo Monteiro, CEO Euro RSCG Group Portugal and CEO Euro RSCC Latin America, and Executive Committee Euro RSCG Worldwide, March 2006

I've been an executive for Euro RSCG Worldwide for the past seven years. I previously worked for BBDO, an American advertising firm, and for Unilever, the consumer goods giant. In my career I've worked in Portugal, Spain, France and have completed my university studies at the Université Catholique de Louvain, in Belgium. I'm currently CEO for Euro RSCG Portugal and CEO for Euro RSCG Latin America, where we employ about 2000 people in 18 countries. We do advertising and provide marketing services across the world to the likes of Peugeot, Citroen, Volvo, Danone, L'Oréal, Reckitt-Benckiser, Airbus, and many others, making us the fifth largest communications conglomerate in the world.

What particular value does southern Europe add to Euro RSCG's activities? Southern Europe is becoming less and less southern Europe in the sense that cultural and social values are, albeit slowly, converging across the European region and, I would even dare say, some Latin American countries, such as Argentina or Chile, and even large groups in North America and Canada. The Latin characteristics that used to stand out are becoming part of everyone's values and only a few things subsist as being peculiar to southern Europe. Among those, I would underline family traits (young people staying at home with parents until they get married, even though they might hold jobs and have a career), eating habits (two full meals a day, long lunch and dinner hours) and a certain 'joie de vivre' that still stands out, particularly when compared with northern countries. These are sufficient for a certain number of industries behaving differently in southern Europe. Banks direct their mortgages to the new graduate from university as opposed to the general population in more northern countries, restaurant advertising is in its infancy, but taking off where McDonald's or Pizza Hut have been an advertising feature in, say, the UK for the best part of the last 20 years, and product categories such as rum or vodka either make

(Continued)

it in Spain and Italy or they're bound to fail in Europe. Keep in mind also that Spain, Italy, Portugal and Greece stand out among the world's favourite tourist destinations. This propels all of these countries to the top of marketing know-how in that category and brings with it a cultural mingling that transforms the atmosphere here into a vibrant location, a true crossroads of peoples and cultures that all create an atmosphere of hospitality and understanding that might justify why, anywhere in the world these days, you'll find Spanish companies on the prowl (they dominate the scene in Latin America) and vast diasporas of Italians, Greeks and Portuguese that have strong positions in restaurants and small 'mom and pop' businesses that proliferate in the landscape. Being a southern European gives one the advantage of centuries' old cultures that have learned to listen, not to impose, to adapt, not to dictate. Don't forget, southern Europeans colonized the world and were first to learn that rule by force will only get you ousted faster. Do we see any particular difference between advertising and communication (its tools, techniques, strategies, targets, etc.) in Europe and that conducted in Latin America? There are things, such as language and folklore, that are shared mainly by Spain and Portugal with Latin America. And they're important. And, most of the African legacy in, for instance, Brazil, can also be found in Angola or on the streets of Lisbon. The Catholic inheritance in the whole of the Latin America region harks back to Spanish missionaries and it has, in many ways, shaped the mentalities. So, the ethics behind advertising messages, the total ignorance of certain important aspects of society today, such as homosexuality, divorce or the rule of the powerful, are still treated or, should I say, ignored by not only advertising but also mainstream media. Therefore, a certain conservatism prevails in the language and only beauty sells – no 'real imagery' or 'real people'. Not the gruesome reality of day-to-day life in the '*favela*' but rather the projective way of the lifestyle anyone would love to have. I think that in southern Europe – a possible line of division with Latin America – we're now getting closer to a certain, 'westernized' reality where social tensions of a basic nature – inequality, rich versus poor, socialism as a solution, fighting corruption – are no longer important. Our (European) speech has moved towards 'employment stability', 'social Europe' whereas in LatAm they're still going for those very basic values. All of this reflects in advertising and communications.

What works better here, what works better there? In southern Europe, indulgence, appeal to luxury and gadgetry, far away places, second cars, second homes. In LatAm, moving up from basics, the first car, the first mobile telephone, the first house. A better detergent, a fuller ice-cream.

Is European diversity (of people, perceptions, cultures and its business environment) an advantage or disadvantage for Euro RSCG's business? It can be an advantage if you come from an open culture such as southern European cultures or

(Continued)

(Continued)

Scandinavian cultures. It can be a terrible hindrance if one comes from France or the UK, where ignorance of other cultures and motivations is prevalent and people tend to concentrate on their national problems and do not see or accept experiences from other countries as valid for their own. Indeed, I always find it more difficult to explain to a Frenchman what Brazil is like – his or her standard reply usually starts with 'In France we . . . ' – than, for instance, to a Swede who will ask all the questions and try to find out as much as possible about your country before he or she ventures into advice. But general ideas are always misleading. There's a growing number of people, mainly young people, who have gone through Erasmus and other European programmes that are coming out as truly diverse and open in their approach and, no matter where they were born, come across as a first generation of 'Europeans' as we like to think of them: open-minded, diverse, with cultural texture and density.

Language barriers, on the contrary, are more difficult to tackle by marketers in Europe who find that for communication campaigns customization is crucial. The other alternative is to find methods to communicate a message that is passepartout (applies quasi-universally), for example using a minimum of text but treating issues that appeal to people across Europe, that is, shared core values (used for beauty and hygiene products for instance, but also for high-tech products or cars).

Language problems can give the wrong impression and images about a product, a service or a company, and can easily be avoided through the help of competent translators of the desired mother-tongue. European legislation requires that the content description on packaging be in all languages of the markets targeted.

In addition to the above, symbols and colours have an impact on promotion and media planning. In this framework, the well-informed advertisement marketer in Europe studies preferences for cinema, commercial or satellite TV. For instance, in Germany 30 per cent of homes view satellite TV. The Internet, newspapers, posters, billboards are supports that work to different degrees; their applicability depends, for instance, on the tendency of people to live outdoors and to travel, in which case billboards and neon signs are attractive tools. Their use in the EU is, however, constrained. Radio and ICT provide important alternatives, mainly at rush hour: Scandinavians finish work at 4 p.m., the French, at 5.30 p.m. Drive times vary from urban to rural regions, and radio and rush hours vary too. Overall, promotion in print is still the biggest single share for advertisement in Europe, while internet advertising has a small but growing percentage (Gillingham, 2005). On an EU scale, it can be observed that media spending is much higher in Germany, the UK and France than it is in Italy.

8.2.7 Geopolitical and geo-historical conditions

In Europe, geopolitical and geo-historical conditions influence the manner in which you can position a product in different markets. As mentioned above, some language barriers stem from sociocultural variations; these are often also based on other conditions. In West Germany between 1945 and 1990, for example, the US government engaged in particular geopolitical interests that were in opposition to the interests of those living on the other side of the Iron Curtain. The Marshall Plan and US forces therefore had a particularly strong influence on economic developments and lifestyles after World War II. As a consequence, English remains an easily accepted language for promotion, and trends that come from an Anglo-Saxon environment are often readily adopted. In another example, in some of the accession countries the socialist past is a rather negative reference point; for subgroups, however, this past reminds them of perceived advantages that the capitalism-focused economies do not provide (full employment, free childcare, etc.).

Perceptions of products or services are influenced by these conditions. In our new era of global terrorism, this threat is vastly perceived and not limited to particular places or regions. 11 September 2001 had its impact on marketing too, on a worldwide level. First, the Madrid and London bombings demonstrated that Europe is at risk; that international terrorism not only targets the US or tourist locations such as Bali, but also Europe. Secondly, the attacks affirmed that some European countries serve as transit places for sleepers, that is, extremists who are covered by neutral well-integrated identities in any society and who may be dispatched for attacks after a certain amount of time. Thirdly, terrorist groups recruit certain young Europeans or second-generation Europeans into their ranks and employ them for their local knowledge and for geopolitical reasons of their own. The challenges stemming from these phenomena force marketers into yet another sensibility about people and perceptions. For example, after the London bombings, the cycle industry was able to position its product by maintaining that it was safer to travel by bicycle than by other forms of transport. (By the way, in other locations, this industry also reacts to people's preoccupations about the environment and about well-being and health into old age.) After each attack, consumers around the world perceived the threat of terrorism as being based on striking with the element of surprise against innocents and attracting as much media impact as possible. For the security sector also, important market opportunities appeared. For the retail industry, a tendency to store more basic food products is measurable. For clothing, fashion stores such as Zara, turned to darker clothes (expressing grief) in Europe after the attacks. In terms of brand marketing, it was recently demonstrated that on a worldwide level US brands have generally lost share while European brands using a multiple brand strategy have improved their place in the market because they are less exposed to the psychological association of the 'prime target' (Suder et al., 2007).

Finally, a particular market can hold promises in terms of image due to the geopolitical interests of governments. For example, the marketing of science parks in Turkey holds the potential for the development of marketing opportunities in the Middle East, and are supported by EU funds that encourage collaboration with or within accession countries.

8.3 The Ps and AIDA: A marketing mix for Europe

Just like the complexities in international marketing, European marketing strategy depends on the number of segments that the company has decided to target. It can be either a standardized marketing strategy with a standardized marketing mix applied to all targeted groups, or a concentrated market dividing a marketing mix to reach a single segment of the global market, or a differentiated global marketing with different marketing mixes for each target group. The crucial deciding factor about being able to standardize marketing strategy is the similarity of the benefits sought by segments in different geographic markets.

When a marketer has defined a specific target, the time comes to develop the marketing answer to the consumer through:

- a product or service that is well designed and adapted;
- its placement;
- at a well-defined price; and
- sold with the right choice for its promotion and communication.

Before the development of this strategy, marketers have to be sure of the targeting process. The best means that may be used in marketing may be classified into three main categories as presented in Box 40: the Pull-strategy, the Push-strategy and the Contact-strategy.

Box 40   Marketing strategies

- the Pull-strategy, creating customer demand through all promotional efforts, 'pulled' demand through distribution channels, that is, leading the consumer to the product, for instance via advertising activity;
- the Push-strategy, pushing the product through the distribution channel into the retailer;
- the Contact-strategy, establishing a direct contact with the consumer through canvassing and follow-up (Kotler, 1988).

Which strategy is the most adapted and why is entirely dependent on the product or service and its target market. Do the size and the growth potential of the targeted market allow for a long-term standardization strategy? If not, high competition might need to be avoided, unless you satisfy an unsatisfied consumer better than the competition. Within your European strategy, is the targeted market compatible with the company's goals?

Non-European companies wishing to establish a European operation may need to adapt the market strategy depending on the company's status, as illustrated in Table 20.

Table 20   Company responses to European markets

Company status	Challenges	Response
Established multinational in one market/multiple markets	Exploit opportunities from improved productivity	Pan-European strategy or regional/country segmentation
	Meet challenge of competitors Cater to customers/intermediaries doing same	
Firm with one European subsidiary	Competition Loss of niche	Expansion Strategic alliances Rationalization Divestment
Exporter to Europe	Competition Access	European branch Selective acquisition Strategic alliance
No interest in Europe	Competition at home Lost opportunity	Entry

Source: material drawn from Magee, 1989, and adapted from Czinkota et al., 2003: 262

Another strategic question is whether a company has the minimum resources (competences/ human resources/financial resources, etc.) to do well? Pricing will be one dependent of this.

8.3.1 The marketing mix in Europe

Decisions on pricing are crucial because of the effect on returns on investment, revenues and hence profits. At the same time, the price of a good or service will shape the perception and willingness of people to engage into a first or a repeat purchase, in terms of quality, image, and positioning vis-à-vis the competition of similar or complementary value. The purchasing power of the market segment needs to be taken into account. By worldwide comparison, price differences in Europe are relatively small, although there are some exceptions as follow:

- goods or services taxed by governments, for example petrol;
- goods or services that have obtained a particular brand recognition in a particular country and are more expensive there than elsewhere, such as cars; and
- goods or services positioned in a more or less deregulated market, such as telephone services.

However, if the brand image is strong in Europe, then a relatively homogeneous pricing can be expected for products (such as Nutella) and for services (such as online purchasing of flowers or books). This is also the case for retail groups that have obtained strong Europe-wide or international buying power, for sales to big European customers, and for cases of parallel imports and grey markets.

Pricing in the form of EU-wide standardization is based on the company setting a price as the product leaves production, with adaptations in terms of foreign exchange rates in non-Euro-zone countries, and in terms of variances in the regulatory field; this is facilitated through the single market and the Euro-zone effects because adjustments are not necessary. Standardization neglects the diversity of the market but, due to its low risk, allows for high-level sales and a coherent price reputation.

Price differentiation is defined, rather, at a regional or local level and is based on the distinction of cultural differences and the perception of the consumer in different markets. This strategy allows for adaptation to the market conditions, local competition, terms and conditions there, and price awareness, but may also invite grey market or parallel import activities across borders. This is the case for, among other examples, the price of tobacco products, which are, again, subject to different levels of national taxes.

Price differences within the Euro-zone tend to reduce with time, which is interesting in terms of sourcing. Prices converge primarily in sectors in which the market is broad and logistics less important, such as in industrial supplies. Also, in mobile and price transparent products and services sold over the Internet, prices converge. However, the attitudes to internet security, to personal spending and savings, and to the choice of the preferred means of payment differ between regions. In France, where credit card payments predominate, the relationship of consumer behaviour and spare change is less developed than in Germany, where most payments are made in cash. Advantageously, we have seen that exchange rate risks only apply to the pricing, to a greater or lesser extent, in those European countries that are not members of the Euro-zone. Nonetheless, differences in VAT still have to be completely eliminated by the EU and, in 2006, varied within a 15 to 20 per cent range; so did excise rates. This is important in transfer pricing, that is, prices set for intra-firm movement of goods and services establish the value of these for taxation purposes when travelling from one country to the other; typically, the ideal solution in setting these prices is to define them on the basis of the tax rates in the countries of manufacturing and distribution (Hollensen, 2004: 509). The difficulty of setting the right price, at cost, at arm's length or at cost plus, can be expected to diminish if the EU is to complete a harmonization of tax regimes. Altogether, the key issue in making price decisions is the question of what price the customer is prepared to pay. If this differs significantly from market to market (for whatever reason that may be), then standardized prices make no sense.

Promotion is crucial to the marketing mix in the two cases developed above, that is, standardization or segmentation by regions or countries. Advertising is key to perception, which in turn is key to competitive positioning and pricing.

Consequently, in the context of brands prestige pricing translates into high pricing for products or services. Examples are Audi TT cars, perfumes, and golf clubs, among others. Positioning and Pricing is the result of a reflection of value and position of the service or good in the market. However, low price-low value strategies, on the other side of the scale, include in Europe particular products that consumers are prepared to accept a low value for, for example, generic brands. The UK's Marks & Spencer and Sweden's Ikea (the largest single furniture retailer in the world) use medium price, good value strategies. Lastly, in penetration pricing strategies, we can find European mobile phones. A quite different strategy has had much success for pre-booking for example: variable pricing means that price in- or decrease as a direct function of demand, for example, in low-cost airlines' online bookings, pioneered in Europe by easyJet and Ryanair.

Altogether, prices reflect what is happening in the market, quality and value, competition, and placement. Benchmark brands influence the pricing of competitors, for example, Perrier in bottled water or companies in commodities with market power. But do not forget that segmentation, discussed earlier, always comes before setting prices, placement and promotion. But even if the core product remains the same, its marketing may differ in accordance with the market and culture. The same product, for example, water, may be sold differently because it may be more or less treated, more or less available, more or less considered valuable and used according to different needs (drinking, cleaning, watering gardens, filling up pools, farming, etc.), and hence at different prices.

In terms of placement, the marketer in Europe recognizes quickly that channel structures and the degree of retailer *power* is not the same in all EU countries. Some national distribution systems are closed networks of producers, transport companies, wholesalers and retailers, but more and more of them are challenged by their European competition. Also, the *means* of distribution are influenced by transport and logistical systems and for consumers goods by wholesaling and retailing systems. Consequently, these systems differ for legal reasons, especially in transport laws, environmental rules on emissions and congestion, planning laws that restrict where production, distribution and retailing operations take place, and technical factors (Harris and McDonald, 2004). For example, in France, hypermarkets were invented because the French did not allow supermarkets in cities.

As mentioned above, good promotion is the key to the most researched perceptions and demand. Their taxonomy influences the behaviour of consumers, who in Europe are exposed typically to receiving between 2000 and 3000 messages per day through advertisements, some of which go unrecognized (most), while others raise awareness.

Legal conditions influence promotion policies because laws on advertising and promotion activities vary across European countries; this was mentioned above in the context of neon boards. But cultural differences often require different types of promotion too. Language differences hinder much of Europe-wide word and mouth, and may hinder large-scale reputation-building and effective promotion. Technical factors often require differences in the demographic and geographical coverage of newspapers, and television and ownership of telephones and connection to the Internet also influence the ability to adopt the same promotion package.

Harris and McDonald (2004) propose the following combination of products and promotion packages in this single but diversified European market:

- the same product and the same means of promotion: is the least cost system and permits economies of scale and scope;
- the adapted product and the same means of promotion;
- the same product and different means of promotion;
- the adapted product and different means of promotion: has the highest cost and limits economies of scale and scope.

The AIDA-toolbox (Weilbacher, 1984) summarizes the main stages in communication and marketing, and consists of:

- **A**wareness raising (how to combat selective perception): the first barrier to pass (Benetton or Barnardo's Child Poverty)
- **I**nterest: does your communication raise interest in your product or service?
- **D**esire: to buy the product or get involved in the service
- **A**ction: getting the consumer to actively seek the product or service.

In all promotion activity, the main questions to analyse are the following: Who is your target market? What is its demography and culture? Does it contain conservative or modern groups, religions, etc.? Could it be that your advertisement offends people? Are the people you may offend your customers? Consumer freedom depends on his or her particular standpoint, culture, and background. If controversial ads are used, this needs to be studied in terms of positive or negative impact on sales. Advertising, personal selling, sales promotion, PR arise as part of AIDA – perhaps the most affected by culture; even if the product is the same your promotion of it is often different.

Is the promotion about brand or product? How saturated are the target customers by your or your competitors' campaigns? Are you as the marketer solely generating revenues or are you also pursuing other goals (for example, stakeholder satisfaction through social or environmental concerns). Do you want to raise awareness or get people straight to buy your product? In Box 41, you will find a non-exhaustive checklist of 'must-dos' in advertising.

Box 41   The 'must-do' in controlling your advertising: a checklist

- Who is the target customer of the advertisement?
- What benefit does the advertisement best emphasize?
- What is the message that is communicated?
- How effective is the advertisement at reaching the target and at communicating the message?
- Can you think of a better way to communicate with the target audience?
- What are the perceptions shown in test marketing with a sample group?

The advertisement's message has to be driven by information, rather than the artistic aspirations of an advertising agency; these aspirations can nevertheless be useful if used positively to attract awareness through creative and innovative approaches. It is crucial to be explicit in the marketer's message to the agency. With perfume, for example, mainly men buy it for their partners; the promotion, therefore, must mainly target men.

The integrated European market gives people a great choice of consumption in terms of quality and quantity, and illustrates its great freedom of expression (Gillingham, 2005).

8.3.2 The future of European marketing

In the diversity of Europe, we can expect that marketing will develop into segments that grow in size due to important harmonization in the environment – without becoming one single segment for all goods and services marketed herein. Interestingly, the US market appears to be developing in the opposite direction, from a generally standardized marketing towards diversity marketing; this phenomenon is due to ethno-demographic and economic developments in recently immigrated communities. We can expect that in the US, marketing will not arrive at the same level of heterogeneity as it does in Europe though, nor vice versa. Consequently, a convergence of marketing approaches will take place in the long-term that – together with the increasing integration of European and North American markets – hold significant promises to the marketer. Again, Europe is a microcosm that allows the development of strategies applicable in the international environment, parting from a sound European base.

Résumé and conclusion

A European market study is the collection of information on a market that is particularly diversified but that also benefits from market group similarities for efficient marketing. These advantages are based on EU integration as well as on conditions that shape the perception of people in Europe. As a selection of these perceptions, we have studied politico-legal, economic, demographic and sociocultural conditions. These conditions help the marketer identify opportunities and challenges according to a product or service's needs, to demand, and to the environment. Knowing these conditions means adapting the 4Ps of the marketing mix efficiently:

- Know the characteristics and needs of customers in order to satisfy them as well as possible.
- Modify a new product according to the consumers' needs.
- Design a new product.
- Test a new product.
- Know the threats and opportunities of a market.
- Analyse sales and forecast the demand.
- Evaluate reputation and firm's brand image.

The situational analysis of the European environment, customers, other actors such as distributors, suppliers, competition, opportunities and threats can be based on a multitude of freely accessible data. The main challenges for market studies may be language barriers for in depth studies in some of the newer Member States.

(Continued)

(Continued)

In accordance with the firm's internal objectives, strengths and weaknesses a segmentation of target markets may be undertaken or a standardized European-wide marketing strategy adopted. The latter option is certainly the most cost-efficient, but only applies to relatively few products and services. Among them, we have found those characterized by strong cross-border brand images, and internet services that allow for high mobility and flexibility. Also, when logistics are unimportant and European harmonization is required, an EU-wide strategy makes sense.

In conclusion, the leakage effects of traditional marketing approaches in a European context make national approaches less effective, but often enough somewhat useful because of important diversities in the perceptions of the European peoples. Any corporation is well advised to market its goods or services in Europe because the flows of trade, investment and sourcing in the EU reduce the specific advantages that a firm would achieve from outsourcing or foreign supply. Marketing can hence be an underpinning of a sound European strategy wherever possible in terms of adapted product or service? Because all efficient marketers use the possibilities that the single market provides (on a regional or EU-wide basis), only those firms that still only act locally lose out on these opportunities.

The true key to success indeed lies in the art of adapting a marketing strategy to either an EU-wide or a country or regional segmentation, in which the marketing mix of the good or service bathes in the perceptions of people, based on long-term similarities. The factor advantages in European marketing are anchored into the best possible compromise between costsavings, quality management and local knowledge. Product or service features, the right price, an efficient promotion, and the place best adapted are dependent on the heterogeneity of successful marketing.

Mini case study: Breaking the ice – how to sell a business development strategy in Greece

When I came back to Europe after many years of working abroad, in particular in South Africa, my activities as consultant for Digital Equipment Corp – Europe led me to conceive business development plans for a vast range of corporations. Selling the proposal for a strategy to a company is just like selling anything. You need to position, adjust, evaluate, and make sure that you target your customer well.

For example, our team was asked to draft a business development strategy for one of the major banks in Greece. As part of this activity, I was to present the technology-based strategy and the implementation strategy to the board of directors. I flew in for this purpose, not knowing the clients but by distance, and only indirectly

(Continued)

through my team. Upon arrival, I was not aware that I had been announced as the 'Einstein' to the solution that was needed for the bank's development.

When I entered the meeting, I was taken aback by the pompous and ceremonial way in which I was received. The meeting was held in a large room in which a half-circular table with numerous participants dominated the space where I was to stand and talk from. You may imagine my feelings of discomfort. In addition, presentations were rather stiff and I could feel the animosity in the room. Members of the board were presented by their titles as well as their prevailing importance in the structure; no doubt was left as to my position as exterior consultant only.

Once presentations were over, I was about to start introducing my project analysis when a fire alarm started to ring. Everyone in the building was evacuated for an emergency exercise, and I found myself outside the building with the board members, this time eye to eye, at the same level. The exercise took a certain amount of time during which we started to talk about my coming to Greece. I was asked whether I knew the country and could advance that my wife has Greek origins.

Over the next few hours, I was able to exchange ideas with the board members over coffees at a local taverna, and finally over dinner. The presentation was rescheduled for the next day. I did indeed sell the development plan to the directors.

The obvious reason for this ostentatious introduction was just to stage a sort of '*rapport de force*' toward the person who had been presented to them as the grand expert especially flown from the European HQ. No special hostility was intended, even though it could have been perceived that way by someone unaccustomed to cultural differences.

This is just one of the many anecdotes that I could tell you about marketing, some more product-oriented and some more project–oriented. Some about management. What counts is to understand the people, to break the ice, to adapt and to know your customer. In Greece, customers tend to like 'impressing' and are expressive; they are proud of their fatherland, local and national competences, and human relations may play an important part in negotiation and sales. In other countries, people are different again. In Germany, for example, people like serious, well-structured and intellectual approaches. In my opinion, 'selling' has the same meaning all over Europe, but knowing the customer helps you recognize opportunities and turn challenges into advantages. Well, if you wish to sell in Europe's diversity, you must be willing to treat all people the same; you must be humane, and get a feeling for the different peoples.

Source: Interview with Daniel Lefevre, VP – EMEA Operations, CRISP Technologies Inc, May 2006

Mini case questions:

1 Judging from Daniel's experience, can marketing in Europe be handled homogeneously?
2 What is the main key to success when selling in Europe?

Review questions

1 **How** does culture impact on consumer behaviour in the buying decision processes?
2 **How** do environmental conditions affect the marketing mix for firms acting in European countries?
3 **What** are the pros and cons of a pan-European marketing strategy?
4 **What** are the fundamental steps to take in conducting a market study (in general and in Europe)?

Assignments

- **Imagine** a product and a service that you wish to market in Europe. Why are the approaches different from those used in other markets?
- **Compare** the promotion of a given product, for example that of a middle-sized car, in Europe and in the USA. What is different in the marketing approach?
- **Case study assignment**: Read and prepare the Schneider Electric case study in Part IV.
- **Internet exercise**: Which Internet sources are most useful for market studies of the European market?

Web guide

http://www.emrc.be/ European Marketing Research Centre.
http://www.emc.be/activities.cfm European Marketing conference.
http://www.consumerpsychologist.com/ Consumer behaviour and marketing.
http://www.maporama.com/home/fr/societe/case+studies.asp Case studies of European firms.

References

Czinkota, M., Ronkainen, I. and Moffett, M. (2003) *International Business.* Mason, OH: South-Western Thomson Learning.

European Communities (2005) *Social Policy Agenda 2005–2010*, Dg Employment, Social Affairs and Equal Opportunities.

Gillingham, D. (2005) *International Marketing Seminar*. Nice: Ceram.

Halliburton, C. and Hünerberg, R. (1993) *European Marketing: Readings and Cases*. Wokingham and Cambridge: Addison-Wesley.

Harris, P. and McDonald, F. (2004) *European Business and Marketing: Strategic Issues*. London: Sage.

Hill, Ch. (2005) *International Business Competing in the Global Marketplace*, 5th edition. Maidenhead: McGraw-Hill.

Hollensen, S. (2004) *Global Marketing – a Decision-oriented Approach*, 3rd edn. Harlow: FT Prentice Hall.

Kotler, P. (1988) *Marketing Management*, 4th edn. London: Longman.

Kotler, P. and Armstrong, G. (1991) *Principles of Marketing*, 5th international edn. London: Prentice Hall.

Magee, J. (1989) '1992 moves Americans must make', *Harvard Business Review,* 67 (May–June): 78–84.

Mercado, S, Welford, R. and Prescott, K. (2001) *European Business*. Upper Saddle River: Prentice Hall.

Monks, J. (2004) *The European Social Model: myth or reality?* May Day Celebration, EU Enlargement, Speech, ETUC General Secretary, Gorizia

Muhlbacher, H., Leihs, H. and Dahringer, L. (2006) *International Marketing: A Global Perspective*, 3rd edn. London: Thomson Business Press.

Onkvisit, S. and Shaw, J. (1988) 'Marketing barriers in international trade', *Business Horizons,* 31 (3): 64–72.

Pardo, P., Rodríguez, L. Serna and Alarcón, E. Toledo (2005) *Marketing in the European Union*. Alicante: Economía Financiera, Contabilidad y Marketing, MEU.

Quelch, J. and Harris, B. (2005) 'Six sigma comes to marketing', *European Business Forum,* 22 (autumn): 33–5.

Schneider, S. and Barsoux, J.-L. (2003) *Managing across Cultures*. London: Pearson Education.

Suder, G. (1994) '*Anti-dumping measures and the politics of EU – Japan create relation in the European consumer electronic sector: the VCR case*'. PhD dissertation, University of Bath; Working Paper, Thomson Consumer Electronics External Relations Department, Bath and Paris.

Suder, G., Chailan, C. and Suder, D. (2007) *Has Terrorism an Effect on Brand Value? An Empirical Study on the 100 Biggest World Brands*, CERAM Working Paper, Sophia Antipolis.

The Economist (1989) '*The myth of the Euro-consumer*', 4 November, p. 79.

Tordjman, A. (1994) 'European retailing: convergences, differences and perspectives', *International Journal of Retail and Distribution Management,* 22 (5): 3–19.

VanderMerwe, S. and L'Huillier, M. (1989) 'Euro-consumers in 1992', *BusinessHorizons,* January/ February: 34–40.

Webb, John R. (1992) *Understanding & Designing Marketing Research*. London: The Dryden Press.

Weilbacher, W. (1984) *Advertising*, 2nd edn, New York: Macmillan.

Other web sources:

http://www.consumerpsychologist.com/international.htm: Lars Perner;

http://www.mckinsey.com/practices/marketing/ourknowledge/pdf/WhitePaper_MarketinginThree Dimensions.pdf

9 Lobbying the Playing Field

> ### What you will learn about in this chapter:
>
> - What is lobbying, and what are the opportunity networks for lobbying?
> - Why is European lobbying increasingly important, and what do you lobby for?
> - How do you lobby the EU?
> - Who lobbies, when, where do you lobby?
> - Further recommendations about contemporary lobbying strategy and action in Europe.

Introduction

The preceding chapter looked at marketing in Europe and highlighted the importance of diversity management tools when it comes to carrying it out. A rather different kind of 'marketing' – this time not that of a product or service, but that of a company and its sector of activity – will now be considered: that of lobbying the EU.

Why is this just as important as those traditional management tools? First of all, both European business and international corporations from non-EU countries have recognized the importance of institutional opportunity networks at EU level. These opportunity networks can be defined as more or less loosely organized relations among (in our case) business and governmental authorities that are potentially beneficial to the involved parties. These networks play an important role in the search for sustainable competitiveness. If you know how to examine these networks, and analyse the arena, players and competitions that prevail in the relations between firms and institutions, then you are capable of playing a role among private and public actors, that is, a relationship that continuously defines the political economy. This relationship is mainly focused on information exchanges, and relies on the interest of each actor to communicate with others and to promote a point of view, comparable to a corporate marketing exercise.

This chapter therefore studies the most efficient and recognized ways of getting a business's voice heard in Brussels, Strasbourg and Luxembourg. This is key to the essential competitive advantages for any firm that is doing business in Europe.

The focus of the subsequent sections is as follows. First, we largely define lobbying and European opportunity networks. European lobbying has increased with each wave of European integration, and with this, the recognition of the EU as an international player and its legitimacy as a supranational organ. 'Interests are happy to ignore Europe until something from Europe hits their wallets!' argues J.J. Richardson in his important work (Richardson, 2001): the more opportunity structures there are, the more corporations will operate on a European scale, and are present in its power centres – at the heart of the institutions, that is, in Brussels and affiliated locations like Strasbourg and Luxembourg, and in the locations of national and regional power. The underlying culture of lobbying originates in Anglo-Saxon models of interest representation; indeed, to date, more US and UK lobbyists work in Brussels than lobbyists from continental Europe. But organizations from all over the world work in this area, increasing their say there. For instance, you will find a person in charge of following up on EU activities in each embassy located in Brussels (those of Arab or Asian countries for example). A number of companies from these countries also employ an in-house lobbyist.

To meet the expectations of shareholders and, more generally, stakeholders, corporations increasingly fear missing out in the intelligence-gathering game that is a key aspect of access to resources. The EU legislator is the biggest market creator in Europe, and any corporation in the European market faces international competition stemming from other business, and that is, of course, also shaped by this regulator. The practice of public affairs management has become both an integral part of effective business strategy and increasingly professional through the creation of training, diploma, a federation of experts and a code of conduct.

In the following text, we examine what lobbying means. In this context, an understanding of the reasons why European lobbying is increasingly important will be enlarged. Business in Europe is indeed experiencing strong trends towards risk-avoidance strategies, anticipation and pro-activity, that are underpinned by Europeanization: Can you take the risk of losing out on the opportunities that Europeanization and lobbying may bring? Can you take the risk of losing out when the public administration decides upon issues? These may make or break your operations and affect your decision making, as well as your customers' choices or investment policies.

Previous chapters have characterized the EU as a mature democratic and integrated system of members with distinct management cultures but that experience complementarities in their objectives: European integration is worthwhile on an economic, social and geopolitical level, and its governance is easy to access when you are in possession of the appropriate knowledge. So why take unnecessary risks? Where, then, does a corporation represent its interests in the EU in the most efficient and effective manner? This chapter teaches about EU lobbying, which is different from lobbying attitudes, techniques and practices in London, Madrid or Prague. The Union is multifaceted, with many arenas in which major decisions that shape the business environment are made; this calls for a sound understanding of the decision-making processes that were introduced in Part II. In this context, we will also analyse the essential When, Who and How questions: you will learn that there is no way to control consistently the trajectory of a policy game. However, there is a stable setting for participation and consultation. That is where corporations develop best practices in what is professionally called 'lobbying'.

9.1 Lobbying and European opportunity networks

What is Lobbying? The term lobbying is generally used interchangeably with public affairs management or interest intermediation. The main function of this activity is to make one's voice heard and known, and to therewith influence a given public administration. The objective of any organization is to ensure that decisions are taken in a way most suitable to its interest. Lobbying is a legal and beneficial activity that allows institutions to receive various inputs that are necessary for the elaboration of a suitably adequate and equitable decision making.

A political opportunity structure can be defined as the degree to which people or groups are able to gain access to power and to manipulate the political system (McAdam, 1996). In this framework, the main lobbying tool is the exchange of information and expertise, transferring in-depth knowledge and competencies, which provide a corporation with the opportunity to benefit from inputs and outputs at the policy level. For a reminder of the theory underpinning this logic, refer back to Chapter 4.

Efficiency in the formulation of public policy and its implementation is directly associated to the need of economies to stimulate competitiveness and consumer welfare, which are typically at the core of occidental governmental intervention. This search for all-over efficiency in political, economic and social terms, gives rise to a necessity for consultation: governmental bodies and institutions need to maintain a strong link to civil society, its business society and the political society, and are hence in a constant search for expertise and support. This can be explained by the lack of certain expertise in-house in the institutions that are not necessarily up to date about innovations and trends; an institutionalized dialogue ensures equity and the respect of law and codes of conduct.

EU 'pressure' groups are generally welcomed if not even sought for, once proof is made that they contribute with high-value information about the 'real' world and its development potential to the administration. Some structures are easily tackled by high-resources groups because they are able to engage in individual and group lobbying on many levels, maximizing contacts. Sometimes, however, less rich, lower-resourced groups are favoured for their unique and down-to-earth expertise, which is valued by many officials in their information gathering because, as we stated above, the most common size of enterprise in Europe is the SME. In general, institutions value representatives in proportion to the uniqueness of expertise and experience, or weight of representation.

The concept of the lobbying 'arena' or 'playing field' visualizes the setting in which this influence process is situated, as the space in which a lobbying campaign is played out. For any party or actor in the arena, efficient and timely lobbying within the public–private matrix and a proactive anticipation of the institutional agenda-setting play an essential role: three keys to long-term competitiveness can be built this way. They are:

- resilience
- flexibility
- speed of action (proactivity and reactivity).

Table 21 A conceptual matrix of structured interrogation

Screening tool (interrogation)	Best-case scenario (targets)	Strategies (means)
WHY	The vision or issue upon which persuasion needs to be instigated	Prioritizing
WHEN	Before the agenda is set Before and during every stage Risk analysis sets the readiness level	Anticipation Multi-timing along life cycle
HOW	Maximize positive input, alliances and forestall opposing lobby	Scenario planning
WHERE	Multiple access points	Venue shopping Alliance
WHAT	Constructive lobbying Dissuasive lobbying	Business firewalls
WHO	Multi-arena, multi-player	Partnerships

All three key factors are necessary to either (a) gain from the political economy or (b) prevent, deflect or minimize potential corporate disaster. This disaster may be, to cite some examples, one of failure to secure support for mergers, for subsidies, for juridical cases, such as anti-trust decisions, or for action against dumping strategies of competitors. Also, business and other players have the opportunity to express opinions about the economic impact of EU legislation and provide their expertise to the policymaker. This is why lobbying, or public affairs management, has obtained more than only a complementary role in European business competitive strategy. Table 21 draws together the main information about successful European lobbying. You may wish to refer to it at certain times of reading and classwork.

9.1.1 Historical and academic background

9.1.1.1 The what and why of EU lobbying

European lobbying issues have attracted the interest of scholars and researchers from diverse backgrounds, and from business and academia in particular. The latter can be distinguished into two main groups: international business scholars and political science scholars. Both find their origins in the thinking of international law and international relations. They play an essential role in raising awareness among corporations, and as consultants to businesses that plan to engage in or improve their lobbying activities. The word 'lobby'

has been since 1640 used to define 'in the House of Commons, and other houses of legislature, a large entrance-hall or apartment open to the public, and chiefly serving for interviews between members and persons not belonging to the house' (OUP, 2005). In the US
in the nineteenth century, the term 'lobbying' developed into the 'influence [of] members
of a house of legislature in the exercise of their legislative function by frequenting the lobby.
Also to procedure the passing of a measure … by means of such influence' (U.S. Congress
1953). Indeed, Washington was and remains the world's hotspot of lobbying, which has
long been regulated by law (Foreign Agents Registration Act 1938; Federal Regulation of
Lobbying Act 1946).

In Europe, lobbying remained a local, regional and national exercise until its art and
techniques were imported from the UK. Its development was shaped by the necessity for
business to tackle issues covered by the step-wise progression of European integration, and
also by its low-politics decisions in regard to corporate and industrial activity. The underlying concepts in the study of lobbying are rooted in expertise of law-making, formal institutions, procedures and (in particular, originally, foreign) policy and power. Most recent
business theorists examine in particular the 'dual roles of both a receiver and a sender of
influence efforts' (Van Schendelen, 2002) in the private sector, the public–private sector,
and the public sector.

Research about corporate lobbying has increased at a pace exponential to that of lobbying itself, and is – as a result of its origins – strongly influenced by Anglo-Saxon literature.
Herein, political scientists typically emphasize the role of government, and traditionally
exclude this power centre from what is considered as legitimate lobbying at the EU (cf.
Laurencell, 1979), that is, private interest groups, pressure groups and NGOs. The lobbyist
is then analysed in his role in the shaping of decision making (Hix, 1999; Rosamund, 2000).

Corporate public affairs management in Europe has a different face to that of the Anglo-
Saxon world, traditionally leading in this field. In Brussels, US businesses have to learn,
social issues, for example, are of greatest interest. The regulator will be interested in a company's working environment and the way its workforce is treated. Also, what is the
company's contribution to environmental protection, to sustainability, and to citizenship?
Does its interest concord with that of a body in charge of Member States?

UK and US lobbyists were for a long time predominant in the corridors of the institutions,
while German and French corporations preferred fostering their relations with their national
institutions. Deregulation and privatizations in a more and more competitive and competing
European business environment have changed this. European and international interests alike
are ferociously defending their positions on issues from the services directive, the REACH
chemicals' registration and evaluation directive for manufactured products, to banana tariffs,
chocolate labels, vegetable sauces and corporate images (*International Herald Tribune*,
5 April 2005, pp. 1–4).

The theory of 'conceptualizing' prevails in the study of European integration: it questions
to what extent Member States are willing to negotiate about sovereignty, state power and federation, as well as consocation (Taylor, 1996), and multilevel governance (Hix, 1999).
'Theorizing' consists mainly of the intellectual frameworks that analyse functionalism, insti-
tutionalism, supranationalism and interdependency theory (Rosamund, 2000): what is

important in practice is that each one of these approaches sets a different priority for and technique of a given actor (and consequently which time frame the lobbyist uses) that allows for efficient lobbying input and output. We will come back to this in more detail below, when we will model lobbying strategy. The analyses of lobbying cited above attempt to function comprehensively, while mid-level research focuses less on a dependency on integration, but on intermediate interpretation work that is often influenced by management and business studies, or the schools of international relations. This has found expression, for instance, in the works on networks (Figstein and McNichol, 1998; Bück, 2003) and garbage-can incrementalism (Richardson and Mazey 1996) in which policymaking processes produce decisions only marginally different from former practice. A number of scholars have also shown a tendency to evolve by synthesizing or changing established theories (Stone Sweet and Sandholtz, 1998). The diversity of roots in these scholarly efforts to conceptualize lobbying is thus a source of fragmentation in research (Van Schendelen, 2002), and is considered by some as a chance for evolution in the field due to the valuable diversity of approaches that help understand the complexity of this art: one that, in itself, is characterized by diversity.

9.1.2 Who lobbies?

Some pressure groups engaged in their first lobbying activity at the same time as European institutions were created; others arrived as the different landmarks of European integration occurred. Even more started to invest resources in lobbying when it became clear that EU-wide regulations influenced a wide range of business and societal interests, specifically for particular cases or in generally influencing the business environment. Pressure groups involved in the EU lobbying process are typically classified into eight categories: European Associations (for example EACEM and the Greenpeace International European Unit), National Associations (for example the Confederation of British Industry), individual firms or groups (for example Microsoft or the EADS group), lobbying consultancy firms (for example Hill & Knowlton and government policy consultants), public representatives (for example regional governments and local authorities), ad hoc coalitions (coming and going for different issues), single issue groups (for example Software Action Group for Europe), and organizations of experts (for example the European Heart network).

Box 42   The role of a European lobbyist, public affairs manager or adviser

- seek to shape democratic decisions in own or clients' best interests;
- collect and disseminate information;
- analyse impacts;
- complement the knowledge of legislators and bureaucrats in the making of laws;
- present and shape a case in accordance with the political and corporate agenda.

While some of these groups are non-profit-making organizations (largely professional and non-governmental associations, and industry federations), some other organizations are profit making, such as legal advisers, public relations and public affairs firms, and consultants. In 1985, 500 European associations were found to have lobbied the EU institutions (Butt-Philip, 1985). In 2000, there were more than 700 European associations, according to CEC figures, among 3000 groups of various kinds. Some sources estimate that in 2005 the number of lobbyists and advisory bodies around the EU institutions amount to between 15,000 and 20,000 (*European Voice*, 2005), making both Washington and Brussels the most densely lobbied locations in the world. Altogether, among special interest groups in Brussels, can be found mainly European and international federations (members belong to more than 5000 national federations), offices representing *Länder* (German provinces), regional and local authorities, individual firms with direct representation, consultants and law firms. It is impossible to know precisely how many groups are accredited given that the accreditation process has been changed.

Operational lobbyists that act for firms, minority associations, workers' unions or expressive groups, such as Greenpeace or workers' educational associations, will normally be involved in minor political issues. However, representative groups like UNICE (Union des industries de la communauté européenne) or propagational ones such as The European Movement get involved in major political decisions and target therefore higher politics debates and higher-level representatives.

'Players' in the lobbying arena are not only lobbyists and pressure groups. In the denomination of actors we find, on the one hand, professionals and NGOs (also known as issue groups), associations, federations and confederations, corporations, citizens and consumers. On the other hand, institutions are also players that seek to influence others, and they are also influenced by actors. All players engage in 'individualist' action that is more often than not complemented or exercised through 'collectivist' ad hoc or permanent partnerships and cooperation agreements. These collaborations serve to increase power and to control potential competition. With '*hostile brotherhoods*', that is, matching up different interests with each other on specific common interests, the partnering of firms in lobbying occurs despite their competition in the marketplace and on other issues. This requires and is based upon an 'open dialogue' in the private–public arena, a term first used by former President of the Commission Jacques Delors, and that has evolved significantly ever since into a necessity of timely and agenda-adapted strategy (Suder and Greenwood, 2004).

9.1.2.1 The practitioner's perspective

At each landmark of European integration (focused on in Chapter 2), the arena has been transformed. More or different actors have joined, and power relations have been altered. For instance, the Treaty of Maastricht modified the arena of EU lobbying through the increased power of the EP, and altered the primacy of the European Commission within the regulatory institutions (Pedler, 2002). Pedler also recognizes that players can have more than one role to play. Therefore, any lobbyist needs to set an action plan along his or her particular place in the arena and the objectives set, resulting in a specific role for each actor. It would be difficult to act in many different fields; as in any research for strategy, a selection of priorities has to be made. Ideally, a corporation or pressure group plays a role in the decision by in participating in lobbying, and/or also plays a role in the decision's implementation. We also note that this player has a role in providing feedback to governance, either directly or via agents such as the Euro Info Centres. In addition, the increasing role of the EU in the global market that we will discuss in Chapter 10, and the interactions of the EU and Member States' public policy output subject to global forces, make lobbying a strategic activity for companies of any size and sector.

Players in the lobbying arena access certain powers, which can lead to *influencing* agendas, but which can also significantly *write* agendas of a policy development. For instance, if your corporation is the leader in a technology that stimulated certain objectives set by the EU (say, best available technology in waste management, good for the environment and sustainable development), you may be able to initiate tighter legislation favouring the use of your technology – at the same time widening your market opportunities (Suder, 2007). Successful firm representations position this strategy within a 'move from reaction to pro-action' (Pedler 2002: 134). This is even easier if a close association of corporate lobbying strategy to institutions is made, that is, when your information input is valuable and rare enough to lead to the 'institutionalizing' of your input, (the systematic association of particular pressure groups to the policy process in a certain field for consultation) (see Richardson and Mazey, 2001).

The following example provides you with a practitioner's view on how to advise the European institutions: when asked to describe the objectives of the European Actuarial Consultative Group as a professional advisory group in the EU, Gijs van IJsel Smits answered:

I would like to start with some detail about the group, the profession it represents and its activities in regard to the European Commission. Thereafter I will answer the questions regarding its role as a professional and technical advisory group on actuarial issues.

The European Actuarial Consultative Group was established in 1978 to represent the actuarial associations of nine EU countries at the European Commission. The purpose of this representation is to give the Commission advice on subjects concerning the actuarial profession as well as on subjects that relate to the business environment of actuaries. This consulting role is both pro-active and reactive, but has – since its start – resulted in a very useful exchange of thoughts with the Commission.

As some of you may never have heard of the actuarial profession, a few words about it seem appropriate. An actuary is someone with a quantitative/statistical economic background whose primary task is to quantify the economic risks related to future uncertain events. In practice this can be applied in a wide range of activities, from determining how much premium you have to pay for your car insurance to which level of provisions is necessary in a company's pension fund in order to ensure payment of the pension rights to their employees in the future. So it is not surprising that the majority of actuaries work for insurance companies, pension funds or have a job as professional advisor to these institutions.

(Continued)

(Continued)

Just like many other groups of professionals, the actuaries have organised themselves on national level in a professional association. The European Actuarial Consultative Group is representing the actuarial associations in the EU.

Why is representation of the actuarial profession at EU-level so desirable?

The answer comes close to the subject of your investigation. The European Actuarial Consultative Group thinks it is important that, at EU-level, awareness is created about the problems connected to the professional environment of actuaries, especially where EU-legislation has an immediate impact on the risks, price and economic circumstances how the financial services industry can operate in the various EU-countries. In addition, in order to secure high professional standards, the group sets admission criteria for the participation of member associations, including the curriculum required to qualify as an actuary according to the international standards adopted by the group and the International Actuarial Association (IAA). Generally speaking the European Actuarial Consultative Group's strategy is to work proactively in a constructive way with the Commission in a spirit of partnership and credibility. As most of the work relates to the financial services industry, examples of their success relate to legislation for insurance and pension funds. An example from the past is the 3rd Directive for Life Insurance Companies that was issued in 1992 (now being revised). The Directive clearly stated that the provisions for future payments of life insurance companies in the EU need to be determined by a qualified person. Supervisory bodies, for example Central Banks, at national level have the authority to determine who is considered to be 'qualified'. However, given the topics in insurance provisions that require a professional opinion it is clear that actuaries have the right education and qualifications to fit into that job. A more recent example, and still ongoing, of professional input by the group is the role of the actuary at the introduction of IFRS reporting standards for insurance companies in the EU. Here again the actuarial profession can claim a role as best qualified to value the liabilities of insurance companies according to the principle of 'Fair Value', because of the specialist knowledge required to give an opinion and because of the internal Code of Conduct for Actuaries that sets professional standards for the work to be delivered by a qualified actuary. Contrary to some years ago, now the need for consultation is more complicated because:

a) The Commission has also to consider whether an open labour market is not conflicting with granting specific work as the exclusive right of any particular profession which sets their own admission requirements for membership;

b) Other specialist groups (for example financial econometricians) might claim to have equivalent qualifications to do that type of work;

c) The right of free movement of labour within the EU should not be constrained by national professional organizations setting their own admission standards.

To convince the Commission of the importance of the role of the actuary, the Groupe has chosen to discuss their agenda with Directorate General XV 'Internal

(Continued)

Market'. DG Internal Market prepares legislation for the Commission that relates to the financial services industry, including insurance companies. By giving comments and proposing amendments on draft legislation, the European Actuarial Consultative Group shows their determination to make proposals that have the support of the whole actuarial profession in the EU and that improves the overall quality of a proposal with the support of a professional group that is at large responsible for a successful implementation of that same legislation in all EU member states. Though not being granted exclusive rights as executor of new legislation, these consultations do strengthen the role of the actuary in the EU as the person to safeguard transparency, quality and uniformity in the EU. In practice, the group is frequently asked for comments on proposed legislation and, in addition to that, participates in discussion platforms set up by the Commission. Also, at least twice a year a meeting takes place between representatives of the European Actuarial Consultative Group and DG Internal Market and there are also regular meetings with the national supervisors of the financial services industry (CEIOPS).

Care must be taken when comparing the group with lobby groups: The main difference is that lobby groups typically represent a certain industry (transport sector, insurance, banks, pension funds) or a group with a common interest (employers' organizations, labour unions). By representing a group of professional associations the Consultative Group must show their relevance – and, above all, their independence from vested interests – to the Commission by providing advice that enhances the quality of the industries in which their members are employed. In the past 28 years the European Actuarial Consultative Group has done so in a successful manner and is therefore increasingly considered as a valuable discussion partner by the Commission. (*Source*: Interview with Gijs van IJsel Smits, Member of the European Actuarial Consultative Group, Representative of the Dutch actuarial association 'Actuarieel Genootschap', 2005, November 8).

This brings us straight from the 'Who' question to the 'How' question.

9.1.3 The 'How' question

The different strategies used in lobbying can be categorized into three predominant techniques that can be separated by their main objectives of being dissuasive (negative), risk minimalizing (reactive) or constructive (proactive) (see Box 43).

Box 43   Lobbying techniques

- Negative strategies – by opposing Commission proposals directly or through counter-proposals: a dissuasive lobbying technique.
- Reactive strategies – monitoring and answering to meetings and consultations prevail: a risk minimalization technique.
- Proactive strategies – taking the initiative, writing agendas and constructively partnering: a constructive lobbying technique.

A standard strategy in public and private lobbying at the European level consists of 'venue shopping' (Baumgartner and Jones, 1991), in which the complexity of the European framework, and the diversity of players and interests is at the origin of a normative multi-level, multifaceted exertion of pressure. This strategy is used in all three techniques, at different intensity. The particular complexity of this lobbying is mainly considered as opportunity-rich (see, for example, Rosamund 2000; Peterson, 2001; Van Schendelen 2002). How do professionals qualify the complexity of EU lobbying? It is 'a chance for those who have been able to develop long lasting relationships based on content, trust and win-win situation. Clever lobbyists know how to diversify their contacts and not to allow disproportionate friendship,' says N. Rougy, Policy Officer, Club of Madrid, while 'it is a is multi-leveled conciliation process between Commissioners and Cabinets, Members of Parliament, the Directorates-General and Services. Each official brings their own cultural, administrative and national filters to any single issue, enforced by the different interest groups involved in any given debate. A lot of the important policy can be skewed by not what is not only best for Europe, but a national interest or departmental need. Multiply this complexity by the many different lobbying groups on each side. Understanding how to navigate through these different schisms will provide valuable intelligence to a lobbyist making important decisions,' writes R. Pinto, Government Affairs Coordinator, Law and Corporate Affairs (LCA), at Microsoft Europe, Middle East and Africa.

Lobbyists attempt to reach satisfaction at the different venues and, ideally, do so simultaneously. This requires an effective functioning of players at the different levels of policymaking.

The way decisions are made can be compared to a project being managed within a corporation, and follows the concepts applying to project management. Decisions are made that either:

- introduce, modify or abolish legislation;
- rule upon an action or measure to be taken;
- distribute, modify or suspend the distribution of specific resources; and/or
- in any other manner alter the economic or political environment of a firm, industry, sector or economy directly or indirectly.

A decision in its infant stage is called an *issue*. This issue may be introduced into public debate by any given actor in the arena. If an issue obtains enough attention to become a social and a political problem and if it is recognized at governmental level, then corporations have a variety of input possibilities that potentially shape the agenda-writing (that is, the sequence and timing of the issue's path through the decision-making process) and the output of the decision maker. This variety and number of actors and strategies in issues explains the increasingly competitive nature of EU lobbying.

But there are many ways of lobbying. The institutionalizing of pressure groups or lobbyists inside of the decision-making process cited above appears to constitute the *best practice*. It establishes vast opportunities, an image close to that of a brand for a product, and a reputation and credibility that is at the source of comparative advantage of any actor enjoying this position. This scenario maximizes the opportunities to be heard and, even better, to be taken into account by the different levels and diverse actors in the policy- and decision-making process. The adoption of strategies is dependent on several vital factors that are mainly defined by the resources available to the actor. Is lobbying exercised by an individual or a group? Is this actor based close to the institutions or not, and is the actor well resourced or not?

Actors seek factor advantages and compete against each other for:

- information
- contact
- networks
- influence
- image
- institutionalization
- resources distribution
- access to actors and agendas
- recourse opportunities
- power.

These factors are interlinked and depend on each other. They are challenging, intensive in nature and may alter at any given moment through interior or exterior 'disaster', which could include anything, from misbehaviour to corporate fraud. Any of these will directly lead to a loss of factor advantages. Again, group strategies may be beneficial for the inexperienced actor in the EU arena: in a collective context, risks are diversified and factor advantages – though shared – may be more sustainable.

Strategies engaged by the different pressure groups vary in tactics depending on looser (in the US) or tighter (for instance in Canada, the UK, Germany and the EU) control of the executive, shaping their preference for bargaining before or behind closed doors.

Reinforced national-level activity therefore influences the preference formation of national governments before delivery to the EU (Richardson and Mazey, 1996). In general, it was observed that national governments sometimes disappoint interest groups in favour of other policy goals in last-minute bargaining; the study of spill-over effects of corporate public affairs management and its time-sensitivity mainly explores those international regimes, using the regime theory definition (Hopkins and Puchala 1983), with its 'principles, norms, rules, and decision-making procedures around which actor expectations converge in a given issue-area.'[1] A corporation can exploit the multiplicity of access points for an issue efficiently, if it engages in writing, influencing and utilizing time frames adapted to the validated strategy of *constructive lobbying, risk minimalization* or *dissuasive lobbying*. It is hence important for any player to:

- screen the arena, and identify actors and their interests;
- analyse the potential ad hoc or permanent agreements that exist or may arise in terms of threats and opportunities;
- evaluate strengths and weaknesses, opportunities and threats (in the same way as the SWOT analysis in corporate strategy) and consider correcting them through appropriate action, partnership or timing strategies;
- set an agenda-oriented time frame of action.

Suder and Greenwood (2004) add that dossier-specific techniques of ad hoc-partnerships are to build '*firewalls*', that is, protect from wider oppositions and playing-off threats in regard to industry- or sector-focused lobbying. In this, particular government–industry patterns may influence the degree to which hostile brotherhoods may be efficient and firewalls can be effective (Cawson et al., 1990: 286): mainly, the public–private (or government–industry) relationship serves to develop responses to market challenges. The power of firms in this context depends on the protectionist or liberal orientation of the economy, because this orientation results in a higher or lower impact of input on the output of the governmental system.

We conclude, once more, that corporate performance is hence directly linked to the political economy in which the corporation is placed. Gilpin (1975) and Spero (1990), among others, argue that the government may, in the context of internationalization, see the corporation as a threat, and therefore needs to be influenced and informed by the private entity to avoid a normative retaliatory approach by the institutions that may attempt to preserve power. This explanation is at the root and the ends of lobbying, and gives insight into the competitive edge that it provides corporations with.

The toolbox of any individual or group engaging in EU lobbying is well furnished for fact-finding, analysis, influencing and follow-up, for networking and reciprocity actions within it, and for creating an atmosphere in which the message is considered as positive. The earlier the lobbyists intervene in the process, the more likely they will be able to influence legislators and other actors, installing trust, credibility and maybe even dependence on others. Monitoring of institutions, issue-and agenda-building is the very basis of efficiency, and is enhanced through communication with policymakers: The knowledge of issues, of access points to legislators and potential partners, and of the legislative process are incomparable values that can yet be enhanced by efficient economic intelligence games. The more your knowledge is rare and distinctive about an issue and about its impact on the business or political environment, the greater are your chances to be heard and taken into account.

The EU lobbyist (different to that at the national level, for example in Paris) is then more like an adviser, advocating and influencing the arena, who will define the strategy and organize the campaign for clients for his or her interests.

Interestingly, a government setting structural objectives in the intervention it chooses, for example through competition policy, will be less concerned with the interests of one single specific firm. This means that, in this context, the individual firm will have less power in the policymaking process (Cawson et al., 1990: 361–3), and will need even more to lobby through groups rather than individually, or combine the two. Also, the higher the degree of concentration in an industry, the more vigorous are its attempts to exclude foreign competition, particularly through high-resourced, highly concentrated lobbying activity (Suder 1994; Suder and Greenwood 2004).

9.2 When is the best time to lobby?

If any interest group or individual, desiring to make a voice heard at governmental level, competes to influence decision making, then agenda-setting defines the competition that takes place at any moment in the decision-making process, its preparatory phase and aftermath. This *time-sensitivity* is based on the matrix of input and output constraints that the corporation or the institution are subject to. It is hence useful to screen the environment early and to draw a matrix of constraints, so as to better structure the message communicated to any of the actors in the arena, and the time-slot that appears most efficient to launch this communication and to repeat it. Figure 12 conceptualizes essential screening tools, targets and ends that are found to help the lobbyist in the formulation of a strategy through

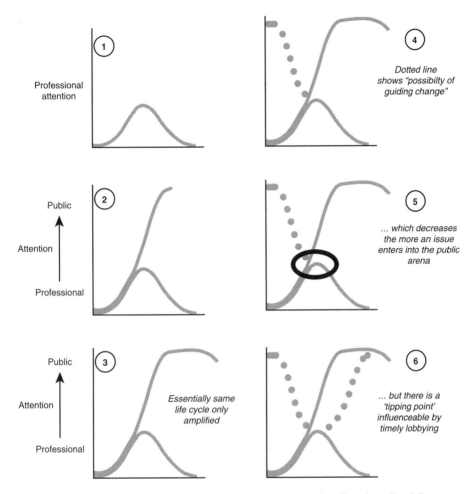

Figure 12   The public affairs life cycle: the nexus of professional and public attention

structured interrogation. The strategy will vary according to the lobbyist and his/her background, the corporation represented, its sector of activity, and the issue in question.

Given the rising number of actors, and policy issues that are targeted by lobbying activity, 'the moment of setting the agenda is the key time to influence process is confirmed' (Pedler, 2002: 315): it is crucial to be well known and valued, and to have your timing right in accordance with the political objectives of the policymaker. A comparison can again be drawn to corporate marketing, in which you need to know your environment, your competition plus the right time for your actions – getting your marketing, or, rather, 'lobbying mix' right.

Any appropriate strategy needs to follow the time frame that surrounds the issue. Van Schendelen (2002) established a life cycle of an issue, which typically may start silently, enter the public arena for a period normally shorter than 10 years, then be settled in some form, and then vanish from agendas, to be replaced by another issue (see also Tombari 1984). On the basis of this issue life cycle, the timeframe surrounding a dossier or issue can be developed in six phases, as illustrated in Figure 12 (adapted from Van Schendelen 2002). The life cycle is herein separated into sub-elements that visualize the development of professional and public attention in more detail.

The life cycle, where applied to a specific dossier, is a powerful tool for the definition of relevant time-slots for individual or collective action. It also helps define the moment in which lobbying may help raise attention, and hence the probability that an issue will be taken into account. This is because interactions of public and private interests are interlinked in bureaucratic politics. They compete on the basis of the resources, the interests, and the needs of each structure, at different venues. This conception includes public awareness of EU lobbying strategy; it includes the need to evaluate the life-cycle programme that defines the key moments for action, for strategies in the:

- long-term (for example for further integration processes);
- medium term (for example the reform of the Human Rights Council of the UN);
- short-term (for example for funding projects);
- ongoing positioning process.

9.3 Where is lobbying most effective?

We have seen that EU lobbying is a crucial activity for corporations doing business in Europe, and for those monitoring EU activities. It was pointed out that this activity required action on various levels applying adapted strategies and using them in particular time-slots. Also, going alone is not always a wise option. Choosing a good partner is essential for optimal results. The different levels of EU decision making ask for a complete knowledge of EU institutions and their interactions. This requires an effective functioning of lobbying at several levels of policymaking: they are those institutional levels that we discussed in Chapter 4.

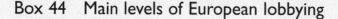

Box 44   Main levels of European lobbying

- the national level(s),
- the Commission (CEC),
- the European Parliament (EP),
- the Council of Ministers, and
- the numerous additional venues at the EU and at national or regional governmental agencies that can be lobbied, including sometimes,
- the European Court of Justice (ECJ) and the Court of First Instance through recourse, or
- any of these levels identified as most strategic to your interests.

The main venues of EU lobbying are concentrated in Brussels, at the EC and the EP for committee meetings and additional sessions, at the EP in Strasbourg, where it holds monthly plenary sessions, at its general secretariat in Luxembourg or anywhere in the EU where its MEPs are located. Another key venue is the ECJ in Luxembourg, and the Court of First Instance. The Council of Ministers can also be approached in Brussels, except in April, June and October when all meetings take place in Luxembourg. All national governments of Member States, their representations and regional or local authorities are also key points. Given the number and distance of these venues, a low-resource representation is generally likely to favour indirect lobbying at local and regional level. Medium-resourced groups will cover these venues and be present in Brussels, the venue of most direct channels of interest representations. High-resources groups cover a maximum of entry points for high input levels.

The CEC is the key venue in Brussels. Its organizational structure emphasizes consultation, because its task (as discussed in detail in earlier chapters) is one of the key policy formation roles that remains mainly unchanged by the more recent treaties (Maastricht, Amsterdam and Nice), despite some shifts in the power balances. The CEC treats problems, policies, interests, and all proposals experience detailed scrutiny and processing. In the assessment and formulation of policy proposals, much technical detail (standards, parameters, procedural rules, etc.) prevails and requires specific expertise. Due to its tasks, the CEC provides a predominantly bureaucratic/technical setting for routine day-to-day policymaking. This establishes a high opportunity for a continuous process of building on, refining, extending existing policies and elaborating new policy to answer to the requirement of an ever-changing business and societal environment. Ongoing consultation is an essential requirement for this institution in this challenge. Also, the CEC is surrounded by consultative bodies like advisory committees, advising on, for instance, safety, hygiene and health protection at work or the Industrial R&D Advisory Committee. We can speak of a European 'committology' as defined by all the expert committees that are working with the institutions for the production of legislations (N. Rougy, Club of Madrid, Brussels).

Further bodies for consultation and identification of key issues and actors are ad hoc groups like the Conference on Environment and Employment (jointly between the CEC and the EP); or the Symposium on aerospace and defence regions and SMEs. These committees, listed on www.europa.eu.int/comm/secretariat_general/regcomito, exercise a high level of power through information shaping and knowledge transfer. Lobbyists and pressure groups therefore strive for input opportunities at these levels, with the procedural ambition of their recognition as key policy shareholders within the EU policy process. At its best, they are involved in the institution's agenda-setting, that is, in the early process of problem identification and options search on a particular issue.

At the Commission level, neo-functionalist expectations (see Chapter 3 for a reminder of this concept) stipulate a preference for working with and through Euro-groups. However, the Commission additionally welcomes direct contributions by companies (McLaughlin et al., 1993: 199) and non-corporate actors (for the EU and civil society, see www.europa.eu.int/comm/civil_society). Companies thus opt ideally for multiple lobbying strategies (p. 195; cf. also Richardson and Mazey, 1991; Butt-Philip and Porter, 1993). The resulting interrelations of actors and levels within the various time-slots are shaped by coordination and cooperative relations, replacing – for the time of a common issue – competition. These relations are fundamentally based on a certain shared sense of interest. The shared sense of interest is reinforced by the very nature of European integration and harmonized policy making and policy application. It is also at the same time one of its strongest driving forces, pressing for further integration, more transparency of the system and open access points to it – in the struggle for higher levels of power.

So, where do you best lobby the EU? The answer to this question depends on the nature of the issue, the actors and the arena as a whole. All regulatory institutions attract interests, and in particular those of business. Corporations cannot afford to be left out, whatever the cost. Firms and groups recognize that governments matter because all business activity is subject to particular rules and practices in what constitutes the business environment. Europeanization has intensified this phenomenon in Europe, adding multiple layers to the playing field. All stages of policy and decision making are targets of lobbying activity, some more and some less, some rather directly and some rather indirectly. You will best lobby at all stages in the policymaking process and at national and international level, complementing your actions with other organizations and actors that may influence preference formation. This requires a constant flow of updated information.

9.4 Resource factors

The CEC has established a set of behavioural norms, rules, procedures (formal and informal), and organizational structures that allow high involvement in any lobbying, and so has the EP (www.europa.eu.int/comm/civil_society/). The register of expert groups is set up by the CEC to provide a transparent overview of advisory bodies. It lists those formal and informal advisory bodies that are established either by CEC decisions or informally by CEC services. The listing helps to find information about groups working in given policy areas, and gives direct links to CEC websites that publish more detail about expert groups on their own websites http://europa.eu.int/comm/secretariat_general/regexp/).

Lobbyists have their own code of conduct which requires them to identify themselves by name and company and to state the client that they represent. The EP also has its own 10-point code of conduct for lobbying.

The level of implication and the strategy of any lobbyist depend strongly on its resources. These resources include financial means, knowledge and economic intelligence, and networks of actors and sympathizers available. The heavy emphasis on consultation at the CEC includes a standard consultation exercise for proposals that are sent out to all relevant groups for comments. Much of this happens by internet. When the main key issues are identified through the feedback received, actors are able to gather in conferences and workshops. Any corporation has a stake to take or defend in this consultation, and it is important also that low-resources SMEs answer to consultations because otherwise, they are subject to decisions made by 'others', which may be fatal to parts of, or all operations. Low financial resources do not stop anyone from monitoring and lobbying the EU. In Brussels, specialized advisory committees (permanent and ad hoc) join forces at the CEC to complement the daily meetings between officials and group representatives; correspondence and telephone conversations make for efficient contacts with the institution for any resource level. At the EP, where most legislative power is shared between the Council and the EP under co-decision, the role of MEPs can be a threat to or a chance for business, whether they debate the adoption of rules on the patenting of new generic material, of chemicals regulations, or of the 'Auto oil programme' to control pollution from motor vehicles. The list of issues that influence the business environment is never-ending. MEPs are thus a decisive target group for lobbyists and are available easily and without complication for their electorate and the different actors of their constituency. A list of MEPs' names and contacts can be obtained from the EU or any national and local authority, and communication is mainly based on e-mails, telephone conferences or direct meetings.

In the numerous EP 'intergroups', informal meetings of MEPs are held to discuss policy issues, such as the Pharmaceutical Intergroup. EP committees also hold public hearings. As a result of these, the EP Committee on External Relations on the Agenda of the WTO Millennium Round, on 22 April 1999, included presentations from Oxfam, Greenpeace, ETUC (European Trade Union Confederation), COPA (Agriculture) and ERT (European Round Table of Industrialists). The EP is hence an interesting option for all types of resource.

The ECJ and the Court of First Instance are, through recourse, part of a standard lobbying strategy when a group fails to get satisfaction at its national venue, at the CEC, EP and the Council of Ministers. This is, however, an option that is costly and time-consuming. Hence, many cases take the form of test cases that are backed by many groups; or else, lobbyists attempt to persuade the CEC to bring the case to court.

The Council of Ministers' task of striking bargains between national governments (through what we earlier named intergovernmentalism) in the decision-making process is either melted into the co-decision, in which the EP takes part, or highly intense when it comes to the most important and historic decisions. In any case, all EU policies are approved in concordance with the Council or Coreper. However, the Council is the EU institution that is the least directly accessible for lobbying, and may be at the low end of priorities for groups that have few resources. Lobbying the Council is based on mainly indirect techniques and target national delegations in Brussels, that is, members of the Permanent Representations, or through participation in Council working groups (more than 200 such groups exist), to prepare meetings of Coreper and ministerial councils. This requires a multiple-level and multiple venue approach that requires relatively important resources. Another technique consists of lobbying members of the many Council working groups that pass on technical expertise to the relevant national representatives. For instance, groups composed of national officials, for example working on vehicle pollution will see Renault lobby its French civil servant.

One lobbying strategy towards the Council that does not require much resource is indirect, targeting national governments. This technique is relatively cheap, close to both EU and domestic affairs, and proves the continuity of use of traditional channels of information and exchange developed over decades. Under the qualified majority vote, lobbyists cannot be sure that its national government delivers the desired outcome (Richardson and Mazey, 1996), because national governments sometimes disappoint interest groups in favour of other policy goals in last-minute bargaining. The national level is therefore important in the long-term and for a multitude of similar issues rather than a guarantee for short-term output. In the same way, lobbyists will set up or attend seminars, conferences, advisory committees, breakfast briefings, and gatherings in the institutions and around them.

A key recognition of the value and importance of pressure groups takes shape when the actor experiences the institutionalizing of its input activity; this translates into the quasi-systematic consultation of the lobbying group by a given EU institution on a given issue (Richardson and Mazey, 1999). An example for institutionalized lobbying at the CEC is the bi-annual meetings with the Platform of European Social NGOs and with the 'Group of Eight' (that is, the biggest pan-European environmental NGOs) and others.

All actors engaged in lobbying for or against a particular issue are helping to construct the strongest links possible with government actors. these contacts may be formal and informal, or both. For instance, on a macro-level, UNICE, the European employer association, enjoys observer status in the Council of Europe, as well as at EFTA, the UN Conference on Trade and Development, the UN Industrial Development Organization, the European Patent Office, and other international organizations, and can therefore be part of a timely and strategic lobbying. At the same time as the influence is exercised upon Europe, the organization may thus benefit from spill-over effects into those markets that are regulated by affiliate institutions. On a micro-level, civil servants, ministries and governmental agents, Member States' Permanent Missions in Brussels and governmental experts are also interlinked by what they do, are affiliated to the consultation and advisory mechanisms within European Member States and institutions, and can be accessed for multiple lobbying purposes, covering various issues and venues.

9.5 And the competition is open: Lobbying strategy in action

Actors are numerous and their knowledge of time spent and competition in lobbying is crucial. Olson (1965) assumes that all pressure groups are equal, and that the health of democracy benefits from the competition between them because the decision maker acts in the role of a referee, who is choosing the most useful input and the best policy presented. However, in reality the actors are not equal, neither in their interests nor in their resources, size or level of influence. This does not imply that low-resources lobbying is condemned and that high-resources groups have the automatic joker card in hand.

Most significant interests in the EU have formed associations, because all areas of public policy are covered by EU regulations, and because the association of interests maximizes entry points into the arena. But Commission officials hardly rely solely on Euro-associations, and because there is no guarantee that your opinion is the most influential one, you need to seek out the most influential person to lobby. Mainly this person is the one who drafts proposals of an issue, and not the person who signs it, who will be lobbied later, because of the opportunity to influence legislation at its very roots.

Lobbying activity depends on resources available to persons, groups or associations who devote amounts of resources (that is, mainly human and financial resources) proportionate to their organization's perception of requirement leading to a win-situation in the EU-policy game. This perception, inherent to the organization in the framework of an issue, shapes the level, time and strategy applied to a lobbying effort, and is a direct result of its environmental screening and scenario-planning in relation to a perceived level of competition in the arena for the issue in question. The chosen lobbying strategy is hence comparable to a function of the perception of the arena, that of competition in the arena, and the resources that are available to the person or group for its lobbying activity (Box 45).

Box 45   The equation defining the choice of a lobbying strategy

Lobbying strategy x = function (perception of arena, a; perception of competition, c; resources available, r; time frame available, t), i.e. $x = f(a;c;r;t)$

Also, geopolitical and societal developments shape the most efficient formula for interest representation. Trade unions, for instance, are interest groups that organized efficiently at EU level so they could counteract already organized business groups, and promote interests that are increasingly difficult to pressure for at national level. The importance of internet and multimedia techniques benefit NGOs and e-governments that are more connected and adept than others. These evolutions underpin the emergence of a dense and mature pressure group system. The density of the lobbying arena is proportionate to the opportunities and venue points that are open to influence and input, therefore defining for every arena a different relation between competitors for power. This is the reason for trends towards risk-avoidance through the op.cit. venue shopping, and an increasing spread of resources.

9.6 Lobbying today

More than ever, doing business in Europe is accompanied by lobbying activity. European regulation may have an adverse affect on interests, but also, new rules may furnish opportunities that may be exploited to the disadvantage of others. Business in Europe has become aware of the competitive advantage that public affairs management on an EU scale offers. The opportunity network is complex and dense. It distributes costs and benefits between interests unevenly, and it is in the interest of any actor to secure all direct benefits where possible.

The involvement in lobbying today requires detailed expertise that accentuates chances to gain rather than lose out on benefits, similar to that in striving for competitiveness in a given market. Actors representing a company need to construct an information network that provides the firm with a crucial alert system and access to essential information. Lobbyists need to be proactive because the earlier you know and engage in an issue, the more effective you will be; even better, you initiate the issue. Representatives need to understand how to communicate to institutions and actors, and how to 'sell' their message best, providing administrations with marked data, industry information and expertise: marrying the interests of all for a win-win situation for all actors by playing the role of actor, supplier and customer at the same time. Herein, alliances and hostile brotherhoods are key to knowing and controlling the competition while enhancing the firm's power.

Lobbying the EU requires a long-term investment. While on the one hand, it is crucial to get known early, on the other, lobbyists must respect the policymaking process and its institutional actors, and try to understand what is required for the issue at hand. Attention to detail and mediation between actors may be key to the willingness of officials to grant access to information, discussion, or permanent representations; they are a valuable resource that needs to be followed up for every issue.

Efficient tools in the complexity of EU lobbying are the Internet and the media. Few genuine media outlets support EU lobbying specially, but there are exceptions such as *European Voice*, edited by *The Economist*. Attempts to influence the news content of newspapers, television and radio guarantees that opinions are communicated.

Writing or advertising in specialized European media for government and lobbying agents helps to:

- influence domestic preference formation;
- influence behaviour of governments;
- influence public perceptions on European issues.

The perceived increase in lobbying activity has given a growing role to tools including press releases, press briefings, press conferences, interviews in the media, public service communications, with advertisement of training sessions, and paid advertisements. Ad hoc groups may favour these methods in addition to grassroots lobbying (activating the relevant contacts in one's personal and professional network), but lobbyists who anticipate attention given to a particular issue that is central to the governmental agenda will also use the media at a specific moment in time.

Résumé and conclusion

Efficient multi-networked public affairs management helps corporations reduce risk and uncertainty in the political economy that they are part of, and recognize the strategic importance of Europeanization. Indeed, the role of firms as political actors is today recognized in international business and international political economy studies alike.

(Continued)

The firm is regulated by an increasing number of actors, at state level as well as multilaterally in the competition of the two for power through the expression of redistributive welfare, and hence, among others, the benefits from wealth creation through corporate activity. Each wave of European integration has given rise to ever more EU-level lobbying activity, at the speed at which EU public policy and the power of institutions have expanded. The landmarks of European integration that we reviewed in the early chapters of this book have incrementally fostered lobbying activity: in 1986 with the SEA, in 1992 with the TEU at Maastricht, in 1997 with the Amsterdam Act, and in particular through the waves of enlargement.

The Europeanized business environment and management have increased corporate awareness of the opportunities that lobbying can bring. Similar to the issues that you studied about cross-cultural management, about marketing and diversity management, and about the important efforts towards financial integration, Europeanization has influenced the way in which business deals with public affairs. Firms need to be aware *which* institutions are the most important to talk to, and *how* institutions matter, and then adapt accordingly. Integration history shifted the power venues and actors that are the most likely to grant an 'output' return on (lobbying) investment.

Corporations need to build a message and transfer this message with the help of other actors in the arena. This happens through, at a minimum, replies to consultations and, at a maximum, EU lobbying that has to be committed to the EU process, procedures and objectives. We note that the EU policy network consists of national and EU institutions and non-governmental actors. It is also heavily influenced by non-EU, international organizations and foreign governments that exercise power. Hence, lobbying activity involves interaction at different levels with directly or indirectly concerned state actors, policy professionals and experts, companies and interest groups of different kinds.

Lobbying means that a person or a group of people tries to influence legislators so that an individual's or organization's point of view is represented in the government. A lobbyist is a person who is, most of the time, paid to influence legislation and public opinion. Most large corporations hire professional lobbyists to help promote their activities as agents, or open their own representation in Brussels, and their main objective is to maintain a positive regulatory environment for their organization.

The activities of lobbyists, that is, the intelligence, can be compared to service functions, of information gathering, direct lobbying functions on the basis of dissuasive, constructive or risk minimalization objectives, implementation functions participating in the policy implementation; as well as a feedback function to the public administration. Lobbyists define their strategies along scenario-planning and best practices that are defined similar to the environmental screening in marketing. The

(Continued)

(Continued)

many access points in the European opportunity structure offer the possibility for all actors to lobby the arena, whether directly or indirectly, whether individually or through partnerships and federations, whether in Brussels or at any other location in Europe, or where the European actors are represented, and finally, whether European or from a non-EU country. For all players, the arena is complex, competitive, dynamic and unpredictable, and unavoidable for any risk minimalization strategy when doing business in Europe. There is, in this 'marketplace' of lobbying, no guarantee of a result. And yet, you need there to be.

Mini case study: Regulatory risk or better look out for consultations

A small local company imports hand pallet trucks exclusively from China. On 18 July 2005, the Council adopted regulation no. 1174 imposing 'a definitive anti-dumping duty and collecting definitely the provisional duty imposed on imports of hand pallet trucks and their essential parts originating in the People's Republic of China'.

Consequence for the company: its costs increased exponentially due to a new anti-dumping duty that amounts to 46.7 per cent if they want to keep on buying products from the same providers, whereas other competitors, who have other Chinese suppliers, pay 'only' 7.6 per cent.

Why such a difference? Could this company have done something to avoid this situation?

The answer is 'yes' because the company knew what was about to happen, but did not take the time to react nor to express its interests or concerns. In short, it did not make its voice heard. Indeed, a one-year investigation of dumping and injury was conducted by the Commission (2003–4). At the time, 'all interested parties' were informed of the EU project for an imposition of an anti-dumping duty on the basis of Council Regulation No. 384/96 of 22 December 1995 on protection against dumped imports from countries not members of the EC. These interested parties were granted a period within which they could give oral and written comments. This company knew that, but did not take the time to respond, to articulate its interests or opinions in the matter, whereas other competitors did act. That is why some European importers – even very small ones – succeeded in having their suppliers individually named on a shortlist of Chinese companies penalized with duties much lower than the 46,7 per cent rate.

Source: Delphine Foucauld, Director of EuroInfoCentre, Nice, France

(Continued)

Mini case questions:

1 What are the consequences of this company's lack of awareness of EU procedures?
2 Despite its restricted resources, how could the company have influenced the outcome of this case?

Review questions

1 **Explain** the strategic difference between short-term and long-term lobbying.
2 **Who** are the key people to approach in the lobbying arena?
3 **What** are the main advantages of collective action?
4 **What** are the advantages of codes of conduct compared with laws regulating lobbying?

Assignments

- **Imagine** that you are the main lobbyist for a confederation of European textile manufacturers, lobbying for quotas against Chinese textile imports. Which institutions will you mainly lobby, and from which actors can you expect competition?
- **Compare** the resources available to an SME and an MNE of your choice. In your opinion, how do differences of resources potentially influence lobbying strategy?
- **Case study assignment**: Read and prepare the Altran case study in Part IV, and discuss the challenges in setting up a representation in Brussels.
- **Internet exercise**: Search for evidence whether the Internet is a main tool in European public affairs management. Which sites are, in your opinion, most relevant? Present your findings and compare them with newspaper support material in this context. What type of readership is the target of those different media (internet, newspapers, radio and so forth)?

Web guide

www

www.eubusiness.com Services, directory, key topics, jobs.

www.eurolegal.org Advice for persons outside the Union who are thinking of launching business operations in the EU.

http://europa.eu.int/comm/secretariat_general/sgc/lobbies/docs/Workingdocparl.pdf Essential information for EU lobbying.

www.gcactuaries.org Website of the Groupe Consultatif Actuariel Européen.

Plus the websites of all embassies and foreign representations in Brussels, trade missions and chambers of commerce, European and foreign associations of manufacturers, NGOs and other actors.

Note

1 Parts of this text are based on Suder and Greenwood (2004).

References

Baumgartner, F. and Jones, B. (1991) 'Agenda dynamics and instability in American politics', *Journal of Politics*, 53: 1044–74.

Bellier, I. (1997) 'The Commission as an Actor: an anthropologist's view', in H. Wallace and A.R. Young (eds), *Participation and Policy-Making in the European Union*. Oxford: Clarendon Press.

Broscheid, A. and Coen, D. (2002) *Business Interest Representation and European Commission For a Game Theoretic Investigation*. Cologne: MPI für Gesellschaftsforschung. Cologne.

Bück, J.Y. (2003) *Le Management des connaissances et des compétences en pratique*, 2nd edn. Paris: Ed. d'Organisation.

Buckley, P.J. (1992) *Studies in International Business*. Basingstoke: Macmillan /Palgrave Macmillan.

Butt-Philip, A. (1985) *Pressure Groups in the European Community*. London: University Association for Contemporary European Studies.

Butt-Philip, A. and Porter, M. (1993) 'Eurogroups, European Integration and Policy Networks'. unpublished, University of Bath, Bath.

Cawson, A., Morgan, K., Webber, D., Holmes, P. and Stevens, A. (1990) *Hostile Brothers. Competition and Closure in the European Electronics Industry*. Oxford: Claredon Press.

Coen, D. (1997) 'Evolution of the large firm as a political actor in the European Union', *Journal of European Public Policy*, 4 (1): 91–108.

Coen, D. and Grant, W. (2000) 'Corporate political strategy and global policy: a case study of the transatlantic business dialogue', *London Business School Regulation Initiative Discussion Chapter*, (November).

Congress of the United States of America (1953) Lobbying Investigation Unconstitutional: Constitutional Law. Free Speech. Lobbying. Congressional Committee Lacks Power to Investigate Indirect Lobbying. Right to Remain Silent before Congressional Committee protected by First Amendment, *Stanford Law Review* 5 (2): 344–39, February 1953.

Cutler, A., Haufler, V. and Porter Tony (eds) (1999) *Private Authority and International Affairs*. New York: Suny Press.

Danton de Rouffignac, P. (1991) *Europe's New Business Culture*. London: Pitman.

European Voice (2005) 'Brussels lobbying', 11 (13) 7 April.

Figstein, N. and McNichol, J. (1998) 'The institutional terrain of the EU', in W. Sandholz and A. Stone Sweet (eds), *European Integration and Supranational Governance*. Oxford: Oxford University Press.

Gardner, J. (1991) *Effective Lobbying in the EC*. Boston: Kluwer.

Gilpin, R. (1975) *US Power and the Multinational Corporation: The Political Economy of Foreign Direct Investment*. New York: Basic Books.

Gray, P. (1985) *Free Trade or Protection? A Pragmatic Analysis*. London: Macmillan Press, and New York: St. Martin's Press.

Greenwood, W. (2003) *Objective Setting*. London: Project World, Imark.

Hix, S. (1999) *The Political System of the EU*. London: Macmillan.

Hopkins, R. and Puchala, D. (1983) 'International regimes: Lessons from inductive analysis', in S. Krasner, (ed.), *International Regimes*. Ithaca: Cornell University Press.

International Herald Tribune, Paris edition, various issues.

Keohane, R. (1984) *After Hegemony: Co-operation and Discord in the World Political Economy*. Princeton: Princeton University Press.

Klemperer, P. (2000) 'What really matters in auction design', *Journal of Economic Literature*, Nos D44 (Auctions), L41 (Antitrust), L96 (Telecommunications).

Laurencell, S. (1979) *Lobbying and Interest Groups: A Selected Annotated Bibliographie*. Washington, DC: Congressional Research Service.

Lawton, T. (1997) *Technology and the New Diplomacy*. Aldershot: Avebury.

McAdam, D. (1996) 'Conceptual origins, current problems, future directions' in D. McAdam, J. McCarthy, and M. Zald, (eds), *Comparative Perspectives on Social Movements. Political Opportunities, Mobilizing Structures, and Cultural Framings*. Cambridge: Cambridge University Press. pp. 23–40.

Mazey, S. (2000) 'Introduction: Integrating gender – intellectual and "real world" mainstreaming', *Journal of European Public Policy*, 7(3): 333–45.

McLaughlin, A. M, Jordan, G. and Maloney. W.A. (1993) 'Corporate lobbying in the European Community', *Journal of Common Market Studies*, 31(2): 192–211.

Moravscik, A. (1998) *The Choice for Europe: Social Purpose and State Power from Messina to Maastricht*. Ithaca: Cornell University Press.

Nugent, N. (1999) *Government and Politics of the EU*, 4th edn. London: Macmillan.

Olson, M. (1965) *The Logic of Collective Action*. Cambridge, MA: Harvard University Press.

OUP (2005) *The Compact Edition of the Oxford English Dictionary*, Oxford: Oxford University Press.

Palan, R. and Abbot, John (1998) *State Strategies in the Global Political Economy*. London: Pinter

Pedler, R. (2002) *European Union Lobbying, Changes in the Arena*. New York: Palgrave.

Peterson, J. (2001) 'The choice for EU theorists: Establishing a common framework for analysis', *European Journal of Political Research*, 39(3): 289–318.

Pollack, M. (1998) 'The engines of integration? Supranational autonomy and influence in the European Union', in: W. Sandholtz, and A. Stone Sweet (eds), *European Integration and Supranational Governance*. Oxford: Oxford University Press.

Porter, M.E. (1985) *Competitive Advantage: Creating and Sustaining Superior Performance*. New York: Free Press.

Rauch, J. (1994) *Demosclerosis: The Silent Killer of American Government*. New York: Times Books.

Richardson, J.J. (ed.) (1993) *Pressure Groups*. Oxford and New York: Oxford University Press.

Richardson, J.J. and Mazey, S. (1996) 'EU policy-making: a garbage can or an anticipatory and consensual policy style?', in Y. Meny et. al. (ed.), *Adjusting to Europe*. London: Routledge. pp. 41–58.

Richardson, J.J. and Mazey, S. (1999) 'Institutionalising promiscuity: Groups and European integration', in W. Sandholz and A. Stone Sweet (eds), *The Institutionalising of European Space*. Oxford: Oxford University Press.

Richardson, J.J.and Mazey, S. (2001) 'Interest groups and EU policy-making: Organisational logic and venue shopping', in L. Cram, D. Dinan and N. Nugent (eds) *European Union: Power and Policy-making*. Oxford: Oxford University Press.

Richardson, J.J. (2001) 'Policy-making in the EU: Interests, ideas and garbage cans of primeval soup', in L.Cram, D. Dinan and N. Nugent (eds) *European Union: Power and Policy-making*. Oxford: Oxford University Press.

Rosamund, B. (2000) *Theories of European Integration*. London: Macmillan.

Schmitter, P.C. (1996) 'Imagining the future of the Euro-polity with the help of new concept', in G. Marks, et al. (ed.), *Governance in the EU*. London: Sage.

Spero, J. (1990) *The Politics of International Economic Relations*. London: Longman.

Stone Sweet, A. and Sandholtz, W. (1998) 'Integration supranational governance and the institutionalization of the European polity', in A. Sandholtz, and W. Stone Sweet, (eds), *The Institutionalising of European Space*. Oxford: Oxford University Press.

Stopford, J. and Strange, S. (1991) *Rival States, Rival Firms: Competition for World Market Shares*. Cambridge: Cambridge University Press.

Strange, S. (1982) 'Cave! Hic Dragones: A critique of regime analysis', *International Organization*, 36 (spring): 479–96.

Schmid, G. (1994) 'Anti-dumping measures and the politics of EU–Japan create relation in the European consumer electronic sector: the VCR case'. PhD dissertation, University of Bath; Working Paper, Thomson Consumer Electronics External Relations Department, Bath and Paris.

Suder, G. (2004) *Public Policy Implications Of Constraint Theorem*, CERAM Working Paper. Sophia Antipolis.

Suder, G. (2007) 'The municipal solid waste incineration sector in Europe: A study of harmonization and its impact', *International Journal of European Waste Management*, Issue 2.

Suder, G. and Greenwood, W. (2004) *Time-sensitive Lobbying: Approaches to Corporate Disaster Impact Reduction*. International Association of the Management of Technology Annual Conference, Washington, DC.

Taylor, P. (1996) *The European Union in the 1990s*. Oxford: Oxford University Press.

Tombari, H. (1984) *Business and Society*. New York: Dryden.

Van Schendelen, R. (2002) *Machiavelli in Brussels: The Art of EU Lobbying*. Amsterdam: Amsterdam: University Press.

Wallace, H. and Young, A.R. (1997) 'The kaleidoscope of European policy-making: Shifting patterns of participation and influence', in H. Wallace, and A.R. Young, (eds) *Participation and Policy-Making in the European Union*. Oxford: Clarendon Press.

Wills, A. and Quittkat, C. (2004) Corporate interests and public affairs: Organised business–government relations in EU Member States, *Journal of Public Affairs*, November.

10 Competing Internationally

What you will learn about in this chapter

- International relations and international trade.
- EU relations with its main trading partners, and a comparison of conditions and sectors.
- Trade partners as competitors on the international scene.
- The EU's link to the WTO and other major international organizations.
- Competitiveness and globalization: the European way.

Introduction: International relations and international trade

This final chapter, 'Competing Internationally', covers issues that are crucial to international competitiveness and the relations that the EU pursues with its trading partners. These issues are placed into a concluding discussion of the role of Europe in advanced globalization. Food for discussion, debate and thought for business students and future and current managers in Europe! Before we come to discuss the issues in this field, you will be asked to remember the basis that defines the very existence of a European Union, and that also defines its international relations. We then discuss the most important trade partners of the EU, which are both partners and competitors on an international scale. In this context, what contribution does Europe make to positive globalization? What role does European business play in this, and how does non-European business enter the playing field? The concluding mini case illustrates, with some final words, the manner in which non-EU country corporations launch doing business in Europe for successful intenational competition.

Let us start by noting that, in its early stage, the foremost concern was to gather the nations and peoples of Europe. European states were to work with other countries and with international organizations in order to remove economic, political and cultural animosities; to develop economic regions and promote worldwide relations ruled by peace. The main objective was (and still is) to spread the European values of freedom, democracy, human rights and peace, based on the dramatic experiences of World War II, and on a resulting strong belief in the benefits of cooperation on a multilateral level. The evolution of European international relations and international trade has gone hand in hand with this belief.

Trade and foreign investments constitute an essential part of those international relations, that is, the relations that countries establish between each other. The meaning of the term 'relation' can take diverse forms and expressions in diplomacy, in propaganda, in military operations, and through economic activities, which can be seen as parts of a state's potential for power. In general, this is to influence other states or actors within them so that they will demonstrate certain behaviour or so that they will become economically dependent on the state exerting the policies. International relations consist of interaction between bodies of decision makers of at least two countries with interests in each other. The actors in international relations are unaccountable, since they depend on the situation and the subject. For instance, in trade and investment, we saw that the multinational company is an important player in international relations.

International trade, that is, the exchange of goods, but now also services, and equity at the cross-border level, is primarily based on international voluntary exchange of assets between parties playing a significant role in the international business environment. Because all international transactions play a role in nations' wealth, much effort is devoted to recording and analysing them, and solving trade frictions. Even more energy goes into competing efficiently within the international business environment. In this, the EU actively deals with the particular challenges of terrorism, international crime, drug trafficking, illegal immigration and also with crucial global issues such as poverty and the preservation of nature and the environment. A potential force for world stability, the EU is characterized by a common belief that economic stability and cooperation are the foundation of geopolitical stability. For this, the EU is entitled to negotiate bilateral trade agreements with countries or regional groups of countries as one self-standing entity. However, the relative failure of the European Constitution project at the beginning of 2000, and the fragmentation of foreign policy outputs (for example, wars in Yugoslavia and in Iraq), weakens the impact of EU power on the international scene, where the EU has relations with many non-EU countries and groups.

Switzerland   No other country has as many agreements with the EU as Switzerland. Funding of EU projects complicated. Liberalization of trade in processed agricultural products and a liberalization of services. Participates in the Schengen and Dublin agreements on border control and asylum policy, and on savings and taxation, and in EUROPOL ECURIE, successor to the Lugano Convention.

Russia, Eastern Europe and Central Asia   Partnership and cooperation agreements (concerning trade, cooperation in science, energy, transport, and the environment), political dialogue, and joint actions to combat crime, drugs and money laundering. The EU provides the Balkan region with financial aid and promotes stabilization. Association and accession agreements between the EU and certain Balkan states.

USA   The EU has intensive trade agreements with the US; on: integration, business dialogue, and dialogue between consumers, trade unionists and environmentalists. Talks about competition law and recognition of technical standards. Agreement on scientific and technological cooperation, on extradition, on mutual legal assistance; cooperation on satellite navigation systems (Galileo and GPS).

Asia   During the financial crisis in Asia, the EU lead international efforts. Frequent Asia–Europe meetings. Aim's to strengthen mutual trade and investment flows, promote the development of the region's less prosperous countries, address causes of poverty, protect human rights, spread democracy, good governance, and the rule of law in particular, see below.

Association of South East Asian Nations (ASEAN)   Exchange on political and security issues. Cooperation Agreement (1980) between the EC and member countries of ASEAN: Brunei, Indonesia, Malaysia, Philippines, Singapore, Thailand and Vietnam only. EC–ASEAN Joint Cooperation Committee (JCC).

Japan   Pressure upon Japan to remove non-tariff barriers; EXPROM to stimulate EU exports. Arrangements in science and technology, competition policy, development assistance, environmental policy, industrial policy, industrial cooperation, macroeconomic and financial affairs, and transport. Close policy cooperation, for example at WTO.

Australia   Science and technology agreement, mutual recognition of conformity assessment (testing, inspection and certification of products traded between Europe and Australia in the exporting country rather than at destination), wine agreement (protect intellectual properties in wine terms, prevent fake representation to consumers). Agreement on export of coal and an agreement on transfer of nuclear material. Cooperation in environmental issues, dialogue on energy issues.

New Zealand   Joint Declaration on Relations as basis of links since 1999. Cooperation in science and technology, sanitary measure agreement, mutual recognition agreement of conformity assessment (cf. Australia). New Zealand's third largest export market.

Canada   Framework Agreement on Economic Cooperation; 1976 commercial and economic agreement established mechanisms for cooperation in trade, industry and science. Joint Political Declaration on EU–Canada Relations and Joint EU–Canada Action Plan 1996 (bilateral and multilateral issues). Large range of sectoral agreements (such as Agreement Regarding the Application of Competition Laws or the Agreement on Customs Cooperation and Mutual Assistance to Customs Matters).

Central and Latin America   Association Agreement between the EU and Central America prepared (Costa Rica, El Salvador, Guatemala, Honduras, Nicaragua and Panama). EU supports the Central America Common Market. Close links with Latin America since the 1960s; EU is leading donor in the region, first foreign investor, and second most important trade partner. Specialized dialogue with Mercosur, Andean community, and specifically Mexico (free trade area in goods and services) and Chile.

Euro-Mediterranean Partnership/Barcelona Process   Create a Euro-Mediterranean free trade area by 2010. Financial support, peace promotion. Framework of political, economic and social relations; Mediterranean partners (Algeria, Egypt, Israel, Jordan, Lebanon, Morocco, Palestinian Authority, Syria, Tunisia and Turkey; Libya under observer status since 1999) part of European Neighborhood Policy (ENP).

Gulf Cooperation Council GCC countries (Saudi Arabia, Kuwait, Bahrain, Qatar, the United Arab Emirates, and the Sultanate of Oman)   Cooperation Agreement to facilitate trade relations and to strengthen stability. Working groups on industrial, energy and environment, university cooperation, business and media cooperation. Negotiations on free trade agreement between GCC and EU. Bilateral relations with the GCC, and with Iran, Iraq and Yemen.

Africa, Caribbean and Pacific (ACP)   The Cotonou Agreement links the EU to 77 ACP countries. Supports ACP governments' aim to create a balanced macroeconomic context, expand the private sector, and improve both the quality and the coverage of social services. The Fourth Lomé Convention frees the ACP countries from customs duties on 94 per cent of their exports to the EU. Among initiatives, the EU is stakeholder in Kimberley Process to hinder circulation of conflict diamonds in African war zones.

The EU has established strong links with the UN, the WTO, NATO, the Organization for Security and Cooperation in Europe (OSCE), the Council of Europe and regional organizations on the other continents to defend its interests and contribute to aid the Third World. Table 23 provides you with an understanding of the compatibility that exists between interests in certain policy areas, using the example of UN millennium development goals.

Table 23   Relationship between the UN millennium development goals and the related actions endorsed by the EU

UN millennium development goals (adopted September 2000)	EU policies in support of these goals
• To develop a global partnership on development	• Trade and development
• To eradicate extreme poverty and hunger	• Regional cooperation
• To achieve universal primary education	• Poverty-reduction policies to support health and education
• To promote gender equality and empower women	• Transport infrastructure
• To reduce child mortality	• Food and general security
• To improve national healthcare	• Sustainable rural development
• To combat HIV/AIDS, malaria and other diseases	• Institutional capacity-building,
• To ensure environmental sustainability	• Good governance and the rule of law
	• Safety
	• Digital opportunities

Source: Commission of the European Communities, 2005. © http//:europa.eu.int/comm/development/body/communications/communications

10.1 The international business environment: Some keys for European business

Compared to its trading partners, the EU enjoys a relatively open economy with an openness degree of almost 27 per cent (exports + Imports/GDP). The trading power of the Member States is embodied by its role as the world's leading exporter of goods, with more than 17 per cent of the world total; the world's leading exporter of services, with about

25 per cent of the world total, and the world's leading source of (FDI) and the second largest home for foreign investment. The EU's members represent approximately 7 per cent of the world's population and account for more than a fifth of global imports and exports. It is the world's largest market, with more than 494 million people. Member States enjoy comparatively sound rates of GDP on a country to country basis and as a whole. In comparison to other trade powers worldwide, Europe benefits from an exceptional business environment that we have studied throughout this book. This environment is as much an opportunity as it is a challenge to business. On the one hand, the unemployment rate in Europe is higher than that in other developed countries (under 4 per cent in the US in 2005, in comparison to a rate of 5 per cent in the UK and 11.4 per cent in Spain). On the other hand, the EU plays a major role in the WTO as one voice. EU tariffs on industrial products are among the lowest in the world and their majority is dismantled.

Table 24   Worldwide exports of the EU

Country	percentage of total EU-15 trade	percentage of total EU-25 trade
1 USA	21.0%	23.3%
2 Switzerland	6.5%	7.4%
3 China	5.8%	6.5%
4 Japan	5.6%	6.4%
5 Russia	3.9%	5.3%

Sources: COMEXT, IMF, European Communities, 2003, URL: http://ec.europa.eu/comm/trade/issues/bilateral/regions/candidates/ff040204_en.htm © European Commission 2004

10.2 Europe's trading partners

The EU is the world's leading exporter, with 19.6 per cent, ahead of the US (13.6 per cent) and Japan (8.5 per cent). Table 24 illustrates the growth of exports to five main partners, pre- and post-2004 enlargement.

Trade and investment relations with other countries, market groupings and emerging countries represent a huge opportunity for the EU firms. This opportunity is generated from international politics that reach out to create and sustain relations worldwide.

10.2.1 Relations with market groupings

Because of its role as a highly integrated and large market, the EU entertains privileged relations not only with major trading partner countries, but also with most other market groupings worldwide. For business that operates in such an enlarged market, the opportunities of other market groupings are part of the life cycle. Market grouping representatives from across the globe come to the EU to understand how regional policy works to successfully stimulate less advanced Member States' growth with the national authorities, such as Spain in the 1980s, Ireland in the 1990s and Poland in the 2000s.

The main trading partner of the EU is NAFTA, comprising the USA, Canada and Mexico. This free trade area, established in 1992, encompasses 390 million inhabitants, with a total GDP of approximately US$11.4 trillion. The main aim of NAFTA is to eliminate impediments to trade of goods and services, to facilitate their movement across Member States and to boost commerce and internal investments. These objectives also characterize the FTAA project, to cover all of the continent except Cuba and French Guyana. NAFTA's dispute settlements concern investment, anti-dumping, and countervailing, among others.

The EU's geographically closest market grouping is EFTA, consisting of Iceland, Liechtenstein, Norway and Switzerland. EFTA members have incorporated two-thirds of EU legislation since 1992, following EFTA's partnership (except for Switzerland) with the Union to form the EEA. Subsequent easy accession to the EU is possible for EFTA members. Many of the countries that joined the EU in the 1980s and 1990s were formerly EFTA members.

The Southern American Common Market, Mercosur, comprising Argentina, Brazil, Paraguay, Uruguay, Chile and Bolivia, was established in 1991 with 210 million inhabitants, with a common total GDP of US$1.9 trillion. The grouping was formed to encourage integration among members via the free movement of goods and services. Members also apply a common external tariff. The main objective is to ensure the economic and political stability of the region. Mercosur influences other regional economic structures, and is looking into an expansion through a pan-American (FTAA) or a Mercosur–EU pact. The most tangible outcomes of the grouping encompass important infrastructural projects such as gas pipelines, bridges and motorways.

APEC, founded in 1989, is the largest market grouping with privileged EU relations. APEC members are Australia, Brunei, Malaysia, Singapore, Thailand, New Zealand, New Guinea, Indonesia, Philippines, Taiwan, Hong Kong, Japan, China, South Korea, Canada, USA, Mexico and Chile: 21 members of over 2.5 billion people, a combined GDP of over US$19 trillion and 47 per cent of world trade (Members Economies, 2006, URL: http://www.apec.org/content/apec/member_economies.html). However, APEC presents a relatively low degree of unification, although its core mission is to facilitate trade and FDI by removing barriers.

The members of (ASEAN) are mostly also members of APEC. Indonesia, Malaysia, Philippines, Singapore, Thailand, Brunei Darrussalam, Laos, Vietnam, Burma and Cambodia regroup in this association, set up since 1967, with 440 million inhabitants and a total GDP of more than $2 trillion. ASEAN was created to accelerate economic growth, social progress and cultural development and is equipped with a dispute settlement. Its free trade area, AFTA, was created in 1993 to stimulate growth through a decrease of government control on national economies, and as a response to the EU's and NAFTA's regional peace and stability initiatives. By 2003, AFTA's trade relations with the EU had evolved into the Trans-Regional EU–ASEAN Trade initiative (TREATI), representing 5.8 per cent of total EU trade (CEC External Relations ASEAN, 2005, URL: http:/ec.european.eu/comm/external_relations/asean/).

Asian–European interests started to take serious shape in the 1980's. From Japanese management models, Asian natural resources and corporate cultures, to the evolution and crisis of the Asian Tigers, the region has attracted Europe with its potential. Contacts between Europe and APEC were established in 1993, from which, in 1996, the first ASia–Europe Summit

(ASEM) in Bangkok evolved. A meeting of the Heads of State and Government of 10 Asian countries and of the EU 15 at the time made an agreement to have regular meetings to stimulate economic, political and social relations. At the ASEM meeting in October 2004, both continents approved the enlargement of each others' grouping for enlarged negotiations. Since October 2004, the Asia–Europe meeting, held every two years, also includes Japan, China and South Korea.

Inside ASEM, the ASia Europe Foundation (ASEF) promotes cultural and intellectual exchanges between Europe and Asia to reduce the risk of cultural misunderstandings. Intellectual exchange is fostered through seminars and conferences, joining together experts from different areas supported by ASEF (for example on issues of security, the environment and cultural dialogue). People and cultural exchange, as well as communication, reinforce the system.

Relations with African market groupings include those with the East African Community (EAC) and the Common Market for Eastern and Southern Africa (COMESA). The EAC was, from December 1999 onwards, re-established among the republics of Kenya, Uganda and the United Republic of Tanzania, with its seat in Arusha, Tanzania. This grouping has the objective to run a customs union. Trade liberalization and EU tariff reductions are practised by COMESA (the eastern and southern African countries). The newest grouping in African integration is the Southern African Free Trade Zone of September 2000; it groups together Angola, Botswana, Congo, Lesotho, Malawi, Mauritius, Mozambique, Namibia, Seychelles, South Africa, Tanzania, Zambia and Zimbabwe.

The 2005 EU Strategy for the first time addressed Africa as one entity for support, aid, security and politico-economic relations.

10.2.2 Relations with selected trading partners

10.2.2.1 The USA

They are allies in a long relationship and the two largest economies in the world and they enjoy the world's biggest bilateral trading and investment relationship (Table 25 compares geographical data). Both partners are also the promoters of generally common goals and interests worldwide. They share common concerns on political and security issues. In accordance with this relationship is the frequency of meetings, negotiations and debate: though the goals are often the same, ideas about the path to take in order to get there differ frequently.

The President of the United States and the Presidency of the European Union meet twice a year for presidential summits. The US Congress confers with the European Parliament.

Table 25 A short comparison: the EU and the US

Country	Population (millions)	Area (1000km²)	Population density (inh./km²)
EU	494	5000	115
US	268	9372	29

Among agreements on political and economic issues, we note the New Transatlantic Agenda (1995) and the Economic Partnership (1998).

It is estimated that trade and investment flow across the Atlantic at a rate of nearly €1 billion a day. US FDI is greater in the EU than in any other region of the world. The US received one-quarter of EU exports and supplies 20 per cent of its imports, and hence serious economic disputes are relatively rare – less than 2 per cent of total transatlantic trade – but make media headlines (such as beef hormones, steel, or the disagreement about the military invasion Iraq in March 2003 that caused the decline of certain French, German and other EU market shares in the US due to a guided change in consumer perceptions.) The EU and the US have trodden a fine line between free trade principles and protectionism in trade for decades.

A comparison of the partners is useful for any cross-Atlantic business. This comparison may be based, for example, on the Lisbon Strategy's dimensions of EU Member States' competitiveness (see Table 26).

Table 26   Lisbon scores comparing the EU and the US

Dimensions	US score	EU average	EU average relative to the US
An information society for all	5.86	4.61	(1.25)
Innovation and R&D	6.08	4.41	(1.67)
Liberalization	5.11	4.69	(0.42)
Completing the single market	5.70	5.13	(0.57)
State aid and competition policy	4.52	4.25	(0.27)
Network industries	5.85	5.81	(0.04)
Telecommunications	5.60	5.96	0.36
Utilities and transportation	8.10	5.85	(0.45)
Efficient and integrated financial services	5.82	5.52	(0.29)
Enterprise environment	5.71	4.74	(0.97)
Business start-up environment	5.83	4.52	(1.32)
Regulatory environment	5.58	4.96	(0.62)
Social inclusion	5.04	4.81	(0.23)
Returning people to the workforce	5.60	5.06	(0.54)
Upgrading skills	5.31	4.96	(0.35)
Modernizing social protection	4.20	4.40	0.21
Sustainable development	4.96	5.16	0.20
Overall Lisbon score	5.55	4.97	(0.58)

Source: Blanke and Lopez-Caros, 2004. Also available online at, www.weforum.org/pdf/Gcr/LisbonReview/Lisbon_Review_2004.pdf © WEForum

Following Table 26, the EU as a whole is less competitive than the US economy. In seven out of eight Lisbon dimensions, including social cohesion, the EU as a group is less competitive than the US. However, the EU outperforms the US in telecommunications, social protection and sustainable development. In this comparison, one may look at individual countries in the EU and compare them to the US: some are progressing better. In particular, the

Nordic countries have comparatively higher scores than the US in all areas. The other Member States either outperform the US in specific areas of the Lisbon criteria (for example Austria, France, Luxembourg) or perform worse in all areas (for example Italy, Greece, Portugal). Although the US economy is separated into different independent large states the economy consists solely of one entity, while the EU consists of many nationalities and economies. The recent accessions of new members to the EU, in the short-term hinders its performance because their existing infrastructure does not support the growth of the economy, especially in the areas of the information society, innovation and R&D, and social inclusion. In the long-term, they are expected to increase prosperity for all.

Table 27   US competitive industries ($ billion)

Industry	World export ranking	World market value (WMV)	US export value	Percentage of WMV
Agriculture	1	783	79.57	10.2%
Chemical	2	976	112.86	11.6%
Electronic data processing (EDP) and office equipment	2	421	43.9	10.5%
IC and electronic components	1	331	49.3	14.9%
Automotive	3	847	76.42	9%

Source: WTO, 2005 data

Based on the world market share of each industry we can compare sectors (see Tables 27 and 28). For instance, if the EU is the second leading exporter in telecommunication equipment (having the largest share in the market) after China, we conclude that the telecommunication equipment industry is one of the most competitive sectors in the EU economy.

Table 28   EU 25 competitive industries ($ billion)

Industry	World export ranking	World market value (WMV)	EU 25 export value	Percentage of WMV
Agriculture	2	783	78.41	10%
Iron & steel	1	266	29.20	11%
Chemical	1	976	190.86	19.6%
Electronic data processing (EDP) and office equipment	3	421	31	7.4%
Telecom equipment	2	383	44	11.5%
Automotive	1	847	125.88	14.9%
Clothing	3	258	19.13	7.4%
Textile	2	195	24.31	12.5%

Source: WTO, 2005 data

Judging from the data in Table 27, the US economy is particularly strong in the integrated circuits (IC) and electronic components industries and in agriculture. American companies like Intel and AMD lead the world in integrated circuits technology. The US is the leading exporter of agricultural products such as grains, oilseed and livestock (the three products account for $36.31 billion in exports). The main market for its agricultural products is Asia. In the automotive sector, the US industry has lost momentum; it is now exporting less than the EU and Japan. Oil prices also have an effect on the world consumption of automotive products and on innovatition needs in the sector.

European car manufacturers such as BMW and Mercedes are performing well in terms of world market share (see Table 28), as the leading exporters of automotive products. In telecommunication equipment the EU is second only to China. Telecommunication companies like Nokia, Ericsson, and Siemens lead in technology, while China does so in production costs. Enlargement adds to the export volumes of the EU, for example in the clothing industries. (The numbers in Table 29 take into consideration only the exports of products from EU 25 to other countries outside the EU and not the export between the EU countries.)

Unfortunately, no similar comparison was published with the Asian trade partners. Therefore, the following analysis of Asian–European relations will be based on European and WTO material.

10.2.2.2 The Asia-Pacific region

The Asian and Asia-Pacific region is home to more than half of the world's population. Moreover, it accounts for a significant part in world trade. In spite of the economic and financial problems it faced in the 1990s, Asia-Pacific is one of the most dynamic regions of the world, accounting for approximately one-third of world value of import–export.

Asia as a whole accounts for 21 per cent of EU external exports, and is the third-largest regional trading partner, after non-EU Europe (31 per cent) and NAFTA (28 per cent). (For a detailed account of EU relations with Asia, see http://europa.eu.int/comm/external_relations/asia) Asia also accounts for a significant share of EU foreign investment flows, while certain Asian countries are important investors in the EU. Within the WTO, Asian countries play an important role, and China's and Vietnam's entry into the WTO strengthen this role; so will Russia's. In particular, China, India, the Republic of Korea, Hong Kong and Singapore all saw higher inflows from worldwide sources. Flows to the region remain unevenly distributed.

The sheer number of consumers and of markets, emerging and more open than ever, make China, Hong Kong and South East Asia fast growing business environments which attract a large amount of foreign investment. Major advantages for trade and investment in Asia are factor advantages that lie in the cost of production. Labour costs in particular are relatively lower than in other regions where the level of development is similar, and often business faces less important bureaucracy for business creation. However, this leads us to the main barrier of entry: some non-transparent factors must be taken into account when investing in certain Asian markets, such as political or socio-political pressures.

Despite the fact that each country in this region has a different policy for foreign investment, most of the countries entertain sound relations with the EU and encourage investment in

Table 29 Business sectors performance; the EU and Asia

Sector	World trade value ($ billion)	EU		ASIA (includes Japan, Taiwan and China)	
		Ranking in world export	Share in world export (%)	Ranking in world export	Share in world export (%)
Agriculture					
Fuel and mining	1281	4	4.62	7	2.46
Manufacturing					
Iron and steel	266	2	10.98	1	22.83
Chemical	976	1	19.60	2	15.40
pharmaceutical	247	1	27.00	3	5.22
EDP and office equipment	420	3	7.38	1	52.83
Telecom equipment	383	2	11.49	1	48.06
Automobile	847	3	14.90	1	19.70
Textile	195	2	12.50	1	41.70
Clothing	258	4	7.40	1	35.80
Commercial services					
Transportation	500	1	32.40	2	17.00
Travel services	625	1	34.00	5	7.90
Others	1000	1	42.60	3	13.40

Source: WTO, STATISTICS: international trade statistics, 2005

the region through tax reduction and incentives. Each country in Asia-Pacific has a different way of doing business: business cultures are very diverse, similar to the situation in Europe, but without experiencing its historic, economic and political integration of the marketplace.

With Japan, the main Asian economy in this area, relations have always been challenging and important. In the post-World War II period the EU had little exchange – limited to textile, cutlery and sewing machines – with Japan. However, during the 1980s and early 1990s, while the Japanese economy was booming, European business became rather fascinated with the Japanese management tools (such as Just-in-Time) and its market. But European business faced strong tariff and non-tariff barriers when approaching the Japanese economy. Through important negotiations and partnership initiatives, the EU significantly improved relations with Japan during the 1990s, and European business has progressively become the major foreign investor there. Since 2001, the EU and Japan are engaged in an action plan that widely expanded bilateral cooperation on trade and investment to political and cultural issues.

Certain Asian countries, notably Japan and South Korea, are also major investors in the EU, while the relationship with China has dramatically increased in political and economic affairs and also in institutional exchanges, in particular in China's run-up to its WTO-membership accession in December 2001. While the US ranks first among its trading partners, the EU is the first source of Chinese foreign investment, in front of both the USA and Japan.

In regard to North Korea (DPRK), the EU supports the inter-Korean reconciliation process and shares international concerns about its uranium enrichment programme, which is in breach of its non-proliferation commitments. The EU's policy of dialogue is underpinned by market accessibility opportunities for North Korea.

With India, current relations are based on the first EU–Indian summit meeting of June 2000 that intensified exchanges on all levels. The EU is India's biggest trading partner and provider of foreign investment. Relations started via trade agreement and now embrace political and business, cultural cooperation and joint research projects. This market excels in technology, engineering competences, and expertise in languages.

The above markets are, apart from the strong consumption potential, interesting for European corporations due to the low cost of material and labour (and its level of education) and the incentives for internationalization given by governments for the developing of competitive expertise and technology infrastructure. The most developed markets for the EU in the region are those of Japan, Korea, Hong Kong, Taiwan, Australia and New Zealand. They typically account for around 10 per cent of EU total exports, about the same share as the developing countries of South and South East Asia, and of China. As a little note, business interests have to take account of the fact that in terms of trade liberalization, Asia-Pacific enjoys also a number of bilateral agreements but suffers from frictions and remaining animosities within the region, for example, between Korea and Japan.

The growing importance of Asia in the world economy calls for a short and selective focus, within this chapter, on the study of its competitiveness vis-à-vis the EU, and vice versa. This study is useful for students and managers of corporations operating in both business environments.

Despite the fact that Asia is a large market, diversities in economic performance are more obvious in the Asia-Pacific region than in the EU, and the continent does not show the same phenomenon of integration. In comparison, the EU therefore enjoys higher degrees of relative homogeneity in its market grouping while Asia is more heterogeneous. The value of the market compared by the average income per capita of EU countries is higher than that in Asian countries. At the same time, the Asian-Pacific region has a considerably high trade: GDP ratio, and in some regions higher growth rates than the EU. There is a significant difference in the level of the trade: GDP ratio among the individual economies within the region. Import tariffs have been significantly reduced in Asia-Pacific over the last decade, largely due to the effects of regional and global trade arrangements. For example, as a result of China's WTO accession, its average tariff dropped by 75 per cent in 2000 in all products (primary and manufactured). On the social side, the EU is more competitive than Asia in education, with a more efficient public health sector and a highly developed infrastructure. But Asia is very quickly catching up, holding important growth potential vis-à-vis the maturity of most European markets and sectors, and its demography.

Altogether, whether doing business in the EU or in Asia, you need to have the understanding and tools for adaptation to the uniqueness of each region, and be experienced in diversity management. Also, you must be able to recognize those specificities that may allow you to benefit from similarities in markets or modes of doing business. The Global Competitiveness Report, in formulating the range of factors that go into explaining the evolution of growth in a country, identifies 'three pillars': the quality of the macroeconomic environment, the state of the country's public institutions, and, given the importance of technology and innovation, the level of its technological development. A Growth Competitive Index position is the comprehensive outcome. As a result of the study, Finland has held the leading position for many years in the global growth competitive ranking followed by the US. Other EU countries are also highly ranked in the chart, as are Singapore, Taiwan and Japan.

Using world trade value and share of world trade statistics from the WTO, trade in the world market has been grouped into five major sectors: only extra EU export is considered when comparing the competitiveness to other regions. Equally, only Asian exports to non-Asian markets are measured. Table 29 illustrates both economic groups' performance in all business sectors.

According to this table, the most competitive sectors in the EU are manufacturing of chemical and pharmaceutical products and commercial services. These competitive sectors draw from the EU's strength in technology competitiveness such as entrepreneurship, information and communication technology (ICT), human resources and sustainability. For example, Finland and Germany are very competitive in the quality and standards of labour, innovation and ICT. On the other hand, small countries like Luxembourg, Poland and Hungary exploit their strength in entrepreneurship. Although single EU Member States are not strong enough in all sectors, it is clear that complementarities can drive further growth potentials in commercial services sectors. Through free movement of resource and capital, the EU encourages the business environment to gain competitive strength in the commercial service sector, including financial and business consulting, and R&D centres. The EU shifts its competitive focus from sectors of manufacturing to a knowledge-based economy. However, the EU also needs to maintain a certain competitiveness in the manufacturing sector for a balanced market.

Again as Table 29 shows, Asia currently excels in the manufacturing sectors. This sector can be sub-sectored into eight generic types as shown in the table. If you consider Asia as one integrated economic group, then it obtains its main share in exports from the many sub-sectors in manufacturing. For example, while Japan makes a big contribution in the automotive sector, China and India count for a major share in Asia's textile and clothing. Despite the small amount of share, other Asian countries like Thailand and Malaysia also contribute significantly to the development of sectors such as office equipment and telecommunication and multimedia equipment. The Asian-Pacific pool of essential resources like human, natural and technological is vast, though unevenly distributed. Lower cost of production, both from labour and material convey Asian competitiveness in mass production, while Australia and New Zealand follow the economic trends of highly developed economies. The fast development of socio-technology, manufacturing technology and raising awareness of the environment sustains investments and improves the quality of products.

Table 30 Share of goods and commercial services in the total trade of selected regions and economies, 2004 ($ billion and percentage, based on balance of payments data)

	Exports			Imports		
	Value		Share	Value		Share
	Total	Goods	Commercial services	Total	Goods	Commercial services
World	11140	80.9	19.1	11060	81.1	18.9
North America	1709	77.8	22.2	2284	85.3	14.7
Canada	378	87.6	12.4	335	83.3	16.7
Mexico	202	93.1	6.9	216	91.1	8.9
United States	1129	71.8	28.2	1733	85.0	15.0
South and Central America	347	83.9	16.1	293	80.3	19.7
Argentina	39	87.7	12.3	28	76.7	23.3
Bolivarian Rep. of Venezuela	40	97.5	2.5	22	80.2	19.8
Brazil	108	89.4	10.6	79	79.6	20.4
Chile	38	84.5	15.5	29	78.2	21.8
Colombia	19	89.2	10.8	20	80.7	19.3
Europe	5032	77.6	22.4	4864	78.9	21.1
Austria	159	69.7	30.3	154	69.4	30.6
Belgium	294	83.2	16.8	284	83.0	17.0
Czech Republic	77	87.4	12.6	77	88.1	11.9
Denmark	111	67.4	32.6	99	66.2	33.8
Finland	70	87.3	12.7	60	80.4	19.6
France	531	79.4	20.6	525	81.7	18.3
Germany	1044	87.2	12.8	911	78.8	21.2
Ireland	146	67.8	32.2	118	50.3	49.7
Italy	428	80.8	19.2	417	80.7	19.3
Netherlands	374	80.5	19.5	344	79.0	21.0
Norway	109	76.2	23.8	73	67.3	32.7
Poland	95	86.0	14.0	99	87.6	12.4
Spain	269	68.6	31.4	302	82.3	17.7
Sweden	161	76.5	23.5	132	75.0	25.0
Switzerland	175	79.0	21.0	144	85.3	14.7
Turkey	91	73.8	26.2	101	89.8	10.2
United Kingdom	521	67.0	33.0	591	77.0	23.0

Source: WTO 2005

In the chemical and pharmaceutical sectors, Asia is catching up with large investments into very important equipment and high levels of education and technology. While EDP, office equipment and telecommunication equipment constitute the world's largest share,

Table 31   Share of goods and commercial services in the total trade of selected regions and economies, 2004 ($ billion and percentage, based on balance of payments data)

	Exports			Imports		
	Value		Share	Value		Share
	Total	Goods	Commercial services	Total	Goods	Commercial services
Commonwealth of Independent States (CIS)	301	88.9	11.1	222	77.6	22.4
Belarus	16	89.0	11.0	17	94.1	5.9
Kazakhstan	22	91.9	8.1	19	73.7	26.3
Russian Federation	204	90.1	9.9	129	74.6	25.4
Ukraine	39	84.7	15.3	34	86.3	13.7
Uzbekistan	5	88.2	11.8	4	88.9	11.1
Africa	275	82.7	17.3	258	78.9	21.1
Egypt	26	46.7	53.3	26	71.4	28.6
Morocco	16	60.3	39.7	19	85.3	14.7
Nigeria	30	95.3	4.7	20	78.5	21.5
South Africa	56	85.7	14.3	58	84.2	15.8
Tunisia	13	73.3	26.7	14	86.6	13.4
Asia	3060	85.3	14.7	2852	82.1	17.9
Australia	112	77.8	22.2	131	80.4	19.6
China	655	90.5	9.5	606	88.2	11.8
Hong Kong, China[a]	314	82.9	17.1	299	90.0	10.0
India	117	66.3	33.7	138	70.3	29.7
Indonesia[b]	76	91.2	8.8	70	69.5	30.5
Japan	634	85.0	15.0	541	75.2	24.8
Korea, Republic of	298	86.6	13.4	269	81.6	18.4
Malaysia	143	88.4	11.6	118	84.1	15.9
New Zealand	28	72.3	27.7	29	76.3	23.7
Philippines	43	90.4	9.6	50	89.9	10.1
Singapore[a]	233	84.3	15.7	200	81.9	18.1
Taipei, Chinese	199	87.2	12.8	187	84.0	16.0
Thailand	115	83.5	16.5	108	78.7	21.3
Memorandum item: EU (25)	4580	77.8	22.2	4443	78.5	21.5

[a] Trade in goods includes significant re-exports or imports for re-exports

[b] Secretariat estimates

Note: Trade in goods is derived from balance of payments statistics and does not correspond to the merchandise trade statistics given elsewhere in this report

Source: WTO, 2005

this to date concerns manufacturing competitiveness. But rates of innovation and techno-logical competitiveness grow.

10.2.2.3 The Third World

The EU reinforced its links with the Third World for trade, investment and political rea-sons in the mid-1990s. It is the leading donor of aid to the Third World providing half of the international help to poor countries. The EU has endorsed programmes to provide, for example, clean water and surfaced roads to support the economic development of opening markets. Encouraging regional trade is part of the EU's objectives in its initia-tives. Trade and aid are thus the two pillars of EU development policy. This policy was ini-tiated in 1971 under the 'Generalized System of Preferences' (GSP). Its main objectives are to reduce and remove tariffs and eliminate quotas on most of its imports from developing countries.

The EU has developed a tied relationship with the ACP countries; a model of how to open markets to poorer countries, and the biggest EU programme to more than half of the world population. However, despite the EU contribution for economic support, the ACP countries' share of EU markets has continued to fall and has contributed to their margin-alization. For these reasons, the European development programme started to focus its aid on the construction of infrastructure and technical equipment to enhance own national economic developments, on the basis of access to food and clean water, improvement of education, health, support of employment, social services, infrastructure and a sound envi-ronment. In 2008, the EU plans to develop new 'economic partnership agreements', com-bining trade support and aid in order to help poor countries to integrate well in the regional economy via DG Development, EuropeAid, AidCo and the EU's Cooperation Instrument. For 2007–3, it replaces the area structures that led EU projects and pro-grammes to 2005 (TACIS, ALA, EDF).

10.3 The role of Europe in positive globalization

10.3.1 Towards a greener, social and diversified face of globalization?

We started the first chapter with an introduction of key terms that were useful for the study of this book and its topics. Globalization was one of them, Europeanization another.

In the context of this book, we spoke of globalization as the compression of time and space that increases the frequency and duration of linkages between any given actors in the international environment. This implied a complex structure of integrated activities, mainly economic, but also those driven by political, environmental and geopolitical con-siderations. The compression of time translates into a high sequence of interaction between any of the given actors; for example, impacting on the rapidity of orders over the Internet or of how long it takes to have a product delivered. The compression of space results in a geographical proximity with countries (and thus markets) that appeared very far away some decades ago. The major advances made in transport, information and communication technology are at the origin of much of this. Therefore, these sectors play an important role in the competitiveness of sectors and markets. Europeanization was a term used in two senses. The first implied the European integration of economies and the development of common policies of EU Member States. Europeanization was considered here as an advanced case of globalization, in comparison to other forms of market grouping and economic integration within regions. Secondly, when used in connection with business corporations, the term Europeanization described advanced forms of organizations that reflect (a) the diversity of markets and cultures and (b) the diversity within the company as well as in the scope of their operations. In any these types of integration, driving and restraining forces result in a push and pull relations between international actors. Table 32 lists some of the main forces.

Table 32   Driving and restraining forces of cross-border business integration

Driving forces	*Restraining forces*
Peace as a means and an end	War and conflict
The logic of profit and sustainability	Market differences
Technology/Investments	Lack of innovation
Market needs and expansions	Inappropriate risk management
Costs (economies of scale) and efficiencies	Lack of resources
Free market initiatives and agreements	National controls and nationalism
Economic integration	Economic protectionism
Management vision, knowledge management and global strategy	Local priorities

Within globalization, some sectors or industries are more touched by the phenomenon than others. This is the case of financial markets and FDI and of trade and production, and concerns mainly corporate organizations such as multinationals. Also, new communication and transport technologies such as satellites, telecom, e-commerce and air travel business are *born global*. Some challenges to globalization are born global too. In Europe they are of great concern and people and companies show high levels of awareness about the role that companies and international institutions play in these fields. Multinationalism and the privatization process of national companies speed up the competition among companies within the same industry. A higher competition inevitably leads to faster research of innovations in order to outperform in the market or as a matter of simple survival. Consumers and emerging countries bear the fruit of those innovations. Moreover, a higher competition reduces the prices of most goods and services and provides better living conditions. That being said, globalization is a debatable development that raises many issues about dramatic divides in dealing with environmental, social and many other challenges. Can Europe influence the international community and add a more social and green touch to globalization?

10.3.2 Environmental issues

Environmental issues know no borders. For instance, the US has not signed up to the Kyoto protocol, which aims to slow down global warming. Among the signatories, many are still far from the set goals because of poor policy implementation. For example, China and India both enjoy very high levels of growth, produce massively and need to tackle pollution issues caused by high manufacturing. To date, Asia is responsible for 34 per cent of pollution, ahead of Europe (27 per cent) and of North America (26 per cent) (*Le Nouvel Observateur Atlas éco*, 2005), but upgraded facilities are expensive and for some of the economies socially unthinkable. The EU therefore promotes social standards so as to rebalance globalization benefits worldwide. One may argue that the integration of our world economy contributes to the promoting of growth, increases incomes and increases social conscientiousness and awareness of environmental challenges. The spread of new technologies helps to reduce pollution and to reduce consumption of resources. Therefore, pollution decreases proportionally.

The EU is actively setting up Best Available Technology references (in BAT Guidelines Document, European Waste Catalogue and seven other main directives) that unify the level of environmental protection. Permits for new incineration plants and process changes, for example, require the use of BAT to protect the environment on a broad level, while remaining economically sensitive. The Integrated Pollution Prevention and Control (IPPC) Directive supports this movement (cf. EEC Council Directives 89/429/EEC, 89/369/EEC on the reduction of air pollution from waste–incineration plants, Directive 2000/76/EEC, Opinion 1998/0289 of 11/10/2000 and Suder, 2007).

Moreover, governments and corporations are increasingly aware of the credibility that can be lost in the international community when ignoring environmental 'good sense' and sound resource management, including that of commodities and the dependence on them. For example, in this framework again, the experience of sound diversity and geopolitical management are crucial: in the 2006 gas crisis, when Russia for a short period cut the supply of gas to Ukraine; this caused transit problems to the EU countries, and the EU was asked to mediate.

10.3.3 Social issues

Before the events of 11 September 2001 turned anti-globalization sour, vivid demonstrations expressed opinions that economic liberalization is leading to the exploitation of millions of workers in countries that do not give workers the rights they deserve. This is the main focus of European social preoccupations, while the interpretation of 'social' concerns in the Anglo-Saxon school of thought implies also cultural and economic network issues. Social responsibility comprises, then, a range of concerns reaching from the environmental to the humanitarian involvement of business (refer back to Chapter 6 for a discussion of these activities).

Staying on the subject of European concern, outsourcing transfers production to countries that have low labour costs but often do not take the respect of human and working rights into account. Also, the concept that free competition may lead to monopoly situations is frequently criticized by anti-globalization activists. For example, in the UK only three banks represent 80 per cent of total household deposits; this phenomenon may lead to closed markets and distortions such as price agreements to the disadvantage of the social society (L'Humanité, http://www.humanite.presse.fr). The European Commission hence reserves the right to approve mergers and takeovers that affect its market. A third concern lies in the increase in the offshore phenomenon that leads to unemployment and de-industrialization in occidental countries. Recent studies published by the Forrester Research Agency and Berkeley University indicate that 3.3 to 14 million jobs in the US will be transferred to emerging countries by 2015, with similar ration expected for Europe (L'Expansion, June 2004). Trade unions, governments, private firms and workers are the main actors in this issue. It is widely relayed by the press, which emphasizes the negative impacts in regions and sectors. In Europe, for example, Michelin in France transferred one of its French factories to India and the explanation for the resulting lay-offs that they were for economic reasons was quickly dismissed by the company's rapid announcement of high profits. However, it is not only the industrial sector that is concerned but also the services sector where more and more telecom services have experienced transfers to India or Africa since 2000. Due to the increasing level of education in some emerging countries (of a part of the population), R&D services are also being transferred. However, economic theory teaches us otherwise. Shifts in international production and investments normally allow economies to evolve towards more competitive sectors; a belief that in the EU still needs to be underpinned by strong incentives from the political economy.

On the social side, Europeans believe strongly in the sound social networks that characterize its economies and protects citizens in terms of health, remuneration, retirement and freedoms as such. Some countries negotiate relatively low levels of weekly working hours, in particular the 35 hour-week in France; Member States such as Cyprus and the Czech Republic show an average of 38 weekly working hours, and some show higher figures, such as Malta, Slovenia and Greece with 40 hours. In France, some companies have proposed to workers that they work more hours for the same pay levels as an alternative to outsourcing.

At the managerial level, in France, Denmark and the UK working hours exceed those of employees exponentially. In Greece, however, managerial staff only work one hour more than non-managerial staff on average. While average working time for non-managerial staff has typically decreased throughout Europe, however, that for managers has increased. European legislation limits a maximum of working hours across its members to 48 hours and grants certain dispensations for the selected managing executives (EURO FOUND, 2000–2006). Paid leave also varies from country to country but averages a minimum of 22 days per annum in Europe, compared with 20 days in India established in 2007, 19.2 days in the US, and 12 to 16 days plus 1 day per each 5 years of service in Vietnam. In Japan, where the number of taken paid annual leave granted averages around 15 days, employees show a tendency not to take the entire holiday period off (rather around 10 days), because of concerns regarding the amount of work left and its distribution during this time, or to preserve leave in case of illness or other emergencies.

Nevertheless, international trade and investments are recognized drivers of world growth over the past 50 years. The growth which stimulates innovations enables people to obtain better living standards and greater levels of freedom, and Europeans – though grudgingly – will always admit that without globalization (European-style!) the social benefits would not be maintainable at the current levels – which are already under strain from demographic problems. Indeed, on a worldwide level the proportion of people living under the poverty threshold (that is to say $1/head/day) has been reduced by half. In 1981, 41 per cent of the world's population was regarded as poor, yet in 2002 they numbered less than 20 per cent. (François Bourguinion; L'Expansion; September 2004). Poor countries, which have lowered their tariff barriers and opened their economies, have reduced their unemployment and increased their national incomes. World exchanges have the potential to help improve the poorest economies. The European example has shown that the integration of poor countries into a market grouping can balance out the divide between economies. European business has driven this phenomenon.

10.3.4 The compression of time and space: Is closer better?
People and knowledge, companies and commerce are spreading around the world to many different places, in a migration that is based on the expansion of freedom, peace and opportunity. Different cultures coexisting in the same area is a more and more common phenomenon that takes value when the value of diversity is recognized among all actors.

The compression of time and space in globalization represents a real opportunity to provide knowledge, goods and services to the peoples of the world. The real challenge is that of economic and geopolitical stability whenever borders are crossed.

Doing business in Europe, experiencing its diversity and the similarities, and knowing how to best tackle the opportunities that result thereof: this is the key to international success.

Mini case study: Joining European competitiveness – the Experience of Dari Couspate, Morocco

The ability to compete internationally, for non-EU firms, can be reinforced when gaining strength through a sound market share in Europe, one of the most important important markets in the world, and a door to many other markets.

After a lifetime working in the pasta industry, and when it was time for me to retire, I decided, in 1994, to create my own company: Dari Couspate specializing in transforming semolina into high-quality couscous.

Thanks to a very good knowledge of the local market, we rapidly earned market share and became one of the two Moroccan leaders. The key objective was to bring a very high-quality product to all the retailers, even in the less accessible regions of Morocco.

However, it was time to expand further: that is, to Europe where the demand for couscous was not fulfilled. Our challenge was to be able to bring couscous to all European kitchens and not exclusively to ethnic groups for whom couscous is a traditional dish. Our main motive to go abroad was the knowledge that the Maghreb communities in Europe were demanding a high-quality couscous and that the supply

(Continued)

there was very limited. We wanted to be the first to offer such a product. And follow the Wider Europe principles.

We decided to concentrate first on France, in 1997, where Maghreb communities were significant. Even if France has its own couscous industry with a large production capacity, there was still a growing demand, particularly from those groups who were looking for a high-quality product. Thus, we started by exhibiting our product in Moroccan and European fairs and trade shows. With the growing demand on our couscous, we decided to supply some wholesalers and small retailers as well as restaurants in the cities where the ethnic groups were important. Those retailers and wholesalers were regularly visited by a Dari representative in France. In addition, the manager took it on himself to visit on a regular basis Dari's clients all over Europe. We also actively participated and sponsored community events and advertised on local radio.

When our product was well established with our primary target, we expanded to mainstream supermarkets and hypermarkets, like Auchan, Cora and Carrefour, which are also competitive worldwide and benefit from the large European market base.

The same strategy has been applied to Belgium as of 1998, Netherlands from 2002 and Spain and Italy since 2004; the relatively harmonized European business environment made our expansion easier. Our annual progression in Europe is 20–25 per cent and we now participate in large food fairs like SIAL in Paris, ANUGA in Cologne and Alimentaria in Barcelona: at these fairs, we target the Maghreb communities living in Europe as well as European restaurants and supermarkets.

In this stream of thought, we keep adapting to the European market by providing packaging that fits better the needs of the European consumers (smaller packages, cooking instructions, etc.). For example, the European market requires 500g packs compared to 1kg or 5kg packs in Morocco, where couscous is a traditional family dish that is prepared for large groups.

The key to our success in Europe is twofold: First, we determined our primary target, focused on it exclusively and strongly established the brand with those customers. Then, we expanded our distribution so that our couscous was no longer considered as an 'exotic' product but as an ingredient that people can use in everyday cooking.

Source: Mohamed Khalil, CEO Dari Couspate, Morocco

Mini case questions:

1   Why did Mr Khali decide to expand into Europe first, rather than into Africa, the Middle East, or other markets in the world? Do international relations and trade relations play a role in this move?

2   Is diversity a value? Discuss this question in terms of Dari Couspate's Europeanization.

Review questions

1 **Explain** the position of the EU in its relations with NAFTA and ASEAN. Compare the objective of these agreements. What is the strategic role of the EU in relation to them?
2 **Why** does the EU have a particular relationship with ACP countries?
3 **To what extent** have relations with Asia evolved and why?
4 **Does** Europeanization potentially have a positive impact on globalization?
5 **To what extent** can non-EU international business benefit from doing business in Europe?

Assignments

• **Imagine** that Europeanization and economic integration came to a halt, and that protectionism and nationalism took over in Europe. Does the international context (international trade relations) have a role to play in the development of a future European Union? What pressure would the international community exercise, and why?
• **Compare** the working hours in Europe with those in emerging countries. Discuss your findings. Can we expect convergence in the future? What would this imply for international business?
• **Case study assignment:** Read and prepare the To Tilt or Not to Tilt case study in Part IV, and discuss the impact of doing business in Europe.
• **Internet exercise:** On http://www.wto.org, review the most recent negotiations at the WTO. What is the European stance on the most recent topics? Analyse the reasons for these standpoints.

Web guide

http://ec.europa.eu/world/enp/index_en.htm European Neighborhood Policy.
http://ec.europa.eu/comm./europeaid/index_en.htm European aid and support for developing countries.
http://www.eurunion.org: The Delegation of the European Commission in the USA and its website.
http//:www.eiro.eurofound.eu.int European Industrial Relations Observatory Online.
www.worldtrademag.com/ L. Sowinski, and J. Smith, *World Trade 100 Annual Trade Review*, 10 January 2004, and more.

http://www.ibeurope.com/Records/7900/7910.htm 'Unemployment Rates in the EU25 and the Euro-zone Remained Unchanged in August 2004', 5 October 2004, and links to other articles.

http://europa.eu.int and http://ec.europa.eu/comm/external_relations/gr/index.htm Trade implications of EU enlargement: facts and figures, and more.

http://europa.eu.int/comm/trade/issues/bilateral/regions/candidates/index_en.htm Candidate Countries.

http://www.wto.org Regionalism: friends or rivals? And more articles, studies and data.

http://www.un.org/ecosocdev/geninfo/afrec/vol14no3/afstocks.htm UN information about competition.

http://www.ewi.info The East–West Institute's site as an example of not-for-profit international networking for the building of fair, peaceful and prosperous civil societies.

References

Alden, J. (2002) *U.S. Competition Policy*. Geneva: Freedom Technologies, Inc., ITU Presentation.

Allegretto, S., Bernstein, J. and Shapiro, I. (2005) *The Lukewarm 2004 Labor Market Despite some Signs of Improvement, Wages Fell, Job Growth Lagged and Unemployment Spells Remained Long*. Washington: Economic Policy Institute and Center for Budget and Policy Priorities.

Blanke, J. and Lopez-Caros, A. (2004) *The Lisbon Review 200': An assessment of Policies and Reforms in Europe*. Cologne/Geneva: World Economic Forum.

Buch, C. (2000) *Financial Market Integration in the US: Lessons from Europe?* Kiel: Kiel Institute for World Economics.

Commission of the European Communities (2005) *EU Report on Millennium Development Goals 2000–2004*. Brussels: Directorate-General Development.

Darrell, M. West (2000) *Assessing e-government: The Internet, Democracy, and Delivery by State Federal Governments*. Providence: Brown University.

Economic Research Service and Foreign Agricultural Service (2005) *Outlook for US Agricultural Trade 2005*, Washington: USDA.

EEC Council Directives 89/429/EEC, 89/369/EEC on the reduction of air pollution from waste-incineration plants, Directive 2000/76/EEC, Opinion 1998/0289 of 11/10/2000.

EUROFOUND (2000–2006), *European foundation for the improvement of living and working conditions 2000–2006*, and *European survey on working time and work-life balance* , http://www.eiro.eurofound.eu, Dublin.

European Commission (2001), *A Sustainable Europe for a Better World: A European Union Strategy for Sustainable Development*, May, COM(2001) 264 final. Luxembourg.

European Commission (2002a) *Report on EU Financial Integration*, European Economy Economic Papers No. 171, May. Brussels Economic and Financial Committee (EFC).

European Commission (2002b) *Manuscript for information brochure*, December. Brussels/ Luxembourg.

European Commission (2005) *Online Availability of Public Services: How is Europe Progressing?* Luxembourg: Directorate General for Information Society and Media.

European Communities, *Decision of 21 November 1997 on code of conduct concerning public access to documents of the European Foundation for the Improvement of Living and Working*. Luxembourg.

Gowan, P. and Anderson, P. (eds) (1997) *The Question of Europe*. London: Verso.

Keegan, W. and Schlegelmilch, B. (2001) *Global Marketing Management*. London: FT Prentice Hall.

Mercadon S., Welford, R. and Prescott, K. (2001) *European Business*, 4th edn. London: FT Prentice Hall.

OCO Consulting (2005) *Attracting FDI to the US: Challenges in a Global Economy*, September, Chicago: IEDC.

Riedmann, A., Bielenski, H., Szczurowska, T. and Wagner, A. (2006) *Working Time and Worklife Balance in European companies*. Dublin: EUROFOUND.

Sen, A. (2000a) *Competition and Demand Change in Selected Asia Pacific Countries*, Presentation, Isik University, Isik.

Sen, A. (2000b) *How applicable is the European Union experiment for a Regional integration form in Asia Pacific*, Isik University, Isik.

Smismans, S. (2004), *EU Employment Policy: Decentralization or Centralization Through the Open Method of Coordination?* Florence: Department of Law, European University Institute.

Suder, G. (2007) 'The municipal solid waste incineration sector in Europe: a study of harmonization and its impact', *International Journal of Environment and Waste Management*, 2(1).

The Federal Government of the Federal Republic of Germany (2004), *EU sustainable development strategy: Position of the Government of the Federal Republic of Germany on the Consultation process 2004*, 1 November, Berlin.

Virmani, A. (2004) *Development of World Economy & Global Governance*, Indian Council for Research on International Economic Relations, ICRIER.

Williams, J. (2005) *Strategy Driver for International or Global Business* (3 of 5), Political Factors Using the EU as an Example, and other topics, on http://www.answers.com/topic/ european-union, download November 2005.

World Trade Organization (2005) *UNCTAD World FDI flows in $ billion* (www.unctad.org/ tdistatistics) and *International Trade Statistics* (2006), Geneva.

Web sources (all downloads from 2005 and 2006):

http://ec.europa.eu/comm/trade/issues/bilateral/regions/candidates/ff040204_en.htm European Communities (2003) The worldwide exportations in 2003.

http://www.answers.com/topic/european-union European Communities (2006) The GDP of European countries.

http://europa.eu.int/abc/keyfigures/economy/trading/index_animated_en.htm European Communities (2001) The EU: A Major Trading Power.

www.weforum.org/pdf/Gcr/LisbonReview/Lisbon_Review_2004.pdf Lisbon Review (2004).

www.waipa.org WAIPA Tenth Annual World Investment Conference (2005).

www.weforum.org/pdf/Gcr/LisbonReview/Lisbon_Review_2004.pdf

WTO, STATISTICS: international trade statistics (2005) Trade by sector, http://www.wto.org/english/res_e/statis_e/its2005_e/its05_bysector_e.htm#top

Asia times online, www.atimes.com European competitiveness report (2004).

http://www.eiro.eurofound.eu.int/2005/03/update/tn0503104u.html Working time developments (2004).

http://www.eurunion.org/infores/euguide/Chapter7.htm

http://europa.eu.int/pol/ext/print_overview_en.htm

http://www.ecdel.org.au/newzealand/EU_NZ_relations/agreements.htm

http://www.ecdel.org.au/eu_and_australia/agreements.htm

http://www.ecdel.org.au/eu_and_australia/index.htm

http://europa.eu.int/comm/external_relations/switzerland/intro/index.htm

http://www.apec.org/content/apec/member_economies.html, 2006

http://epp.eurostat.cec.eu.int/

http://local.de.eea.eu.int/

http://europa.eu.int/comm/avpolicy/media/index_en.html

http://europa.eu.int/comm/external_relations/gulf_cooperation/intro/index.htm

http://europa.eu.int/comm/external_relations/mercosur/intro/index.htm

http://www.europa.eu.int/pol/ext/index_de.htm

http://www.sba.gov/sbir/indexsbir-sttr.html

http://usinfo.state.gov/wh/Archive/2005/Jun/02-875391.html

http://www2.salliemae.com/news/highereducationstats/

http://www.tiaonline.org/resources/stats.cfm

http://www.pulse.tiaonline.org/article.cfm?ID=573

http://usinfo.state.gov/products/pubs/oecon/chap3.html

http://europa.eu.int/abc/history/index_en.html

http://www.sdi.gov/lpBin22/lpext.dll/Folder1/Infobase7/1?fn=main-j.htm&f=
    templates&2.0

http://trendchart.cordis.lu/scoreboards/scoreboard2002/index.cfm

http://www.dti.gov.uk/ewt/diff.htm

http://europa.eu.int/pol/trans/overview_en.html

http://europa.eu.int/comm/economy_finance/publications/economic_papers/2002/ecp17
    1en.pdf

http://www.finfacts.com/irelandbusinessnews/publish/article_10003880.shtml

http://europa.eu.int/comm/employment_social/emplweb/news/news_en.cfm?id=82

http://europa.eu.int/comm/sustainable/pages/review_en.htm

http://www.dol.gov

http://www.dot.gov/stratplan2008/strategic_plan.htm#_Toc52257031

http://www.doingbusiness.org/ExploreEconomies/Default.aspx?economyid=197

http://europa.eu.int/comm/employment_social/social_inclusion/index_en.htm

http://fbweb.cityu.edu.hk/hkapec/Conference/Papers/Asli%20Sen.pdf

Media sources:

L'Express, 'Délocalisations et mal français', 1/7 November 2004.

Le Nouvel Observateur, 14/20October 2004.

Le Nouvel Observateur Atlas éco 2005.

Le Nouvel Observateur, 'L'allemagne licencie en force', 23 to 29 October 2004.

Le Nouvel Observateur Atlas éco 2005, October 2004.

Marianne, Jack Dion, 'Quand Chirac et Lula désignent les véritables armes de destruction
    massive', 25 September to 1 October 2004.

Marianne, Jack Dion, 'Allemagne. Les patrons se plantent, les salaries trinquent', 24/29 October 2004.

L'Expansion, 'La Mondialisation uniformise les produits', September 2004.

L'expansion, François Bourguinion, September 2004.

Le Nouvel Observateur, Doan Bui, 'Délocalisations la filière roumaine', 9/15 September 2004.

L'Expansion, 'Les délocalisations déroutent les politiques', June 2004.

Le Nouvel Observateur, Bruno Birolli, 'La croissance chinoise fait peur', 17/23 June 2004.

World Economic Forum: Global Competitiveness Report 2005–2006.

Part IV

CORPORATE CASE STUDIES

Airbus: A Catalyst of European Integration

By Dr Gabriele Suder

The first A380 flight has announced a European success story that has evolved with the deepening of European integration, and the resulting business opportunities and challenges. The European Aerospace and Defence sector is a significant catalyst of an integration that has gained business recognition over time, and that has been driven by business. This case therefore studies the link between the two, the growing role of the European aerospace industry and European integration, by promoting cooperation and accelerating the phenomenon of business Europeanization. Defence is at the very origin of the European settlements after World War II: peacekeeping and security concerns were the main driving force behind post-war economic cooperation.

Over time, the EU has set out clear objectives that aim to improve the security and economic prosperity of its members. The Cologne European Council recognised the need for sustained efforts for a competitive and dynamic industrial and technological defence industry in support of Europe's capacity to respond to international crises. At the Lisbon Council, the Heads of State and Government set the Union the strategic goal of becoming the most competitive and dynamic knowledge-based economy in the world within a decade. This message was reinforced at the Barcelona Council, which called for a significant boost in the overall R&D and innovation effort in the Union. More recently still, the Thessaloniki Council decided that the time had come to take concrete steps in the field of defence, of which the aerospace industry is the most integrated part. Why aerospace? As a high-technology and highly skilled, dual-use industry, the European aerospace industry is uniquely placed to contribute significantly to these economic and strategic objectives as it had played a great role in European integration: it is a crucial component in maintaining Europe's industrial and technological capability for transportation, communication, observation, security and defence. Airbus was one of the first firms created as a truly European company. Constituted of four major European nations (Germany, Spain, UK and France), it is now one of two aircraft manufacturers in the market for large commercial airliners that designs, builds, sells and provides support for commercial aircraft with a capacity of 100 seats or more. Airbus boasts the most modern and comprehensive airliner families in the world and consistently captures about half of all commercial airliner orders.

This case is based on documentary research: internal information and documents, web and press articles. It is exclusively descriptive and analytical. Most material was directly made accessible by Airbus.

Airbus history

Airbus Industrie, as it was formerly known, began as a consortium of European aviation firms that joined together to compete with American companies such as Boeing and McDonnell Douglas. In the 1960s European aircraft manufacturers had been competing as much with each other as they competed with the American firms that were already giants in the sector. In the mid-1960s tentative negotiations commenced that were to give birth to a true European collaboration.

At its very beginnings, in September 1967, the British, French and German governments signed a Memorandum of Understanding (MoU) to start the initial development of a 300-seat Airbus A300. This was the second major joint aircraft programme in Europe, following only that of Concorde, for which no ongoing consortium was devised. An earlier announcement had been made in July 1967 but was condemned by the British Aircraft Corporation (BAC). The British government refused to back its proposed competitor, a development of the BAC 1-11, and instead waited to support the Airbus aircraft. In the months following the agreement, both the French and British governments continued to express some doubts about the aircraft project. One of the issues was the development and requirement for a new engine that was to be developed by Rolls-Royce, the RB207. In December 1968 the French and British partner companies, Sud Aviation and Hawker Siddeley proposed a revised configuration, the 250-seat Airbus A250. Renamed the A300B the aircraft would not require new engines, and hence reduced development risks and costs, and the project went ahead. In 1969 the partnership was shattered by the withdrawal from the project of Hawker Siddeley. Given the participation by the British partner up to that point, France and Germany were reluctant to take over its wing design. Finally, the British company was accepted to continue as a major subcontractor.

Airbus formed: Changing mindsets

Airbus Industrie was set up formally in 1970 following an agreement between Aerospatiale France and Deutsche Aerospace (Germany); they were joined by CASA of Spain in 1971. Each company would deliver its sections as fully equipped, ready to fly items. The name 'Airbus' was taken from a non-proprietary term used by the airline industry in the 1960s to refer to a commercial aircraft of a certain size and range. The term was acceptable to both French and Germans linguistically.

In 1972, the A300 made its maiden flight and the first production model, the A300B2, entered service in 1974. Initially the success of the consortium appeared to be short-lived but, over time and by 1979, 81 aircraft had entered into service. The launch of the A320 in 1981 confirmed Airbus as a growing competitor in the aircraft market: the aircraft had over 400 orders before its first flight, compared to 15 for the A300 in 1972.

In 1977 Hawker Siddeley merged with BAC to form British Aerospace (BAe). In 1979 BAe (now BAE SYSTEMS) formally rejoined the consortium, taking a 20 per cent stake in it. This left the Germans and the French with 38 per cent each, and the Spanish firm with 4 per cent. It was a fairly loose alliance that only significantly changed in 2000 (when DASA, Aerospatiale and CASA merged to form EADS) and in 2001 (when BAE and EADS formed the Airbus Integrated Company). This was to coincide with the development of the Airbus A380, as yet the world's largest commercial passenger jet. Airbus was ripe for an ambitious European adventure with this mega-jumbo.

Federating a spirit over time

Driven by high R&D costs, aerospace companies started to cooperate much earlier than their counterparts in other sectors. Over several decades, from soon **after World War II**, firms learned to work together, first for controlling each other's activities (also from a political point of view), and then for efficiency reasons. They gradually developed a dense network of joint ventures that served as an excellent base for the consolidation wave at the end of the 1990s. Land system companies and naval shipyards, in contrast, have never reached a similar degree of cooperation: during **the cold war**, R&D costs in these sectors were lower and (as far as land armaments are concerned) production runs longer, making purely national programmes and production facilities sustainable. This situation changed with procurement cuts in the **early 1990s**. The ensuing period, however, has been too short to make up for the delay taken over several decades, in particular since there were almost no intergovernmental programmes launched that could have structured industrial cooperation.

The aerospace industry though, having military origins, realises more than 70 per cent of its turnover in the civil market. The importance of commercial business is due not only to a reduction in military orders in Europe, but also to the growth of civil aviation in general, and to the huge success of Airbus in particular. Airbus was in many ways both the result and the driving element for cross-border consolidation. First, cooperation within the consortium has led to a considerable degree of specialization among the partner companies, binding them together in a core area of activity. Secondly, the transformation of Airbus into an integrated company implied the wider restructuring of the whole aerospace sector, including defence activities. This stands in opposition to the land systems or naval shipbuilding sectors where producers are often highly specialized, with little diversification, and rarely associated with big commercial groups (except in Germany). As a consequence, civil activities could never become a driving force for transnational consolidation.

A market under pressure

Between **1993 and 1997**, a wave of consolidation in the US led to the creation of aerospace and defence giants with turnovers several times greater than those of the biggest European groups. The only way for Europe's national champions to sustain competition with companies the size of Boeing, Lockheed-Martin and Raytheon was to pool R&D resources, broaden market access and reform the Airbus system. The temptation to move from cooperation to integration was all the more irresistible because competition with the US was high across both the civil and the defence markets. Since the announcement of the MDD-Boeing merger in particular, European governments actively supported the Europeanization of their aerospace industries.

Historical opportunities and challenges

The early evolutions of European integration allowed gradually for the creation of crucial freedoms: in 2007, companies can sell their products anywhere in the Member States and consumers can buy where they want with no penalty; citizens of the Member States can live and work in any other country and their professional qualifications should be recognized; currencies and capital flow freely between the Member States and European citizens can use financial services anywhere in the Union. European integration has cared for professional services such as banking, insurance, architecture and advertising, and these can be offered in any Member State for use by the citizens of any other Member State.

In 1992 companies were given further leeway. A company could organize its structure, or establish subsidiaries or branches, across national borders without any extra costs resulting from different national regulatory requirements on company organization. Specifically, this is a point on which European industry like that of aerospace relies on, to have a better distribution of its activities – for the benefit of increasing productivity.

The power of the integrated market underlies the capacity of Airbus to establish strategic cooperation agreements with firms based in other Member States. In that way, 2002 and 2003 marked two essential events with the adherence of the EU to Eurocontrol and the signature of a cooperation memorandum between the two on 22 December 2003. The cooperation memorandum stimulates five fields of cooperation essential to Airbus: the settlement of a Single European Sky, R&D, gathering and data analysis in the fields of air traffic and environment, aerial navigation by satellite (like Galileo), and international cooperation in aerospace fields.

Due to the increasing demand of aerial space capacity, the European Commission also launched a major initiative with the creation of the Advisory Council for Aeronautics Research in Europe (ACARE) that could guarantee a close collaboration between major R&D players in aeronautical fields. ACARE defines and updates the Strategic Research Agenda (SRA) that maps out plans for research programmes. The SRA takes accounts of five principal challenges: quality and economic access, environment, security, safety, and the efficiency of the air transport system in Europe. It aims to create innovative means to improve the efficacy of the current research system, setting up further mechanisms inside the European area of research thanks to additional public and private investment. This agreement is fundamental because it provides the solid basis to reinforce those agreements between different firms of the aeronautical sector inside Europe that are the backbone of Airbus.

The political achievements have also translated into the possibility for any company to establish stages of its supply chain across European Member State borders, using production factors located or sold in other Member States wherever suitable and economically advantageous. This opportunity has not only generated delocalisation but also contributed to balance out some economic differences between the European states. The firm is able to define and determine a product's specification and how to market it without consideration of national barriers. Thanks to the integrated market, Airbus has the possibility to promote, distribute and sell its products, goods and services to wherever its management finds it desirable or profitable without any extra costs other than those due to geography and local preferences, such as the costs of broadcasting advertisements in national markets.

Concretizing cooperation

The creation of Airbus and its structure was first organized by Natco, a network of dispatched specialized sites of manufacturing coordinated by a Central Entity, that is, one nation named to be responsible for the production of aircraft parts. Airbus Manufacturing manages the production of Airbus aircraft, which takes place at different sites in Europe. Typically, manufacturing is organized as a transnational process, structured around key manufacturing units. Each one is responsible for producing a complete section of the aircraft for delivery to the final assembly lines. Airbus organizes its structure, operations and manufacturing through Centres of Excellence. These are transnational in several fields and thus represent a still greater path in European corporate integration: Airbus employs around 40,000 people in several European countries. Construction takes place at a number of plants across Europe – Airbus sites are located throughout Europe, while its main factory is situated in Toulouse, France. The two final assembly plants of Airbus are located in Toulouse, France and Hamburg, Germany.

Given distance and diversity, the corporation has worked and is still working to strengthen cooperation, and to harmonize the processes, ways of working, procedures, cultural differences and operations for increased productivity. For instance, specially enlarged jets, called 'Beluga', were created to move aircraft parts between the different factories and the assembly plants; the system relies on an aircraft that is capable of carrying entire sections of fuselage of the Airbus aircraft. This means it is not in use for the A380, which has exceptional width of fuselage and wings; the parts are mainly shipped to Bordeaux and then transported to assembly via a specially enlarged road to Toulouse.

Civilian and military products

Within 30 years, Airbus has developed from the role of challenger to market leader in both civilian and military sectors, and has profited from a unique integration based on EU history and political will.

While the Airbus product line started with the A300, a shorter variant of it known as the A310 was also conceived to confirm market presence. Airbus then launched the very successful A320 with its innovative fly-by-wire control system. The A318 and A319 followed as shorter derivatives with some of the latter under construction for the corporate *biz-jet* market (Airbus Corporate jet). A stretched version is known as the A321 and is proving competitive with later models of the Boeing 737.

In January 1999 Airbus Military SAS was launched to conceive and support development and production of a turboprop powered military transport aircraft (the Airbus Military A400M). The aircraft represents a joint development of seven NATO members, that is, Belgium, France, Germany, Luxembourg, Spain, Turkey and the UK, as is an alternative to the C-130 Hercules. Longer-range products in civil aircraft, the twin-jet A330 and the four-jet A340, have efficient wings, enhanced by winglets. The Airbus A340-500 excels with an operating range of 13,921 km (8650 miles), which is the second longest range of any commercial jet after the Boeing 777-200LR (which has a range of 17,446 km, or 9420 nautical miles). Here, integration is further illustrated inside civilian and military planes with the use of fly-by-wire technologies and the common cockpit systems in use throughout the aircraft family.

International challenges

Boeing has continually protested over the support that Airbus receives from the governments of the partner nations. In July 2004, for instance, Airbus was accused of abusing a 1992 non-binding agreement covering launch aid. Airbus is given launch aid from European governments, which it must repay through strict commercial contracts, and contends that this is fully compliant with the 1992 agreement and WTO rules. The agreement allows up to 33 per cent of the programme cost to be met through government loans, which are to be fully repaid within 17 years with interest and royalties. These loans are held at a minimum interest rate equal to the cost of government borrowing plus 0.25 per cent, which would be below market rates available to Airbus without government support.

Airbus, on the other hand, argues that some of the government-funded (directly or indirectly) military contracts awarded to Boeing (the second largest US defence contractor) are in effect a form of subsidy (see the Boeing KC-767 military contracting scandal). The significant US government support of technology development via NASA also provides significant support to Boeing, as do the large tax breaks offered to Boeing that are suspected of violating the 1992 agreement and WTO rules. For its recent products, such as the 787, Boeing has also been offered substantial support from local and state governments. Airbus and Boeing also dispute the American company's latest offering, the 787 Dreamliner. EU trade officials are questioning the funding provided by the Japanese government and Japanese companies for the launch of the is aircraft.

The competition is fierce. For the first time in its 33-year history, Airbus delivered more jet-powered airliners in 2003 than Boeing. After losing supremacy to America in the battle of commercial airliner sales in the 1950s and 1960s, Europe seems to have regained the upper hand. Industry analysts widely attribute this to Airbus's more efficient product line, compared to many of Boeing's older designs; the 737, for example, still uses components designed in the 1980s. The 747 was designed in the late 1960s and the 757 and 767 were conceived in the late 1970s. Boeing claims the Boeing 777 has outsold its Airbus counterparts, which include the entire A340 series, as well as the A330-300. The smaller A330-200 competes with the 767, and has dominated that class until the sales introduction of the 787. Currently there are around 3800 Airbus aircraft in service. But its products are still outnumbered six to one by in-service Boeings (there are over 4000 Boeing 737s in service, for example). Airbus entered the modern jet airliner market relatively late (in 1972 compared to 1958 for Boeing) and Airbus's sales are almost completely civilian (as compared to the numerous Boeing aircraft used by the military in the US and other countries). However, the company has won a relatively greater share of orders and delivered more aircraft in 2003, 2004 and 2005 than its main competitor.

More than just commercial competition, the challenges for Airbus and Boeing are frequently perceived as a political and geopolitical quarrel. In this duopoly, Airbus is an emblem of EU influence on the economic and geopolitical scene and helps Europe to gain influence, to improve its image and to build a true identity.

Key success factors

At Airbus, European values and the integration of market, labour, capital and services represent a great tool in the search for efficiencies, such as in human resources (HR). The Airbus corporate culture and philosophy are critical success factors in its integration. Internal corporate communications are heavily based on European values and identity, and with it a feeling of Europeanisms is created internally. Airbus internally promotes a strong message to its staff to get involved in multicultural teams, cooperating and sharing experiences, to move internationally and to recognize and use beneficial differences as complementarities. The resulting feeling of cohesion and an appreciation of diversity is actively used within initiatives that aim to motivate people to actively participate in company integration. For instance, personal training sessions for managers and operational staff are regularly organized to enhance people's intercultural management skills: how to collaborate efficiently with those many different cultures that make up the corporation. The corporate website underlines that '*Airbus' corporate culture is built on innovation, creativity and freethinking. Our organisation reinforces trans-national working patterns while preserving the diversity of cultures and languages which has proved a key asset in the company's development and growth.*' (Source: http://www.airbus.com/about/philosophy.asp).

Cultural diversity and European progressive integration constitute a value to the company and are represented as such:

Company culture

√   Proud of our Past

–   Thirty years of European partnership producing a family of aircraft
–   Making history with new technology
–   Changing the face of the industry

√ Confidence in a challenging future

- One organisation working together as a truly integrated team
- Taking advantage of and developing our cultural diversity
- Taking a leading part on the world stage
- Designing and manufacturing the world's largest commercial airliner

(Source: http://www.airbus.com/careers/life/company.asp)

Opportunities in human resources

In an interview in 2005, the Human Resources Director of the Central Entity explained the extent to which Airbus's HR management is based on EU-created opportunities:

Question: What sort of working environment does Airbus offer?

Airbus strongly believes in the multicultural value of its workforce. With 45,000 employees, representing more than 30 nationalities speaking 20 languages, we are creating a business culture of openness, originality, drive and enthusiasm. We do not believe in forcing everyone into a company mould. Our cultural diversity is a major business advantage – enabling us to work closely with a wide range of customers, understanding their needs and speaking their own languages. We offer exciting opportunities for international 'players' who are able to adapt to a multicultural team, enjoy working on a project basis and are willing to learn from others, while contributing their own ideas and experience.

The transfer of knowledge and cross-cultural co-operation are key factors in our success. We promote cross-functional and international mobility and we seek to recruit graduates with an international mindset. International experience is increasingly needed for a successful career within Airbus.

Question: What does cultural diversity mean at Airbus?

Over the past 30 years, we have mastered the art of creating effective teams of individuals with different nationalities, backgrounds and skills. Airbus boasts at least 80 different nationalities and 20 languages amongst its employees.

We do not try to standardise our employees. On the contrary, we encourage individual originality, drive and enthusiasm. Preserving diversity also presents a key business advantage. It enables us to work closely with customers by understanding their needs and speaking their language.

Question: What are the opportunities for working internationally?

Within Airbus, there are a number of opportunities to work internationally – via trans-national work teams, exchange programmes and international transfers. Vacancies are advertised internally across the Airbus organisation worldwide. Trans-national and cross-functional moves are encouraged throughout the company.

(Source: Interview release of Airbus.com: www.airbus.com/careers, information L. Darnis, February 2005)

The location of its headquarters in Toulouse is a key element. The main aerospace schools (ENAC, Sup Aero, etc.) are located in this attractive south-western city of France which attracts engineers from all over Europe. Airbus Central Entity and Airbus France are both also located in Toulouse.

Cooperation, integration and innovation

Of equal importance to borderless HR management for Airbus is innovation and innovativeness. The one may go in hand with the other through a diversity of educational backgrounds, cultures and ways of thinking and doing.

The need for innovation and continuous technological development is crucial for the satisfaction of the customer. As much as competitors and customers are relatively scarce in this market, research and development programmes represent very heavy costs. To respond to this problem, the European Commission decided to get involved with the STAR 21 programme, launched in July 2002. STAR 21 deals with five prime objectives:

- Opening of markets with a single set of competition rules and relaxation of the 'buy American Act'.
- Development of a coordinated research policy in order to secure €100 billion of R&D finance over 20 years.
- Creation of a single sky with the EU as the decision-making and control authority in all areas of civil aviation.
- Harmonization of operational requirements, equipment and defence budget, reduction of capability deficits.
- Development of a coherent space policy along with the necessary funding based on the Galileo and GMES projects (Global Monitoring for Environment and Security).

The harmonization of industrial policy favours innovation and R&D, and clearly helps its industry to maintain market share. For example, the A380 competes directly with the B747 on the long-distance carriers with a far bigger passenger capacity (from 550 passengers to 800). Due to a high degree of innovation, it is an economical aircraft. In the middle-distance carriers market, the 7E7 by Boeing, which is launched in 2008 to compete with the A330, will be able to carry between 200 and 250 passengers. A kerosene consumption lower than 20 per cent to its competitors for a 0.85 mach speed decreases the kilometre price per passenger. Innovation is key.

European and international suppliers

The quality and flexibility of subcontractors and suppliers, too, is crucial because they provide Airbus with all the parts of the final product: it is composed of thousands of parts or components provided by different firms, including engine, electronic (for semi-conductors for instance) and information technology (IT) systems manufacturers. About one thousand subcontractors are involved in an aircraft's manufacture.

The corporation has links with suppliers from all over the world. For instance, some parts supplied in 2003/4 originated from:

- USA: engines in collaboration with SNECMA, security, navigation system;
- Europe: electronics, development, fuselage, opening door system;
- Asia Pacific: front doors, access doors, wings, body, tools;
- Africa: cables.

For the A380, Airbus has reorganized its purchasing policy by widening some of its vetting of tender for new suppliers. It has also tried to minimize the number of its suppliers. The firm's aim is to negotiate as best as possible in order to have products at the best prices to be the most cost efficient. Thus, building a real partnership is necessary. The evolution of European integration and its administrative procedures facilitate this increasingly. On the supplier side, EU integration offers to those suppliers three main options for cost and operational efficiency:

- Joining the firm, to reduce costs and benefiting from each other's capabilities.
- Relocating their production into eastern countries, to use lower-cost labour.
- Offering innovative products to the firm, to differentiate themselves from competitors.

In the supply chain process, the integrated system chosen by Airbus has an objective to reduce costs for both parties. Programmes, operations and functions are thus transversal and transnational, and are reinforced by means of conference-call, video-conference, very regular shuttles, networking, and air-bridges from site to site, e-portals and e-room collaboration.

IT tools infrastructure: linking people and knowledge for greater and faster integration

IT plays a key role in corporate integration, particularly to strengthen transnational cooperation and to enhance reactivity and constant and regular communication and exchanges. Airbus has created an integrated internal portal named 'Airbus People' and e-rooms offering to all employees a shared secure space of collaboration, to exchange data, documents and planning. Airbus People and other portals open to external stakeholders (suppliers, customers, etc.) are now the basis and structure of 'Airbus Collaboration'. These tools provide the drive to harmonize ways of working, processes and procedures, documents, messages and identity.

Altogether, Airbus makes extensive use of portal technology to work with three different groups: the air transport community (airlines and legal authorities), worldwide suppliers (subcontractors and forwarders), and employees and onsite subcontractors. The company's portals promote cultural integration, enable process optimization, and facilitate information systems harmonization and file sharing.

Sup@irWorld Solutions

Sup@irWorld, one of the main integration projects, provides web-based collaborative tools to enhance working efficiency between Airbus and suppliers. Its solutions have been running since March 2005. It provides solutions for integration internally and externally by harmonizing all the procurement processes on every international sites and entity. With such tools and solutions, Airbus's suppliers obtain one common strategic policy and objective which ever site they deal with. Internally, this tool and shared solutions enhances inter-site cooperation offering one way of working for all the Airbus entities.

Airbus manages this tool as one policy regarding procurement, customer relationship, human resources, and other fields – creating a single point of contact, a working place and a source of information for its corporate activities and its stakeholders.

Sup@irWorld covers all exchanges for both flying and non-flying materials/goods/ services and acts as the 'backbone' of both the procurement channel in the Airbus people and the Airbus supply chain through its supplier portal.

Sup@irWorld consists of four interlinked domains, which address four key channels with suppliers: sourcing, e-procurement for non-flying goods, e-collaboration for flying goods, and procurement master data management.

- *Sourcing*   The sourcing domain allows current and potential suppliers to register with Airbus and tells buyers about their products and capabilities. Suppliers and buyers can also exchange information about requirements through a secure connection.
- *BuySide*   This e-procurement domain covers the purchase of general, non-flying goods and services from initial request through final approval of payment. By simplifying and standardizing procurement processes, BuySide has significantly reduced administrative costs and purchasing lead times. Requisitioners order from electronic catalogues, which are created and updated by suppliers, and which Airbus hosts free of charge. Automation has reduced the time required to process an order from five days to two hours, and cut delivery time from 72 to 24 hours. BuySide automates specific e-procurement terms and conditions, resulting in purchasing that is automatically fully compliant with the contracts set by the European Aeronautic Defence and Space Company, which owns 80 per cent of Airbus.
- *eSupplyChain collaboration*   This domain allows Airbus and suppliers of flying goods to collaborate through the entire supply-chain cycle. They can exchange information in real time about forecasts, purchase orders, physical logistics, and the receipt and storage of goods and invoices. Airbus sends immediate notification of changes in requirements or quantities to its suppliers, so that procurement plans can quickly adapt to production changes. It tracks the shipping of purchased goods after they have left the supplier. The supplier has to commit himself to the procurement plan or propose some recovery plan. Inventory is reduced and visibility on forecast and the ability to track logistics flows also reduces the risk that shortages and late deliveries pose for manufacturing. Reduced risk also means greater assurance that schedules are met for final delivery of airplanes to customers.
- *Found@tion*   By consolidating data from 70 different databases in Airbus across France, Germany, the UK and Spain, this domain gives the company, for the first time, a comprehensive view of its suppliers. The constantly updated database provides cross-referenced information about the nature and quality of the suppliers' products and services, purchasing history, comprehensive reporting, and

the status of the approval process for the suppliers and their products. These services are the cornerstone of the BuySide and eSupplyChain operations.

Sup@irWorld gives Airbus a common way of dealing with suppliers across the organization. The company acts as a single integrated entity in its procurement and presents a single face to its suppliers.

Airbus: 'A European adventure'

The development of Airbus has required gradual cohesion and cooperation over time in concordance with the evolution of the single market. The development of the A380, the world's largest passenger jet, has required significant, if not unique, investments in skills, research and technology. Industrial cooperation in the EU is the basis for the success of new aerospace products within an intensively competitive global market. The French President, Jacques Chirac, expressed this, in March 2005 at the official unveiling of the Airbus A380:

'The launch of this giant of the airways is the crowning achievement of a fantastic human and industrial adventure. A European adventure of perseverance, innovative spirit and ardent determination … Today I share the enthusiasm, the emotion and the deserved pride of all the men and women who are part of this immense industrial success story: the engineers, journeymen, assemblers, sales and administrative staff of Airbus and its suppliers. All of you, who have given the best of yourselves to bring this aeroplane into being, I pay you the warmest homage. Whether you work in Germany, the United Kingdom, Spain, France or other countries, notably in Europe, it is your common dream that is taking shape here at AéroConstellation, the A380 assembly site. This is the culmination, I know, of years of effort, imagination, sacrifice and willpower … First of all, it is the success of a European company: EADS, the parent company of Airbus with BAE Systems, is probably the first truly European company, in its ownership structure, its working methods and the common culture that has developed between the French, Germans, Spanish, British and their partners from other countries of the EU. It is also the success of an innovative Europe. A Europe where every nation contributes what it does best. A Europe that is demonstrating its capacity to master and integrate the most advanced technology.'

(*Source*: www.ambafrance-au.org/article.php3?id_article=888)

Note

The author would like to thank Laetitia Darnis, CERAM and Airbus, for their valuable assistance by providing the material for this case study.

Altran: Launching a Corporate Representation Office in Brussels

By Dr Gabriele Suder

Introduction

In 2001, the decision was taken by the Belgian Executive Management of Altran to entrust the analysis of 'the opportunity for Altran to position itself at European Institution level' to a business development manager. This was the beginning of a project for the launch of the company's representation office in Brussels at the heart of European policymaking. A group of more than 180 companies serving more than 500 partners worldwide, Altran engages into technology and engineering consultancy as one of Europe's main players.

This decision to move into the heart of Europe was motivated by various factors. Among these were: the physical position of Altran in Brussels, close to the European decision-making process, and the proposal of the Business Development Manager to create a representation office for the group. This manager was, at the time, in charge of Space and Defence at Altran's offices in Belgium and had graduated from business school, specializing in European Affairs.

An analysis of the opportunities indicated potentially good conditions for Altran to start developing its contribution to European policies and projects following a professional and organised process that included the following:

- increase of allocated resources for research;
- focus on small and medium sized enterprises (SMEs) and innovation;
- Altran geographical coverage;
- international crisis: a need to find new markets; reorientation to public sectors;
- change in the European institutions in 2004 (new Commission, new Parliament);
- refocus of the Lisbon agenda.

The high degree of diversification of the group's business domains and its geographical coverage were indicators for Altran's main opportunities in the project: with its various competencies of technical consultation in fields such as energy and environment, telecommunication and information, and transport, the group was leading the European market in its sector of technology and engineering consulting. Also, Altran's geographical diversification into markets reached from the EU, throughout regions such as those of Eastern Europe and the Mediterranean, to North and Latin America, and into the Asia-Pacific region. A remarkable development of Altran's revenues on a year-on-year sales basis reinforced its operations: a great increase in its US market share of 75 per cent and its Latin American of 50 per cent at the turn of the millennium provided the corporation with sound international weight, while Altran was still to reach its full potential and advance into new markets such as Oceania and the ACP countries.

The Belgian branch of Altran analysed and examined the project's potential and their findings led to the decision to focus on short-term return on the investment, given the lack of experience in the field of EU corporate representation.

However, the success rate was to remain insignificant, and the group's internal and external challenges at this time forced it to reconsider its strategy, and to realize what potential was to be exploited through new objectives for the project.

Altran's target business area, coverage field or coverage clients were unlimited from the beginning. However, at the second stage, the group concentrated on a small pilot project with a limited number of companies so as to create a sound and solicited expertise. Altran focused on EU contribution and image investment for business development. Only then, it was recognized, would it be sensible to diversify its target business area and partners so that both short-term and long-term return on investment could be met for Altran itself, its future clients and partners (the term used by the firm for existing clients). This case will now give valuable insight into the complex and difficult path that leads to the launch of a successful corporate representation office in Brussels.

The Project

With an analysis of the group's opportunities for a launch of a corporate representation office in Brussels, during 2001, the project was rapidly considered worthwhile though not strategic for the whole group. In the short term, the go-ahead was given for a focus on high-quality proposals to public institutions' calls for tender and proposals, and for the development of new expertise and know-how with rapid returns on investment. In the long-term, this was potentially to widen into the further development of services and new competencies at Altran, and a proposal to the clients to act as an interface for European programmes.

The main objectives were hence two-fold: first, to ascertain Altran's expertise in EU affairs management and second, to then also serve its clientele.

In Phase 1 of the project, the European office was created and operated with six Altran pilot companies. From January 2002 to December 2003, this analysis and test phase analysed the potential for effective business in Brussels, aiming to prove the concept following a 'strategy in action 'approach, that is, to design the concept by starting to produce actions and results. The focus was mainly on business development and short-term return on investment. Altran companies were selected for their interest, their knowledge and their capacity to work on European projects, and an external partner was added, working in a cluster approach. The European office started to produce projects proposals concerning services for the European institutions. After a year of activities, the success rate was rather low.

In Phase 2, the involvement of more Altran companies (more than 180) came to broaden the scope of action (Figure 13). A Phase 3 was to enter the collaboration with clients, and to develop new services by targeting the private sector.

Given the low success rate of the European office at the beginning, the Altran European office team analysed the concurrent key factors of future success, and with this the needs that were to be satisfied to obtain efficiency in its operations. These factors were noted to be the:

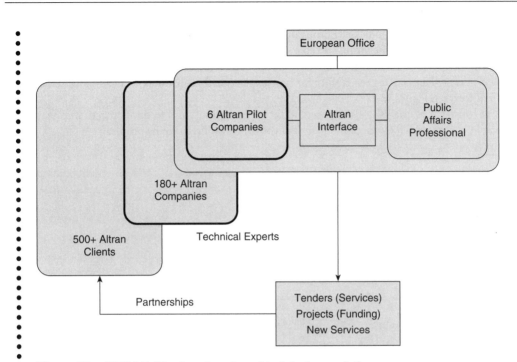

Figure 13   ALTRAN Client and partnership interface relations

- commitment of the companies to provide key human resources during the entire proposal preparation;
- commitment of the Board = decision-making on strategy and action plan and convergence with group strategy;
- industrialization of the process starting with one key sector (pilot project then growth);
- thorough process/methodology with tools;
- anticipation and coordinated action between business and representation actions (building image to make business which develops image).

In addition, management recognized that the project's future was based not only on technical competencies, but also on networking skills and experience at the EU institutions. On the one hand, the high quality of human resources and skill of its employees were necessary, on the other hand, an external partner selection process was to add the missing experience. Hence, the European office analysed 50 European public affairs companies, of which it interviewed 10. Seven of these companies were interviewed by recruitment to reinforce the focus on their compatibility with the Altran corporate culture, and finally, with seven proposals having been received and presented, one company was selected to work with the European team.

In a similar fashion, the Altran companies selection process, of those companies to be part of the six pilot companies in the project, followed the EU tendering approach. Six companies in six different key European markets were selected, that is, France, the UK, Spain, Italy, Germany, Belgium, and shared investments every month.

The structure of this organization was developed as illustrated in Figure 14. This two-step strategy has a strong readability for non-experienced individuals as it can be summarized through Figure 15.

It consisted of analysis of the potential for its operations, and to develop activities that would ensure return on investment so that the office would make its proofs.

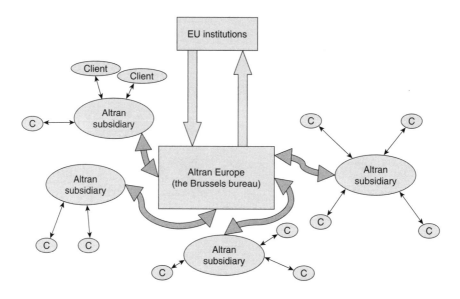

Figure 14　Strategy in action

In analysing the potential, the team highlighted the main areas of development that its office would offer to the group. Probably one of the most important features to be aware of was the potential for a strong and close relationship with EU institutions. What would such a relationship possibly deliver to Altran?

As part of the analysis, the team studied the methodology of the EU's funding policy, the main actors, and the way in which the Union discloses information on funding programmes with a call for tenders that only allows for a short delay for interested organizations. Anticipation and follow-up of annual calls were found to be essential in this field of activity, which requires a medium- to long-term approach of the office's intelligence. Moreover, the great diversity in the range of programmes likely to co-finance projects of Altran's entities involves specialization and selectivity.

The internal structure of the Altran group is composed of an exceptionally wide range of companies. Each of them is specialized in one or more fields of activity, that may find affinity with EU sectoral and horizontal policies. Also, Altran's geographic development

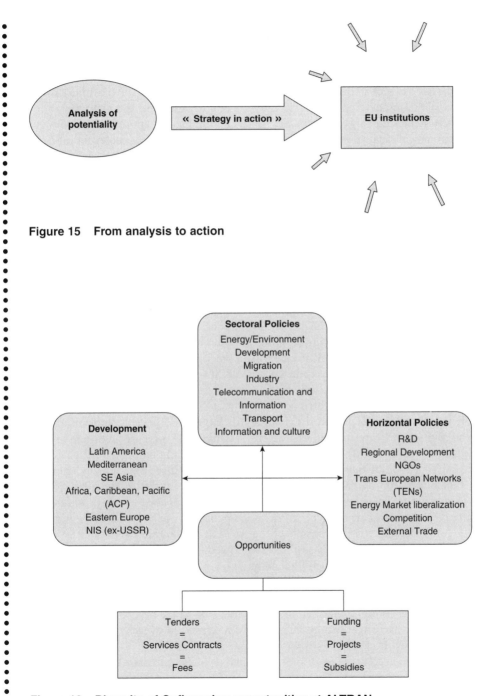

Figure 15   From analysis to action

Figure 16   Diversity of Cofinancing opportunities at ALTRAN

evolves in areas that are part of the EU's strategic interests. This establishes the 'portfolio' of Altran's competencies that can contribute to EU expertise and, vice versa, benefit from European partnerships, funding, services and market contracts, and the international political agenda. Nonetheless, reaching this type of relationship needs the excellent knowledge of the two sides; of all the players in the EU policymaking arena, and of Altran's structures, specializations, developments, engineers. It needs organization and planning.

The 'strategy in action' was meant to be a 'learning from failures' approach. The objective was to learn how to do by doing. This strategy had to directly link Altran's domains of competence with the direct implementation of returns. Hence, from January 2004 to January 2005, this second launch phase concentrated on conceptualization. During this phase, the European office dedicated its activities to the reformulation of objectives and design of a new concept, and the structuring and creation of a modus operandi. The main focus was to define Altran's contribution to the EU, and to invest in an image for its business development

Company specificities shape the methodology

Altran specializes in scientific consulting, and has acquired great experience in this domain, particularly in Europe. The group's internal organization is relatively fragmented given the more than 180 entities that constitute the group. Altran is hence, to some extent, comparable to a grouping of SMEs: each entity specializes in a precise field of activity(ies).

In 2002, Altran was hit by an accounting scandal. It was alleged that various members of the board of directors of the time were accomplices in manipulating and falsifying the company accounts. On 11 September 2002, the COB (the French market supervisory authority, now called AMF – Autorité des Marchés Financiers) filed a complaint against three of the group's directors on charges of dissemination of false information and manipulating quotations. By October 2002, Altran's shares had plummeted with a 45 per cent loss in value. Altran then allowed for external auditing to check the company accounts.

On 30 January 2003, a legal inquiry was initiated against the directors and Altran joined in as civil plaintiff. These legal proceedings followed a case opened by the prosecutor in October 2002, the same date that a press article was published on the results of the first half of 2002 (on 8 October 2002, the results of the first half of 2002 were published with the comment 'audited figures under review'). Altran immediately asked its auditors, in concert with the COB, to perform a thorough audit of the 2001 accounts and the accounts for the first half of 2002. When the audit was completed and the results corrected, the auditors confirmed the authenticity of the 2001 accounts and those of the first half of 2002 published on 15 October 2002. The auditors informed the prosecutor that to the best of their knowledge, no other item was likely to attract his attention. At the end of 2004, each of the three directors were subsequently cleared of any wrongdoing.

This scandal undeniably affected Altran's image and reputation. To make matters worse, the Altran scandal occurred in the shadow of the Enron and WorldCom accounting scandals, which shook the financial world. The case also highlighted two very concerning problems within the Altran structure. The first was a lack of accounting checks and regulations at the time. This is illustrated by the ease with which the employees involved in the scandal appeared to have falsified and manipulated the accounts. The second was poor corporate governance and a lack of communication with the business world and shareholders. This last problem no doubt created further damage to Altran: the corporation's secrecy in the case and about their affairs in general did nothing to fan the speculation and rumours during the scandal nor the negative publicity that Altran received from the media. Rumours circulated about highest annual turnovers of employees in the industry. The direct impact of this was that Altran's financial results were very unconvincing in the 2002, 2003 and 2004 exercises.

Indirectly, the European office project suffered from the necessity of the group to dedicate its main financial and human efforts to redressing the company, minimizing and reducing damage done to the company by the scandal, and replacing its management. Since the EU lobbying project is a project with a long-term aim with little possibility of significant immediate results, Altran's priorities were elsewhere.

However, the new top management recognizes that, for Altran's aim to be the European market leader in innovation, European representation, European credibility and European influences are vital. Logic dictates that only credible, ethical, trustworthy and valuable actors are permitted into the microcosm of successful public affairs managers at the EU. The name-and-shame principle of Brussels has a reputation!

The European office of Altran was, after the low rate of success in its early years, forced to set new objectives that would extend from the short- to the long-term on the timeline, and be complemented by an internal lobbying for the office's cause in the long run. In 2005, Altran went under an important reorganization and analysis of its strategic orientations, after the appointment of Christophe Aulnette, former CEO of Microsoft France, as new CEO for the group. A new board was recruited and the management decided to change the governance of the organization. After three years of discussions, preparation and development of the project, Altran decided to officially launch its European office.

The European office now focused on a revised timeline:

- In the short-term: Altran is aiming in the short-term at developing high-quality proposals and projects to public institutions, while benefiting from the expertise of an EU professional through a reinforced partnership with non-Altran competencies. Moreover, Altran experience and know-how can be considered as a 'push power' to create new projects and programmes.
- In the ST/MT: In the short-term/medium-term, the aim of Altran is to influence the development and innovation of European technological trends. Thus, there exists a real will to become a partner of the EU in the field of scientific consulting.
- In the long-term: Finally, in the long-term, Altran is to develop new services and competencies by choosing more specific partners inside the group, thus choosing more fields of competencies. Another aim is to propose an interface on European programmes to Altran clients, helping them improve their understanding of these sometime policies and their opportunities (Figure 17).

The strategic relevance 'fighting on all fronts' at the EU level can only be based on a corporate culture, and may otherwise well be classified as a waste of resources and energy. A company such as Altran, composed of more than 16,000 employees, can be well advised to

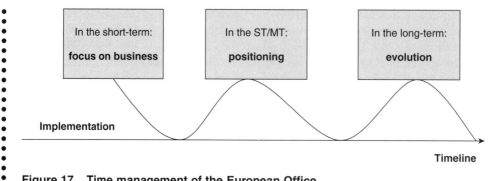

Figure 17 Time management of the European Office

create a small conglomerate of preferred partners for a set of European affairs. Only strong links between fewer companies allow the necessary level of collaboration that is required to implement an efficient bureau in Brussels.

The difference in the timelines lies in the fact that public institutions think in terms of months and years, when companies have shorter periods. This feature stems from the fact that companies and public institutions diverge in terms of objectives: the former needs to be profitable, the latter to represent the interests of the citizens. This divergence has to be taken into account and developed to sort out a strategy coherent with collaboration with EU institutions.

There it has exactly the same 'mental gymnastic' as a business plan: you need to think about processes before applying them. The creation of a modus operandi is probably the best way to see all the issues that are about to rise, and solve them with anticipation. The interpretation of objectives, methods and timelines can make or break the relations between the corporate and the public sector in Europe.

Note

The author would like to thank Nicolas Rougy for his insights and support, as well the students from the MIM European Business programme for their input into the case analysis.

Synops6 International: A Company at the Service of Companies

By Dr Gabriele Suder

Introduction

Synops6 International is a small company, based in the French Riviera technology park of Sophia Antipolis. It was set up in 2003 by Jérôme Reboul to help manufacturing businesses in Europe export their products to other countries. Its creation was also motivated by the desire to help other SMEs in Europe by providing procurement, consulting and outsourcing services to companies who wish to internationalize. The aim of Synops6 is to help the client companies improve their efficiency and expand their operations by improving their procurement process. Clients originate from Europe and its neighbouring countries, but also from elsewhere in the world.

The modus operandi of Synops6 consists of doing market research for its clients: the firm engages in identifying new suppliers in a selected host country or wherever desired by the client. It also identifies trends for new products that apply to the customer's industry or sector of activity. It helps companies who wish to outsource, to find new suppliers or products (sourcing) that are the most appropriate to bring efficiency and provides the client with accurate market insights (trends).

In 2007, the company has been in business for little more than three years; therefore its networking skills and capabilities have necessarily grown. But, the main development since the outset has been the *change of scope of its activities, its markets and its clients*: when it was set up in 2003, there were only 15 EU members, since 1 May 2004, that number has risen to 27 (details of the new entrants will be given in the second part of this case study). This enlargement by the EU represented the biggest opportunity but also the biggest challenge that the Synops6 team had to face to date. Would, and if so, how and why, this firm expand towards Eastern Europe, and if so, how and why? What are the main threats or opportunities and how does Synops6 face them?

Internal analysis

The structure of Synops6 is fairly small; Jerome expected it to have great potential to adapt to fast-changing environments and markets such as those of the new EU Member States from Eastern Europe where growth rates in particular are much higher than in Western Europe in general.

In addition, he believed that there was an obvious client/market match with Synops6's clients who produced products that were the major imported goods of the 10 new entrants.

This indicates that Synops6 could help its clients expand successfully towards these new markets and, therefore, for Synops6's activity to be prosperous.

However, Jerome also knew that he would lack resources, and needed to find solutions: the financial and informational resources were small, and for a consulting company especially, this represents a big drawback for its potential of growth and financial health. Indeed, since the information research concerning the 10 new entrants was very heavy and costly, for it to be efficient and precise the appropriate financial resources were vital. With the 10 new entrants now obeying some of the same rules and regulations as all other EU Member States, the opportunities appeared vast, though. But the language differences appeared important, and indeed appeared as soon as the firm started to look for market information in Poland and in the Czech Republic. Language problems remain and will not disappear quickly. Synops6 needed to overcome them: by hiring local staff, having translators or going through governmental institutions in order to have information in English or French. Last but not least, Jerome analysed his infrastructure. Would Synops6 have the logistics and distribution infrastructure adapted to a consulting company which is supposed to give up-to-date and precise information to its clients?

It transpired that existing networks of the firm and its home base in an older EU Member State allowed it to benefit from existing networks and commercial bilateral agreements with specific countries that are now part of the EU.

Common regulation, since May 2004, applied to 25 EU countries concerning customs and transport especially, but also, for example, quality standards (EU norms and quality standards). This legal harmonization acts as a real catalyst for exports and outscourcing activities, and therefore is a huge advantage for Synops6's business development opportunities. However, for certain products such as raw materials (one of Synops6's main segments), the competition was extremely intense. It could be local, like for the cement industry, or international, like for the petroleum industry. This competition needed to be clearly identified in order to manage and minimize any threat. In addition, the markets had to be well chosen so as not to enter one that was too risky.

The way of doing business in the new Member States can be very different from the way it is done in France or other EU Member States. Synops6's clients have to be made aware of these differences and so does Synops6 itself.

Decisions to be made: Synops6's evolution

Given the potential advantages of the enlarged market, Synops6 turned more and more towards Eastern Europe and especially the new entrant countries. Poland has become one of the main destinations of Synops6's clients' products.

Common EU legislation was finally the main cause of this move towards Poland and other new entrants. In terms of risk minimalization of this internationalization, no longer do problems of different standards (ISO, EU, etc.) hinder the acceptance of produce or components, which means products no longer need to be altered before crossing borders, that is, decreasing cost and risk of non-conformity. The common tariffs ease the circulation of goods and services, and at no tariff cost within the EU, for Synops6 clients. Transportation also improved through EU initiatives to improve infrastructures, and information research concerning country specifications started to improve (Chambers of Commerce, Economic Missions, Ministries of Trade, etc.) – a crucial advantage for Synops6 activities.

For the company, the new entrants constitute *high-potential markets*, by their growth rate, existing size and growth potential. Often, too, these countries try to attract foreign companies and therefore some firms can benefit from government subsidies or tax cuts if they set up activities there. The new entrants offer *reduced costs* (not only wages, but also transportation, raw material, infrastructures, services, etc.). Production costs are therefore greatly reduced compared to Western European countries. Sometimes, fiscal reasons also motivate this move towards the east. This phenomenon has been observed increasingly within the EU, with many factories (shoes, electronic equipment, car manufacturing, etc.) moving towards Poland, Bulgaria or other new EU members. This is seen as a negative aspect by many countries since local production leaves and creates unemployment. But, for companies facing global competition and huge price wars with Asian countries especially, this is not just an opportunity but a necessity in order to survive.

In response to these elements, Jerome decided to split Synops6's activities into six product ranges, that is, *raw materials*, *industrial products*, *companies services*, *consumer goods* (food, cosmetic, appliances...), *private label* and, finally, *innovative products*. In order for Synops6's activities to be successful, it needed to ensure a stable and accurate flow of information for its clients. To do so, it needed to have links with local or EU institutions, NGOs, local companies, consulting companies already in the targeted market. The method of work and therefore the whole of Synops6's business relies on the *networking* capacity of the team.

A key issue for Synops6 since EU enlargement

Synops6 mainly had to decide upon the manner in which to take advantage of apparently attractive conditions and opportunities brought along by the enlargement of the EU? The market growth potential for the new entrants was very attractive but given the threats inherent to these markets (currency, political demonstrations, such as in Poland in 2005, etc.), Synops6 needed to minimize its weaknesses, especially concerning the lack of financial and informational resources (both linked), which are the backbone of the firm's business. Therefore, Jerome picked four of the new entrants for an initial analysis that appeared to present an important potential for Synops6 and its clients, in terms of growth rates, population, consumption habits, but most importantly the growth potential of these markets and the economic opportunities that come with this expansion. The main objective was to identify the three main raw material imports into these countries, so as to be able to not only identify the main purchasers and distributors, but also establish contacts related to clients of Synops6 and their products, and vice versa for their exports. The next four sections analyse what Jerome found.

New EU entrant countries' analysis: Hungary

- *Population:* around 10 million
- *GDP:* over US$150 million with an average of 3.5 per cent growth in the last five years. The IMF projection for 2006 is a growth average of 3.6 per cent

- *Currency exchange*: 1€ = 250.512 HU

  The EU accession has driven a truly liberal policy development in the countries that have allowed the creation of a strong and dynamic private industrial network. The privatization of the state companies, the reinforcement of the banking system, the property right security, the legal system development and a low taxation system (16 per cent company tax) have encouraged many companies to come to Hungary. In the early years of the twenty-first century, about 85 per cent of GDP comes from the private sector and 50 per cent from FDI. The flow of FDI has increased by 165 per cent since 2003, Germany is the leading investor, the French are fourth. In addition, the sustained level of consumption has also enabled the country to preserve a high growth rate.

- *Export flows*

  Exports increased by 14.1 per cent last year and their average growth is about 5 per cent per year over the past five years. The main clients are Germany with more than 30 per cent, the US with 8 per cent and then EU partners, such as France, Italy or Austria, with 5 per cent each. More than 80 per cent of exports go to the EU and this trend will probably increase with the EU accession. The export trade is largely sustained by the automotive industry with 11.2 per cent, which includes not only car engines and other automotive components but also electric appliances and computer materials.

- *Import flows*

  Imports have increased proportionally to exports. The volume of exports is more important than that of imports but the difference in value gave a negative balance for Hungary. Hungary's main suppliers are Germany with 30 per cent, Austria and Italy with 6 per cent, Russia, mainly for energy resources, with 6 per cent and France and China with 5 per cent. 70 per cent of imports arrive from the old EU 15 countries. Hungary is dependent on others for energy supplies and its import flow has increased by 69.5 per cent since 1998 as well as the import flow of electrical appliances and automotive components to sustain its manufacturing production.

- *Synops6 activities*

  The lack of natural resources in oil and heavy petroleum is a real issue for Hungary. On an economic level this is a problem because it needs to maintain a high level of production in the manufacturing industry and on a political scale this lack of natural resources maintains a Russian dependency. Companies like Synops6 must source in this sector and develop activities in this way because the EU accession will encourage internal trading and will be well received from Hungary in order to reduce its dependency on Russia.

  The high demand of automotive components and electrical appliances should also be taken into consideration because a lot of French SMEs are performing in this sector and this is a way for them to diversify their activity and also save costs (labour cost €3.8).

New EU entrant countries' analysis: Czech Republic

- *Population*: 10 million
- *GDP*: growth of 3.3 per cent since 2000 and more than 4 per cent in 2004, US$134 billion for 2005

- *Currency exchange*: 1 € = 29.5973 CZK

The EU accession has put some difficulties in the management of the budget, the governmental expenses and the inflation rate (which has increased from 0.4 per cent to 2.1 per cent in five years). These difficulties have slowed down the privatization process and the reinvestment in industrial equipment and infrastructure a little.

- *Export flows*

The Czech Republic has a strong industrial tradition and a well-educated population, which is a real advantage compared to most Eastern European emerging countries. Exports represent 40 per cent of GDP and have increased by 0.9 per cent this last year. It exports 90 per cent of its furniture production to the EU. Exports are mainly sustained by foreign investments (50 per cent of GDP comes from foreign companies) such as the important Toyota, Peugeot/Citroen factory which produces 400 cars per day. The economy is also highly competitive in the electrical appliances sector which has increased exports by 368.8 per cent in four years.

The taxation system is less attractive than that in Hungary, but even so, FDI statistics are very positive there: French companies are the biggest investors, while Dutch firms comparatively score the first place with 34.1 per cent of total FDI.

Germany is the main client with almost 40 per cent of the export flow, then Slovakia with 7.7 per cent, followed by EU partners, such as Austria or France, with 5 per cent.

The economic sector is also characterized by being very competitive in metal production, for example, iron and steel, much of which is exported to countries like Slovakia.

- *Import flows*

The Czech Republic has a true energy policy; and it is making a sustained effort to decrease its dependency on nuclear energy. Because of this its energy imports have only increased by 173.6 per cent in four years. However, the country still has a need for natural gas and petroleum. Germany is the main supplier with 34.9 per cent, then Slovakia and Russia with more than 6 per cent, slightly more than French companies which supply less than 5 per cent.

Even if exports are more dynamic than imports, however, the trade balance is still negative.

- *Synaps6 activities*

The development of a nuclear policy is clearly a sector in which Synops6 must enter. In fact France, and therefore French companies, have real expertise in this area. In the automotive sector large production plants are already established, and French subcontractors should be attempting to liaise with potential clients with the help of Synops6.

New EU entrant countries' analysis: Slovakia

- *Population*: 5 million in 2003
- *GDP*: US$51.6 billion in 2004
- *Currency exchange*: 1€ = 38.9047 SKK

Slovakia is the country chosen by most German investors because of its proximity and because of its government's efforts to reinforce the country's infrastructure and education system and to make its banking system and legal system more secure. Other EU investors do not appear to have the same point of view because it has received the least investment from them, even though its growth rate over the past few years has been the highest.

Contrary to the other countries, export (+ 11.5 per cent) growth is lower than that of imports (+ 13.7 per cent) in 2004. This is mainly due to its dependency on the European automotive market which represents 16.2 per cent of its exports.

Main clients and suppliers are Germany (30.5 per cent of exports, 24.2 per cent of imports) and the Czech Republic (18.7 per cent of exports, 18.3 per cent of imports). Russia is also a major supplier with 13.3 per cent of imports; this is because it is an important energy supplier of natural gas and petroleum. Slovakia is very competitive in the export of iron and refinery products.

- *Synops6 activities*

Slovakia already has powerful partnerships with Germany and the Czech Republic. This is the reason why it may be difficult to establish trade activities there. In fact, France is a relatively minor partner with around 4 per cent of the trade in both imports and exports.

New EU entrant countries' analysis: Poland

- *Population*: 39 million
- *GDP*: 4.5 per cent for the last 10 years
- *Currency exchange*: 1€ = 3.90371 PLN

Poland is without doubt the leading Eastern European partner of France for several reasons. Most of all, it was the most implicated country in the economic transition and the most dynamic. Its growth dynamic is mainly sustained by a high consumption level and export trade (24.9 per cent of growth in 2003) with its EU partners and with China and the US. Unfortunately, the restructuring of the country, particularly in retooling and infrastructure, has increased the value of imports which gave a negative trade balance. These elements are an incentive to keep encouraging companies to invest in Poland.

The development of special economic zones that encourage businesses dealing in export, warehousing and finance also made the country attractive to investors. Poland is also a market in which companies can invest in and extend their sales activities. Table 33 highlights the advantages and disadvantage of the Polish market.

Currently, more than 660 French companies are established in Poland and employ 164,000 people. Among the corporate leaders are France Telecom and Vivendi Universal, as well as companies in the distribution sector, and the main countries engaging in imports and exports are, in descending order, Germany, Italy, France, the UK, the Czech Republic, the Netherlands and Russia. In terms of suppliers, the leaders are Germany, Russia, Italy, France, China, the Czech Republic and the Netherlands.

- *Synops6 activities*

Poland is a very attractive partner for French companies. In fact, opening subsidiaries there would prove to be economically advantageous because the market is huge and qualified manpower is less expensive than French staff. All actors in the international value chain appear to welcome French contractors, and the image of France in the region is very positive.

Poland needs to renovate its infrastructure: roads, highways, railways (the average speed on the rail network is 80 km per hour, the same as in China), areas in which France has a lot of expertise. France already exports more to Poland than it imports from there and Synops6 could really take advantage of this existing partnership.

Table 33   Advantages and disadvantages of the Polish market

Positive points	Negative points
Labour market	Bureaucracy
Creation of 14 special economic zones	Lack of efficient infrastructure – highway and train
Positioned at heart of Europe	Judicial system
Large domestic market	Delay in privatization process

Witnessing: An important learning curve

Of course, the small company is still confronting several challenges in its expansion. Given the limited resources available, a certain lack of pertinent resources may hinder efficient market research. For example, verified and accurate information is available from the Internet only when selecting sources carefully and writing off some sources that are susceptible to being subjective or lack accuracy. The relevant information must come from scientific, institutional or academic sources to grant as much validity as possible. Brick walls become apparent to free information sourcing, when information is only complete when paid for. The need for cross-checking of data from different sources requires resources that need to be multilingual or require translation from external services. For example, the Polish information search proved to be particularly challenging for non-Polish speakers, which is the case for Synops6 staff.

Despite these difficulties, it is quite clear that the EU enlargement undertaken in May 2004 represents a huge opportunity for EU companies and, in Jerome's opinion, for Synops6 International. Indeed, he saw the advantages of these 10 new countries joining the EU to be relevant for his clients from all over the world (common quality standards, cheap labour, etc.).

The finding that Synops6's clients produce the same products and materials that are traded on these countries' markets made the decision to extend the company's reach definitive. In addition, Synops6 was able to benefit from the knowledge of some markets through past trade agreements between France and these countries (Poland for example); wisely, the learning curve of political and market integration has become that of the company.

'Through EU enlargement, Synops6 International was able to develop its consulting activities towards new markets, relatively secure markets – because [they are] part of the EU – adding on new clients,' witnesses Jerome.

Microsoft and the Lisbon Dialogue: Accelerating the EU Institutional Agenda

By Dr Gabriele Suder and Vojtech Jirku

Background

Only a few years after EU leaders launched the Lisbon Agenda to make Europe globally more competitive and dynamic as a place to do business, it is clear that a new urgency and commitment are required to reinforce the drive for increased innovation, jobs and growth in Europe that is at the very heart of the Lisbon goals. The prize is a healthy, growing and world-leading knowledge economy that creates rewarding jobs and spreads prosperity and opportunity for all Europeans. President Barroso and his Commission team defined the situation very clearly: the current delivery gap demands new decisive action to set priorities; high-impact initiatives must be initiated rapidly; and everyone has to contribute at EU, national, regional and business level.

Microsoft decided to support this emphasis on acceleration of practical initiatives: the commonality for the EU and the firm is to enable stronger links between research, industry and education and encourage more public–private partnerships in research and innovation, SME development, education and lifelong e-skills learning, announced in detail by Bill Gates during his visit to Europe in January 2005.

The company positions itself as part of a large and very rich technology and innovation ecosystem comprising thousands of small, medium and large businesses, research institutions, education providers and community partners across the European continent. Fostering growth in this ecosystem is a key part of its business model as a question of corporate sustainability and responsible business in society. A sound ecosystem enables the European knowledge-based economy through R&D, innovation, job creation and deployment of ICT into other sectors of the economy and the community. 'But more is needed,' decided the CEO of the EMEA region at the time, Jean Philippe Courtois, 'since it is clear that expanding public and private investment in ICT, research and innovation is absolutely critical to Europe's future growth and competitiveness, and to sharing the tangible income benefits throughout European society.' (Since 2005, Jean Philippe Courtois has been President of Microsoft International.) With this in mind, and the call by President Barroso for business to 'stand up for Lisbon', the corporation started to intensify its internal focus and collaboration with partners across Europe: to deepen and broaden business contributions to Europe's core Lisbon goals. In this case study, we offer a vision of how innovative public–private partnerships support R&D, SMEs, education and lifelong learning contribute to the institutional agenda of the EU and can accelerate Europe's overall Lisbon goals alongside government-led acceleration of vital regulatory reforms. The partnership initiatives outlined in this case study focus on the three key dimensions of growth, competitiveness and inclusion, and on working in partnership with key stakeholders to enable more technological research and innovation, more access to ICT for SMEs and wider opportunity for ICT-based learning for everyone in society.

The needs

There is a clear new technology gap between the USA and the EU, but also within the EU and among its Member States.

On the one hand, regarding Internet use frequency, while the majority of the US population is online over six hours a week, most citizens of the EU use the web only between one and five hours a week. On the other hand, if 45 per cent of internet users in the USA have already bought through eCommerce, the situation is completely different in the EU where only 20 per cent of the EU population connected to the web has already done so.

Moreover, as more and more people are connected to the Internet around the world, eLearning has become a new, interesting, fast and economical way for students of all ages and backgrounds to have access to a lot of information that can make them more efficient in their studies or job. In the USA, more than 17 per cent of the employed population use electronic learning material for work-related learning, while the average for the EU is at less than 9 per cent. There is no denying that if the EU strives to maintain an attractive level regarding many fields such as science, economy, education, its Member States have to make considerable efforts to catch up with their direct competitors (USA, Japan) by consolidating the diffusion of all the services provided by the ICT industry to people. In fact, wherever individuals go (especially in developed countries), the ICT industry surrounds them: at home, at their workplace, at school, etc. Thus, European society cannot afford to ignore it and has to integrate this component to its lifestyle as soon as possible. This concerns the public and the private sector: it is where EU institutions play a significant role, setting the agenda and legislation that is to stimulate all actors to strive for those goals.

Given the dynamism of the ICT sector, there are many technological developments to come that will require policies and regulation adjustment. Examples of the types of necessary adjustment are clearly pictured with the deployment of technologies such as broadband, 3rd Generation (3G) mobile services, or any disruptive technologies that come from outside the mainstream. In addition to this point, there are important developments at the global level. New players and competition are quickly building up on the world ICT market. Other regulatory issues including the protection of copyright, the rules applying to mobile and micro payments, the protection of privacy and the needs of law enforcement agencies are crucial points that have to be tackled.

But vice versa, the sector can contribute much to the priorities that the EU institutions define for their community. Overall, given the relatively weaker position of the EU compared to the US and Asia, a strong presence in R&D is essential. Two main needs have been identified to fill in the gaps; firstly there is a strong need for a favourable scientific, financial and entrepreneurial environment, and secondly, the EU would necessitate efforts to promote ICT-driven innovations. In shorter terms, the EU regulatory framework would have to be appropriate in an environment where technologies evolve rapidly. In addition, linking the different EU information society initiatives is another challenge. Only a networked economy will allow an even take-up of ICT in society.

Threats of open networks and IT systems' weaknesses and vulnerabilities are central preoccupations in the ICT world as well. Close international cooperation across market sectors is needed to address security threats and to prevent cyber-crime. In a more general line of thought, governments need to develop a comprehensive approach to exploit the potential of ICT. eGovernment, eHealth, eLearning, etc. should be online services that allow the public sector to function more efficiently and effectively, while adapting online services to individual needs of businesses and citizens.

Since the use of ICT has gradually become more complex, there is a constant need to follow up these changes and adapt to the new standards and tools existing, as well as making sure that interoperability is maintained. The main challenge here is to offer small businesses access to a support service that would provide expertise at a relatively low price for the functioning of their business as well as for their customers' ICT offering.

Lisbon Agenda needs accelerate partnerships

The Lisbon Agenda for innovation, sustainable and inclusive growth and job creation is, as the Kok High Level Group Report states, an integral and vital part of the European project and the most important EU economic topic for the next five years.

There is widespread recognition that the incremental progress so far requires the Lisbon Agenda to become much more tangible for European citizens through bold and practical initiatives that touch them individually: at work, in the home, in interacting with their governments, at school and university, in the laboratory, in healthcare, and through culture and entertainment. At the same time, there are many calls to increase the pace of the Lisbon reforms, which would also enable innovation, growth and job creation.

Ultimately innovation and knowledge value creation is vested in people; and the next phase of Lisbon should indeed focus on removing long-standing barriers to their potential and capabilities. Some of these barriers are structural, requiring regulatory reform; and some are capacity barriers, requiring broader partnership initiatives. In addition, over the next decade a new wave of ICT innovation can be expected to take place. Today, all of the science, technology and engineering disciplines are increasingly being driven by computing and when we look forward five to ten years the private sector will be absorbing the impact and benefits of wireless connectivity and mobility, multi-core processors, natural language, speech recognition, improved search functions, infinite storage, increased programmer productivity, interoperability and enhanced security. In other words, an ICT environment that surpasses the expectations of the past two decades. For Europe this will create opportunities to achieve many substantial breakthroughs in growth and job creation, particularly if barriers to the deployment of innovation and technology across the whole economy can be removed. It also exposes the need to move forward much faster along the path of the Lisbon Agenda.

In addition to those core goals, there is the wider and implicit goal of helping European partner economies to move forward, particularly neighbourhood regions already receiving support from Europe because of close geographic or historic ties (for example in the Mediterranean, the Middle East and Africa). Addressing their needs brings many benefits to Europe, such as increased demand for goods and services from Europe, reduced economic migration and increased political stability. This must also be done much faster than at present, to outpace the demographic and other challenges facing those regions.

Therefore, a key focus for what may be termed a Lisbon Acceleration Agenda will include leading companies helping to initiate the next generation of innovative public–private partnership models for enabling people in all walks and stages of life. Students, teachers, professors, scientists, innovators, entrepreneurs, product designers and makers, office workers, community volunteers, farmers and artisans, doctors and nurses, artists and entertainers, journalists, and retired people from these and other fields. Technology, innovation and ICT will be key to the way people learn, work and relax, the incomes they can create for themselves and the value they can create for the economy and society as a whole.

The European Commission consultation document on a Competitiveness and Innovation Framework Programme (CIP) points out three areas where a new generation of public–private partnership can particularly help to accelerate the ICT value-creation cycle in Europe. They are science-based research and innovation, the SME sector and lifelong e-skills learning (see Figure 18). These are all critical individual and dynamically linked components of growth, competitiveness and inclusion in the knowledge-based society.

Microsoft proposes that, through high-level partnership initiatives to support the CIP, Europe can envisage making great progress during the next decade in building its knowledge-based society.

From school to further education, in the community and in the workplace, people will have the opportunity to learn and upgrade their e-skills, enabling better matching of training and job creation initiatives; and faster and more effective bridging of current gaps between the skills needs of European employers and job-seekers, and the skills needs of all citizens to be active in the information economy.

People with good ideas will be using e-skills and technology-support services to start businesses and creating more thriving small firms. And workers in all kinds of businesses will have tools to locate, compare and update past, present and projected business-critical information at greater scale, speed and ease.

Scientists, innovators, industry and venture capitalists will be working together to bring European research breakthroughs in medicine, biology and agriculture to global markets in the form of novel products, materials, technologies and processes that reduce environmental stress, help prevent and cure disease, and improve farming and food. Breakthroughs in computational science will enable scientists to manage and manipulate vast amounts of data in modelling and predicting complex trends, problems and solutions, including those to protect our planet's life-support systems. And companies optimistic about their prospects for future growth inside and outside the EU will hire more workers, invest more in their training and education and be more willing and able to increase investments in research and development that, in turn, will fuel future growth and investment.

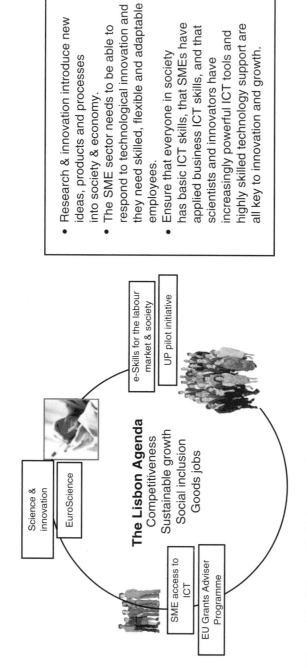

- Research & innovation introduce new ideas, products and processes into society & economy.
- The SME sector needs to be able to respond to technological innovation and they need skilled, flexible and adaptable employees.
- Ensure that everyone in society has basic ICT skills, that SMEs have applied business ICT skills, and that scientists and innovators have increasingly powerful ICT tools and highly skilled technology support are all key to innovation and growth.

e-Skills for the labour market & society

UP pilot initiative

Science & innovation

EuroScience

The Lisbon Agenda
Competitiveness
Sustainable growth
Social inclusion
Goods jobs

SME access to ICT

EU Grants Adviser Programme

Figure 18   Microsoft's Lisbon accelerators

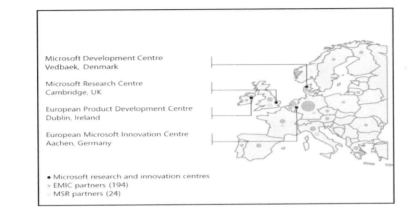

Figure 19   Research and Innovation Centres in EMEA

The tools and means: Objective 'accelerating research and innovation'

Microsoft has established a number of research and innovation centres in Europe:

- *Microsoft Research (MSR) Cambridge, UK*   Bringing together Europe's most creative minds, MSR-Cambridge has over 80 full-time staff of 16 different nationalities. The facility aims to accelerate the next generation of software innovation, driven by fundamental challenges and long-term vision. Research areas include operating systems, networks and distributed computing; machine learning and perception; programming principles and theory; and interactive systems. The facility has produced significant and tangible results including inventing the Tablet PC, powerful new algorithms for computer vision with applications ranging from medical imaging, videoconferencing and games to new computer languages.
- *European Microsoft Innovation Centre (EMIC), Aachen, Germany*   EMIC provides a focal point for Microsoft's collaborative efforts with industry and academia in Europe on applied research projects such as those sponsored by the European Commission and national research programmes. EMIC participates in EC co-funded projects involving eLearning, eHealth, security and privacy and networking technologies, and is a member of the Integrated Projects and Networks of Excellence selected by the European Commission for the first call of the 6th Framework Programme. EMIC is developing strong relationships with the University of Aachen and has academic partnerships with a number of other institutions.
- *Microsoft Development Centre, Vedbaek, Denmark*   Microsoft's campus at Vedbaek employs more than 700 people and is Microsoft's largest development facility outside of the main campus in Redmond (US). It focuses on supply chain management strategy, Microsoft Business Framework, and Project Green – building the next generation of Business Solutions. The Microsoft Business Solutions division works with Europe's developer community to produce solutions to help foster growth in the region's SME sector.
- *European Product Development Centre (EPDC), Dublin, Ireland*   The EPDC is charged with ensuring that Microsoft products are available in different versions across Europe, reflecting local languages and culture. The EPDC employs linguistic specialists to localize software into over 35 national and regional languages.

- *Microsoft Technology Centres (MTCs), Munich, Germany and Reading, UK* MTCs support local IT industries competing in the global market. They work side by side with customers, architects and developers to find solutions to their technology challenges. The MTCs have formed alliances with industry leaders to provide comprehensive resources such as hardware, software and services to MTC customers from local IT industries.

A Brand new initiative: EuroScience

The Lisbon Agenda sets a key marker for increasing Europe's innovation investment – from 1.9 per cent of GDP to 3 per cent by 2010, with the private sector contributing two-thirds of the increased investment. Achieving this involves several fundamental competitiveness challenges:

- keeping a sustained pace in innovation investment;
- retaining and attracting the best researchers;
- improving the foundations for commercialization of research.

Microsoft's new EuroScience Initiative is focused on creating, stimulating and accelerating fundamental innovation in science and computing that will underpin the next quarter century of fundamental technological, scientific, economic and social growth.

The founding vision of EuroScience is that in the next 25 years computing has the potential to make a far broader and greater positive impact on the fabric of society than the last 25 years of the computing revolution, which transformed business productivity and the workplace. This new era holds the promise and potential to accelerate 'new kinds of science', to create a new revolution in computing, to transform medicine and healthcare, to enhance learning and transform the creative sectors and the creative process, and to play a vital role in helping protect and sustain the planet's life-support system.

Guiding this view are two fundamental principles of EuroScience: that advances in computing can revolutionize science, and that 'new kinds' of science can fundamentally revolutionize computing. But it is increasingly clear that realizing the enormous potential that this 'next wave' will afford requires us to accelerate not only how science is done, but also what science is done, to rethink current assumptions in computing, and to rethink and accelerate the business of innovation. This is what EuroScience is all about.

Accelerating innovation: EuroScience research focus

- *Building blocks of the next century of computing* Long-term advanced research into new and exciting areas at the frontiers of science and technology that have the potential to dramatically revolutionize and redefine the future of computing beyond current 'classical' computing assumptions and architectures.
- *New tools for advancing science* Working with the science community in Europe and around the world to build the next generation of advanced computing tools to accelerate the 'new kinds' of

- science that will underpin the emerging era of 'science-based innovation', and new discoveries and breakthroughs in medicine, prevention of disease, agriculture, engineering and aerospace.
- *The 'new everyday'* Creating devices that will become tomorrow's everyday, from 'things that think' to 'invisible computers' and 'ambient intelligence'.

EuroScience partnerships

The EuroScience model is centred on accelerating innovation, and achieving this through a collaboration model based on Open Innovation. The Open Innovation concept is based on the premise that in an increasingly complex scientific, technological and competitive environment, and as advances in basic science lead the innovation chain, firms are unlikely to be able to create all the innovation they require through a predominantly internal model of R&D. Instead, they will need to work much closer to basic science, by combining the strengths of internal R&D with strategic collaborations with external institutions, groups and individuals in universities, industry and government to generate long-term economic, technological and social value creation. It is a model that crosses traditional boundaries – institutional and organizational R&D, traditional scientific and technological, market and national – through new forms of public – private partnerships between universities, industry and government:

- *Universities* Strategic collaboration with world-leading scientific departments, groups and individuals in Europe, and where appropriate elsewhere around the world to engage in ambitious, key new fields of science and technology research to address important social, scientific and technological challenges and opportunities. This will include establishing new research centres where they can act as innovation catalysts. Such partnerships are already being established in the EuroScience Initiative.
- *Government* Working with governments, government science agencies and regional development agencies in co-investing in and making contributions to the broad strategic science and technology agenda in Europe.
- *Industry* Form partnerships with start-ups, SMEs and industry leaders in Europe, including the pharmaceutical, aerospace, consumer electronics and health sectors, in joint research ventures and co-investments that can accelerate innovation in Europe.

Developing intellectual capital

To support the vital role of scientific research and innovation in building Europe's knowledge-based economy, the EuroScience Initiative also includes a set of programmes to help develop and support Europe's intellectual capital required to realize the EuroScience vision and underpin Europe's science-based innovation era:

- *European PhD Studentship Programme* Launched in November 2004 to support the development of future scientists in Europe. Starting with the 2005 intake, up to 30 awards will be made each year

- for some of Europe's brightest scholars to undertake scientific training in European institutions. The programme offers encouragement to PhD research at the intersection of computing and the sciences as a way to catalyse growth in the 'next wave' of scientific innovation that will be so important for global competitiveness.
- *Career Development Fellowship Programme*   Launched in February 2005 to support, develop and retain tomorrow's key scientists in Europe – up to 10 highly promising young post-doctoral European scientists in Europe who are quickly establishing a track record and international reputation of world-leading research in key emerging science and technology areas will be eligible for significant support that includes up to 0.25m euros.
- *European Scientist of the Year Award*   EuroScience will sponsor a prestigious award to recognize the achievements of an individual who has been nominated for making a fundamentally important contribution to science and society in Europe.
- *Scientific Workshops*   An annual workshop series has begun to bring together the spectrum of student researchers, leading academics, government officials and industry to discuss, debate and inform on key scientific, policy and societal issues and topics arising from the EuroScience Initiative's research agenda.

'As part of our research partnerships across Europe,' Jean Philippe Courtois explains, 'we will also be supporting a number of local competitions and class prize awards to encourage both undergraduates and post-graduate students.'

Accelerating innovation exploitation

EuroScience is an important Microsoft Research initiative focused on creating and accelerating fundamental innovation. As such, Microsoft Research and its EuroScience Programme Management Office is engaged in defining equally innovative ways to develop a 'pipeline' of future downstream technological product innovation for Microsoft, for Europe and for European business that can benefit from EuroScience and lead the generation of real economic and social value. This will take the form of new tools for Europe's science-led businesses and sectors and new building blocks for entirely new applications and sectors in the IT and computing sector.

It will also involve innovation in the business of innovation itself. To this end, EuroScience has developed the concept of an online marketplace to help creators of ideas and innovation to find each other.

The ability to generate value from intellectual property (IP) is vital, but currently difficult for universities, small firms and even large firms. Much needed is a better, more efficient form of IP valuation, exploitation and value extraction. Essentially this means what is needed is a marketplace for IP-based ideas, so that universities, governments and firms who create IP of value are able to come together freely and easily with the firms who need IP to derive competitive advantage. The concept of an online 'innovation marketplace' could benefit Europe significantly. 'We believe it requires joint discussion with Government, other industry players and universities around the region,' states Microsoft, 'We would like to commence this discussion.'

Also accelerating SME growth

In September 2004, International Data Corp. (IDC) released the third update to its Economic Impact model, which assesses the ICT industry's impact in 58 countries. The latest study examines the ICT sector's impact on job creation, company formation, local ICT spending and taxation revenues in 15 EU Member States, as well as Russia, Israel, Turkey and South Africa.

According to the study, ICT-related activities in the 19 countries analysed are the source of nearly nine million jobs and US$200 billion in taxation receipts in 2004. The nine million jobs are provided by more than 356,000 companies in the hardware, software, services and channels segments, or as ICT professionals in end-user organizations. Roughly half of all ICT-related jobs are engaged in creating, distributing or servicing software, for either external customers or internal corporate users. Similarly, more than half of all their ICT-related taxation revenues come from software-related activities. And the ICT industry's economic impact is expected to grow: over the next four years, the EMEA ICT sector is expected to generate two million new jobs and an additional US$160 billion in tax revenue.

The IDC study also shows that companies selling or servicing hardware or software implementing Microsoft technology contribute to these figures, accounting for over a third of 2004 ICT employment and tax revenues in the 19 countries. This Microsoft-related employment ranges from approximately 36,000 people in countries such as Hungary and Turkey, to more than half a million in the UK or Germany. In addition, 'for every $1 of Microsoft revenue in the region another $7.5 is generated by other companies in related businesses'. Further, 10 of the leading systems integrators, representing 33 per cent of the European services market, ranked Microsoft as the vendor providing the greatest business opportunity through strategic alliances.

The challenge for the next 5–10 years is to help this ecosystem to grow even further.

New initiative: The EU Grants Advisor programme

The Lisbon Agenda emphasizes both the vital role of SMEs in the quest for growth and jobs and the need for enhanced channels to support SMEs, particularly for technology deployment, employment generation, new business start-ups and other information society objectives such as employee training. This is essential because the nearly 20 million SMEs in the EU employ more than 140 million people and are undeniably the motor of the European economy, contributing 60 per cent of GDP and nearly two-thirds of employment.

Further, as reinforced in the Kok High Level Group Report, the Lisbon Agenda calls for a regulatory climate conducive to investment, innovation and entrepreneurship, facilitating access to low-cost finance, taking into account the specific nature of SMEs and lowering the costs of doing business, as well as reducing time and costs for setting up a company.

Indeed, research reveals that one of the most pressing needs that SMEs have is access to finance for expansion or implementation of new ideas and technology, and many SMEs manage with basic ICT capabilities due to financing constraints.

From 2000 to 2006, approximately €117 billion in EU funds and Member State co-financing funds has been made available to SMEs (and local and regional governments – LRGs) for technology-related, innovation, employment and business start-up projects in order to stimulate efficiency, growth and modernization. Yet recent estimates find that only 45 per cent of European SMEs have some awareness of the available EU financing instruments, that around 4 per cent have applied for such financing, and that of those applicants around 25 per cent have been successful in their applications.

In response, and to address the challenges highlighted by the Lisbon Agenda and the Kok Report, Microsoft has developed the European Union Grants Advisor Programme, designed to increase SME awareness and understanding of EU funds, as well as to facilitate the administrative process for those wishing to benefit from the funds for which they are eligible. Through this initiative, Microsoft, in partnership with other leading ICT and financial services companies, as well as community partners, such as chambers of commerce and business associations, offers broad information and resources on available funds, provides consultancy and streamlined application support, and offers ICT guidance for productivity enhancement programmes.

The goal is to make it easier for European entrepreneurs to gain informed access to the funds they need to startup their business, grow and thrive, thereby stimulating overall market and economic growth. As eGovernment services are critical for SMEs in an accelerated Lisbon Agenda, the EU Grants Advisor (EUGA) is also open to LRGs.

SME and consortium partners' views on the EU Grants Advisor programme

The following views were given about the EUGA

- *Ana Patricia Botin – CEO Banesto Bank (Spain)* 'We want to thank … Microsoft for the commitment towards the Small Businesses and its support towards the Banesto SME School, a business school aimed to facilitate the adoption of the ICT amongst the SMEs in Spain.'
- *Danuta Anglart – County Information Centre, Wolsztyn (Poland)* 'We do greatly appreciate the contribution in preparation of training on "Building of IT society using European Union structural funds" provided for local governments and companies.'
- *Renata Pawlaczyk – Mars Computer Systems, Słupsk (Poland)* 'In Słupsk and the nearby area the people know little on structural funds and this knowledge is a barrier for the further development. Perhaps, owing to ITeraz Europa project [local name of the EUGA initiative in Poland] something will change.'
- *Jose Manuel Fernandez Norniella, President of the Spanish Chambers of Commerce* 'We need to be in the vanguard of IT. With the agreement we are signing today endorsing OASI [local name of one of the EUGA initiatives in Spain], I am confident we will be able to make the Technology more accessible to the SMEs. This is an encomiastic initiative.'
- *Róbert Bobrovniczki, Sales Manager VT-Soft Ltd. (Microsoft partner)* 'The training and the predefined templates provided by Microsoft facilitated the identification of the most appropriate

grant and reduced the necessary administration of our clients connected to the EU funds applications. That was a great help for our clients (mainly Hungarian SMEs) to implement customised
IT solutions.'

Through the EUGA's online services, SMEs and LRGs can find extensive information, in
local languages, about the various EU funds and can start to better ascertain for which funds
they may be eligible. Further, the EUGA provides access to independent and specialized
consultancy regarding the grants available; helps SMEs and LRGs define their needs and
appropriate solutions; and provides a service that assists with the formalities and steps for
technology grant applications.

The EUGA initiative was first launched in 2003 in Spain, followed by a similar programme
in Poland during 2004. Experts consulted by Microsoft assess that the application time is
reduced ten-fold and application rate was doubled using the specialized consultants. The
results achieved in Spain and Poland in terms of benefits and positive feedback from both the
SMEs and the national and regional governments, encouraged Microsoft to move ahead with
deployment of the EUGA initiative in other EU countries.

The most beneficial way of implementing such a programme would be through consortia,
as truly public–private partnerships are necessary for leveraging synergies, argues Microsoft's
leadership. The consortia are established taking into consideration that a balance of global
and local expertise will resonate more appropriately with SMEs. For example, in Spain
consortia were set up with HP, Intel, BBVA, Banesto and Telefonica; in Hungary Microsoft
teamed up with MBS Partners, HP and Matav; and in Poland Intel and Cisco were involved.

Accelerating e-Skills, employability and digital inclusion

Just as ICT innovation and the widespread use of ICT in the general population increasingly
drives growth and job creation, so ICT skills are now recognized as the third essential educational life skill, after literacy and numeracy.

Furthermore, a key challenge facing SMEs is their lack of 'absorptive capacity', meaning
they do not have enough staff with the right skills to get full benefit from SME development
schemes. There is a particularly large gap in the area of ICT skills that needs to be overcome
rapidly if Europe is to get full business value from the large investments it is making in ICT.
The ICT skills gap cannot be overcome by relying on people to teach themselves by trial and
error, which is commonplace today in SMEs and for individual citizens.

This is important, since overall EU skill shortages and gaps with US and Asian skills and
education performance persist despite the emphasis on access and skills investment. In
addition, the low skilled still account for very large proportions of the working age populations in certain Member States; and average unemployment rates for the low skilled are more
than double those for the high skilled. For example, the youth unemployment rate in the EU
25 has risen to 18.3 per cent and is twice as high as the overall EU 25 unemployment rate.

Partnership investments and initiatives need to lead to rapid improvement in availability
of these 'e-skills'; but despite the considerable public and private investment to date, particularly

in enabling technology access, the majority of non-adopters cite skills development, confidence and motivation as the real barriers to online opportunity. This calls for more rapid and extensive effort, to encourage the further growth of skill-intensive sectors, and the acquisition of higher skills throughout the population.

Indeed, the European Employment Guidelines established by the Council in 2003 include a recommendation for 'Investing more and more effectively in human capital and lifelong learning, inter alia by sharing costs and responsibilities between public authorities, companies and individuals by broadening the supply of training in particular for those most in need such as the low-skilled, women and older workers.'

'At Microsoft we believe that e-skills investment partnerships need to focus on enabling a fast track between training, job creation and delivering the business value that underpins competitiveness. Sharing knowledge of innovation and good practice is a key part of this.' The higher the speed of diffusion of knowledge about best practice, innovation and available resources, the higher the agility of an organization and the higher its potential competitiveness. These are acknowledged to be major factors in the success of the 'hyper-growth' companies that eventually become large employers.

Europe needs companies of all sizes to be innovative and competitive. On the whole, SMEs' performance is constrained, often through poor systems for learning about opportunities (part of knowledge sharing), coupled with lack of skilled staff able to exploit those opportunities. Therefore a particular focus for action is the need to create a better and faster match between the skills-gap needs of European SMEs and the skills set acquisition of young unemployed people. With many young people still not in formal education, employment or training, it is crucial to create new ways of supporting young people who leave school with no qualifications and few opportunities to secure work and grow small businesses.

Unlimited Potential

Unlimited Potential (UP) is Microsoft's global initiative to help narrow the technology skills gap and help everyone develop by providing technology skills through community-based technology and learning centres (CTLCs).

Over the last two years, Microsoft has supported 98 skills training projects in 58 countries across Europe, the Middle East and Africa, working with over 200 partners, and supporting over 1000 community learning centres. UP offers a comprehensive approach to bridging the digital divide by bringing together the following critical components to support Community Technology Learning Centres:

- UP training grants – enhancing access and training opportunities for individuals underserved by technology.
- Software donations – providing community centres and NGOs with access to the most current productivity applications necessary to train people for the global economy.
- UP community learning curriculum – localized in eight languages to date, it provides support for training on computer fundamentals, and real-world applications and course material.

- Community Technology Support Network – in partnerships with IDRC and UNESCO, Microsoft is offering capacity building services to the community of telecentres world wide.

Building on the Microsoft UP programme, which focuses on the provision of IT skills training opportunities and solutions for disadvantaged groups, Microsoft intends to pilot an 'ICT skills for employment and entrepreneurship' programme in an EU Member State. Such projects require the creation of a strategic alliance of key players and interested parties to focus in an integrated way on innovative training and support for disadvantaged and marginalized groups, including young unemployed people, immigrants and people with disabilities. Examples of similar initiatives are the Prince's Trust partnership with The Royal Bank of Scotland Group to provide enterprise-related training in the UK's most deprived areas. The initiative aims to help 16–18 year olds who leave school with no qualifications and face a 'poverty of opportunity' in areas of high unemployment. In Belgium, the Plato programme works through partnership in similar ways to provide support for the creation of self-employment opportunities.

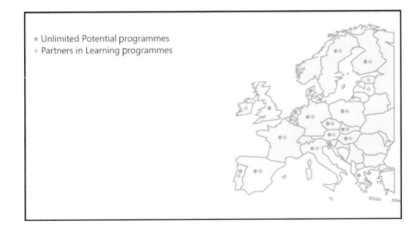

- Unlimited Potential programmes
- Partners in Learning programmes

Figure 20   Unlimited Potential and Partners in Learning programme in EMEA

Microsoft's pilot programme in the EU will be based on a blueprint that aims to devise and test out locally driven partnership schemes and easily actionable measures in specific locations of unemployment (Figure 20). The goal is to engage the young unemployed (or other marginalized low-skilled groups) in vocational education and training catered to employability needs and self employment requirements.

The blueprint specifically involves multi-party partnership between business, national and regional governments and third party organisations, such as chambers of commerce, federations of small enterprises, employment offices and community organizations, that together can foster the identification of a skills base and the creation of linkages to the skills needed for local business, training in information and communication technologies. In such a way they can devise locally based best practice, innovation, and networking.

Using the assets and tools of UP, the goal is to build a specific blueprint programme that will support the skills-gap needs of the labour market with crucial objectives:

- *Closing the skills gap* Working with unemployment offices, chambers of commerce and federations of small and medium enterprises is important to provide the platform to tailor IT skills training programmes to the needs of the local population of young unemployed, marginalized groups and young entrepreneurs. First, these organizations have a unique view on the supply and demand of skills, labour and training programmes for the target groups in need. Secondly, they are also the natural channel to market for existing basic skills training programmes, vocational programmes and entrepreneurship mentoring programmes.

- *IT skills training programmes and skills certification* Leveraging UP training grants and the UP curriculum in the national language, the programme seeks to work with the organizations mentioned above as a springboard to mainstream IT skills into other training opportunities. Working with NGOs and community organizations the UP IT skills training grants can be structured in a way to provide formal IT skills training and learning, access to technology content, skills and solutions, practical skills development, community work and the support of a mentor. A certificate of completion of the UP Curriculum will be awarded on completion of the course. The programme will aim to train 50,000 young unemployed and people from marginalized groups. A multiplier effect will be set in place by an exponential train the trainer programme to ensure the scalability and transferability of the programme in other parts of the country.

- *Fast track experience to the labour market* Working in partnership with local associations of SMEs, other business networks and employment offices, the blueprint would seek to help young people into the labour market. Young people completing the initial three months of training should be able to engage in internship experiences in local SMEs and larger businesses so as to continue their experience through a three-month work and development placement for socially excluded young people.

Note

This case study was prepared for CERAM based on white papers prepared by Microsoft's EU/legal team and the work of the CERAM study group for this topic.

EU Transport Policy and the Europeanization of a Business

By Dr Gabriele Suder

Because transportation plays a vital role in the daily personal and professional lives of people and in business, the EU strives to harmonize its sky, road, sea and train networks. With a surface area of 4.5 million km^2 (1.7 msqm) in one single market becoming more and more integrated every day, transportation is ever more important and takes place on a broad scale. Ideally, as Europe continues to integrate, transportation and transport policy will integrate with it. Transportation within and between Member States stimulates the ideals of a unified Europe, of cross-cultural and cross-national exchanges, and of peace and prosperity among its peoples, and is a determinant of harmonious cross-market commerce. When we speak of the free movement of goods, services, capital and labour, much of that movement is dependent on transportation. Much has been done to accommodate the European transport system to business realities that serve the purpose of competitiveness, but there are still many objectives to achieve and obstacles to overcome. More often than not, national systems, interests and politics hinder the smooth logistics that could be those of the European single market.

European integration has created and been created through a compression of time and space in which both virtual and real distances have been reduced. The Internet has played a huge role in the reduction of virtual distances, while the emergence of low-cost airlines, serving many routes, has created new and faster ways of travelling through Europe. They aim to counteract congestion, saturation, red tape through administrative cross-frontier bureaucracy, and the incompatibility of trans-European transport systems. Competition, open across the EU Member States, has Europeanized transport and logistics business. Still, even in this single market, transportation is not at an identical level in every Member State.

This case study examines the role that transport plays in Europe: What are the objectives of the transport policy, what has been achieved, why does Europe need a common policy? The current EU transport policy developed on the basis of the Maastricht Treaty's legislation but had existed in an earlier form since the Treaty of Rome. It is to strengthen competition, increase safety and improve the environment. A constant increase in rail transport is used as an example to demonstrate the challenges for public policy and business in this field.

Transportation trends in Europe

Transport is a vital industry in the EU. It represents 7 per cent of its GDP, and is mainly generated through freight. Transport comprises 7.5 million jobs in the EU, representing 7 per cent of total employment. This concentrates 61 per cent of these jobs in land transport (road, rail, inland waterways), 2 per cent in sea transport, 5 per cent in air transport, and about another third in supporting or auxiliary employment such as cargo handling, storage, warehousing and transport agents. Transport represents on average 40 per cent of Member States' investment and private households spend about €745 billion on it. About one-third of energy consumption is used on transportation.

Transport volumes have continued to rise within the EU for the past two decades, road and air travel growing at a higher rate than rail, bus, and inland waterways, which actually declined in some cases. To balance this trend, which may lead to saturation and high logistics costs for European business if not managed at EU level across the continent, the Trans-European Transport Network (TEN) has grown significantly over the last 10 years. Investments have focused mainly on creating new high-speed road and rail connections between Member States.

Furthermore, price structures do not always equally support the goals of EU transport policy; they may favour private transport instead of public. Costs for private transport have remained relatively stable, while the cost of using public transport has increased, meaning that people and businesses that depend on the use of public transport have become less mobile. In freight, a fuel tax on air transport may shift demands yet again.

EU transport policy

The Directorate General of Transport is attached to that of Energy, serving the sound management of critical infrastructures across the EU. The objectives of EU transport policy are ends within themselves as well as serving the greater aim of further integrating the Member States. Some of the most important objectives are to:

- provide a modern and competitive system that satisfies the economic, social, and environmental needs of society;
- encourage the liberalization of rail transport;
- harmonize legislation of safety and transport infrastructures;
- reduce environmental impact (emissions, noise, pollution);
- encourage the creation of modern transportation routes between the EU and neighbouring countries;
- develop technology to improve efficiency and quality of services (for example, through the Galileo satellite navigation project).

Perhaps most important to the Europeanization of transportation is the opening up of markets and their connection to EU commercial development. The Maastricht Treaty started a significant evolution in the field, because political, institutional and budgetary foundations for transport policy were augmented, and the focus on quality voting in the decision-making process raised the responsiveness of the public policymaker to the requirements of the market. The amendments to the EU decision-making process also empowered the European Parliament in the reinforcement of a co-decision mode that became particularly important in the vote on the rail freight liberalization in 2000, to be fully implemented by 2008. Indeed, the European Commission's 1992 White Paper that focused on the opening up of these markets has led to a decrease in the cost of transportation as well as an increase in the number of choices available to consumers and business. However, this phenomenon has not sufficiently concerned a rail sector that was fragmented through a privatization process.

Achievements so far

Successes have been achieved in all areas of transport. All sectors have been granted to varying degrees the right of cabotage, that is, the right to carry goods freely from another Member State, which prevents a container returning home empty, and hence increases efficiency and cuts costs significantly.

EU transport policy uses several tools, or 'instruments', to achieve and enhance this type of result in the promotion of business facilitation, and aims simultaneously for safety and environmental protection. These instruments are fiscal (tax, monetary, in conjunction with national governments; EU subsidies), strategic (sub-policies and programmes), legislative (laws; regulations on safety such as NCAP crash safety test, toxic emission levels) and others (such as voluntary agreements, campaigns). For example, the Maastricht Treaty set the basis for the construction of a trans-European transport network (TEN) (Art. 154 ff.); Regulation No 2236/95 of 18 September 1995 then introduced the rules for the granting of EU financial assistance for TENs. Five years later, Agenda 2000 supported the expansion of TENs with a view to linking accession countries. TENs include communications networks, and are an interesting source of EU funding for adapted business initiatives.

To cite another example for the evolution of the EU transport business, haulage companies are authorized to freely transport freight to other EU Member States if established in the EU. Before 1993, these firms had to ask for special authorization on the basis of bilateral agreements and community quotas. The free transport principle find their applicability limited by quality and safety conditions that need to be satisfied before an EU transport licence can be obtained. The Council's surveillance system monitors these trans-European operations to limit market disequilibrium.

Rail

Rail is an interesting sector to the EU because it allows for the accomplishment of its three main goals: to strengthen competition, increase safety and improve the environment.

Consequently, rail has been subject to EU attention and the use of its main tools: the sector has undergone the separation of infrastructure and operation, thus increasing competition by allowing several operators to use the same infrastructure. The focus on safety and maintenance of open markets has also enhanced competitiveness. In the inland waterway sector, cheaper transport costs are an increasing phenomenon. The air travel sector has benefited the most from EU transport policy, resulting in a liberalized industry that favours the interoperability of supply chains, trade and partnerships across Europe. In rail, more safety is sought by a certification system for locomotive conductors and more efficiency is sought by introducing an operating licence that facilitates the provision of a network while giving unrestricted access to infrastructures. Also, users pay the full real cost of facilities then. The 'infrastructure package' of the 2001 White Paper was to open rail freight markets, and is enhanced by the 2006 White Paper. The main goal of EU transport policy is the improvement of the quality of transport by promoting free competition among the operators in this sector, while reducing the environmental impact of transportation methods. The railway sector is the most environmentally friendly in the transportation industry, therefore much emphasis has now been placed on improving its operations. The two main tools that are used to do this are privatization and separating the operation and the possession of infrastructure; they have been the dominant methods of promoting competition thus far and have been operating for about 15 years. There are several examples of how these tools have increased competition and improved the quality of the railways throughout Europe. There are also examples to show that the EU still has a way to go in order to refine these tools to achieve the objectives efficiently.

Privatization

One example of privatization in the railway sector took place in Germany in 1994 with the reforming of Deutsche Bahn, German Railways; the first reform of its kind. The goal was to increase railway market share by improving the quality of rail transport, especially in East Germany. Also, a shift from road to rail was encouraged for environmental concerns. Privatization spurred the creation of five separate companies within the DB group that allowed each to specialize in a certain area of rail transport. This reform effectively increased rail usage by 11 per cent from 1993 to 2003, which in turn caused a decrease in car and bus transport but a step in the right direction for environmental protection. Germany now counts more than 200 operators that provide freight transport services throughout Germany and integrated freight transport (for example, maritime and rail, or air and rail) across the EU and the world.

Privatization in the UK is another interesting example to look at. Due to large deficits in the UK government in the late 1980s as well as recurring train accidents, privatization was sought as a way to cut costs and improve safety. The organization and governance of British Rail were eventually entirely reviewed in 1994 and competition was increased dramatically, with the number of train operating companies (TOCs) rising to 27 throughout the UK. However, the increase in competition was not sufficient to improve service, with significant delays in the network, nor safety, as demonstrated by the train derailment in Hatfield in 2000. This example demonstrates that any improvement in productivity is easily overshadowed when the most basic needs of transportation, such as safety and customer convenience, are not properly maintained.

Separation of ownership

The French railway system illustrates that the separation of ownership of infrastructure and the operation of the railways can be very effective. Throughout the early 1990s, SNCF, the sole railway operator in France, was accumulating large amounts of debt and was not able to commit the investment necessary to improve the quality of rail transportation. The national government decided to implement reforms in this sector and in 1997 a new organization, RFF, was established to take possession of the railway infrastructure and all related maintenance. SNCF subsequently transferred a large portion of its debt to RFF and therefore was able to invest in improving customer service in railway operations.

Separating the possession of infrastructure and the operation of railways can be positive for several reasons. The SNCF case shows how restructuring allowed the operating company to focus on improving service without the burden of infrastructure maintenance. This separation, which is now mandatory in the EU, is also a method of improving competition because several operators can use the same infrastructure. The operators pay a fee for using the infrastructure, so all qualified operators have open access. Also, given that railway infrastructure is a substation or telecommunication-related business, its liberalization opens opportunities to companies other than rail operators.

Access charges, that is, charges for maintenance and use of rail tracks upon railway transporters, still differ on a country to country basis depending upon market conditions, with a prohibition to discriminate among operators, and upon the basic principles stipulated in detail in EU Directive 95/19. For example, the French SNCF and the British Rail pay two charges to Eurotunnel plc for using the Eurotunnel: one charge is fixed, the other is variable, with its revenues allocated to repay liabilities of construction and for maintenance. Both operators enjoy equal rights.

In Sweden also, two types of charge are common, in that the fixed part is charged upon operator's rolling stocks and the variable part is charged upon elements including the speed and weight of the train. The charges include not only maintenance but also a fee for pollution and accidents, and are directly payable to the government.

Airline competition

A significant boost to competition in the transportation industry has resulted from the introduction of low-cost airlines. Traditionally the EU has seen many barriers to entry and regulations surrounding the airline industry. This has ensured that competition remained low and prices remained high for air travel. The liberalization brought about by EU transportation policy has changed the situation and caused meaningful competition to develop in this sector, on the basis of fare, frequency and time. The establishment of low-cost carriers has lowered prices such that there is now competition between the airlines and the railways. While each sector still has its unique appeal, the new competition has forced improvement across all industries that influences the passenger and freight services.

Why a common policy?

We have discussed examples of how EU transport policy has taken steps to improve transportation across the continent and achieve the goals of the EU; however, many would argue that a common policy is unnecessary. Other government initiatives such as health and social programmes are handled easily by the Member States themselves, so why should transportation be controlled by a common policy?

There are a few issues that demonstrate the need for further cooperation in this sector. First, the discrepancy between quality of infrastructure across the EU is a problem that needs to be addressed. For example, the motorway network in the UK is 10 times the length of that in Poland, which is actually a larger country, but where rail is prevalant. Latvia has a larger rail network than Lithuania, but no motorways as of 2006. This type of comparison has its limits, of course: Malta has no rail network but, given its size, has little or no need for any. In order to pursue further economic integration across Europe, the transportation infrastructure in the Eastern European states must be improved, and a common policy is one way to make it happen.

Secondly, greater efficiency can be realized by standardizing transport legislation. The differences in speed limits, maximum vehicle weights, toxic emissions regulations, and blood alcohol levels only serve to slow down business between countries. As with many other steps towards integration, a common transport policy is another method of improving speed and efficiency of commerce in Europe. Petrol prices differ as widely in Europe as transport costs. Using a Slovakian transport company is generally cheaper than using a French one.

The third issue to be considered is the environmental impact of transportation in Europe. This has been the most unsuccessful of the EU's goals for its transport policy, which demonstrates the need for even greater cooperation. Creating a shift from passenger cars and road freight towards rail transport is a huge task and will take a vast improvement of the rail network with a common budget: only a common policy could facilitate the cooperation needed to make a meaningful difference in the environmental impact of transportation.

Transportation network: a business facilitator

Transportation in the EU, both as an industry in itself and as a service for business and trade, has had many challenges to master. Keeping up with EU integration and the Europeanization of businesses within the EU is a challenge and an opportunity for public policy and private structures. Developing a common policy is a very long and slow process, especially considering the ongoing expansion of the EU and the increasing complexity of the transport networks. Not all of the Member States have the same goals. They have different priorities, different transportation needs and different systems. As a result, some goals have been very difficult to achieve, namely those in the environmental area. If the EU is to be competitive in the long run, then transportation and its policies need to improve and advance on a supranational level, so that all may benefit.

Note

The information in this case study was compiled from various CEC, SNCF, RFF, DB, JR-West, and other transportation data.

References

Brooks, M. and Button, K. (1995) 'Separating transport track from operations: A typology of international experiences', *International Journal of Transport Economics*, 22 (3), October; 235–60.
Gorinson, S.M. (1990) 'Overview: essential facilities and regulations', *Antitrust Law Journal*, 58; 871–7.

A Corporate Challenge Resulting from the Introduction of the Euro

By Michael Payte

A 'Hobson's choice':[1] An apparently free choice when there in fact is no choice at all.

'Being between a rock and a hard place':[2] Being in a difficult to impossible position or situation such as being stuck between two opposing forces; being confronted or faced with a choice between equally unpleasant alternatives or unsatisfactory options with few or no opportunities to evade or circumvent them.

Not exactly a 'catch-22' where all choices apparently contradict each other, but close!

It is mid-summer 1999; you are the CEO of a leading financial services organization. Under your direction, the new product development group of your organization has spent most of the past two years, since early 1997, on marketing research, product and software design, and initial customer marketing. So far this has involved the investment of tens of millions in financial terms, thousands of personnel hours, as well as a great deal of your own personal capital.

First, extensive initial market research was conducted with the target market user group. This was followed by the product design and extensive systems development work commissioned in parallel with the introduction and planned implementation of this service, which is the largest and most important new service/product provided to your current and target customer/user base. Your phased target launch and implementation timetable is for spring/summer 2000. This major product's development and introduction is highly visible and has significant implications on the industry prestige of your company, on your executive position at the company, as on well as on your professional reputation and the reputation of your organization in the marketplace. Of equal importance to the organization is the need to recapture the many millions that have been spent on the research, development, marketing and planned implementation of this important new service.

To date, all your group's market research has been telling you that the market and your customer base, which consists of the leading international commercial and investment banks, are very interested and in need of this new service. In addition, you are expecting that the most important of these companies is expected to sign on for real-time system testing, as well as early users, and once you have its approval as market leader, the product would then be open to and easily accepted by the rest of the market. On this basis, you have allocated significant resources directly to this specific product, and externally contracted for the software development and systems interface. There has been significant publicity and speculation both inside your organization and in the marketplace about the introduction of this service.

Now, as CEO you have begun receiving feedback, both through your staff and directly from your target customers that many of them are beginning to have internal difficulties with being able to confirm that they can meet the previously agreed upon target-testing and implementation dates of spring/summer 2000. These indications are that the market leader is going to be unable to test and implement the service. This information is quickly developing into the potential for major political, organizational and financial problems for both you and your company. The launch and implementation of your product and service requires the customer users to implement significant software and systems updates and enhancements in the systems at each of their own companies. However, as the end of the millennium is approaching and as the timetable for the implementation of the euro is now also in place, all of the resources of the systems departments of your target customer base are being directed by the senior management of their companies to hold off or push back any new product or service enhancements that are not absolutely critical or that are not being mandated by the industry regulators during the time period between 1 January 2000 and 31 December 2001. This directive/constraint has gone out virtually worldwide because of the problems of the immediate threat and widespread concern of the 'Y2K Millennium Bug'. This is widely forecast to strike as computer systems clicked over from midnight 31 December 1999 to 1 January 2000 and there is a fear that those that are not programmed to recognize the new millennium will either shut down or alternatively turn their internal clocks back to 1900 and not forward to 2000. This immediate problem is accompanied by the considerable systems work required for the imminent introduction of the euro, which has corporate executives and industry regulators deeply concerned around the world.

The Y2K Millennium Bug represented the global concern that the thousands and thousands of computer programs that had been written over the past decades never considered or provided for the four digit fields required for the change of century. In many cases, these old programs were still serving as the nerve centre and primal brain of the software that had basically been added to and patched over the years for most international organizations, governments and financial institutions. Generally, these computer programs, some of which had been written as far back as the 1970s, were structured with economy of 'bytes' in mind, such that the data fields for the year were generally written with just two data fields that would only accommodate the last two digits of the designated year. So, whether you were referencing 1967, 1987 or 1997, only the 67, 87 or 97 was being recorded with the century (19XX); the implication being that the software was never expected to last into the new century at the time it was programmed. As time for the change in century drew near, along with the introduction of the new European currency, the general global expectation/fear was that when 1999 ended and the calendar moved to 2000, the world's computers would not recognize the new dates as beginning with 20XX without massive and specific reprogramming.

There was very real and widespread global concern that when the world's computers clicked over in the new century to 00 they would read this either as 1900, not the year 2000, or worse, and that there would be systematic computer crashes creating global economic disruption as the computers would simply shut down creating a form of global paralysis in defence, economics and finance.

Now, as CEO you are receiving strong signals from your most important and target companies that because of the twin problems of the possibilities of widespread computer failure from the Y2K Millennium Bug and the massive systems updates required for the revolutionary introduction of the new currency, the euro(€), you are being faced either with market pressures to delay the introduction of your new product/service for as long as a year, to spring 2001, or with a customer base unable/unwilling to implement or endorse your new product and system. You are also being faced with massive 'loss of face' both internally, with the Board of Directors, company executives and employees that had been strongly supporting this new effort, and externally, as you clearly anticipate the financial press and the marketplace to heavily criticize you once information on the potential for this significant delay begins to circulate. In addition, as this is a swiftly moving industry, you also run the risk that with a full year delay either the market dynamics might change or some competitor might steal your market leadership position and leave you unable to recover your company's investment.

It was the sort of 'Perfect Storm' of the systems world, two massive technical enhancements requiring all the systems experts and technicians around the globe to work nearly round the clock: to 'fix' the forecast Y2K Millennium Bug to prevent the possibility of global computer and systems meltdown and simultaneously to prepare these systems for the introduction of the euro. At the same time you are attempting to introduce and implement one of the most important new products in your company's history.

Now, while the introduction of the euro on a day-to-day transactional basis for the general public will not occur until 1 January 2002, for business and economic purposes, the currency will become administratively operational well in advance of its introduction to the public. Thus, during 2000 all legal and financial documents, all computers and all financial calculations going back in time retrospectively as well as moving forward in time prospectively will have to be amended to reflect the new currency values of the Euro-zone countries. The participating Euro-zone countries will not be the only ones to be affected, each and every company and country that does any business in Euro-zone currencies or with Euro-zone entities will have to amend the financial values of all their documentation, contacts, legal and financial agreements, as well as all their computer systems to reflect this change.

So, as the ultimate decision maker, you are now faced with these massive newly identified external obstacles, as well as the serious financial, public relations and organizational consequences and repercussions that a significant delay in the introduction and implementation of your new service could cause.

Your options include either sticking to the current and announced timetable of introduction and launch of this major new product/system during spring/summer 2000 without the guarantee of the important support of the market and your primary customers or pushing the testing, launch and implementation as far as a year into the future and risk losing organization momentum, significant market and organizational credibility as well as possible market position.

Either decision could result in tremendous negative financial, career, administrative, publicity, organizational implications and repercussions for you.

Notes

1 The origin of 'Hobson's choice' dates back to sixteenth-century England and is often used by economists to describe difficult, hard or impossible choices faced by business executives, central bankers, economic and finance ministers or governments.

2 The phrase 'Being between a rock and a hard place' has a very similar meaning to the above and apparently dates back to the American southwest, where it first appeared in print in the early 1920s and concerned a miner's strike where the mineworkers were faced with a choice between harsh and underpaid work at the rock-face, on the one hand, and unemployment and poverty, on the other (The Phrase Finder: http://www.phrases.org.uk/meanings/62900.html). It is a contemporary version of the classic reference to Odysseus' dilemma of passing between Scylla and Charybdis (figuratively a rock and a hard place). Scylla being a monster on the cliffs and Charybdis a dangerous whirlpool. Neither fate was more attractive, as both were difficult to overcome (Origin of Phrases: http://members.aol.com/MorelandC/Have Origins.htm, Kymberli Drummond).

European Chief Executives in the Merger Maze: Coping with Multiple Realities

By Jacqueline Fendt

In a global economy characterized by liberalization and consolidation, many leaders today are busy reinventing their organizations, preparing or digesting a merger, attacking new markets or outsourcing tasks and downsizing their workforce. But many such experiences, especially mergers, still fail to deliver on their promise and often destroy substantial human and financial corporate value. The reasons – more often than not – lie in the social, psychological and cultural challenges of the post-merger process. These are particularly challenging in European companies, given their extreme plurality in language, culture and – last but not least – the diverse European visions of capitalism that are so different from the Anglo-Saxon model. European leaders in a globalizing world, and especially in the increasingly frequent transatlantic mergers, have to marry the European notion of capitalism, the Social or *Rhine capitalism*, based on corporatism and stakeholder consensus, with the exigencies of the more shareholder-based Anglo-Saxon capitalism.

A seven-year empirical research project on German and Swiss CEOs in global post-merger situations uncovered some powerful challenges these executives faced in their complex integration endeavours. 40 mergers in such varied industries as banking, airline, automotive, IT, engineering, life sciences, hotel management and food manufacturing were studied and the actors themselves, CEOs and top executives, spoke up and candidly shared how they went about solving problems and how they struggled between art and science in their thought processes. The research identified three generic types of leadership patterns – the *cartel*, the *aesthetic* and the *videogame* executive – and proposed a taxonomy of leadership behaviour that seem particularly propitious to post-merger performance, dubbed the *holistic* executive.

The Cartel Executive: 'Life is Power'

Cartel executives have a strong desire for control and power maximization. They are solitary, no-nonsense, facts-and-figures executives who do not mingle much, except in their restrained circles. Such leaders grew up in protected markets, trade organizations and barriers, and have a low tolerance for ambiguity. Their leadership is instrumental, utilitarian and focused on the conservation of power and unconditional control. Their secretive, power-based lobby has been highly successful in a stable world where this leadership style had served well for decades. In the management team, they usually form a coalition with the Chief Financial Officer. Such leaders are hard workers, bold decision makers and have an unflinching determination, a well-oiled network among highest political and economic leaders and a long-term strategic perspective.

The Aesthetic Executive: 'Life is Beauty'

This type of leader is all about image. Their day's work begins with a thorough reading of the press that largely determines actions and priorities. They have multiple personal media appearances, often as carefully staged as those of a pop star. Their rhetoric is smooth, their metaphors well-oiled and their PR consultant never far away. This style posits a dualism with the leader on one side and the followers on the other, which mystifies leadership and jeopardizes true collaboration. Such leaders believe that they can use the media for their purposes but often end up being used by the media. Also, their successful public appearances bring them to mistake their perceptions for realities and thus the curtain over the stark truth often remains closed until it's too late. Still, the *aesthetic* executive has distinct strengths, namely a high awareness for effective, systematically planned communication with various stakeholders, a process-view of change, intuition and loads of charisma.

The Videogame Executive: 'Life is a Game'

Videogame executives are acutely lucid, very well informed, anti-authoritarian and unsparing with classic leaders, which they consider mediocre, cynical and mendacious. To them, change is not a programme but simply a fact of life. They aptly use visual, symbolic communications first hand and by all available electronic means, and aptly raise their mission at hand to a level of worthwhile human adventure rather than an astute business deal. They have a playful but effective capacity to enthuse and want to have fun above all. They believe that doing a good job and being a good citizen does not have to come at the price of cynicism and sacrifice of family life and bonding with friends. It goes without saying that they tell the truth, even when it's ugly: they see themselves and their followers as 'in it together'. Videogamers don't think in hierarchies and terms of 'moving to the top' but rather prefer multiple experiences. They believe in diversity, do not mind losing face before colleagues and easily volunteer unfinished bits and pieces of solutions in management meetings. In their logic, to make mistakes is essential and helps them to progress. Videogamers are explorers, not exploiters: they hop from project to project and get bored rather quickly as soon as the task gets repetitive. They stick it out as long as the game lasts.

The Holistic Executive: 'Life is Multiple Realities'

Leaders who performed best in complex, constantly shifting environments were those who combined the strengths of the three foregoing leadership styles (see Box 46). These *holistic* executives have a long-term vision, have a powerful network, are highly determined and have the tenacity to stick it out as the cartel leaders did. They work equally closely with all management team members, including the HR manager. Like the aesthetic leaders, holistic executives are process-conscious, know the value of planning and communication with diverse stakeholders and use their charisma to the full to gather rank and file around a strong, shared higher-echelon goal. Like videogamers, they are technology savvy, creative and view mistakes as opportunities for growth and innovation, and inspire colleagues through tough times with their candour, vulnerability and empathy. Above all, holistic leaders are pathological and passionate learners: they have a high tolerance for ambiguity, refuse to cede to complexity with binary 'either–or' decoys and instead support diverse alternatives. Incorporating plural viewpoints brings enjoyment to the merger process, which becomes a social and factual discovery trip. Choice is presented as a configuration of value rather than a selection from mutually exclusive alternatives and permits to innovate with hitherto untested third positions.

A People Focus

Merger integration is above all a social and thereby a leadership challenge. In leadership theory, different sets of behaviour are said to be particularly apt at coping with different company life stages, for example, transitional situations require analytical leadership, start-up companies thrive on creative behaviour, adaptive situations need conceptual leadership, growth companies need a production focus and consolidation situations require a behavioural style. The problem is that a post-merger situation is simultaneously consolidative, starting, adaptive, growing and transitional. In this maze of juxtaposed entrepreneurial situations, the CEO would have to concurrently be analytic, conceptual, behavioural, production-focused and creative! The holistic executive comes closest to this as he or she manages the critical post-merger challenges, namely to:

- tap to the full the immense learning potential of two companies combining resources: this necessitates a learning vision and new management and learning processes and structures;
- move the organization from hierarchies to networks, that is to bring more accountability; and power to the workplace. In poorly managed mergers, the contrary happens;
- keep the best talents on board and attract new ones from the market. Many companies plan to acquire human assets, which are then drained by poor integration. Talent turnover, which is normally at about 20 per cent, can rise to 75 per cent in post-merger phases;
- shape a new culture. The way change and uncertainty are managed, how the CEO treats people, the clarity, integrity and coherence of management action and the solutions found for the inevitable losers in a merger process, will determine staff commitment and the future culture of the merged company.

HR managers are ideally placed to second the CEO in these issues (see Box 47): they show a richer insight into how to manage the human factor in mergers than CEOs, as they are the turnstile between top management and the organization. Yet, except with holistic leaders, HR is still often involved late, sometimes only when human problems escalate. Holistic executives recognize the value of an early HR involvement and attribute a key role to the HR manager.

Box 46 Taxonomy of European leadership behaviour in mergers

Characteristic, dimension	Cartel	Aesthetic	Videogame	Holistic
Value system	Life is power and control	Life is beauty	Life is a game	Life is multiple realities
Ethics	Within the law	Code of conduct	Add value	Add value, respect
Social embeddedness	Solitary	Elitist	Unselective	Diverse, selective
Purpose of learning	To obtain something	To be someone	To become someone	
Knowledge	Is a possession, a means to an end	Is a product to be acquired	Is constructed	
Leadership	Directive	Analytic	Conceptual	Integrated
CEOs personal merger involvement	Until closing of deal	Until communication and integration plan	Until boredom	Permanent
Organizational perspective	Systemic organization	Systemic self-organization	Systemic networking	Coactive self-organization
Communication	By head of comm.	By CEO		
Communication means	Formal verbal statements	Multiple personal appearances	By images, symbolic acts, systems	Mixture of verbal and image, systems
Main entrepreneurial focus	Degree of control	Degree of media support	Degree of excitement	Integrated

Box 46   (Continued)

Time dimension term	Decades	Next quarter	The time of a game	Long and short-term
Subconscious learning mode	Instinct	Intuition (automated expertise)	Intuition (holistic hunch)	Both types of intuition
Human diversity	Little diversity	Diversity		
Medium diversity	Single medium (verbal)	Reduced media (verb. Some images)	Multimedia	Integrated
Degree of planning	High		Low	High to permit improvization
Vision	Long-term dominance	Short-term results	Adventure	Integrated
Determination	High, permanent		High, until boredom	High
Internet literacy	Low	Medium	High	High
Rhetoric	Poor	Excellent, universal	Excellent but addresses only the 'young'	Excellent, diverse
Attitude towards mistakes	No mistakes		Mistake-making as a resource	
Networking	Stable, long-term, confined to few peers	Reduced network	Intense, multiple partners, alternating, temporary	Both long-term and alternating networking
Perception of uncertainty	Is an inhibitor and must be reduced	Is related to some temporary factor and must be managed	Is a fact of life and must be integrated in the game tactics	Is a fact of life

Box 46 (Continued)

Characteristic, dimension	Cartel	Aesthetic	Videogame	Holistic
Relationship with ext stakeholders	Lobby	Communication, negotiation	Invited to join the game or ignored	Communication, negotiation
Notion of complexity	Reduce	Communicate, explain	Discover, enjoy, drop when bored	Discover, communicate, explain
Task dimension	Exploitation and exploration (sequential)		Exploration	Exploration and exploitation (simult.)
Films	*The Godfather* trilogy *Wall Street*	*Sideways, American Beauty, Kageshuma*	*Martix, Erin Brockovich*	All types
Videogames	None	Chess, flight stimulator	All types	All types

Source: Fendt, 2005

Box 47   Critical HR tasks in mergers

Before the merger:

- contribute to defining the merger objectives;
- bring an HR and a knowledge view to the selection of a potential merging partner;
- assess the human and skills value of the potential partner (HR due diligence);
- advise CEO on human and cultural merger issues;
- plan the integration process as a learning process.

During the integration phase:

- assist CEO in structure and design of the new company from a knowledge perspective;
- assist CEO in acculturation leadership;
- select the integration manager, design and manage the teams;
- retain key managers and talent, recruit new talent, promote diversity;
- manage the change process, negotiate with and motivate stakeholders;
- examine extant HR policies and practices, select and implement the new policies and practices.

During stabilization:

- be a knowledge and learning ambassador to the CEO and the organization;
- solidify culture, leadership and staffing;
- assess strategies, structure and processes from a knowledge perspective;
- assess and adapt HR policies and practice;
- monitor stakeholder concerns;
- manage learning.

Source: adapted from Schuler et al., 2005

References

Fendt, J. (2005) *The CEO in Post-Merger Situations: An Emerging Theory on the Management of Multiple Realities.* Delft: Eburon.

Schuler, R.S., Jackson, S.E. and Fendt, J. (2005) 'Managing human resources in cross-border alliances', In H. Scullion and M. Linehan (eds), *International Human Resource Management: A Critical Text.* Basingstoke: Palgrave Macmillan.

The Case of Schneider Electric: Industrial Marketing in Europe – A Pack Solution?

By Dr Gabriele Suder

Effective marketing is a key factor in the success of any company, and marketing within Europe is no exception. Some may even argue that marketing in Europe is more complex than in other parts of the world, as each European country has a distinct culture and language, as opposed to the United States, for example, in which English is the main language. This case study focuses on a particular company, Schneider Electric, and analyses the difficulties and successes that the company has to master in its European marketing: how to be competitive in a mature market through a new pack approach.

A company overview

Schneider Electric is a French company that was founded in 1836. It is one of the largest in its industry of electrics and automation with over 85,000 employees and a leading international presence in 130 countries worldwide. In 2004, the corporation had reached a sales figure of €10,365 million, with 54 per cent of those sales originating in European countries, 21 per cent in North America, 18 per cent in Asia and the Pacific, and 7 per cent in the rest of the world. A closer analysis of Schneider Electric's presence within Europe clearly shows that this is indeed its principal market. Furthermore, 52 per cent of its employees are based in Europe. Knowing the importance of this market to the firm's success and sustainability, the company merged with different European companies in order to gain local competencies and ensure that it remained a key player in an ever-increasing market. One example of a proposed merger, which was actually rejected by the European Commission, was that with Legrand in 2001. This attempted merger, however, was declared 'incompatible with the common market', as the European Commission thought it would create a potential monopoly. While the decision was eventually turned over by the European Court, it was too late for Schneider Electric to finalize this merger because Legrand had already been taken over by another company. Schneider Electric, however, has been successful in other mergers.

The company has two core businesses. The first, 'electrical distribution', accounts for 63 per cent of overall sales and operates under the names of Merlin Gerin and Square D. The second, 'automation and control', accounts for 26 per cent of overall sales and operates under the names Square D and Telemecanique. While the company is present in four markets altogether, the focus of this case study is the *industrial market* of Schneider Electric.

A basis for industrial marketing

For the industrial market, the multinational Schneider Electric has developed a specific sales strategy. With its main clients based all around Europe, this strategy takes account of the main challenges that these markets and the different expectations may hold. The expressed desire is primarily to 'improve performance' by 'developing a local and global offer, forming partnerships and pushing back frontiers'. Pursuing these goals has translated into the forming of solid partnerships with distributors, contractors and systems integrators, and global strategic accounts.

Schneider Electric asked its management about the ways to maintain its leading position in Europe through its marketing strategies and through its various projects within the European market. This is how the firm came to play a key role in very diverse projects regarding control navigation on the Meuse river in Belgium, lighting for the Sophia Hilton in Bulgaria, optimization of electric components at Square Crossroads, Senart in France, and other large projects throughout Europe that have a strong significance for global communication, as well as public and private partner- and image-building. In terms of Schneider Electric's mass market, a new momentum was also to be found, in the everlasting challenge of doing better than the strong European competition, such as that of Siemens. New ways were to be found to attract clients and position products across a highly competitive and mature European market.

Selling pack solutions to industrial clients?

In 2004, Schneider Electric decided to release a brand new industrial package formula, also called the 'pack', which required a new marketing strategy and special attention. This is because the idea of a pack in the industrial market was brand new, and its innovativeness translated into new risks, and potentially new important returns. The concept was to be similar to that of buying a pack that included a satellite dish with all technical equipments provided, a subscription and after-sales service, or a pack that included a mobile phone with earphones, hands-free and other equipment plus the subscription.

While packs have existed in the mass market for quite some time, the idea had never been tried in the industrial market. In addition to the risk that Schneider Electric's management decided to take with this move, it took an additional risk in launching this idea on a Europe-wide level and with the product itself; this made it necessary to carefully plan the appropriate marketing strategy. The *main* objective was therefore to decipher the key success factors of launching a new pack in Europe with 'Twido', its first pack release. After looking closely at these factors, management was able to answer a fundamental question: What are the best conditions for implementing a pack on a European level which can, on the basis of this experience, also be sold globally?

The Twido pack

The Twido pack, which was designed for the industrial market, had a European focus. Its purpose was centred on operating industrial machinery, so its contents included an automate, a display terminal, a power supply unit, cables, and software. Approximately 70 per cent of the packs sales went through the European market, making it an ideal example for future packs to be launched in Europe. Key success factors of the Twido pack give some insight for launching future packs. Apparently, success was based on creating a pack that would simplify the life of customers and that was cheaper than purchasing the components separately. Also, special services or gifts were offered to incite first purchases and then, to establish customer loyalty, the firm put strong emphasis on customer relationships.

At the technical level, it was important to obtain interoperability between components (they must work together); on the customer level, a large distribution base helped target the industrial market efficiently and Schneider Electric had the 'first mover' advantage on its side, as no other pack had been launched in this market before. While these were the success factors of Schneider Electric's Twido pack, it was also felt that it would be worthwhile to evaluate the success factors of Schneider Electric's competitors' packs. As no other company had launched a pack in the industrial market, examples of other companies' packs in the mass market helped find additional tools for expanding Schneider Electric's marketing strategy successfully.

The mass market: A learning experience

Three of Schneider Electric's main competitors in the mass market are Netgear, Darty and Canal Plus (Canal+). At the same time as Schneider Electric launched its pack, Netgear was already providing packs, but in the field of networking solutions for small businesses and homes. Darty was already involved and was a market leader in the distribution of electronic in France. Canal + had developed into one of Europe's largest pay-TV operators. The key success of these packs centred on the following factors: ease of use, quality, reliability, performance, affordability, a 24-hour hotline, a 30-day lowest price guarantee, free delivery, warranty, customization, and a focus on services.

Of the mass market packs, Netgear's pack, a router modem, is the product of a worldwide provider of technologically advanced networking products. The firm was founded in 1996 and is a significant provider of networking solutions for small businesses and home users. The company's products are designed for ease of use, reliability, performance, quality and affordability. Netgear products are grouped into three segments: Ethernet networking, Broadband, and Wireless networking. What could be presumed from Netgear in regard to its marketing of a pack/package in the mass consumer market? This particular package was only offered in France, meaning that Netgear selected a particular market first, before any European ambitions, and customized its packs to the specific needs of that market. Netgear altered its router package accordingly for the UK market: it did not include the antenna because the antenna was not adapted to the UK market and was not required. Also, in the

US, the router modem was only sold as a single item, which again is part of the marketing strategy of Netgear to customize its products to the needs of its customers in different cultures and countries.

Interestingly, it could be concluded that the main success factors from Netgear's router pack were: Netgear's objective focused on brand awareness in France by offering a special package, getting its name known in the large market that France offered; the package was then customized for both the French and UK markets – this is important because Netgear appears to soundly study its market prior to introducing new products, and varies its strategies accordingly. In the Netgear example in France, the package was created by a distributor that possesses the local knowledge necessary to find the best ways in which to market the package. On the downside, the Netgear package formula was more expensive than buying individual components separately: the package cost €205 as opposed to €185 for the three separate components at that time. However, the customer received a 'free' bonus USB key with the package as well as an upgraded antenna and free hotline. The point here, therefore was that it would be important to portray the price of a package as being cheaper than buying individual components. If customers could easily compare prices and distinguish that separate components are cheaper, their perception of clear company policy was most likely to favour other packs.

Darty's Home Cinema Pack, by the market leader in France, constituted another crucial comparison in understanding the pack market. The Darty pack was quite different in nature but comparable for the purpose of marketing strategy. A strong distribution network within France allowed for quick delivery anywhere. The pack could be customized by the distributor, with a consultant ensuring flexibility to meet customer needs. The package was cheaper, by about €50, when purchased as a complete unit as opposed to separate components. The only problem that could be found was not a minor problem: the exact individual components were not available in retail outlets for customers to compare prices. On the other hand, this is part of the Darty strategy to position these cinema packs.

Finally, a third mass market pack that was examined was different again. It was not a tangible product but a cable service provider, Canal+. The Canal+ group was found to be one of Europe's largest cable TV providers and was the original cable provider in Europe. Several packages were developed by Canal+ and four different cable packages were offered at that time, meeting various consumer needs and desires: the Movie channel, Family channel, 'Grand Spectacles' and 'Thematiques' . Particularly useful were the many selections from 290 channels, which could be added to the four packs. Customers love choice, especially when it comes to entertainment. Also, within the pack, customers could obtain a perception that the antenna was free, because it was provided with all the packages.

In terms of pricing, Canal+ favoured the promotion of limited time offers adapted to the right time of year (for example Christmas) or special events (for example football's World Cup). For instance, in a special deal, customers could subscribe to a pack for only €20 per month if they signed up prior to a given deadline. However, customers mostly need to sign up for a year's subscription. This may deter some people from buying packs, although this did not appear a big problem, because most people can be expected to look for a long-term cable TV service.

A direct competitor in the industrial market

All the success factors mentioned would be worth consideration by Schneider Electric; even though they are success factors from packs within the mass market, they provide some important input for industrial pack marketing within Europe too.

A direct competitor of Schneider Electric, the German corporation Siemens – the world's largest supplier of electrical solutions and products – was also beginning to sell industrial packs at this time. The pack sold by Siemens had four standard varieties for operating industrial machines in Germany. In France and Belgium the firm only sold two standard packs. The main reason found for this difference was the fact that France and Belgium both have different machines that are not adaptable to other 'vertical' machines. While Germany was the main market for Siemens, so too were Austria and Switzerland, which were close to Germany both geographically and culturally and were in a way the same market. Italy appeared also to be a very dynamic market for Siemens, which made the market yet more European-encompassing. France had become part of the Siemens market because of the company's strategy to win and maintain market share vis-à-vis its competition.

In these various markets, the Siemens approach of 'know your markets' translated into highly customized packs adapted to different cultures and technology. Distributors handle the marketing when customers are used to purchasing through distributors; in France customers would prefer to buy through a dealer than directly from the manufacturer.

A Market analysis for Schneider Electric's pack in Europe

Through the analysis of a previous survey with a local distributor, Cecci in Antibes, France, some key findings shortly after its launch complemented the knowledge acquired for a pack approach and for its European implementation. In 2004, 80 per cent of products were sold here as separate components. But while consumers preferred separate units, producers started to prefer selling packs because of easier interoperability and because they could sell them through promotion. Customers at that time appeared to be more attracted to the gift and attractive price than the pack composition itself. Hence, promotion became a key success factor in selling packs.

The overall strengths of the new *European Pack* from Schneider Electric were its all-in-one formula as a general idea, making things easier for consumer and distributor. The lower price of the pack compared to separate components was determined and attributed to the pack via consequential economies of scale (in production and packaging and a resulting quick inventory turnover). Also, Schneider Electric added value to the pack through services, gifts and software.

However, questions appeared with this market analysis. Would the European Pack be adaptable to a global market? If the pack is standardized, does it allow for customization if packaged centrally? Are the right components in the pack then? In that case, doesn't it lag behind the competition in terms of consideration of different cultures and technology requirements?

Expanding industrial marketing for Schneider Electric

The main opportunities for Schneider Electric were found in its capabilities to create strong customer distributor relationships. Its European and global customer base provided several key access channels to the various markets. Within this, distributors preferred selling packs. Contrary to this, the competition from Siemens and others appeared important and packs were new to the industrial market, in particular with a European approach. Also, ever-evolving technologies for industrial machines were a threat to a pack approach.

From the beginning, the question was what would be the best conditions for implementing a new European pack which can also be sold globally. The conclusion to the marketing analysis and the answer to this question appeared not to be 'black and white', but rather complex. It appeared that standard packs needed some flexibility for customization in different countries, for technicalities, customer preferences and also distribution habits. Value-added services entice customers to buy (for example free software, helpline, gifts, etc.) packs, and this is everywhere. Promotional parties and special offers can build relationships with customers that will ensure word-of-mouth advertising and repeat business.

In addition, packs should always be (or give the impression of being) cheaper than buying separate parts; savings could be passed on from less packaging and economies of scale. The pack should be considered a product in itself: by educating the consumer that a package is a separate product, there would be opportunities to expand the pack market. Industrial marketing via a Europe-wide pack solution seemed to have a great future but Schneider Electric's management needed to consider some key elements. The European market represents over half of the firm's business. Further expansion and growth in new European markets, such as Turkey and Romania, would help justify the investment made in a new industrial pack.

Exporting High-Segment Wine to Europe: Early Internationalization of an Old Lebanese Winery with a New Management

By Dr Gabriele Suder

In 1868, the French engineer François-Eugene Brun came to Lebanon through his work with an Ottoman company that opened the Beirut–Damascus main road. He finally settled in the village of Jditta– Chtaura – on the main road in the Bekaa Valley – fascinated by the beauty of its environment. The surroundings reminded him of his home in Chézery (Ain, France), which he had left many years before.

It appeared to him that this was a good place to start producing wine, and Arak, traditional Lebanese alcohol. He was soon also engaged in producing liquors and high-quality wine vinegar. The French Napoleonic army that sojourned in Lebanon was a regular customer for his products; the location of the winery was particularly well chosen because it constituted the first stop on the Beirut–Damascus highway. His wines were soon well known for their superior quality and received a number of gold, silver and bronze medals.

However, Pierre L. Brun, the last descendant of François (third generation), died in 2000. The domain was then inherited by his cousins living in Paris and in the French colony of New Caledonia. They sold the old property in late 2000 to Elie F. Issa and Nayla Issa el-Khoury, two families who had been close contacts of Pierre L. Brun for 50 years, and who had been given the opportunity to learn the secrets behind the Domaine des Tourelles label and the know-how to produce it, as they had worked intesively for the winery from 1980 to 2000, when the health of M. Brun started to deteriorate.

The families invested in this field in a move to obtain a secure future and a challenging working environment that was to connect the ancestral know-how with the young generation that graduated from engineering, viniculture, viticulture, business and marketing. Also, this was to counteract migration to other countries, which is a phenomenon that weighs heavily on the country's economy.

In 2001 the wine production of the Domaine became a joint venture between the fruit of ancestral know-how and the expertise of a team from Bordeaux. Arak production was reinvigorated, and 125 additional earth jars aiming to market in 2006 a special version of this unique product were purchased. However, liquors, brandy, and Carthagene remain high segment products distinguishing Domaine des Tourelles. A small-scale production of 10,000 bottles of each type of wine (rosé and white), 50,000 bottles of red wine (2 types) plus Arak (9000 cases/year), and liquors in small quantities was reached in 2006.

In Lebanon, the wines are only distributed at the Domaine in Jdita-Chtaura and in one sole exclusive boutique in Monot-Achrafieh, Beirut. Given the Domaine's positioning as a select, low-quantity and high-quality winery, its competition in Lebanon is mainly constituted by other small family-owned producers. They are essentially Cave Komoum, Clos St Thomas, Chateau Nakad, Domaine Wardy, Clos de Cana, and Massaya. The big producers on the market are Chateau Ksara, Chateau Kefraya and Chateau Musar. These are, rather, competitors in the international markets.

The Domaine soon decided to start exporting, for wine and Arak only, and this began in 2003. Its destinations a couple of years later (in the order of importance by market share) encompass France, the USA, Canada, Arab neighbours where possible (Jordan, United Arab Emirates, etc.), and the winery's management has started to look into exporting to Australia and the UK very soon.

For the European market, Domaine des Tourelles focused primarily on conquering the French market, as of 2003. This market was selected due to the historic links that the vineyard's original owner had with France, but the decision was also based on the privileged relationship between the Lebanese and the French as well as the particular distribution potential of many French distributors.

The significant image of France in terms of wine enhances the probability that, once successful there, the expansion of exports to its neighbouring countries will be easier. The single market would hence be useful and France the springboard across Europe. Also, a sound knowledge of the country through their university education and visits to France motivated the young generation to focus on this market first. The choice of France as the European entrance country for the Domaine's wine was hence a strategic decision. (Pierre L. Brun was a graduate from Montpellier's ENSAM school.)

So was the choice of the produce to send there. In contrast to the domestic market, the winery decided to position itself in a slightly less select segment at the beginning, though high level, and not to send out its Grande Cuvée immediately. However, the Grande Cuvée is the subject of a current negotiation to present it at selected points of sale.

Rather, its special selection wines are distributed in Europe. They can also be found in supermarkets; word of mouth spreads faster and accessibility to the product is be easier for the consumer.

'In Lebanon, consumers like to feel that they are buying a rare, snob kind of product,' Christine Issa, the young and dynamic marketing manager explains. 'In France, our positioning is different; to start the word-of-mouth. In the near future, we wish to use our French footing as a base to benefit from the single market and ship our wine and Arak throughout the EU.'

When comparing the French wine market with others in Europe and abroad, Christiane points out that it is a rather more simple business environment than that of Italy or Canada, for example, because less sampling and visits are necessary. Once the distributor is contracted, it is possible to control the activities there from the home market and to pay relatively few visits per year, which keeps the costs down in these young internationalization efforts. This is an important advantage for the Domaine des Tourelles. Indeed, in Italy the winery tried to establish distribution networks but, at this stage, considers that this requires too much networking and expensive visits.

The Domaine's management is now targeting other countries in the EU as a new market. In the UK, the very active Circle of Wine Writers when touring Lebanon approached the Domaine and, satisfied, ranked the wine positively in its publications. The Domaine's rosé was nominated to be one of the 100 most exciting wines by Mickael Karam in the *Wine Report* (2007). The wine is also increasingly distributed thanks to an article in *Impressions*.

For European tastes, the wine is slightly different. Its red version, round and fruity, reminds one a little of Merlot of a dark ruby colour, but stronger and with a higher alcohol content. The Domaine's products differentiate themselves well from the old wines. The winery needs to comply with certain specific norms and regulations to export its produce to Europe, different from those in its domestic market, in particular the VI1 FORM (it contains a health certificate). The bottle size should be 50 cl and 35 cl, but new bottle sizes are being used for France and Europe because their domestic standard size is 75 cl and 37.5 cl.

The winery is combining the values of traditional procedures and prestige with the concepts of modern management and a dynamic internationalization that is at the same time opportunist and strategic. It is the phenomenon of an increasing demand of Lebanese products in the international market. Regionally speaking, the neighbouring countries are also part of the Greater Free Trade Agreement (GAFTA, fully implemented in 2005, the umbrella agreement between 17 countries of the region). This allows for stronger demand for local products, but also creates stern competition from the Arab countries, in which generally costs are lower and in particular electricity is a cheap and more reliable resource. Customs tariffs among the GAFTA are minimal and Lebanese communities appreciate food from home. The food industries sector of Lebanon has grown by 20 per cent, reports *Lebanese Opportunities* in its March 2006 issue, with food products and beverages accounting for US$1 billion and exports for US$ 191 million (Chamber of Trade and Commerce, 2005 figures), only beaten by the construction materials sector.

Given the relatively limited local market, Lebanese business searches for sustainable growth and revenue abroad. The experience of market integration in the area shows that it simultaneously challenges performance and opens opportunities. The export market is more profitable in that it allows business to reach economies of scale; many raise revenues through value added and through the increase of output capacity.

This is the case of the Domaine des Tourelles. Aware of the opportunities that sound relations, market stability and market grouping can offer, the winery's young internationalization efforts aim at the high potential that the EU offers. However, to date its early export operations are less profitable than the sales in the domestic market.

The 2012 liberalization of trade with the EU is most interesting for a company that prepares its markets well in advance, and in accordance with the conditions that a small family business works in: the Euro-Med agreement signed with the EU furnishes the gradual reduction of customs duties within a 12-year period, and allows for a five-year grace period for Lebanon, also granting the country's industry an immediate tariff exemption and removal of import quotas once the agreement is enforced. Preparing for this future is an important strategic objective for Lebanon's business sectors.

Notes

The information in this case study was compiled from internal sources of Domaine des Tourelles and an interview by the author with Christiane Issa; *Lebanon Opportunities* (March 2006, Issue 108).

To Tilt or Not to Tilt: The Grand Velocity Question

By Dr Wladimir Sachs

It was July 1986 and I was in Paris, away from home on the East Coast of the United States. Lunch was with an old business acquaintance, who made it high into the hierarchy of the French foreign trade establishment, and who used (or abused) my sympathetic ear to hurl a long litany of the usual complaints about US protectionist barriers and their prosecution of French products. Why did they not authorize Concorde to fly at supersonic speed on overland routes to Los Angeles and San Francisco? How come they don't use Minitel, the French pre-internet proprietary information retrieval system? Why don't they use smart credit cards with chips built into them, instead of those old-fashioned magnetic-strip based ones? Why do they prefer hamburgers to decent food? And why don't they travel in high speed trains, preferably the French TGV? As on previous occasions, my attempts to explain each of those cases in terms of its own logic, drawing on the specifics of the US economy and society, fell onto deaf ears. 'What is good for France must be excellent for the United States' seemed the deeply held belief of my friend.

Dinner was with a US TV and radio correspondent, excitedly telling me how she got to ride in the engineer's cab of the Train à Grande Vitesse (TGV) between Paris and Lyon, accompanying Elizabeth Dole, then the United States Secretary of Transportation, former Miss North Carolina, wife of Senator Bob Dole, a prominent Republican. 'I should avoid my lunch companion for a while,' I thought to myself; 'Once again they are trying to sell the wrong product in the wrong way, and they will be even more frustrated when they fail.'

Very fast trains – traveling at speeds over 200 km/h (recently the definition was upgraded to 250 km/h) – are an attractive alternative to air travel when they connect high population-density areas that are no further apart than about 700 km. Indeed – if you figure the hassle of getting to and from the airport and the complicated airline check-in procedures – it takes less time to cover such distances by a fast train, it is better for one's health and certainly more convenient in terms of space to sit and move around. Add a modicum of environmental consciousness, and the train is a winner.

The Japanese, crowded as they were on a densely populated island with lots of compli-cated topography, were the first to build a rapid train, which went into operation between Tokyo and Osaka just before the start of the Olympics in 1964. The pre-existing Japanese train network was built on narrow tracks ('narrow gauge' in railroad jargon), inappropri-ate for higher speeds, and to make things worse it was sinuous, going around obstacles rather than using viaducts and tunnels. There was no choice: the Japanese had to build new dedicated track to travel at high speeds.

At about the time of the inauguration of the Tokyo–Osaka line the French and the Germans started thinking about their own fast trains. In both countries the teams that developed the initial projects had a similar reasoning, settling for the following three basic objectives: (1) to travel as fast as possible with comfort and safety; (2) to use to the maximum existing track and (3) to favour smaller trains with higher frequency over larger less frequent ones.

The first objective is obvious, being the essence itself of rapid rail travel. The second objective is not difficult to understand: if one builds new dedicated track, as opposed to upgrading existing one, the amount of capital required for investment increases dramatically. Also, when building a new connection between points A and B, one must wait to use it for the entire project to be completed. When simply upgrading existing lines, one may gradually improve service without waiting for the whole to be completed.

There also is another, more subtle, reason to support using existing lines over building new ones. It is obvious to anyone who ever rode a bicycle, that speed can be more easily achieved on a straight line than on a curvy one, and riding downhill or on even terrain is faster than riding uphill. The same holds true for trains, and therefore building new lines would make sense only if one had them fairly straight, with curves when unavoidable very gentle, and slopes not too steep. But this implies getting land for the new train line where it makes most sense from an engineering point of view. In old and densely populated countries like France and Germany this would necessarily involve expropriating private land owners, riding over socially valued relics, such as cemeteries or antique buildings, spoiling pristine views, and other nuisances. Many infrastructure projects are realized at such costs, and most societies agree that a larger social good should override lesser good or private interests, but democracies also insist that such decisions be carefully weighed, avoided when possible and that those expropriated be properly compensated. The lesser is the power of the government, the harder it is to realize projects requiring massive expropriations. Conversely, strong or authoritarian governments are not hampered by such considerations. There is a popular legend that the train line between Moscow and St Petersburg was once the straightest in the world: the tsar, bored with engineers and their detailed presentations of the project lost patience one day and drew with the aid of a ruler a straight line on the map, and that is how the track was built. The problem is that His Majesty held his finger on the side of the ruler on which he ran the pencil, and therefore at midpoint, and for no apparent topographical reason, the train had to slow down to a crawl and go through a very tight semi-circle.

Advocates of new and 'straighter' lines argue that riding a train fast on a curve is unpleasant, since centrifugal forces destabilize passengers and loosely lying objects. Opponents respond by arguing that it is possible to build train cars whose cabin tilts in the sense contrary to the centrifugal forces, tampering thus the effect. If you are a structural engineer, comfortable with building things from steel and concrete, you favour the first view. If you are a mechanical engineer, especially one with knowledge of electronics and regulating devices, you favour the second view. One implies spending a lot of money on tracks, and less on trains; the other is the exact opposite. It is not difficult to imagine lobbies of professional bodies and subcontractor companies forming around this issue.

The idea of favouring frequent smaller trains over less frequent large ones was the result of a vision of future spatial development of the country. The French planners had a very clear vision of short trains carrying relatively few people that would connect cities frequently, working a little bit like the subway, only on a national rather than metropolitan scale. They also wanted to serve not only large cities, but also smaller ones, where demand would not justify large trains. The French Agency for Territorial Development (DATAR) pushed this vision very strongly, wanting to reverse the historical Paris-centricity of the country. The original development team, working directly for the President of the National Rail Company (SNCF), was fully attuned into this vision.

Over time, however, the mainstream bureaucracy of the National Rail Company took over the project, and the original development team was eventually disbanded in 1975, well before the first train ran in 1981. The traditionalists in the company were more at ease with developing new track than with sophisticated vehicles (although both are required for the project to work). Also, they wanted to replicate on a bigger scale familiar operating patterns, serving large cities, with not too high a frequency, and large trains. Such an approach required little or no renegotiation of labour practices and other operating procedures, could be managed with existing logistical procedures, and generally required very little change to the 'soft' aspects of the company.

While French trains can travel on conventional track they require special track to travel at high speeds. They are long (consisting of several carriages) and travel at relatively low frequency. The French state is very centralized, wielding far greater power over individual citizens or local governments than in most comparable democracies, so initially the building of special high speed rail tracks went relatively smoothly, but with the progress of political decentralization the more recent projects are far more difficult to realize. TGV lines in France have curves with a minimal radius of 4 km, increased on newer lines to 7 km. The French do not use tilting technology, opting instead for construction of adequate routes.

The pragmatic Germans, with a strongly decentralized political system and much higher population density, remained more faithful to the initial project, upgrading existing infrastructure at the cost of lower speed, comfort and even safety, and introducing tilting technology. But even so, bitter political fights caused the Inter City Express (ICE) to be introduced 10 years after the French TGV. One of the political controversies – but not the only one – was criticism that Germany and France, allegedly working so closely in building the EU and successfully launching joint industrial ventures such as Airbus, have failed to coordinate their fast train projects. The Germans would not buy TGV technology and the French delayed for years technical and safety certification of the German ICE. This is not one of the proudest instances of European cooperation.

It was natural for Elizabeth Dole to be interested in the fast train. The US has an area that is vastly greater than the EU, and a population that is smaller, and therefore early on it favoured air transportation over rail. However, there are a few areas of the country that resemble Europe in that they have high density of population concentrated in large metropolitan areas. One in particular, the so-called North-Eastern corridor, spreading from Boston to Washington, D.C, comprising Providence, Stanford, New Haven, New York, Princeton, Newark, Philadelphia, Wilmington, Baltimore and other less known cities, was an obvious candidate for a high speed train. The French were eyeing the market for a long time, arguing, not without reason, that their TGV and the engineering firm Alstom producing it were world champions.

But the US is not France, not even Germany. It has a highly complex system of intertwined governmental jurisdictions, and the federal level has very little power to impose anything on lower levels. Approving new projects and expropriating land can be hell. The idea of building a motorway bypassing Philadelphia (now known as the Blue Route, about 30 km long) was discussed as early as during the Roosevelt infrastructure projects of the 1930s. In 1951 the 'final tracing' of the route was approved, but opposition of local interest groups delayed the approval of the budget till 1957. The route was completed in 1991 after six decades of planning and controversy at a cost of $600 million, 15 times the original estimate. About 375 families had to be displaced to build the route.

This and other experiences help explain why there was no appetite for the French approach, even if there was great admiration for the technology. It was simply not possible to envision building dedicated track with its gentle curves. After decades of studies and discussion the existing track from Boston to Washington was upgraded and the Acela train service was introduced at the end of 2000. The equipment is built by a consortium in which Alstom has only a 25 per cent stake, the rest belonging to the Canadian firm Bombardier. And the trains tilt …

The hero of the French system is the National Rail Company, and Alstom – the company building the trains – is a secondary player. In Germany the bulk of innovation comes from Siemens, the company that designed a train to run on just about any well-built and maintained track. In countries neighbouring Germany, with the notable exception of France, the ICE system has also been implemented, although the French TGV has inroads into Belgium, the Netherlands and soon into England and Italy, but only on lines connecting to France. Spain has both TGV and ICE.

Index

Please note that page references to non-textual information such as Figures or Tables are in italic print. Titles of publications beginning with 'A' or 'The' will be filed under the first significant word. Numbers (e.g. 20) are filed as if spelled out (e.g. twenty)